SHOW BOAT

Geoffrey Block, Series Editor

Series Board

Stephen Banfield   Jeffrey Magee
Tim Carter   Carol Oja
Kim Kowalke   Larry Starr

"South Pacific": Paradise Rewritten
Jim Lovensheimer

Pick Yourself Up: Dorothy Fields and the American Musical
Charlotte Greenspan

To Broadway, to Life! The Musical Theater of Bock and Harnick
Philip Lambert

Irving Berlin's American Musical Theater
Jeffrey Magee

Loverly: The Life and Times of "My Fair Lady"
Dominic McHugh

"Show Boat": Performing Race in an American Musical
Todd Decker

SHOW BOAT

Performing Race in an American Musical

TODD DECKER

OXFORD
UNIVERSITY PRESS

OXFORD

UNIVERSITY PRESS

Oxford University Press is a department of the University of Oxford.
It furthers the University's objective of excellence in research,
scholarship, and education by publishing worldwide.

Oxford   New York

Auckland   Cape Town   Dar es Salaam   Hong Kong   Karachi
Kuala Lumpur   Madrid   Melbourne   Mexico City   Nairobi
New Delhi   Shanghai   Taipei   Toronto

With offices in

Argentina   Austria   Brazil   Chile   Czech Republic   France   Greece
Guatemala   Hungary   Italy   Japan   Poland   Portugal   Singapore
South Korea   Switzerland   Thailand   Turkey   Ukraine   Vietnam

Oxford is a registered trade mark of Oxford University Press in the UK and certain other countries.

Published in the United States of America by Oxford University Press
198 Madison Avenue, New York, NY 10016

© Oxford University Press 2013

Library of Congress Cataloging-in-Publication Data
Decker, Todd R.
Show boat: performing race in an American musical /Todd Decker.
pages; cm.—(Broadway legacies)
Includes bibliographical references and index.
ISBN 978-0-19-975937-8 (alk. paper)
1. Kern, Jerome, 1885–1945. Show boat.
2. Ferber, Edna, 1887–1968. Show boat.
3. African Americans in musical theater.
4. Music and race.
5. Musical theater—History—20th century. I. Title.
ML410.K385D43   2012
782.1′4—dc23   2012000392

Publication of this book was supported in part by the
Lloyd Hibberd Endowment of the American Musicological Society.

1 3 5 7 9 8 6 4 2

Printed in the United States of America
on acid-free paper

For

MY PARENTS

CONTENTS

* * *

Foreword by Geoffrey Block   ix

Acknowledgments   xiii

Introduction: Magnolia's Black Voice   1

PART 1 Making

1. A Ferber Plot   13

2. The Robeson Plan   29

3. The Morgan Plan   57

4. A Ziegfeld Soprano and a Shubert Tenor   71

5. Colored Chorus Curtains   101

PART 2 Remaking

6. Featuring Robeson: 1928–1940   125

7. Broadway Black, Hollywood White: 1943–1957   166

8. Landmark Status: 1954–1989   196

9. Queenie's Laugh: 1966–1998   212

Epilogue   242

Appendix 1 Cast of Characters   251

Appendix 2 Archival Sources for the 1927
   Broadway Production   253

Appendix 3 Select Stage and Screen Versions (1928–1998)   257

Notes   263

References   285

Index   293

FOREWORD

• • •

Although it added the word "perhaps" in the event of an undisclosed rival to the throne, the 1980 edition of the *New Grove Dictionary of Music* proclaimed *Show Boat* to be "the most successful and influential Broadway musical play ever written." A little earlier, to mark the golden anniversary of the show's 1927 premiere, Miles Kreuger, the author of what is probably the first book-length study of a Broadway musical, *Show Boat: The Story of a Classic American Musical* (Oxford, 1977), considered this epic work's significance to go "far beyond fleeting artistic and social fashions." Twenty years later in *Enchanted Evenings: The Broadway Musical from "Show Boat" to Sondheim and Lloyd Webber* (Oxford, 1997; 2nd ed., 2009), the author of this Foreword lauded *Show Boat*'s "convincing use of American vernacular appropriate to the changing world (including the African-Americanization of culture) from the late 1880s to 1927" and, for its day, its "sensitive portrayal of race relations that range from the plight of the black underclass to miscegenation" and concluded that this work "has long since earned its coveted historical position as the foundation of the modern American musical." Nearly thirty years after the 1980 *Grove* and Kreuger canonization, Thomas Hischak boldly introduced his entry on *Show Boat* in *The Oxford Companion to the American Musical* by calling it "the first masterpiece and arguably still the finest musical play."

In this thoughtful and passionate book, *Show Boat: Performing Race in an American Musical* (2012), Todd Decker, assistant professor of music at Washington University in St. Louis and the author of *Music Makes Me: Fred Astaire and Jazz* (2011), like his predecessors, considers the treatment of race and the performance of race as central to both the original and continuing importance of this 1927 musical by Oscar Hammerstein (book and lyrics) and Jerome Kern (music), but he goes further in his emphasis that *Show Boat* deserves recognition as "the first in a line of shows to use music and dance to explore what it has meant to be black *and* white in the United States." For Decker, it is the "long-lived resonance" of this racial component and the evolving performances of race, more than its considerable artistic merits, that "makes *Show Boat* the most important musical ever made and also made its remaking a necessity again and again." The profound importance of race in Edna Ferber's original novel, in which the central female character, who is white, makes her way in the entertainment world by adopting the musical voice of a black servant, retained its pivotal incorporation of black musical culture in its first realization on the musical stage. In the first part of *Show Boat: Performing Race in an American Musical* ("Making"), Decker deftly uses archival materials to uncover the complex social and artistic journey of this work from novel to stage, beginning with its conception as a showcase for the famous African American actor and singer Paul Robeson, unavailable and perhaps unwilling to accept this honor, followed by the unprecedented development of a black chorus in a racially mixed show, strongly influenced by black musicals of the day.

In the second half of the book ("Remaking") Decker explores how *Show Boat* evolved over its eighty-plus-year history along the river and far beyond, a history that includes no less than nine New York revivals, six London productions, productions in Houston, Los Angeles, Chicago, and St. Louis, three Hollywood films and a television broadcast, and John McGlinn's historic recorded reconstruction. In each case Decker "privileges performers" as he explores the symbiotic "relationship between how *Show Boat* used and shaped the performers brought into its orbit and how those same performers used and shaped *Show Boat* for their own ends." In his exploration of the legacy of blackface minstrelsy, Decker "relies on the idea that musical and performance styles can be read as indexes of race." For example, as Decker explains, actresses playing a number of key roles have adopted "a performance style understood by the audience to be black," perhaps most notably Magnolia, Cap'n Andy's white daughter and the central female protagonist in the story, who learned to adopt a black voice when singing such black songs as the blues-inflected "Can't Help Lovin' Dat Man," a centerpiece of all the stage versions, and "Gallivantin' Aroun'," newly written for the 1936 film. The role of the mulatto Julie was "initially required" to be played by a white actress and would not be performed by a black woman for decades to come, and even the role of the black cook Queenie at first demanded a white actress to perform in blackface. Decker goes on to develop "an important subplot in the history of *Show Boat*" crucial to our understanding of this work: "the process whereby black women claimed both roles [Julie's and Queenie's] as their own." Of comparable interest is the parallel story Decker has to tell in which white performers, including those who play Magnolia, over the years have also adopted a contrasting musical style in order to "perform white." In his Epilogue Decker discusses the historical "triumph of black music and dance in *Hairspray* and *Memphis*" (the former situated in 1962 Baltimore and the latter in mid-1950s Memphis, premiering respectively in 2002 and 2009), two musicals of the early twenty-first century in which, like their primogenitor *Show Boat*, a presentation of racial issues and the performance of popular music from an earlier era reflect current values and sensitivities.

The chapter on *Show Boat* that concludes Ethan Mordden's *Make Believe* (Oxford, 1997), a comprehensive survey of the Broadway musical in the 1920s, considers *Show Boat* a "culmination of two energies" that have worked in tandem throughout the history of the genre: "one was devoted to artistic development and the other to a social agenda." More than any musical of its era, and more than most since, Kern and Hammerstein served Broadway's artistic energy by producing a musical that possessed a desire "to advance the integration of story, character, music, and dance" and a social energy most evident in their desire "to promote the musical as a form of inherently progressive socialistic sympathies." Scholars have tended to focus on *Show Boat*'s artistic qualities and its place in the Broadway pantheon. In *Show Boat: Performing Race in an American Musical* Decker offers a compelling and well-documented social history, which not only tells us a great deal about how *Show Boat* has evolved from 1927 to the present but also about our own progress as a nation, as we continue, like the Mississippi River, to keep rolling along.

GEOFFREY BLOCK
Series Editor, Broadway Legacies

ACKNOWLEDGMENTS

• • •

Show Boat's archival legacy is vast. This book is the product of many journeys to many libraries. I am grateful for the welcome I received in Washington, D.C., at the Music Division of the Library of Congress (Mark Horowitz) and the Moorland-Spingarn Research Center at Howard University (Joellen Elbashir); in New York City, at the New York Public Library for the Performing Arts, the Schomburg Center for Research in Black Culture of the New York Public Library, and The Paley Center, Manhattan branch; in Los Angeles, at the Margaret Herrick Library of the Academy of Motion Picture Arts and Sciences, the Cinematic Arts Library of the University of Southern California (Edward Comstock), and The Paley Center, Beverly Hills branch; in Madison, at the Wisconsin Historical Society; and in London, at the British Museum, the London Metropolitan Archives, and the Theatre and Performance Collection of the Victoria and Albert Museum at Blythe House. Jean M. Gosebrink at the St. Louis Public Library quickly located a valuable source, and my home library at Washington University in St. Louis (Brad Short) was, as always, essential.

Financial support from many sources made my work on *Show Boat* possible. An Alvin H. Johnson AMS 50 Fellowship from the American Musicological Society supported the project during the dissertation stage. Research funds and a semester of junior leave from the Washington University School of Arts and Sciences allowed for many research trips. A Faculty Fellowship from the Washington University Center for the Humanities provided a further semester of leave during which most of the book was written. My thanks to Gerald Early, Erin McGlothin, Jian Leng, and Barbara Liebmann for a productive time at the center and an office into the summer.

Valuable opportunities to share this study as a work in progress were provided by the American Musicological Society (2006, 2011), the Society for Cinema and Media Studies (2006), and two specialist meetings: Classic Broadway and Those Who Built It (Sixth Triennial Susan Porter Symposium at the American Music Research Center, University of Colorado, Boulder), and The American and British Musical: An International Colloquium (University of Bristol).

I started working on *Show Boat* at the University of Michigan in a class on musical theater taught by Steven Whiting. Professor Whiting went on to co-chair my dissertation committee with Richard Crawford. I have great memories of sharing early discoveries in the archives with both of these esteemed mentors. When it counted most, Professors Whiting and Crawford moved my work on *Show Boat* and my career in academia forward. Their guidance during that time made all the difference in the world.

Geoffrey Block suggested I write this book. I am grateful for his confidence in me and his sound advice these past years. Norm Hirschy was a great editor, shepherding the book from prospectus to print with an energetic hand. Mary Sutherland perceptively copyedited the manuscript. Production editor Joellyn Ausanka improved the book in the final stages.

William Everett, Charlotte Greenspan, Raymond Knapp, Jeffrey Magee, Carol Oja, Thomas Riis, and Rose Rosengard Subotnik were welcoming senior colleagues and inspiring role models for how to think and write about musical theater. Daniel Goldmark offered good advice. Nathan Platte was, as always, a good friend. Paige McGinley, Maya Gibson, Julia Walker, Lutz Koepnick, Linda Nicholson, Anca Parvalescu, and Erin McGlothin vetted chapter 1 at the Washington University Center for the Humanities. As they always have, my colleagues in music and film and media studies at Washington University encouraged my work and kept track of my progress. Danny Gurwin made certain my family and I had great seats for *Show Boat* at the St. Louis Muny in 2010. Zachary Colonius helped with research. David Chapman did the musical examples. Emily Lenz assisted with acquisition of the cover image. I am grateful to the estate of Doris Lee for generously allowing me to reproduce Lee's lovely 1939 painting of the final dress rehearsal of the Ziegfeld *Show Boat*, a piece of the show's visual legacy, which has not, until now, been reproduced.

Bruce Pomahac, music director of the Rogers and Hammerstein Organization, has continually aided my work on *Show Boat* from my first meeting with him more than six years ago. His knowledge of *Show Boat* is vast, his enthusiasm for the show infectious. Visiting Bruce's New York office to talk about *Show Boat* has been one of the primary pleasures of this project.

I dedicate this book to my parents, Ron and Linda Decker, who have supported my interest in musical theater from its earliest beginnings.

For six weeks in 1984, I played the role of Jake the piano player in a production of *Show Boat* mounted by the Good Company Players in Roger Rocka's Music Hall in Fresno, California. I spent about three years with the Good Company Players while in junior high and high school: performing six shows a week, learning the Broadway tradition from the inside by singing, dancing, playing piano, and running lights, spotlight, props, and sound. Whatever I have come to think or know about the Broadway musical begins with the training I received from Dan and Laurie Pessano, Fred Bologna, Steve Pepper, Kaye Migaki, Chris Moad, Alta Parrot, Beverly Broughton, and Veronica Smida.

My wife, Kelly, and sons, David and James, provided the underlying motivation for writing this book. Their love and support—and comical renditions of "Ol' Man Baby"—helped keep everything in perspective.

THE TRUSTEES OF THE ESTATES OF EDNA FERBER, OSCAR HAMMER-STEIN II, AND JEROME KERN GRACIOUSLY CONSENTED TO THE REPRO-DUCTION OF MUSIC, LYRICS, DIALOGUE, AND CORRESPONDENCE RELATING TO *SHOW BOAT*. THE AUTHOR IS DEEPLY GRATEFUL FOR THEIR GENEROUS SUPPORT OF THIS STUDY.

SHOW BOAT

Al Hirschfeld's 1956 caricature of the outdoor Jones Beach production highlighted Show Boat's *black dance chorus, who charge onto the stage from the right performing the African tribal dance "In Dahomey" while Andy looks on impassively at left. Steam from the tow boat, the Mollie Able, and the fireworks that ended each performance frame the* Cotton Blossom, *a massive floating set built on a barge and towed into place during the opening scene. © Al Hirschfeld, reproduced by arrangement with Hirschfeld's exclusive representative, the Margo Feiden Galleries Ltd., New York. www.alhirschfeld.com.*

INTRODUCTION

• • •

MAGNOLIA'S BLACK VOICE

It's an old story. A white, popular music star makes a career by singing the songs and emulating the style of black performers who never receive the fame or money they deserve. This is the plot of *Show Boat* as found in the 1926 novel by Edna Ferber. At that time, in the midst of an explosion of African American visibility in popular culture, it was a new story—at least for the readers of best sellers. The actual history of white Americans copying (or stealing) the musical innovations of black Americans reached back to the roots of the entertainment industry. *Show Boat* told and was itself part of this popular music narrative that forms one strand of the story of blacks and whites in the United States.

Blackface minstrelsy, born a generation before the Civil War, capitalized on African American enslavement: enslaved blacks could not represent themselves in popular culture, so white Americans blacked up and set about creating a set of lasting, pernicious, unsettlingly attractive stereotypes purporting to capture how black Americans sang and danced. Blackface minstrel troupes proliferated, and the musical theater genre of the minstrel show spread like wildfire in the North. In the decades after Emancipation, blacks in blackface took to the stage, initially in minstrel troupes, which were commonly segregated by color. As a national entertainment infrastructure formed around railroads and vaudeville theaters, African Americans on the variety stage slowly began to alter the stereotypes of minstrelsy, representing themselves and their race before audiences both black and white but seldom mixed (and if mixed, usually in segregated seating). With the hope of stardom on the stage among the few American dreams open to them, African American show business professionals found national fame within reach if they modulated their acts to meet white expectations and accepted the indignities of life off the stage. Black audiences celebrated such performers—among them Bert Williams, star of the *Ziegfeld Follies* from 1910 to 1919—as trailblazers.[1]

In a parallel development, African American musical practices began to transform American popular music, initiating a cultural juggernaut still unfolding today. With the emergence of ragtime—the first syncopated dance music to remake the landscape of popular culture—black musicians began to shape national identity, and what started out as African American became simply American. Jazz followed ragtime, generating similar excitement among the young and similar fears among the guardians of white culture. Swing, rock and roll, soul, and hip-hop came after, moving along familiar paths.

Among the black musics making a mark along this way was the Negro spiritual. In the 1920s, when *Show Boat*'s story ends and the history of *Show Boat* begins, Negro spirituals were experiencing a vogue among white audiences, coinciding with a movement in black arts and letters that came to be known as the Harlem Renaissance. When Edna Ferber sat down to write *Show Boat*, African American music and musicians—especially male singers of spirituals— were firmly installed on the New York scene. First among them was Paul Robeson: a 1920s phenomenon, equal parts singer and dramatic actor, arguably the most famous black man in America or, at least, New York. Ferber capitalized on the still new figure of the black concert spiritual singer, and in a surprising narrative move, she gave *Show Boat*'s self-reliant, white heroine Magnolia Hawks Ravenal a black voice.

> Kim Ravenal [Magnolia's daughter] was probably the only white child north of the Mason and Dixon line who was sung to sleep to the tune of those plaintive, wistful Negro plantation songs which later were to come into such vogue as spirituals. They were the songs that Magnolia had learned from black Jo and from Queenie, the erstwhile rulers of the *Cotton Blossom* galley. Swing Low, Sweet Chariot, she sang. O, Wasn't Dat a Wide River! And, of course, All God's Chillun Got Wings. . . . Magnolia sang these songs, always, as she had learned to sing them in unconscious imitation of the soft husky Negro voice of her teacher. Once, when they were living at the Sherman [House in Chicago], Magnolia, seated in a rocking chair with Kim in her arms, had stopped suddenly in her song at a curious sound in the corridor. She had gone swiftly to the door, had opened it, and had been unable to stifle a little shriek of surprise and terror mingled. There stood a knot of black faces, teeth gleaming, eyes rolling. Attracted by the songs so rarely heard in the North, the Sherman House bell boys and waiters had eagerly gathered outside the closed door in what was, perhaps, as flattering and sincere a compliment as ever a singer received.[2]

(Ferber habitually used the trope of rolling eyes to describe the black figures in her fiction, a measure of minstrelsy's lingering power to limit the imagination of white writers with little knowledge of actual black Americans.) Abandoned by her husband, Gaylord Ravenal, Magnolia would build a solo career as a vaudeville star on her ability to mimic the black voice. White theft of black music underlay Magnolia's success. Of course, Ferber never calls it theft. Magnolia receives her black voice as a free gift of the river world where she grows into a genuine American artist (whatever that might mean). The issue of equity or fairness never enters the tale, although Ferber holds out the possibility that "Born fifty years later [Jo] might have known brief fame in some midnight revue or Club Alabam' on Broadway."[3]

Ferber's story is best known today for its retelling as a musical. Just weeks after the novel was published, the composer Jerome Kern and the lyricist and author Oscar Hammerstein II set about making Ferber's interracial cast of characters sing and dance on the Broadway stage. Their approach to the phenomenon of Magnolia's black voice took off in a different direction from Ferber, but both the novel and the original stage musical were steeped in the same Manhattan milieu. *Show Boat* as a musical proved a tremendous and enduring hit, the single most revived and revised work of the Broadway stage, successful multiple times in London's West End, as a Hollywood musical film, and in the opera house. All these remakings had to deal with the original *Show Boat* forged in the crucible of the Jazz Age, when black music and musicians arrived in the white mainstream in powerful new ways. And because the importance of black music and musicians in national culture continued to grow as the twentieth century unfolded, *Show Boat*—remade and reimagined—continued to have something to say, both about the roots of American popular culture and the present state of the nation. This larger theme of race, music, and national identity, captured in Ferber's white girl with the black voice, was hardwired into the musical by Hammerstein, whose vision for *Show Boat* consistently circled back to the colored roots of America's popular music. This narrative thread—what I call Hammerstein's popular music plot—will return again and again in this book.

Two surprisingly frank admissions about race underlay Ferber's story and every version of it. First, in the United States blacks and whites have lived side by side. Our national experience is fundamentally interracial. Stories, plays, films, and musicals that do not account for this diversity, among them the vast majority of Broadway and Hollywood musicals, offer a convenient fiction. No version of *Show Boat* can create the illusory world of an all-white or all-black America so often encountered on the musical stage and screen. Second, the color line separating black from white has played an active role shaping the life of the nation. Both the story of *Show Boat* and the history of its telling on the musical stage and screen draw attention to the power of the color line as a destiny-shaping force affecting both black and white individuals. Assuredly, race relations in the United States are more complex than simply black and white. But in the realm of popular culture where *Show Boat* has played its part, black and white remain the two most significant categories. African American performers have always aspired to stardom on stage and screen in numbers disproportionate to their share of the population, and there is no Latino-, Asian-, or Native American–cast musical tradition to speak of. Indeed, African Americans are the only racially defined minority group with a Broadway genre reserved just for them—the black-cast musical—and the color line endures on the Great White Way and the Silver Screen despite strides made elsewhere in American society over the last eighty years. Color-blind casting has never conquered Broadway, much less Hollywood, like it has the international and American opera stage. One powerful contribution black performers have made to the musical lies in the expressive register of the black voice, a changing and vibrant part of American popular singing. *Show Boat* is one place where this voice found, indeed still finds, an outlet. And while a handful of Broadway musicals call for both black and white performers in numbers, only a few have dealt with the realities of racial discrimination in the United States, used racially coded music to express the contrasting experiences of black and white characters, or given comparable stage time to black and white performers. *Show Boat* did (and does) all these things.

This book is about *Show Boat*: the novel (1926); the original Broadway production (1927); eight major New York revivals (1932, 1946, 1954, 1956/57, 1961, 1966, 1983, 1994); five London productions (1928, 1943, 1971, 1989, 1998); four Hollywood films (1929, 1936, 1951, and *Till the Clouds Roll By* from 1946, which included extended excerpts from *Show Boat*); important stage productions in Houston (1982, 1989) and Los Angeles (1940, 1944, 1960, 1967); a televised stage production originating in New Jersey (1989); and an ambitious recorded version made in London (1988). The dynamic of the color line provides the vantage point from which I consider *Show Boat*'s many lives. This approach remains relatively new. Race has not always been a key element for historians, critics, and scholars of *Show Boat*, the majority of whom have focused on the notion that *Show Boat* was the first musical play to successfully integrate music, dance, and dramatic story—a claim now on the way out.[4]

The original makers of *Show Boat* ignored a defining racial practice on the American musical stage: they flouted the unwritten rule that blacks and whites address the Broadway audience separately, that the races not share the stage. From their earliest drafts, Hammerstein and Kern imagined *Show Boat* as an interracial musical, and the show they created heads a short list of memorable shows that put blacks and whites into the same cast, among them

Lost in the Stars (1949), *Golden Boy* (1964), *Dreamgirls* (1981), *Big River* (1985), *Ragtime* (1998), *Hairspray* (2002) and *Memphis* (2009).[5] With its interracial cast, *Show Boat* has proved an uncomfortable fit in histories of the musical, which have been largely written along divided racial lines. This situation is not unique to the musical; the dance historian Susan Manning identifies a similarly "segregated historiography" in the area of American modern dance.[6]

Scholars of the black-cast stage have generally ignored *Show Boat*.[7] But when considered in historical perspective, *Show Boat*'s black-cast numbers prove crucial to the show's initial and enduring success. The black chorus opens the show and has anywhere from one to seven numbers depending on the production or film. Up to three major roles in *Show Boat*'s large cast— each with prominent musical numbers—are the province of performers who identify as black in their larger careers. Omitting *Show Boat* from the history of black-cast Broadway eliminates a control of sorts against which innovations in the black-cast musical might be measured. For example, *Show Boat* and *Dreamgirls* played Broadway simultaneously in the 1980s. These two woman-centered shows about race and show business have much to say to each other. Scholars of the white-cast musical—otherwise known as the racially unmarked Broadway or Hollywood musical—have embraced *Show Boat* without emphasizing its black-cast elements (except for "Ol' Man River" and the miscegenation subplot) and spilled much ink trying to define the show's genre. *Show Boat* has been variously categorized as an operetta, a musical play, a folk operetta, and even a sort of failed opera.[8] Most, if not all scholars, overlook the musical comedy dimension, even though the 1927 opening night program defined the show's genre as "An All-American Musical Comedy."[9] The racially mixed origins of musical comedy—built on the rhythms of ragtime and jazz but usually peopled by whites—come to the fore when *Show Boat* is set within both the white and black Broadway traditions.

Understanding how race has worked in the history of *Show Boat* begins with the admission that "whites are raced" as well as blacks.[10] Racial performance is part of every role in a creative realm as tied up with national identity as the musical. Raymond Knapp and Andrea Most, among others, have explored this notion.[11] But the performed distinction between black and white as an essential and constructive element of the American musical in its totality—black-cast and white-cast shows taken together—has not been broached in any systematic way, certainly not in the manner of virtually every other area of popular music studies, where the construction and interaction of black and white remains a fundamental question. The story of *Show Boat*'s making and remaking proves an ideal place to begin the effort to understand how black-cast shows and white-cast shows, blackness and whiteness, blacks and whites, have played against and with each other in the creative realm of the musical over the last eighty years. Only *Show Boat* can do this because only *Show Boat* has endured for so long, and only *Show Boat* among canonic musicals was built so squarely across the color line.

Even as *Show Boat* challenges the segregation of black-cast and white-cast Broadway, the story of its making and remaking brings performers to the fore with particular force. The abundant archival record contains persuasive evidence for how individual performers, black and white, shaped *Show Boat* all along its history. Performers made each version of *Show Boat* into an unrepeatable event, forcing historical consideration of each version on its own terms and rendering moot the effort to define an ideal or definitive version.[12] A history of *Show Boat* that privileges performers reveals an ongoing relationship between the way *Show Boat* used and shaped the performers brought into its orbit and how those same performers used and shaped *Show Boat* for their own ends. The place of this most-revived work in the professional lives of performers, especially African Americans, forms an essential strand of *Show Boat*'s history. *Show Boat*'s mixed-race cast is not equally balanced. Whites dominate the story; blacks are featured in many of its most effective musical moments. This combination of featured blacks in musical highlights and leading whites carrying the plot proves an enduring aspect of *Show Boat*'s innovative structure, copied in later shows and important for black performers's careers.

My approach to *Show Boat* relies on the idea that musical and performance styles can be read as indexes of race. Performance "of a type" or "in a style" is a learned skill, not something inherent or authentic, and songwriters underwrite performance by providing material that supports particular poses, be they race-, gender-, or class-based. The musicologist Raymond Knapp has pointed out that the musical has never enjoyed or suffered under the pretentions to authenticity typical of other, less baldly commercial popular music spheres.[13] And Toni Morrison said in a discussion of the lyric stage, "stereotypes, that's what musical comedy is."[14] This is particularly true in the United States, where native musical theater traditions began with blackface minstrelsy. Playing a black role in *Show Boat* necessarily entails adopting a performance style understood by the audience to be black. In a wide-ranging discussion of African American music, Albert Murray memorably described the "very specific technology of stylization" professional performers call upon when singing the blues.[15] Jayna Brown has recently explored "how expressive artistry brings into view the staged nature of racialization."[16] Professional African American performers on the musical stage and screen have historically called upon a set of techniques that signaled their identities as black. *Show Boat* is a space where these techniques have been employed to various and changing effect, frequently in innovative ways and often in a manner that tested the limits of racial stereotype. But Murray's and Brown's formulations—developed as responses to ideologies of natural rhythm or talent that might undermine the artistic control or skill of black performers—can also be deployed for white performers who perform white roles. The technologies of whiteness on the musical stage and screen are learned as well. Trained or "legitimate" singing, an important element of Magnolia and Ravenal's love duets, defines the pair as white just as much as the flowery imagery and proper grammar of their lyrics. The Jerome Kern scholar Stephen Banfield has described passages requiring high notes like the kind Magnolia and Ravenal sing as needing "real singers."[17] Historically, it's also accurate to describe this kind of voice as "white." And anyone can learn to sing that way. Remember that the trained opera singers Todd Duncan and Anne Brown, the first Porgy and Bess, had to be taught by George Gershwin to sing in black dialect. Among *Show Boat*'s cast of characters, Queenie and Julie prove especially interesting here, as both these roles initially required white performers to play black types. An important subplot in the history of *Show Boat* has been the process whereby black women claimed both roles as their own.

Most all the recent scholarship on *Show Boat* taking up the question of race has been critical and theoretical rather than historical. Scholars such as Linda Williams, Raymond Knapp, M. Nourbese Philip, and Robin Breon have, for the most part, relied on Miles Kreuger's *Show Boat: The Story of a Classic American Musical* (1977)—a compendium of facts and pictures—and John McGlinn's 1988 omnibus recording of all the surviving music created by Kern and Hammerstein for versions made between 1927 and 1946.[18] Kreuger and McGlinn are essential, but they leave much out of the story and have their own embedded biases. This book follows the lead of the late Scott McMillin, the first *Show Boat* scholar to bring practical, show-making questions of race into an archival study of the show. In a *Theatre Survey* article from 2000, McMillin described an early version of the 1927 script, which demonstrated how important race and performance were to Hammerstein and Kern's conception of the show.[19] His study marked a new direction in *Show Boat* research, where archival discoveries rather than critical readings open up the meaning of the show.

An entire substratum of *Show Boat* history lies buried in the papers of Kern, Hammerstein, Ziegfeld, Ferber, and others. Several archival finds stand out. I describe for the first time in print a previously unknown script dating from the start of rehearsals for the original Broadway production, as well as a rediscovered copy of the conductor's score also from 1927 and a heavily marked vocal score that belonged to the assistant conductor for the 1928 London production, the first to include Paul Robeson.[20] Beyond these new sources, phantom *Show Boats* that never sailed survive in treatments and scripts produced by Hollywood screenwriters tasked with transferring *Show Boat* to the screen. These writers—Hammerstein prominent among them—often imagined versions of Ferber's tale that were stunningly different from the finished films. Their rejected ideas trace out some of the limits put on the retelling of this tale of race, music, theater, and America at given times in its Hollywood history.

Part 1 puts the making of the novel and original Broadway musical into a detailed 1920s context, describing how Ferber's story was transformed by Hammerstein and Kern, the producer Florenz Ziegfeld, and the interracial group of performers who introduced and shaped *Show Boat*'s large cast of characters. Part 2 considers key moments in the remaking of *Show Boat* over the ensuing seventy years, zeroing in on how questions of race and performance answered one way in the 1920s were responded to by new generations of performers, producers, choreographers, and directors, all endeavoring to make *Show Boat* into a hit one more time. Race—employed here as a one-word marker for ongoing issues of black and white on the segregated musical stage and screen—proves an enduringly salient point of entry. The color line defines the field for practical reasons in this show, which forces a black cast and a white cast to coexist on the same stage and in the same story. My emphasis on race rests equally on definitions of blackness and whiteness. Magnolia and Ravenal perform their whiteness every bit as much as Joe performs his blackness and any actress playing Julie must perform that character's mixed-race identity, whatever that has meant in particular times and places.

In 1939, the American artist Doris Lee was commissioned by *Life* magazine to paint a grand picture of the final dress rehearsal of the original 1927 *Show Boat*. The result—published in full color as the centerpiece of the November 27 issue—appears on the cover of this book. Lee did meticulous research and included all the important players who made the original show. Ziegfeld, Hammerstein, and Kern are at bottom center in the orchestra pit, gesticulating broadly, clearly in charge of the entire enterprise. At center stage, Magnolia and Ravenal (played by Norma Terris and Howard Marsh) and Joe (played by Jules Bledsoe) seem to be simultaneously offering the balcony scene love duet "Make Believe" and the anthem-like "Ol' Man River," musical numbers heard in succession in act 1 scene 1. In refusing to choose between a moment of high musical romance and the quasi-spiritual signature song from the score, Lee captured the creative tension between black featured performers and white main characters that accounts for *Show Boat*'s length and fuels its constant variety. Lee surrounded her central group of Joe, Magnolia, and Ravenal with various ladies from the cast: on the right, some members of the white chorus, Edna Mae Oliver as Parthy (a disapproving column in pink and white stripes), and Tess Gardella in blackface as Queenie (in the white-with-red-polka-dots costume she wore in her vaudeville act as Aunt Jemima); on the left, a lone black chorister with dark brown skin in a yellow dress with red polka dots provides some balance to the composition, posed as she is beneath an American flag (which visually rhymes with Parthy's dress). Lee's vision of *Show Boat* is colorful and honest. She combined all the essential elements at center stage; refusing to choose white over black, recognizing the diversity of skin colors in the cast—even including blackface—in effect reminding *Life*'s readership of what made the show so unusual in its time (and, of course, after). Most of the illustrations in this book similarly picture black and white together. Almost all, like Lee's painting, have not been previously reproduced. These interracial images repeat in visual form the defining element of *Show Boat* as an American musical, affording glimpses of black and white performers alike performing race while enacting *Show Boat*'s tale of American music and theater.

PART I

MAKING

1

A FERBER PLOT

• • •

Show Boat was conceived on August 20, 1924, after the desultory out-of-town tryout opening of Edna Ferber and George S. Kaufman's *Minick* (a play adapted from Ferber's story "Old Man Minick"). Commiserating with the cast and authors after the show, the producer Winthrop Ames joked that if *Minick* flopped they could all join a show boat. Ferber recalled her response in her 1939 autobiography *A Peculiar Treasure:* "'What's a show boat?' I asked, sourly. I'd never heard of them." Ames's description of floating theaters plying America's inland waterways during the nineteenth century captivated Ferber, who felt the thrill of new material. "Here was news of a romantic and dramatic aspect of America . . . one of the most melodramatic and gorgeous bits of Americana that had ever come my way."[1]

Ferber took up the new project with dispatch. She traveled to Maryland in October, only to find the show boat she sought was tying up for the winter. With a promise to revisit the James Adams Floating Palace Theatre—Charles Hunter, proprietor—the next spring, Ferber returned to New York and started doing research. She made inquiries about steam ships on the Mississippi on which she could catch a ride, but in the end Ferber never felt it necessary to make even a short visit to the river at the center of her story.[2] Come April 1925, Ferber spent four days on Hunter's show boat as honored guest and member of the company. Ever the stage-struck frustrated actress, Ferber took to life on the boat immediately: "Show folks. My heart leaped toward them, like Tiny Tim I loved them every one, from Jo, the colored cook, to the pilot of the tugboat. . . . It seemed to me a lovely life as we floated down the river. . . . New York was another planet."[3] In one marathon session, Ferber got Hunter to sit down and tell stories of his life on the river, yielding, she wrote, "a stream of pure gold."[4] Then it was off to Europe. Ferber started writing *Show Boat* in a Basque seaside village, worked in Paris for a while, then returned to Manhattan. She finished the book at 50 Central Park

West—the luxurious Prasada building at Sixty-fifth Street—in her six-room apartment, which had eight windows facing the park. Ferber wrote in a small back room.

It was almost without precedent for Ferber to bring black characters into her fiction. By 1925 she had published four novels and more than sixty short stories, most set in the Midwest with Chicago as the primary urban locale. The only characters of color she had created to this point were the black washerwoman Canary in "Old Man Minick" who became the black maid Alma in *Minick*. Canary is written with a thick dialect and has the "rolling eye" that persists like a tic in Ferber's descriptions of African Americans. Alma sings spirituals as she works around the house, and her connection with the title character brings the play to a gentle close. Ferber noted in her autobiography how innovative it was to cast the black actress Emma Wise in the role, a decision that gave *Minick* an unusual mixed-race cast.

The southward flow of the Mississippi necessarily pulled Ferber out of her midwestern comfort zone. Writing *Show Boat* encouraged, perhaps constrained her, to address racial issues more directly than she ever had. She did so in three ways: inserting anonymous black figures into her descriptive passages of life along the river, giving Magnolia a black voice, and creating a subplot around the mixed-race character Julie.

Julie and the "passing" plot have received the lion's share of commentary on race in *Show Boat* the musical. Julie, an actress in the show boat company, resists the advances of Pete, a member of the crew. Pete retaliates by telling the sheriff that Julie is of mixed racial parentage, that she is "passing" as white. Warned in advance of the sheriff's impending visit to arrest the pair, Julie's husband, Steve, a white actor on the boat, cuts her hand and sucks some of her blood. Performance of this melodramatic, symbolic act in the presence of the *Cotton Blossom* company allows Steve to claim under Mississippi's "one drop" rule that he, himself, is black. (Windy, the vessel's crusty old pilot, can truthfully attest to the sheriff that Steve has "Negro blood in him.") Successfully dodging the accusation they are guilty of miscegenation, Steve and Julie must now leave the show boat because they are both considered black, and the *Cotton Blossom* acting troupe is all white. Ferber's source for the story survives in a letter Hunter wrote her offering several stories of race mixture or racial performance.[5] She opted for the one that skirted questions of interracial sex—rejecting tales involving the children of interracial coupling—and cleaned up the story as Hunter had told it. For example, Hunter's Julie leaves Steve in the end and takes up with a "big black negro."

In transferring the confrontation between Julie, Steve, and the sheriff to the musical stage, Hammerstein put dialogue, stage action, even descriptive language from the novel directly into the show's libretto—with one important exception. Ferber's Elly—the childish, self-indulgent leading lady of the boat—reacts to Julie's unmasking with explicitly racist anger, losing control to the point where her husband, Schultzy, physically restrains her and carries her out of the room "like a sack of meal."[6] But Elly roars back in, confronting Julie directly: "'She's black! She's black! God, I was a fool not to see it all the time. Look at her, the nasty yellow—' A steam of abuse, vile, obscene, born of the dregs of river talk heard through the years, now welled to Elly's lips, distorting them horribly."[7] In the musical, Ellie (spelled with an "ie") plays a very different role. She runs in ahead of the sheriff to warn Julie and Steve of the situation—giving them time for the business with the knife—and matter-of-factly fingers Pete as the "river rat" who gave Julie away to the sheriff. Ellie, like everyone on the stage except for Pete, is thoroughly sympathetic to Julie and Steve's predicament. (Even the starchy matron of the boat Parthy tacitly joins the united front the *Cotton Blossom* players present to the sheriff.) By rewriting Elly's moral character, Hammerstein eliminated the one individual in Ferber's version who articulated a racist response to the revelation of Julie's racial identity. This surely played into Hammerstein's own beliefs on racial questions. He eliminated a view of the situation that some, perhaps many, in the Broadway audience might have shared, and instead directed the audience to read the story of Julie and Steve as tragic, as absurd, as an instance of injustice. Musical support in the form of underscoring drawing on the mournful "Mis'ry's Comin' Aroun'," a cut number for Queenie and the black chorus (see chap. 5), also enhanced the moment. As a reviewer of the Boston tour noted, the "little tragedy of Julie, Steve and their negro blood devotedly commingled is acted not without a sympathetic thrill."[8] Hammerstein's rewriting of Ferber's tale closed the door on racist readings of Julie's situation, a crucial revision that would stand the scene in good stead in later years when the miscegenation plot would be pointed to as an example of a serious topic treated in a serious manner in line with Broadway's brand of liberal sentiment.

The Julie subplot is more important in the musical than in the novel. For Ferber, Magnolia's black voice plays a more central role, directly articulating a major theme of the book. But before examining this story of race and popular culture in detail, we need to get a general sense for how *Show Boat* and its heroine fit into Ferber's fictional universe, for Ferber's fascination with show boats did not guarantee she would write anything resembling an authentic show boat story. Indeed, she wrote a typical Ferber story, centered on a strong, independent woman who succeeds in business without a man to help or hinder her. In *Show Boat*, the business in question is show business.

Ferber's pre-1926 heroines were American girls who grew to womanhood within the time frame of the story. These high-spirited females typically marry, but the marriage seldom—almost never—turns out well. Ferber's antihero husbands have less imagination, less commitment, or less healthy constitutions than their wives. Sooner or later these men pass neatly out of the narrative but not before fathering a child, almost always a boy, who adds to the story a malleable subject to be molded into adulthood by the now solitary heroine. Husbandless, Ferber's heroines must find the resolve and marketable skills to support themselves and whatever children they may have. They always manage to do both. Professional success is a given: Ferber never created a woman who couldn't win on her own terms in the world of men. The children are disappointing but never embarrassing. *Show Boat* has two possible Ferber heroines: Parthenia Ann Hawks and her daughter, Magnolia, each live a version of Ferber's favorite tale.

Parthy, a New England school mistress, marries Captain Andy Hawks rather late in life and the couple has one child, Magnolia. The story of Parthy and Andy's marriage occupies much of chapters 2 through 6. Parthy is enticed onto the *Cotton Blossom* by a vision of authority over others: her first glimpse of the kitchen inspires in her eyes "the unholy light of the housewife who beholds for the first time the domain of her dreams."[9] When, at the midpoint of the novel, Andy is swept overboard to his death in a storm, Parthy takes over, managing the *Cotton Blossom* into the most profitable floating theater on the Mississippi. At her death she leaves Magnolia a half a million dollars. But Parthy is too severe, too negative, too spiteful to be a true Ferber heroine. As Ferber notes of Parthy, "always she was to resent loveliness; fight the influence of each new experience; combat the lure of each new face. Tight-lipped, belligerent, she met beauty and adventure and defied them to work a change in her."[10]

Magnolia is Ferber's real heroine, and it is difficult to overestimate the extent to which *Show Boat* the novel, unlike the musical, is about her to the exclusion of the other characters. Ferber's Magnolia is a headstrong but always sympathetic girl, raised on the river and filled with a passion for living reflected in her irresistible smile. The incident with Julie serves as the only shadow over her otherwise sunny childhood. After Elly departs unexpectedly, Magnolia takes her place as leading lady. Shortly thereafter, Schultzy also leaves to care for Elly, who has fallen ill. The boat thus needs a new leading man, and a gambler fallen on hard times named Gaylord Ravenal enters the story. Magnolia, already an accomplished actress, falls in love with Ravenal, a figure of shabby romance. (In the novel, the Julie episode occurs when Magnolia is a young girl. Hammerstein's telescoped plot for the musical connects

Julie's departure, Magnolia's selection as the new leading lady, and Ravenal's hiring as leading man, three junctures in the plot that remain discrete from each other in the novel.) Ravenal and Magnolia elope and return to the boat, now an unsustainably tense environment as Parthy and Ravenal refuse to make peace. Magnolia gives birth to Kim and soon thereafter Andy dies. Unwilling to remain on the river under his mother-in-law's control, Ravenal convinces Magnolia to leave the river with a sizable legacy in hand.

The family moves to Chicago. After a year or so of high living, the money is gone, and the fortunes of the Ravenals henceforth ride on Gaylord's success as a gambler. Looking for some stability for her daughter, Magnolia enrolls Kim in a convent school, a not particularly respectable place filled with the daughters of show people and high-class prostitutes. When Parthy writes of her intent to visit, Ravenal takes off for good, never to return. All versions of *Show Boat* except the original novel rehabilitate Ravenal at the close, a change that flies in the face of Ferber's imaginative universe, which up to and including *Show Boat* was populated by weak, ineffectual men. Ferber puts her final verdict on Ravenal in his grown daughter's mouth. Kim dismisses the father who abandoned her as a shallow albeit romantic figure: "Gaylord Ravenal. A lovely name. What a tinhorn sport he must have been. Charming though, probably."[11]

When Ravenal abandons Magnolia, she confronts the same questions previous Ferber heroines had faced: How will I live? and how will I support my child? Again, the principal theme of Ferber's writing is the interplay of personal destiny with economic reality.[12] William Allen White, a well-known journalist and editor, commented, "All her people do something for a living. She is the goddess of the worker. . . . And her stories chiefly tell what a fine time these hardworking Americans have with their day's work."[13] Previous Ferber heroines facing the "how will I live?" question responded by selling coal or insurance, by managing rental properties, or by running a small town store. One raised and sold asparagus to fancy hotel restaurants; another opened a successful restaurant in her home. Magnolia opts for the stage.

Magnolia's embrace of show business as a means to survive as a single mother is directly linked to Ferber's use of black music to characterize her heroine. Magnolia's black voice thus proves a defining aspect of Ferber's main character and a central pillar of the novel's structure and larger themes. Magnolia's story and the plot of *Show Boat* alike trace the course of American life across the divide separating the nineteenth century from the twentieth, an epochal shift felt with particular power in the 1920s when the effects of World War I and a series of overlapping transformations in daily life were altering the fabric of the nation. *Show Boat* was about these transformations, offering its original readers a history of the present, specifically as reflected in the American theater. Magnolia's performance of blackness—defined in contemporary 1920s terms—was used by Ferber as a means to critique the present. This critique was of a largely aesthetic nature and directed chiefly at the Broadway stage. Hence, *Show Boat* was not, by intention, a political or socially engaged novel. When transferred to the musical stage by a politically engaged figure like Hammerstein, Ferber's story would have the potential to address the history of American race relations from a particular angle. But before the story of making the novel into a musical can be told, a precise understanding of how Ferber used Magnolia's performance of blackness must be set forth.

The crucial scene where Magnolia embarks on a professional career as a singer is laid at Jopper's Variety in Chicago circa 1904. (In the musical, the location is the Trocadero, a Chicago venue Ziegfeld had once owned.) Magnolia auditions with a song she learned as a child from Jo, the black cook on the boat. Magnolia's choice of song harkens back to a scene early in the book, part of a two-chapter idyll of life on the river, which was extravagantly praised by reviewers. There, the reader learns how Magnolia learned to sing just like Jo, who also taught her to play the banjo. Ferber spends several pages describing Jo's musical style and vocal timbre. She defines his repertoire, and even prints the words and music for his favorite song "All God's Chillun Got Shoes"—a spiritual Jo calls "I Got Shoes." (Other titles for this popular and widely published Negro spiritual include "All God's Chillun Got Wings," "I Got a Robe," and "Heav'n, Heav'n"). Magnolia finds her voice by copying Jo:

> Jo's voice was a reedy tenor, but soft and husky with the indescribable Negro vocal quality. Magnolia soon knew the tune and the words of every song in Jo's repertoire. Unconsciously, being an excellent mimic, she sang as Jo and Queenie sang, her head thrown slightly back, her eyes rolling or half closed, one foot beating rhythmic time to the music's cadence. Her voice was true, though mediocre; but she got into this the hoarsely sweet Negro overtone—purple velvet muffling a flute.[14]

At the Jopper's audition many years later, Magnolia picks up a banjo, throws her head back—just like Jo did—and sings the song Jo taught her. The manager's reaction assures the reader that Magnolia is a fine mimic. More important, her performance raises questions from the listeners about her racial status:

> "What kind of a coon song do you call that?" inquired the [man in a] gray derby.
> "Why, it's a Negro melody—they sing them in the South."

"Sounds like a church hymn to me." He paused. His pale shrewd eyes searched her face. "You a nigger?"

The unaccustomed red surged into Magnolia's cheeks, dyed her forehead, her throat, painfully. "No, I'm not a—nigger."

"Well, you cer'nly sing like one. Voice and—I don't know—way you sing."[15]

Magnolia's performance does not square with the stereotypes of the variety stage: she's not a "coon-song shouter." The novel's original readers would have made a distinction the man in the gray derby could not: Magnolia was singing a spiritual.

In two other scenes earlier in the novel, the adult Magnolia similarly startles two contrasting groups of listeners. The scene with the black bellhops listening outside her hotel room was quoted earlier in the introduction. Ferber includes a contrasting moment with a white audience in the same section of the novel. During a chance encounter with a group of Ravenal's gambler friends at a restaurant, Magnolia performs the spiritual "Deep River" in "an unconscious imitation of old Jo's attitude." The men are unsure how to respond. One echoes the gray derby's confusion at the audition. "You call that a coon song and maybe it is. I don't dispute you, mind. But I never heard any song like *that* called a coon song, and I heard a good many coon songs in my day. I Want Them Presents Back, and A Hot Time, and Mistah Johnson, Turn Me Loose."[16] Magnolia next plays and sings "All God's Chillun Got Wings," a spiritual that permits up-tempo performance, and everyone agrees this one is better. Again and again, Ferber emphasizes the gap between Magnolia's performances of spirituals and the turn-of-the-century genre of the coon song—ragtime songs in black dialect frequently containing extremely racist lyrics and typically sung by whites in blackface—in short, the antithesis of the spiritual.

What purpose did a heroine who could sing spirituals like a black man serve in Ferber's novel? Several answers present themselves when *Show Boat* is placed within its precise time and place—mid-1920s Manhattan—and within Ferber's output. Magnolia's black voice is firstly connected to black musical styles, performers, and themes that were gaining a new visibility in mainstream (white) popular culture in the mid-1920s. The southern critic Donald Davidson took Ferber to task for what he saw, not inaccurately, as a strategic use of black music. "Miss Ferber does not play fair, either, in introducing at various points in the narrative certain prescient references to the Negro spirituals so popular nowadays. It seems an illegitimate foresight, even a truckling to the mood of the moment, to equip her heroine with a perhaps unnatural admiration for 'I Got Shoes,' 'Go Down, Moses,' and 'Deep River.' It is a cheap trick. . . . It looks as if Miss Ferber had carefully mixed her ingredients for a large popular audience."[17]

Ferber worked on the novel between September 1924 and August 1926, a period that saw a high-water mark in the vogue for concert spirituals and black male spiritual singers in New York City. Ferber built this vogue into her heroine's identity as part of a critique of the present that was unrelated to larger debates about the status of blacks in the nation. Ferber wrote neither an antiracist novel nor a sentimental evocation of the South. *Show Boat* is neither *Uncle Tom's Cabin* nor *The Clansman* (Thomas Dixon's novel, which was turned into the film *The Birth of a Nation*). Rather, Ferber uses black music and attendant ideas of its authenticity—its immediacy and spontaneity, for example—as a means to critique the sterility of modern New York in general and the Broadway dramatic theater in particular. While Ferber may deploy black music and ideas about black music as part of her story, this does not mean she put any substantial investment in racial issues in *Show Boat*. She had no axe to grind about race in the American present or past. Ferber's main concerns are much narrower. Masquerading as a picturesque historical novel, *Show Boat* was, in the end, more about the contemporary (white) New York dramatic stage than anything else.

Ferber's use of black music in a critique of white theater finds its precise historical context in the ubiquitous presence of Negro spirituals and African American singers in Manhattan during the period when Ferber was researching and writing. This innovative milieu built on interracial encounter—black singers of a particular type attracting enthusiastic white audiences—similarly informed Kern and Hammerstein's work on the musical. A brief description of spirituals in Jazz Age New York helps contextualize both *Show Boat* the novel and the musical.

Negro spirituals performed as solos in the concert hall were a new sensation in New York in the mid-1920s. The black tenor Roland Hayes initiated the practice of offering spirituals, usually a single, concluding set, in recitals otherwise dominated by the music of Handel and nineteenth-century German and French art songs. Hayes studied and launched his career in Europe in the early 1920s, where critics hailed his artistry. In 1924 he returned home to the United States and took the northeastern urban centers by storm. He sang his New York debut at Aeolian Hall in April, just months before Ferber started work on the novel.[18] On December 6, 1924, Jules Bledsoe, another trained African American singer, made his solo recital debut at Town Hall. Four months later Paul Robeson, not classically trained but possessing a powerful bass voice, took spirituals singing a step farther. On April 19, 1925, Robeson performed an all-spirituals recital at the Greenwich Village Theatre. The event was a sold-out sensation and Robeson repeated the program twice in the following four weeks.[19] Ferber, though out of town for four days in April visiting Hunter's show boat, was otherwise in New York during the period of Robeson's triumphant debut as a singer of spirituals. (She left for Europe in June of that year.)

The advance of spirituals singers continued unabated while Ferber worked on *Show Boat*. The Urban League's journal, *Opportunity*, declared in November 1925, "This year marks the feverish awakening of America to the poignant charm of Negro folk songs."[20] Carl Van Vechten, a white advocate for black musicians and writers, declared the winter of 1925/26 to be a "spiritual winter."[21] By January 1926, white New York newspapers were casting a slightly jaundiced eye at the vogue. The *Herald Tribune* wrote, "No week of the present season seems complete without its Negro Spirituals," the same day the *Sun* announced "Rival exponents in the interpretation of negro [sic] spirituals are on the march and the battle is waxing strong."[22]

Spirituals singing and their singers also found their way onto the dramatic stage. Bledsoe and Robeson alike pieced together performing careers out of concert singing and acting in dramas featuring strong, frequently tragic, black characters, such as Eugene O'Neill's *The Emperor Jones* (1920) and *All Gods Chillun Got Wings* (1924). It was not uncommon for black characters in these plays to start singing a spiritual. Alma in Ferber's own *Minick* does so as well. The appearance of words and music for a spiritual in the text of *Show Boat* brought this kind of interpolated black song from the theater into the novel.

By the mid-1920s the Negro spiritual was an attractive, popular, and still novel sort of black music filling several different niches on the New York scene—just like jazz. Both were understood to be uniquely African American, and thus uniquely American. Black leaders saw the spiritual as a lever of sorts, able to change the way whites thought about blacks. Already in January 1925, *Opportunity* was declaring, "Roland Hayes is now an institution. His concerts have swiftly become the classic example of the power of art over the barriers of race."[23] But spirituals could also be seen as just another mode of blackness on the New York scene, taking their place beside jungle motifs, decadent displays by the denizens of Harlem, and lingering minstrelsy stereotypes. All of these would find a spot in the musical *Show Boat*.

Spirituals were even showing up in fashionable magazines. In the July 1925 issue of *Vanity Fair*, Van Vechten made connections between spirituals and vaudeville that Ferber may have found helpful. "Such a joyous number as *All God's Chillun Got Wings* is even sung in vaudeville, occasionally with an added infectious but impious verse to the effect that All God's Chillun got a Ford! . . . It is not novel to state that the Spirituals are the source of our modern popular music."[24] The article was published with a picture of Robeson. Ferber definitely did not agree with Van Vechten's views concerning spirituals and white singers when he wrote, "I do not think white singers can sing Spirituals. Women, with few exceptions, should not attempt to sing them at all."[25] Perhaps this declaration of what women should not attempt to do influenced Ferber's decision to give Magnolia a black voice. (Ferber mentions *Vanity Fair* twice in *Show Boat* as an exemplar of the fashionable present.)

Immediately before and after the printed music for "I Got Shoes" appears in the novel, Ferber described in detail the sound of Jo and Queenie's voices. Virtually all of her characterizations of black music here and throughout *Show Boat* are drawn from a 1919 *Musical Quarterly* article by Natalie Curtis Burlin, a widely published scholar known for her research on the music of Native Americans and African Americans.[26] Ferber closely followed Curtis's lead. Curtis's four-page article "Negro Music at Birth" describes her experience attending a musical gathering of African Americans in the woods of Alabama. She categorizes the songs she hears as "old plantation melodies."[27] Ferber initially identifies Jo's repertoire as "Negro plantation songs" and writes in a later passage of "those plaintive, wistful Negro plantation songs."[28] Curtis writes of the meeting's Pentecostal character: "It was spirited singing and it was devout; but the inspirational quality of the group-feeling made this music seem a lambent, living thing, a bit of 'divine fire' that descended upon these black people like the gift of tongues." In an atmospheric passage describing the sights and sounds of life on the river, Ferber literalizes the image, pointing to an actual fire, rather than a sacred visitation: "At night you heard them singing plantation songs in the fitful glare of their camp fires in the woods; simple songs full of hope."[29] Curtis wrote, "with song he has colored his shadowed life, evoking hope, joy, beauty even, from within himself."[30] Curtis mentions a "Campmeet'n of the olden time," and Ferber describes Queenie's "high rich campmeeting voice."[31] More shared words confirm Ferber's borrowing from Curtis:

Curtis Burlin: Rough sons and daughters of toil, **ragged** and unkempt, no one could accuse them of ever having come under the smooth influence of refined white environment. . . . Yet in the voices of these toilers lingered an **indescribable** pathos, a something both **child-like** and touching.[32]

Ferber: Jo's voice was a reedy tenor, but soft and husky with the **indescribable** Negro vocal quality. . . . The longing of a footsore, **ragged**, driven race expressed in the tragically **childlike** terms of shoes, white robes, wings, and the wise and simple insight into hypocrisy: "Ev'rybody talkin 'bout Heav'n ain't goin' there . . ."[33]

Even Ferber's description of the timbre of Jo's voice as "reedy" comes from Curtis, who describes the "penetrating, reed-like beauty of quality" she heard in the black voices in the forest clearing.[34]

Curtis's description of the black singers in the woods centers on the idea that in their spontaneous singing, African Americans are overwhelmed by music. She writes about the music being "possessed so completely by them all (or so utterly possessing them!) that they were free to abandon themselves to the inspiration of their own creative instinct."[35] Ferber borrows this notion of blacks being overcome by music in a passage of local color describing the show boat's arrival at a new dock: "Almost invariably some magic-footed Negro, overcome by the music, could be seen on the wharf executing the complicated and rhythmic steps of a double shuffle, his rags flapping grotesquely about him, his mouth a gash of white."[36]

Both Ferber and Curtis argued that authentic musical expression was untrained, spontaneous, and (often) black, while music that was learned formally was destined to be refined, soulless, and (absent genius) likely to be white. Curtis wrote, "With the Negro, it would seem that the further back one traces the current of musical inspiration that runs through the race, (that is, the more primitive the people and thus the more instinctive the gift,) the nearer does one come to the divine source of song,—intuition, which is in turn the wellspring of all genius. So often does education deaden and even utterly destroy intuitive art in individuals as in races, that one might affirm that the genius is he who can survive the attrition of scholastic training!"[37] Magnolia resists "scholastic training" and remains an intuitive performer. Ferber's description of Jo and Queenie's musical influence on Magnolia precedes an account of Parthy's unsuccessful attempts to get Magnolia to take piano lessons. Like an archetypal white American parent fearing the black music their child loves, Parthy exclaims, "I declare I don't know where you get your low ways from! White people aren't good enough for you, I suppose, that you've got to run with blacks in the kitchen. Now you sit yourself down on that [piano] stool."[38] (Kern and Hammerstein introduce Magnolia from offstage with the sound of her less than fluent piano playing.) The little girl rejects formal musical instruction just as she does any and all schooling. Magnolia's reward is a black voice granted an authenticity by all who hear her.

Raised off the river in the cities of the North, Kim does not inherit her mother's black voice. She is, instead, defined as an artist by her studies at the fictional "National Theatre School of Acting" in New York, described in detail in the novel's final chapter. Magnolia watches in amazement as Kim studies to be an actress. "Fencing lessons. Gymnastic dancing. Interpretive dancing. Singing lessons. Voice placing. French lessons. . . . [Kim's] voice was 'placed.' Magnolia, listening and beholding, would not have been surprised to see her remove her voice, an entity, from her throat and hold it up for inspection. It was a thing so artificial, so studied, so manufactured."[39] This scene of mechanical and passionless precision, which Ferber's authorial voice casts as frightening and laughable, is Kim's equivalent to Magnolia's childhood lessons at the feet of Jo and Queenie.

In this fashion, Ferber redeployed Curtis's argument about the intuitive genius of American blacks into a critique of the overschooled 1920s stage. Ferber was a Broadway playwright as well as a novelist, and on the somewhat precious title page of the original edition of *Show Boat* Ferber noted that her story concluded in "the modern theatrical centre of America, the Times Square district of New York City." A primary concern of the novel—conceived as it was during a Broadway tryout—was an analysis of the state of the American theater, surely not a terribly compelling topic for a broad readership. (The theater was on Ferber's mind in the mid-1920s. After writing *Show Boat*, she collaborated with George S. Kaufman on *The Royal Family*, a play about a multigenerational acting family that opened to critical and commercial success the night after the musical *Show Boat*.) In *Show Boat*, Ferber used a racial argument about the sources of musical inspiration and authentic voice to support her thesis about the sources of inspired versus uninspired acting in the almost entirely white realm of the Broadway theater.

Blackness proves instrumental but not essential to Ferber's argument about white theatrical culture. In several places, she describes the show boat performers and audience using Greek-derived terms that make her comparative point sufficiently well. For example, in one ode-like passage the effect of the show boat performances are linked to the deepest roots of the Western theater: "It was the theatre, perhaps, as the theatre was meant to be. A place in which one saw one's dreams come true. A place in which one could live a vicarious life of splendour and achievement; winning in love, foiling the evildoer; a place in which one could weep unashamed, laugh aloud, give way to emotions long pentup. . . . Here were blood, lust, love, passion. Here were warmth, enchantment, laughter, music. It was Anodyne. It was Lethe. It was Escape. It was the Theatre."[40] Descriptions of the river players of the past and the contemporary New York stage would have been enough, it seems, to make her point.

But Ferber went farther and added the element of Negro spirituals, giving Magnolia a black voice. This decision gave Ferber's *Show Boat* an of-the-moment feel and opened the story to critics who saw opportunism in her use of black music. But Ferber's deployment of spirituals and a spiritual-singing black man also likely drew Hammerstein and Kern to the novel as well, suggesting it might be suitable for adaptation to the musical stage. Ferber makes no mention of Broadway musical theater in the novel. Her critique, like her career as a playwright, is entirely concerned with straight plays. Hammerstein's transformation of Kim from serious actress to musical comedy star would foil Ferber's critique entirely, leading to a totally different conclusion as to how the past and present related to each other. In Hammerstein's revised reading of history (see chap. 2), black music played an essential part and Joe's voice and Kim's voice—if not Magnolia's—would play a major role in bringing *Show Boat*'s tale to a conclusion in the present.

Before shifting focus to the musical *Show Boat*, it is important to recognize how arbitrary and problematic the presence of black music is in Ferber's novel. The primary difficulty with Ferber's gift of a black voice to Magnolia comes in the details, or more precisely, in the lack of detail at the very point where, in her other stories of independent women, Ferber is usually painstakingly specific. The moment when a Ferber heroine steps out alone into the male-dominated economy and makes her way under her own power is always laden with drama and a flood of supportive details. Trained as a newspaper reporter, Ferber makes the mechanics of her heroines' success central to the telling of their stories. In *Fanny Herself* (1917), Molly Brandeis must revive the fortunes of her recently deceased husband's general store. Molly goes on a buying trip to Chicago and, on an impulse, buys a variety of gaudy, oversized Catholic holiday figurines. She displays the garish objects in her shop window, and they sell out almost overnight. This prompts the local priest to praise the Jewish shopkeeper while also confirming for Molly her own instincts as a retailer. In *So Big* (1924), the heroine Selina decides to take over her dead husband's truck farm. She rises before dawn, loads her wagon, and heads for Chicago. Selina's physical and mental exhaustion, the risk of failure, and the moral danger she faces sleeping alone in the back of her wagon on a noisy Chicago street crowded with prostitutes and rowdy men are all described in detail. And in Ferber's Emma McChesney stories, the constant business calculations of her "drummer" heroine serve as the substance of most of the plots. Emma, a traveling representative of the Featherloom Petticoat Company, enlightens the reader about how to survive cold train compartments, dingy hotel rooms, and rich hotel food, all the while outsmarting every male salesman in the trade and rising to the top of the firm. Of such detail is the world of Ferber's fiction made. Indeed, her readers came to expect fine-grained depictions from an author who told stories about real people in concrete, identifiably American situations.

And yet, even the closest reading of *Show Boat* yields frustratingly few details about how Magnolia went from abandoned wife to singing star. This should be a central thread in the story, relating precisely how Magnolia conquered the glamorous and seamy world of show business *off* the idealized river. No stranger to tales of women in show business, Ferber celebrated and critiqued this world in several stories prior to *Show Boat*. She knew the ins and outs of theatrical life.[41] But at precisely the moment when Magnolia steps onto the variety stage to support herself and Kim, *Show Boat* takes a huge leap forward in time. The gap between chapters 17 and 18 amounts to twenty years, a period never sufficiently filled in for the reader. In chapter 17, Magnolia auditions unsuccessfully at Jopper's Variety. The chapter ends with Magnolia buying a banjo and sitting down to learn the coon song "Whose Black Baby Are You?" from the sheet music. On the next page, the start of chapter 18, the story shifts abruptly to Kim, now grown up and being interviewed "at the Booth between the second and third acts of Needles and Pins," an "English comedy" already in its sixth month. With this sentence, Ferber all at once assumes a Broadway savvy reader—someone familiar with the Booth Theatre and "English comedy." Kim's transition from convent girl to Broadway star is dispatched by way of celebrity biography shorthand.

What's missing for Ferber's readers is any explanation of how Magnolia managed to parlay her show boat training and much-described black voice into success as a singer on the vaudeville stage. The hints Ferber gives only complicate the question of Magnolia's supposed career in the early decades of the twentieth century. On page 2, Magnolia is described as having been a "soubrette" in Chicago during the "naughty '90s." Vaudeville soubrettes of the 1880s and '90s, among them Lottie Gilson, were white women who sang popular tunes—"cute songs"—in solo acts that were on the cutting edge of popular culture and stylishness.[42] Some 360 pages later, the reader is told that a year after her Jopper's audition, Magnolia was "singing American coon songs in the Masonic Roof bill, her name on the programme with those of Cissie Loftus and Marshall Wilder and the Four Cohans."[43] (Loftus, a singer known for performing imitations, appeared on an old-timers bill at the Palace in April 1925 when Ferber was writing the novel.[44]) The reporter interviewing Kim describes Magnolia as "a show boat actress and later famous singer of coon—," breaking off just when more detail would be welcome.[45] As a final clue, Ferber notes that Magnolia's "vaudeville days" ended when a "roaring tide of ragtime and jazz-time youngsters [came] surging now toward the footlights."[46] In musical terms, coon songs were ragtime tunes, so the notion that a new syncopated style drove Magnolia from the stage makes little sense. This is all the reader is ever told about Magnolia's career on the stage. She is never described performing. Her repertoire is never detailed. Her career is never given shape.

Magnolia's musical performances in the novel are framed in contradictory terms: authentically black enough to startle both black and white audiences while simultaneously confronting those listeners with a kind of black music they found difficult to categorize. What qualifications does Magnolia have to sell coon songs on the vaudeville stage? Did she black up? It's never clear whether Magnolia parlayed Jo's musical voice into fame and success or whether she put aside everything she learned on the river to become a coon shouter like every other white woman singing black songs in vaudeville. If Magnolia was a coon shouter, then the silence of the text is understandable. It would radically change Magnolia as a character to fill in such details. Yet, if Magnolia did make a career singing Jo's spirituals, then the credibility of the narrative collapses—no one, male or female, was singing spirituals on the variety stage in those ragtime years—and Magnolia loses her place in the ranks of Ferber heroines who attain economic independence in a reasonably realistic economic context. Silence at the point in the story where Ferber was typically voluble was perhaps the only alternative if the theme of black music as authentic, intuitive expression were to be combined with Ferber's characteristic plot centering on a white woman who succeeds on her own in a man's world. This credibility gap in the narrative would come to haunt the film and musical adaptations made just after the novel came out. Audiences for a stage or screen version of Magnolia's story wanted to see and hear her onstage, to experience her magic. Ferber, though, provided little guidance. Hammerstein and Kern (influenced by Norma Terris, who introduced the role) solved the problem one way in the 1927 musical. The Universal film of 1929 came up with a different solution (see chaps. 4 and 6).

Ferber insisted on several occasions that *Show Boat* was a frivolous, escapist book. On a 1939 radio version of the book directed by Orson Welles—Ferber played Parthy—she said "*Show Boat* carries no message. It is just a romantic novel about a rather glamorous phase of American life."[47] In a 1945 interview, Ferber noted, "But as for themes in fiction—every one of my books has had a theme deep in it that was very important to me. I should say every book except *Show Boat*, which hadn't any theme, which was just fun."[48] As noted above, Ferber's deployment of black music in *Show Boat* does not suggest she took any principled stand on race. When asked to pen an article describing "the world she would like to live in" for the *Nation* in 1928 as *Show Boat* was running on Broadway, Ferber made no reference to race prejudice, nor did her later work deal with black/white issues or questions of race prejudice as a continuing theme (as Hammerstein's did).[49] In sum, the sources of

"Ol' Man River" are not to be found in Ferber's novel. Ferber used black music to serve her own limited purposes.

But once out in the world, Magnolia, Jo, Queenie, Julie, and the other characters in *Show Boat* were there to be turned to other purposes—principally the filling of theaters and movie palaces. In those venues, where her characters were made to sing and dance by creative figures such as Oscar Hammerstein, the implications of Ferber's story of a white girl with a black voice would take *Show Boat* in unexpected directions.

2
THE ROBESON PLAN
• • •

Show Boat the musical was conceived around the talents and star power of Paul Robeson, a black male singing star who appeared most often in concert halls and theaters accompanied only by a piano.

Show Boat the musical as presented to the American theatergoing public for the first time ended up hitched to the talents and star power of Helen Morgan, a white female singing star who appeared most often in nightclubs and theaters accompanied only by a piano.

Paul Robeson was a major star of mid-1920s Manhattan, enjoying in the most public of ways the white fascination with blacks that fueled the so-called Harlem Renaissance. Hammerstein and Kern tried to tap into this fascination from the beginning of their work on *Show Boat*. Beyond retelling Ferber's tale of Magnolia and Ravenal, the earliest draft librettos expanded the role of Joe, spelled with a final *e*, as Robeson would play it, reimagining the character in broad, historical terms, going far beyond Ferber, and drawing on the history of popular music in an attempt to round out the story in a dramatically effective, musically diverse, thematically satisfying, thoroughly commercial manner. I call this effort the Robeson plan. Hammerstein and Kern only relinquished the Robeson plan late in the production process—it was still there when rehearsals began in October 1927—and they clung to the idea beyond the successful opening of the show without it. But Robeson himself rejected the Robeson plan, agreeing to play Joe only after certain elements that referred to him specifically had been removed (and after *Show Boat* had proved a solid hit with audiences). The remnants of the Robeson plan—"Ol' Man River" and its many reprises—served Robeson and generations of black basses after him, creating a reliable role and underwriting the revivability of *Show Boat* itself. The Robeson plan was multifaceted, designed to both feature Robeson and underscore Hammerstein's popular music plot, which tied the multigenerational story of Magnolia and Kim to the larger history of American music (echoing Ferber's tale of the legitimate theater; see chap. 1). Later attempts to incorporate Hammerstein's popular music plot into *Show Boat* would, of course, not rely on Robeson. Still, the story line initially designed to feature the singer has endured as an element of the musical up to the present. In this way, even without Robeson himself, remnants of the Robeson plan and permutations of Hammerstein's popular music plot would reappear again and again in the making and remaking of *Show Boat*.

Like Robeson, Helen Morgan was a major star of mid-1920s Manhattan. Unlike Robeson, who stood in front of the piano, Morgan sat atop—some said "rode"—the piano, usually with silk scarf in hand. In the process of shaping the role of Julie around Morgan's unique talents, the makers of *Show Boat* presented the singer to the Broadway public in a tremendously effective manner. For an entire generation of American audiences, Morgan was the standout star of *Show Boat*. The decision to feature her in a particular way constitutes a separate strand in the making of the show, a series of creative choices that I call the Morgan plan. The Morgan plan did not have much effect on the overall theme or plot trajectory of *Show Boat*. It wasn't as conceptual as the Robeson plan, lacked any relation to Hammerstein's popular music plot, and succeeded only in expanding the role of Julie to the point where the actress playing the part could be more than a minor player. In later remakings, the Morgan plan worked to the benefit of a string of actresses—most hailing from nightclubs—who used the featured role to build or sustain their careers. In story terms, the Morgan plan introduced a musical and emotional high point—the interpolated song "Bill"—that bore little connection to the rest of the show and yet became an essential part of the whole. The Morgan plan also brought media notoriety to *Show Boat* that could not have been anticipated by Ziegfeld, Hammerstein, and Kern when they cast Morgan. On a practical level, the Morgan plan ended up selling tickets.

The Robeson and Morgan plans—the *Show Boat* that could have been, the *Show Boat* that came to be—were built on new song-centered, thoroughly gendered performance personas: the spiritual-singing black man and the torch song-singing white woman, both of which marked out new areas of racially defined performance. These were innovative voices and figures, expressions of the changing popular culture landscape of Jazz Age Manhattan. Robeson embodied like no one else the black performance insurgency of the 1920s, where new opportunities given black performers were tempered by the imperative that they show restraint when seeking acceptance from white audiences. Morgan carried the torch for Prohibition-resisting white Manhattan, her life and performance persona embodying the predicament faced by middle-class wets. *Show Boat* could accommodate both because it made room for black *and* white performers. Kern, Hammerstein, and Ziegfeld had no prior connection to either the black male concert spiritual singer or the white female nightclub singer. These were performed racial types on the New York scene primed for insertion into musical shows. *Show Boat* embraced both: Robeson by strong intention and ultimately without success; Morgan for convenience sake and to unexpectedly great benefit.

On a flyer advertising two 1929 Carnegie Hall appearances, Robeson's white management offered a selective biography of the singer. As to the facts, it was accurate enough and bears quoting from at length (with annotations) as an introduction to the phenomenon that was Paul Robeson in the 1920s:

> Paul Robeson was born in Princeton, N.J. [in 1898]. He was the youngest son of a Methodist minister [and former slave] who had earned his way through Lincoln University [an all-black college]. . . .
>
> Once [Robeson] brought home a report card with seven A's and one B. "Son, what's the B doing there?" asked his father. "Nothing less than perfection" became Paul's motto. Perfection came easily to him. His brilliance at high school won him a scholarship. He went to Rutgers College [only the third African American student in the school's history]. He won his "R" in football, baseball, basketball and track sports, being one of Rutgers' few 4-letter men. . . .
>
> His logical brain, convincing language and endearing personality made him Rutgers' star debater. He was graduated as "the perfect college man." A brilliant career as a lawyer was predicted for him. He completed the two-year law course at Columbia University and took his degree. In the meantime he consented to act in a play being given at the Y.M.C.A. By chance Eugene O'Neill was in the audience. He came backstage and insisted that Paul Robeson should act in *Emperor Jones*. Robeson laughed at the idea.
>
> In 1923 he consented to play *Emperor Jones*. To his astonishment the audience went mad over him! *Emperor Jones* was followed by *All God's Chillun [Got Wings]*, . . . and *Black Boy* (written especially for him). His law career [which had never really interested Robeson and was inevitably limited by racism] was definitely abandoned for the stage. Though all admired his acting and his appearance, it was the marvelous quality of his voice that thrilled them most. "Why don't you give a concert?" clamored critics and audiences. In 1925 he gave his first concert, in New York [a program entirely made up of Negro spirituals accompanied by the African American pianist Lawrence Brown, a seasoned professional]. His gloriously pure and velvet voice flooded the hall with magic beauty. People shouted

and stamped until he had given an hour of encores. For his next concert they lined up in a snowstorm to buy standing room.

A brief concert-tour of Europe stretched itself into two years. He became the rage, winning new thousands of devotees wherever he sang. London, Paris, Berlin, all cities acclaimed his genius. [During this period, Robeson played Joe in the first London *Show Boat*.][1]

This press agent's Cinderella story leaves something out, of course: the fact that Robeson was black. The text suppresses Robeson's race, both as an attraction for audiences and as a barrier to advancement. Perhaps Robeson left the law because he saw little future in the profession after encountering endemic racism in his first job with a white firm rather than fate knocking on the door in the person of Eugene O'Neill. Perhaps he went into concert singing because of the limited number of parts available for a black dramatic actor. Perhaps his path was more subtle than the triumphal procession hailed by the cries of besotted critics and audiences, understood by the text to be white. The common impulse among successful blacks of the period to suppress references to discrimination for fear of alienating white patrons surely hangs over this narrative. Still, there is an attempt here to write the life of Robeson as a man rather than a black man, a celebrity rather than a black celebrity. In living that life, Robeson was never able to dispense with his color, and a parallel text from 1925 offers a contemporary gloss to the boosterish bio.

Walter White's contribution to Alain Locke's 1925 anthology *The New Negro* was an essay "The Paradox of Color." White used Robeson as his prime example, beginning with the Broadway audience's response to Robeson in *The Emperor Jones*. "Wave after wave of applause, almost hysterical with relief, brought Paul Robeson time and time again before the curtain to receive the acclaim his art had merited. . . . His color—his race—all, all were forgotten by those he has stirred so deeply with his art."[2] White's wishful thinking that the white audience had somehow forgotten Robeson's race (this after seeing a play about a black man going mad in the jungle) serves a rhetorical purpose, for after the cheers fall silent, the essay follows Robeson, his wife Eslanda, and White and his wife as they exited the stage door together.

We wanted supper and a place to talk. All about us blinked invitingly the lights of restaurants and inns of New York's Bohemia. Place after place was suggested and discarded. Here a colored man and his companion had been made to wait interminably until, disgusted, they had left. There a party of four colored people, all university graduates, had been told flatly by the proprietress, late of North Carolina, she did not serve "niggers." At another,

other colored people had been stared at so rudely they had bolted their food and left in confusion. The Civil Rights Act of New York would have protected us—but we were too much under the spell of the theatre we had just quitted to want to insist on the rights the law gave us. So we mounted a bus and rode seven miles or more to colored Harlem where we could be served with food without fear of insult or contumely. The man whose art had brought homage to his feet from sophisticated New York could not enter even the cheapest of the eating places of lower New York with the assurance that some unpleasantness might not come to him before he left.[3]

The story of Robeson and *Show Boat* epitomizes the power performers can wield even as it marks the limits within which black actors (and characters) operated in the period when *Show Boat* was made. All subsequent versions of *Show Boat* had to renegotiate structures first laid out around Robeson. Within those bounds, Joe—a character with few precedents in American musical theater, built on both the Negro spiritual and Robeson's star persona—could articulate a specifically racial message that spoke to the injustice faced by black men and women in the American past and present. Before detailing how the figure of Robeson captured Kern and Hammerstein's imagination in their initial work on *Show Boat*, the place and shape of that figure on the New York scene must be explored in more detail.

Robeson's meteoric career on Midtown stages in the mid-1920s embodied the notoriety African Americans were newly able to claim and the narrow limits within which they might express themselves. It was also testament to Robeson's sheer star quality, something that should not be underestimated. Nothing if not ambitious, Robeson famously said his law degree was meaningless because he would never make it to the Supreme Court. The desire to be at the center of things led him to the theater. Robeson recognized that finding a spot in the white-cast realm of serious drama was the only way to transcend the black-cast musical shows of the time. Black-cast dramas were emerging in the 1920s, and Robeson appeared in *Roseanne* (1924) with the all-black Lafayette Players in Harlem; for an ambitious young actor, though, the goal had to be Broadway, which Robeson entered by way of Greenwich Village.[4]

From the start of his acting career, Robeson appeared in interracial shows where, without fail, his singing voice was also heard. His first professional appearance came in 1922 with *Taboo*; here he co-starred with Margaret Wycherly, the only white in an otherwise all-black cast. The show flopped—it closed after four performances—but provided "timely exposure" that launched Robeson with the critics.[5] The powerful Alexander Woollcott, a friend of Ferber, even invited Robeson over for tea and facilitated introductions to major figures such as Irving Berlin.[6] Early on, Robeson was comfortable moving in elite white circles. When *Taboo* went to London as *Voodoo*, Robeson went along on his first trip abroad. Efforts to fix the play were soon reduced to a single strategy: have Robeson sing a spiritual whenever the story lagged. London opened up a new world for Robeson, who reveled in the absence of segregation and the general racial tolerance of the British. He quickly became part of the black expatriate community, which included the baritone John C. Payne who was singing recitals with the pianist and spiritual arranger Lawrence Brown. Brown would shortly return to America and shape Robeson's recital career.

Back in New York, Eugene O'Neill contacted Robeson, initially while looking for a black actor to replace Charles Gilpin in the title role for a revival of *The Emperor Jones*. O'Neill's play, which premiered in 1920 by the Provincetown Players and featured a small, interracial cast, simultaneously made Gilpin's career and invented the category of the black male tragic character in American drama. Gilpin kept on with the part—there were few others for him to play—but was proving unable to sustain high standards because of his drinking. Gilpin also had a habit, annoying to the playwright, of changing the words "nigger" and "black boy" to "negro" and "colored man."[7] Despite Robeson's inexperience, O'Neill cast him as the lead in a new play, *All God's Chillun Got Wings*, a story of interracial romance ending badly as there was really no other way for it to end in the 1920s. The play sparked tremendous pre-production controversy. Robeson, more concerned with simply playing the part than the frenzy surrounding the play, became a well-known name before appearing in either show. The run-up to *All God's Chillun* was so intense that Robeson's white co-star became seriously ill, postponing the opening for six weeks. Robeson quickly learned *Emperor Jones* under the direction of James Light and opened to wide acclaim. Overnight the breakthrough role for black actors—previously synonymous with Gilpin—belonged to Robeson. *All God's Chillun* eventually ran without incident in repertory with *Emperor Jones* through October 1924. In 1925 Robeson took *Emperor Jones* to London under producer Sir Alfred Butt, who would produce the 1928 London *Show Boat* in which Robeson played Joe for the first time.

Emperor Jones and *All God's Chillun* initiated a close connection between Robeson and the creative circle associated with the Provincetown Players and the bohemian scene in Greenwich Village. Robeson found the art studios, theaters, and coffee houses below Manhattan's Fourteenth Street a comfortable place to wait until the next opportunity arose, even though he and his wife, Eslanda, could not have lived in the neighborhood. (Eslanda supported the couple throughout the early 1920s working as a chemist at Columbia Presbyterian Hospital.) Robeson reacted positively to the attentions of O'Neill, James Light, the sculptor Antonio Salemme, and others associated with the Village, and the artistic pretensions of the group shaped his relationship to the commercial stage. Robeson's early successes were causes célèbres, not big box office. Big-time Broadway of the kind represented by Hammerstein, Kern, and Ziegfeld was well beyond anything Robeson knew.

By 1925 Robeson's acting career, barely two years old, was already circling around the very few parts open to a black leading man. He needed a new means to reach an audience clearly fascinated with him, and so Robeson became a concert singer. His concert career began on April 19, 1925, at the Greenwich Village Theatre, not a standard concert venue but the modest theater (seating around four hundred) near Washington Square Park where he had appeared in *All God's Chillun* and *Emperor Jones*. The day before the concert, the columnist Heywood Broun—like Ferber, a member of the Algonquin Roundtable—told his readers to go if they liked spirituals: "It seems to me that Robeson does a little better with such a song than any one [*sic*] I know. Even such a finished artist as Roland Hayes is a shade less exciting in singing these chants of the camp meetings. Robeson is closer, I think, to the fundamental spirit of the music."[8] The *World* registered a cosmic shift the morning after Robeson and Brown's concert: "So all those who listened last night to the first concert in this country made entirely of Negro music—if one may count out the chorals [*sic*] from Fisk and so forth—may have been present at a turning point—one of those thin points of time in which a star is born and not yet visible—the first appearance of this folk wealth to be made without deference or apology. Paul Robeson's voice is difficult to describe. It is a voice in which deep bells ring. It has all it needs, perfect pace, beautiful enunciation."[9] Two more concerts were hastily arranged: the first again in the Village, the second at the 48th Street Theatre (with more than double the seating capacity of the Greenwich Village Theatre), which took Robeson and Brown into the heart of Times Square.

Robeson and Brown followed their New York successes with tours of the Northeast and Midwest, Broadway's hinterland where shows had tryouts and where touring companies, often with Broadway casts, regularly visited. Reviews from the first eighteen months of Robeson and Brown's partnership capture Robeson's effect on critics at exactly the time when Ferber, Kern, and Hammerstein were occupied with *Show Boat*. The reaction of critics can be sorted into four overlapping categories: (1) responses to Robeson's physical presence, (2) efforts to define his technique and artistry, (3) positive reactions to his redefinition of the concert platform, and (4) descriptions of the authority he brought to the music by virtue of his race.

Robeson was described as having a mighty instrument and being a mighty man. His voice and physical presence were frequently commented upon together: Robeson was "a rugged athletic figure," "a very monolith of a baritone," and "a huge man physically" with a voice "as great as his physique and on those rare intervals when he chose to release it to its full power, he fairly shook the hall with its volume."[10] The experience of being in the room with Robeson weighed heavily on several of these no doubt jaded critics: "It will be long before any of us will forget the spectacle of this magnificently built man and the soft beauty of his voice."[11]

Robeson's effortless vocal production, dynamic subtlety, and especially his clear diction were praised for their artlessness; his evident control and restraint allowing him to bring out the inner depths of his material rather than celebrate his own talent. He was at once technically skilled and humble before his often lowly material. Two critics similarly highlighted his "diligent restraint [which] toned down to the necessary proportions a voice of great power and strength" and his "effortless bass baritone which he uses with skill and with due regard for but without emphasis upon the drama of what he sings."[12] *Musical America* added, "His enunciation is a thing to marvel at, and there is no escaping the emotional appeal always quietly and untheatrically achieved, of many of his numbers."[13] The emotional appeal was inevitably tied up with the content of the spirituals Robeson sang—the black experience as defined by resigned suffering and the hope of glory. His vocal and emotional restraint delivered this appeal with not a trace of confrontation. Robeson embodied the New Negro ideology of the Talented Tenth put forth by the African American intellectual W. E. B. DuBois—reaching out to whites by means of uniquely black artistic expression with undeniable artistry in a way whites could understand and always within a nonthreatening demeanor. While singing the soul of his people, Robeson, a physically imposing, obviously gifted individual, was a figure with whom white audiences could feel comfortable.

Several critics praised Robeson's concerts for enlivening the sometimes stuffy concert stage with a freshness and directness that never breached the bounds of decorum. Robeson and Brown managed to strike a balance between the seriousness of the concert hall and the audience interaction central to vaudeville, a context where the comparatively simple tunes they offered might have seemed a better fit. "His solos were sincerely given and void of platformism. Even his lighter and more humorous spirituals were done with a certain reserve and dignity."[14] "Mr. Robeson is a versatile genius. We do not know where to look for an artist who is freer from affectation, who gives to all he does a more splendid dignity, who seeks and obtains his effects in a more legitimate way."[15] "These two men are genuine artists—and their singing (to Brown's playing) is something more than art, while it is as well delightful and stimulating diversion."[16]

Finally, there was, of course, the racial rightness of the event, a match between performer and repertoire that Robeson exploited to his advantage. Robeson captured the quality of the material in a way that matched the expectations of white critics and audiences, and led them to what they saw as deeper conclusions about the black experience. Black music was everywhere in New York in the mid-1920s as an avatar of the contemporary moment. Robeson delivered an unusual take on race music in this context, dignifying the Negro at a time when popular music was selling jazzed-up stereotypes. Here was nothing of the nightclub or Harlem dive; indeed, nothing of the city at all. Here the Negro stood forth as new and sophisticated even as this old music expressed what most whites understood to be the fundamental character of the race. Robeson's "accents were deeply mournful without being lugubrious; his utterances were those of a prophet bowed with the cares and aspirations of his race."[17] "Mr. Robeson is an effective interpreter of the music of his race because he presents that music with the utmost simplicity and directness. A strain of wistful melancholy pervades his sonorous bass baritone voice, and his readings have a peculiarly pathetic poignancy."[18] Robeson was praised for expressing "all the plaintiveness of the colored race" and "a haunting tenderness, a wistful longing, an indescribable seeking for something just beyond, to be found in the voice of the Negro, and in no other voice."[19] Speechlessness was also an option: "Criticism is silent before such beauty."[20]

Robeson's singing had deep roots in his childhood experiences singing in his father's churches, but the origins of his recital act lay with his accompanist Lawrence Brown, who innovated the all-spirituals concert in Britain with John C. Payne. An accomplished musician, Brown fled the American South after a childhood haunted by racial violence. He ended up in England, where he accompanied on occasion for Roland Hayes. But Negro folk music was not a defining repertory for Hayes, who typically sang a set of spirituals at the end of otherwise all-classical programs. Brown found a more congenial collaborator in Payne, and the earliest surviving program for their all-spirituals concerts dates to January 1923 in London. The event was billed as a "Programme of Negro Music." Robeson and Brown's first concert was billed similarly. Payne and Brown's program was divided into four sets featuring three sorts of songs: "Spirituals" (of which there were two sets), "Negro Dialect

Songs," and "Negro Folk Songs." Robeson and Brown's concerts were structured around the same categories. Robeson's and Payne's repertories were substantially the same. Programs for Payne and Brown's concerts included a short text by Harry T. Burleigh—"Printed by request of Mr. Brown."— explaining the origin of the spirituals.[21] The same text appears in the program for Robeson and Brown's first New York concert. Robeson's biographers emphasize the important role played by white benefactors like the singer's Village supporters, who encouraged and enabled the event, and Broun and Van Vechten, who aroused public interest in the white press. But the substance of the concerts—what Robeson did and how he did it—owed much to Brown, who found in Robeson a charismatic singer who could launch the deceptively modest all-spirituals recital format on a path to worldwide success.

Robeson and Brown performing spirituals on the concert stage created a new kind of black man on the American concert platform, just as O'Neill had done on the dramatic stage, only this time the effect for white audiences was neither threatening nor controversial but revelatory. Robeson singing slave songs in formal dress was at once timeless and modern, a living statue with a voice to shake the rafters who preferred to whisper songs of resignation and hope beyond the grave. Others sang these songs around this time—among them Jules Bledsoe—but no one had Robeson's magnetism. Robeson was sui generis, neither entertainer nor classical singer. The consensus, as one publicity flyer put it, was that Robeson and Brown offered "Not just a concert— but an experience."[22] (The added frisson of Robeson's sexual attractiveness for white women is captured in Dorothy Parker's 1927 story "Arrangement in Black and White," in which the white female narrator's encounter with a black concert spiritual singer modeled on Robeson climaxes when she shakes his hand at a party and reflects on the shock her husband will feel when he learns she addressed a black man as "mister."[23])

In a perceptive profile for the *New Republic*—reprinted in a 1927 collection, Robeson the only African American included—Elizabeth Shepley Sergeant summed up the paradox of Robeson at the moment when *Show Boat* was being made. She extolled Robeson as uniquely grounded in an age of anxiety: "Unlike most complex moderns, Paul Robeson does not appear half a dozen men in a torn and striving body. As a singer of Negro Spirituals, above all, he is one and clear-cut in the Greek or primordial sense. . . . I have never seen on the stage a more civilized, a more finished artistic gesture than his nod to his accompanist, the signal to begin the song. This gesture is the final seal of Paul Robeson's personal ease in the world."[24] Taking a surprisingly clear-eyed view for a white writer, Sargeant noted "Paul Robeson is lucky, so they say, and one of his luckiest strikes is to have been born into the best age that the American

Negro has yet known. That is not saying much."[25] She acknowledged that "the moment came when he, too, had to take his place on one side or the other of the colour [sic] line," and that even at a time "when the Black Man is in fashion," Robeson can "walk not too easily" on the street.[26] But, Sargeant stated unequivocally, "He is a symbol of the New Age of the Negro, a figure of our year and hour."[27] This was also the "year and hour" of *Show Boat*, and the above detailed description of Robeson's mid-1920s persona serves to ground the making of Hammerstein and Kern's show in the particulars of this moment. Concrete connections between Robeson, "the Black Man" on Broadway, and the conception of *Show Boat* demonstrate how this historical nexus came to be inscribed in the musical, despite the fact that Robeson himself initially declined to be in the show. Robeson's extraordinary presence haunted *Show Boat*'s making, put a powerful mark on more than a decade's worth of versions, and lingers on in most every subsequent remaking. Audiences for *Show Boat* still respond to "Ol' Man River" as if it were not just a song but an "experience." These ovations resound with those first given Robeson in the mid 1920s.

Robeson had a new show in fall 1926: *Black Boy*, a drama by Jim Tully and Frank Mitchell Dazey, again with a mixed cast. Robeson played a boxer (loosely based on the black champ Jack Johnson) who rises to the top only to be sabotaged before his big fight (against a white opponent) by the woman he loves (who he thinks is white but is revealed at the end to have "colored blood").[28] Woollcott noted that Robeson "was at once the occasion for, and, to a reasonable extent, the justification of "the entire enterprise. Alan Dale cited his "dominant personality that many a star might envy."[29] If critics noted Robeson's ability to carry a weak show, surely theatrical producers and creators noticed the same.

Sergeant described an interesting scene at a performance of *Black Boy*. "Here is a Black Boy who is sublimating the least acceptable of American destinies. When, in the first act of Tully's piece, that deep and gentle voice of primitive innocence came out of the tattered figure of the Negro, the man beside me began to weep."[30] Jerome Kern saw Robeson in *Black Boy* and like the gentleman seated next to Sergeant, responded strongly to Robeson's voice—presumably without tears. In a written reply to a 1938 inquiry about his compositional methods, Kern pointed to the experience of seeing *Black Boy* as the impetus for the composition of "Ol' Man River," the defining song in *Show Boat*'s score. In the body of the letter Kern listed the "characterizations and personalities of interpretive artists" as one source of inspiration. In a postscript, he added, "the melody of OL' MAN RIVER was conceived immediately after my first hearing Paul Robeson's speaking voice . . . Robeson's organ-like tones are entitled to no small share of 'that thing called inspira-tion.'"[31] (Writers often evoked the organ in their descriptions of Robeson's voice, and Kern's use of the trope suggests he was familiar with the critical reception of Robeson.) Kern saw *Black Boy* in the last week of September during its tryout run in Mamaroneck, New York. The show opened on Broad-way on October 6 and ran a disappointing thirty-seven performances.

Two days before *Black Boy*'s Manhattan opening, another new stage work featuring a black male spiritual singer and a mixed cast had its premiere: *Deep River* (book and lyrics by Laurence Stallings, music by Frank Harling). Billed as both "A Jazz Opera" and a "Native Opera, written on a native topic," *Deep River* was an expensive, high-profile production with a large cast in-cluding Jules (Julius at the time) Bledsoe and the black actress Rose McClen-don in a highly praised dramatic role.[32] The show's opening was a major event covered by all the New York papers. The *Morning Telegraph* noted that *Deep River* "represented the first grand opera to be presented on the stage of a le-gitimate theatre in the roaring Forties [the Times Square theater district]. . . . Virtually every Broadway composer, from Jerome Kern to Harry Ruby, also had promised—or threatened, as the case may be—to be in the offing when the first strains were played."[33] Bledsoe's singing was uniformly praised, with Burns Mantle stating that Bledsoe "lends verisimilitude . . . to the occasion."[34] The black press followed *Deep River* closely as well. The *Afro-American* stated "the nature of the story demands that the two races be on the stage at the same time," a phenomenon unusual enough to warrant comment.[35] Set in New Orleans in the 1830s, *Deep River* was criticized for having a weak plot on which were hung picturesque scenes that did not quite add up to a show. The show's lack of a clear generic identity—was it musical comedy, opera, or operetta?—also came in for criticism. A volume of "vocal gems" from the score was published and likely available for purchase in the theater lobby, as was the custom with musical shows. *Deep River* failed commercially, closing after only thirty-two performances, but advance publicity was heavy, and the prominence of producer/director Arthur Hopkins guaranteed press coverage. Shortly after the show closed, a think piece in the *Times*, "Native Opera Proves Elusive," described *Deep River* as "the most ambitious effort of the present season . . . a highly valuable and interesting experiment."[36] Brooks Atkinson noted the promise of *Deep River*'s setting: "As always, the glowing colors of pre-Rebellion Southern costumery, the flounces, the head-dresses, the long coats, gay trousers and resplendent neck-cloths set the mood for relaxed enjoyment. And, although the play is too slender for a full evening of opera, it points the way to a rich mine of American dramatic material."[37] For Kern and Hammerstein this widely discussed, experimental, and serious musical show—which both surely saw—with a mixed cast set in New Orleans in the 1830s came at just the right time, stimulating their own ideas for a large-scale show with a mixed cast also set along the Mississippi in the nineteenth century. Perhaps *Deep River*'s unsuccessful investment in a Broadway version of New Orleans is one reason *Show Boat* never visits that particular port.

Kern's *Criss Cross* opened on October 12, 1926, at the Globe Theatre on Forty-sixth Street. *Deep River* was at the Imperial on Forty-fifth Street; Robeson's *Black Boy* at the Comedy just five blocks farther downtown. It was at the *Criss Cross* opening night that Kern famously asked Ferber for the rights to make *Show Boat* into a musical, an encounter evoked in almost every history of *Show Boat* simply for the pleasure of repeating Ferber's supposed reaction: she thought the idea was "fantastic," as in crazy.[38] Ferber's novel had hit the shelves only in mid-August, less than two months earlier. (Serialization of the complete text in the *Women's Home Companion* ran between April and September, although it's unlikely Kern encountered it there.) *Show Boat* would rapidly emerge as a best seller, heralded by Doubleday in Christmastime advertisements as "the most popular book of the year" and topping the *Bookman* best-sellers list for five months beginning in December.[39] That same month, *Show Boat* was ranked as the third most requested title at the Harlem branch of the New York Public Library.[40] But when Kern asked Ferber for the rights to *Show Boat*, the novel's great success with readers still lay in the future. Kern responded to the content of the story and not the public success of the book; odds are Kern had already contacted Hammerstein before approaching Ferber. (The duo had collaborated for the first time on *Sunny* the previous year.) Given Kern's enduring memory that Robeson's voice inspired him to write "Ol' Man River" and musical evidence (see ex. 2.1) that a tune from *Deep River* was in Kern's ear at the time, the impetus for *Show Boat* can be rather precisely attributed to a combination of Ferber's novel, Robeson's unique prominence as a black actor singing on the Broadway stage, and the example of the daring, large-scale, mixed-cast *Deep River*.

Kern and Hammerstein set to work even before signing a contract with Ferber on November 17.[41] That contract suggested that Florenz Ziegfeld produce what was sure to be a mammoth production. Just nine days later, Hammerstein and Kern auditioned act 1 for Ziegfeld, who proved eager to participate.[42] In early December, Ziegfeld inked a contract with Kern and Hammerstein for delivery of a usable script by the first of the year, with opening night occurring by the first of April.[43] On December 15 *Variety* announced that Robeson had been signed to play Joe.[44] He hadn't, but what evidence is there for Robeson's importance to *Show Boat* at this very early stage? Ziegfeld's eagerness to herald the planned spring production with Robeson's name fits with the archival evidence for *Show Boat* at this point in its creation. The earliest complete script for *Show Boat* can be dated to January 1927. (The extant complete drafts for the 1927 *Show Boat* are detailed in appendix 2.) The January draft, together with music materials from Kern's papers, provides a glimpse of *Show Boat* as Kern and Hammerstein first imagined it and likely contains much of the show as pitched to Ziegfeld in late November 1926.

As Kern and Hammerstein were preparing for their appointment with Ziegfeld, Robeson and Brown gave a pair of concerts at the Comedy Theatre where *Black Boy* had recently closed: the first on November 14, the second on November 25 (the night before Kern and Hammerstein auditioned their score for Ziegfeld). A third concert followed on December 5.[45] The seating was segregated with blacks relegated to the balcony. Theater critics who had praised Robeson in *Black Boy* received complimentary tickets.[46] The *Herald* commented on the event: "The spiritual invasion of New York received some advancement last evening . . . through the tender ministration of Paul Robeson [and Lawrence Brown] . . . The work of these two is too well known to need comment. The house was full and there were more request numbers than the most amiable of singers could possibly fill in an evening. . . . It is not, of course, possible to avoid in such an entertainment a somewhat oppressive atmosphere of monotony, but for those addicted to it (apparently the clamoring majority), it could only prove a satisfactory repetition."[47] Kern and Hammerstein may have attended one of these spiritual concerts in a Broadway theater for their earliest known draft of act 2—the January draft— included the wholesale importation of Robeson and Brown's recital routine into *Show Boat*. Doing so would capture Robeson's cachet with Broadway audiences for the benefit of *Show Boat* and allow the musical to reconfigure Ferber's narrative in a bold, overwhelmingly positive way.

How to end *Show Boat* was always, and has always remained, a problem. Beyond what to do with Ravenal—no one seems to have seriously considered not reuniting the central white couple at the close—the need to bring the story to a close in the 1927 present shaped Hammerstein's thinking profoundly, both initially and throughout the almost twenty years he tinkered with *Show Boat*. As the January draft shows, *Show Boat* with Robeson as its star was to be a musical tale of the triumphant 1920s arrival of black music and musicians at the center of Broadway musical culture. The intent of the Robeson plan can be summarized in a note scribbled by Kern in the margin of a sketch for the song "Can't Help Lovin' Dat Man," one of the first songs composed for the show. Here, in the midst of writing a song designed to hint at

Julie's racial identity, Kern reminded Hammerstein, "In other words, we must feature Paul Robeson."[48] Featuring Robeson by building up the role of Joe was the priority, even though Ferber's book offered little guidance.

Like any musical comedy or operetta of the time, *Show Boat* opened with a chorus number, the difference being the use of a full black chorus who sang the provocative lyric "Niggers all work on de Mississippi / Niggers all work while de white folks play." Joe is not listed among the stevedores and gals onstage at curtain's rise, but fronting the show with a strong black presence and previewing words and music from Joe's "Ol' Man River" served notice that the black characters and performers were essential rather than decorative elements. (The opening chorus alone, present in the earliest drafts of this scene, marks a sharp departure from Ferber's original.[49]) Closing the long opening scene with "Ol' Man River" rather than the operetta-like duet "Make Believe" effectively bracketed *Show Boat*'s exposition with powerful statements from the black cast. Musically, Joe was presented as the de facto leader of the black ensemble and an important figure in the show as a whole.

The January draft includes "Ol' Man River" in three other scenes, all of which survived to the Broadway opening. They remained as pillars of the show's dramatic structure in almost every subsequent version as well. (An early reviewer praised the repetitions as a "modernization of the Greek chorus."[50]) Joe sings "Ol' Man River" at the close of the long miscegenation scene while Magnolia and Ravenal rehearse together for the first time under Andy's supervision. The song's final phrase is heard while the soon-to-be lovers engage in a kiss—to Andy's delight and Parthy's horror. Stage directions pull the emphasis off the kissing couple and onto Joe, whose face is to be illuminated by a pin spot while the rest of the stage goes to black. A second reprise— a complete singing of the chorus with a partially rewritten lyric—occurs during the transition from 1904 to 1927 in act 2, just after Magnolia's debut at the Trocadero. Hammerstein imagined a variation on the Ziegfeld costume parade for this sequence marked "Interlude" in the January draft. Hammerstein took the *Follies* formula of show girls parading in fantastic costumes while a male solo singer delivered a tune in a spotlight downstage and put it to work dramatically. An aged Joe takes the role of boy singer, revealed in a pin spot (a motif continued from act 1) which widens to illuminate his entire body as he sits and whittles. While Joe sings, white girls parade behind him, "visions of the passing years" demonstrating the radical changes in fashion of the two decades being traversed. Hammerstein stressed that the costumes should be real clothes, not fanciful creations, recommending a boy in uniform and a female ambulance driver to mark the war years, and a flapper to denote arrival at the present. The costume parade was eventually cut, replaced by the expedient placement of Joe next to a newspaper office displaying headlines of 1927. A third reprise of "Ol' Man River," with Joe's voice augmented by the entire chorus, brought the show to a close, the final cutoff timed to match the moment the descending curtain hit the floor. Reviewers across the history of *Show Boat* have noted how these reprises help hold the show together; they also effectively feature Joe, giving the actor playing the role multiple opportunities to make an impression despite the fact that Joe as a character plays no substantive part in the plot.

Underwriting the power of Joe's many reprises is the song "Ol' Man River" itself, a brilliant cross-fertilization of the Negro spiritual and the Broadway song built on the dimensions of Robeson's persona. Kern's tune begins at the bottom of its almost two-octave range and rises to its highest note in the final phrase, encouraging a performance shaded generally from very soft to very loud. "Ol' Man River" is an ideal vehicle for a singer with Robeson's famed dynamic control. The melody's long lines demand a singer with superior breath control and the ability to shape phrases built on repeated, gently syncopated rhythmic motifs while sounding neither like a "jazz" nor a "trained" singer. These qualities defined Robeson's concert persona: at once technically controlled and yet without the veneer of artistic sophistication or the razzmatazz of popular music. Hammerstein's lyrics are unfailingly serious and speak of the black experience as defined by weariness, sorrow, and waiting. Notions of hope for a better life beyond death or struggle for a better world in the here and now are notably missing, casting the singer as a monolithic figure locked in time and space. (Robeson would try to add a sense of racial protest to the lyrics in later revisions of the lyric).[51] The song as described in the January draft fairly insists on a concert-style delivery each time it recurs. Pin spots generally constrain movement about the stage. The solemn character of "Ol' Man River" casts a mantle of seriousness over any moment when it is heard, and Joe is essentially pinned into place by this song, which hems the character in on several sides.

Whatever inspiration Kern and Hammerstein took from Robeson, his recitals, and his repertory, the duo took more concrete ideas for "Ol' Man River" from *Deep River*. The sources for *Deep River* include a draft script and published vocal selections. At least three numbers were written for Bledsoe: "Ashes and Fire," "Po' Lil' Black Chile," and "De Old Clay Road." His character has no name in the draft script, where he is referred to as "BLEDSOE," and he does not participate in the drama in any meaningful way in the outer two acts.[52] The Philadelphia *Inquirer* praised the effectiveness of *Deep River*'s first moments: "The opening number is 'The Old Clay Road,' [sic] a song of Old Kentucky, sung by Julius Bledsoe, the noted negro baritone, of rich and resonant voice . . . in a spotlight on a darkened stage, with a chorus heard with softened tone and much beauty of effect behind the scenes."[53] Bledsoe simply stood and sang: a formula applied to Joe in every use of "Ol' Man River." Woollcott remembered Bledsoe's performance in *Deep River* in a 1933 letter to Ferber, where he described how Bledsoe "walked forward to the footlights, squared his shoulders, threw back his head, and emitted his song."[54] Woollcott's description applies equally well to most Joes in the history of *Show Boat*. In truth, there is no one to sing "Ol' Man River" to—except the audience watching *Show Boat*. Hammerstein and Kern had a model for this approach in Bledsoe's performance at the opening of *Deep River*, which effectively established time and place while featuring the black male voice in a quasi-spiritual song. The arrangement also demonstrated the effectiveness of a full black chorus singing in support of such a figure. Hammerstein's persistent reference to pin spots in the January draft may also draw upon *Deep River*, the draft libretto for which describes Bledsoe singing "Ashes and Fire" in a "head spot" in front of a black curtain. Head spots and pin spots are identical descriptions of lighting that emphasizes a singer's head, requiring complete physical stillness and forcing the singer to just stand and sing.

Beyond the dramaturgical similarities, Kern knew and borrowed musical material from "De Old Clay Road." Example 2.1 reprints the complete sheet music for the song, with the musical phrase Kern borrowed marked in brackets throughout. Kern's closest approximation of Harling's original is given above the first appearance of the phrase in the vocal part. Kern borrows from Harling in a manner reminiscent of the Baroque composer Georg Frederic Handel's appropriation of musical material from his peers. Like Handel, Kern improves upon his sources, using Harling's gently syncopated rhythmic figure and general melodic direction to create a vastly more satisfying melody that ebbs and flows, only to climax at the close, providing a reliable show piece for singers. Kern's melody rewards the listener and has worked to tremendous advantage for *Show Boat* as a whole over its entire history.[55]

Kern also drew inspiration from well-known black-themed popular songs. As shown in example 2.2a, b, the bridge from "Ol' Man River" uses the identical pitch content as the bridge of "Goin' Home," a popular song adapted from Antonín Dvořák's *New World Symphony*, itself a touchstone of black spiritual topics in classical music. Both passages convey a certain melodic futility reflected in their respective lyrics—penned by whites—expressing a particular view of the black experience.

But creating a one-song role was not enough no matter how good the song nor how many reprises, and Hammerstein arrived at an ingenious way to tap directly into Robeson's recital notoriety. Late in act 2, after the story had

Example 2.1 "De Old Clay Road" from Deep River *(1926, music by Laurence Stallings, lyrics by Frank Harling), with borrowing by Kern in "Ol' Man River" noted above the vocal line.*

Example 2.1 (continued)

Example 2.2a The bridge of "Goin' Home," a quasi-spiritual popular song adapted from a pseudo-Negro melody from Antonín Dvořák's New World Symphony.

Example 2.2b First half of the bridge of "Ol' Man River."

arrived in the present, Hammerstein envisioned a dramatically integrated specialty for Robeson. In a scene that works against every fiber of Ferber's tale, Andy (who does not die in the musical) has brought Ravenal (who likewise doesn't disappear for good) back to the *Cotton Blossom*. The two are conversing quietly on deck while listening to Magnolia, now a national star, singing live on the radio from New York. Networks were still new then, and the moment would have been startlingly modern in 1927. Going slightly off topic in a scene chiefly contrived to absolve Ravenal of his abandonment of wife and child, Andy provides a lead in for Robeson's big moment in act 2.

> ANDY: Joe's son—'member him when he was a little pickaninny wouldn't study 'rithmetic wouldn't learn to read but he knew all the river songs, that ever was. Parthy used to have to keep shuttin' him up wel, [*sic*] sir—he's now singin' in concerts all over the country, and makin' good money, too an' you know what he sings? The same dem fool old songs they sung forty years ago on these levees.

(The lights have gradually dimmed to a blackout—Joe's voice continues in the darkness until scene changed—It is timed so at end of refrain the lights iris up revealing PAUL ROBESON in evening clothes in front of a piano, with his accompanist, Lawrence Brown, in a velvet drop, as he appears at his recitals.)
(SCENE VIII: A PAUL ROBESON RECITAL)

In addition to playing Joe, Robeson was to play himself—a 1920s spiritual singing star—outfitted with a fictional biography as a show boat "pickaninny" who could neither read nor do math. Robeson, of course, had lived a very different life of great, even historic achievement before carving out his singular place on the concert platform. But in *Show Boat*, Robeson as composite celebrity and made-up character—at once himself and Joe and Queenie's son—would step forward toward the end of the evening and entertain the audience with a specialty.

Inserting the Robeson recital in *Show Boat* was a brilliant if predictable idea. Broadway book shows were regularly hosting popular music figures as added attractions in the mid-1920s. Kern's *Lucky*, produced in March 1927, included Paul Whiteman and his Orchestra. The Gershwins' *Lady, Be Good* (1924) included Cliff "Ukelele Ike" Edwards in the specialty number "Fascinatin' Rhythm," which was scheduled around Edwards's nightly performances elsewhere. Inserting a specialty act in *Show Boat* act 2 also would have appealed to Ziegfeld's background as a producer of revues. In fact. the Robeson recital was little more than a vaudeville act given the superior setting of a high-class Broadway show.[56] And the recital is also reminiscent of the landmark black-cast musical *Shuffle Along* (1921), which paused in act 2 for "A Few Minutes with Sissle and Blake." Like Robeson and Brown, Noble Sissle and Eubie Blake were black men who appeared in formal attire, offering songs at the piano in a refined but engaging manner. (Sissle and Blake performed chiefly on white vaudeville circuits.) Both Robeson-Brown and Sissle-Blake brought new versions of black musical masculinity to white audiences, who would welcome a short musical offering from famous performers in the middle of a book show. The Robeson recital also made sense if you read Ferber carefully, as Hammerstein did. Ferber got it wrong when she imagined her Jo might have found fame in the "Club Alabam' or some midnight revue." Hammerstein correctly read Jo's musical style and put him where he belonged—on the concert stage. Bringing Brown into the mix demonstrated the desire for complete authenticity. *Show Boat* would offer the Robeson-Brown experience eight times a week, potentially garnering for the pair a vastly larger audience than even years of concertizing might offer.

The Robeson-Brown recital specialty necessitated a willingness on Kern's part to share his score with Negro spirituals. The plan to interpolate popular songs from the American past into *Show Boat* seems to have been agreed on from the start. The January draft lists ten different titles—most all white popular tunes—to be used in various ways. (One precedent for this was O'Neill's *All God's Chillun Got Wings*, which used white and black offstage voices singing popular tunes to mark the passage of time.) Hammerstein did not, however, speculate in the January draft on which songs Robeson would sing in his recital. It is hard to believe he would not have requested "I Got Shoes," which was reprinted in Ferber's novel, listed in the January draft as Magnolia's audition tune at the Trocadero and a favorite with Robeson's audiences. The short recital specialty would perhaps have closed with "Ol' Man River," which would be heard in context with the spirituals informing its music and lyrics. Kern and Hammerstein must have been confident their song could stand the comparison, and beginning in 1931, Robeson and Brown would include "Ol' Man River" in their concerts for a decade and more.[57]

But the Robeson recital was not the end of the story; Hammerstein's extension of the idea suggests further engagement with popular music history on the part of the bookwriter, who was rewriting Ferber's tale of the dramatic stage in the very different terms of the musical theater. After the Robeson recital—which would necessarily be flexible in length, responding to the audience, perhaps involving calls for encores that had the capacity to disrupt the production altogether—there was to be a scene set in "Kim's Apartment, New York City, That evening." Here, the Robeson plan intersected with Hammerstein's popular music plot. A big party is in progress, complete with "some life of the party . . . shaking a cocktail—perhaps the composer can make the rhythmic clink-clink a part of the orchestration." This ultramodern scene introduced two new characters: the adult Kim, a Broadway star who makes a big "conventional musical comedy" entrance, and a pianist and composer named George, just finishing his "Rhapsody in Blue" as the lights come up. The musical segue out of the Robeson recital would thus be the already familiar strains of *Rhapsody in Blue*, a work just over two years old when Hammerstein imagined putting it into *Show Boat*. Surely Hammerstein and Kern had no plans to entice George Gershwin himself to join the cast of *Show Boat*, but they did plan to put a stand-in for the famous composer into the scene as the composer of Kim's latest show.

Before the musical highlight of the scene, Kim and the partygoers engage in banter intended to catch the audience up on the story. Kim and Magnolia (who is absent from the scene for practical reasons) are off to Natchez to visit the *Cotton Blossom* the next day. A "Man with Glass of Sarsparilla"—a conspicuous figure in Prohibition New York—shouts out "Show Boat? What's 'at?," nicely setting up a reliable laugh line for Kim, who replies, "Now listen, Moron—D'you mean to tell me you haven't read Edna Ferber's book?" What follows demonstrates how seriously Hammerstein and Kern took the musical implications of Ferber's story.

GEORGE: Did you know that the song hit of Kim's show was based on an old Show Boat tune?

KIM: That's right—it's an old southern song my mother taught me—I hummed it to George and he used it as a theme—

ALEC: Old southern song your mother taught you—sounds like an old gag your press agent taught you—

GEORGE: It's true—Come on Kim—Let's show them the original—

(They all plead—she assents. She starts to sing it in the old way.)

MAN WITH HIGHBALL: That's fine—Now let's hear it the way you do it in the show—

(She sings the modernized version)

MAN WITH HIGHBALL: Come on girls—snap into your number—

(Girls join in—built to big dancing number)

(BLACK OUT)

In Hammerstein's plan, the Robeson recital and Kim's big number acted as pendants: both marked the show's arrival at the present, both displayed how the roots of the present reached back to the world of the show boats and ultimately to the sources of American popular music in black music making. Together they make up one version of Hammerstein's popular music plot. Hammerstein's initial presentation was breathtakingly direct: the African American sources of American music would be presented first by Robeson in the form of spirituals and then by Kim, who would state in so many words that the sources of her style lay in "old southern songs" updated by the most contemporary (white) musical mind of the decade. (Kern apparently had no compunction about letting a few bars of Gershwin's trendy *Rhapsody* into the score as well.) The reliance of contemporary Broadway musical comedy on black models could hardly be more explicitly stated. Both the Robeson recital and the party at Kim's were eventually cut, but Kim's up-to-date number—a sung and danced illustration of Hammerstein's popular music plot—survived to be inserted into the final scene on the levee. Spotted in that scene, Kim's number would be continuously reinterpreted across the entire history of the show. (Several of these attempts to end *Show Boat* with a modern musical showstopper are discussed in part 2.)

The generational nature of this double tale received further emphasis in a casting strategy that redefined conventional Broadway practice. Robeson would play Joe and himself as the son of Joe. Magnolia and the grown Kim were similarly to be played by the same performer. Norma Terris did so in the Broadway original. There were abundant precedents for the same actor playing two roles, representing two generations of the same family. The operettas *The Blue Paradise* (1915), *Maytime* (1917), and *The Magic Melody* (1919), all longrunning hits with scores by Sigmund Romberg, built bittersweet stories on the conceit of having a single pair of actors play two couples with different romantic destinies: an initial pair whose love was denied, and a second pair, in some way descended from the first, who united in love at the close of the show in a more tolerant time closer to the present. Hammerstein and Kern were surely familiar with these shows, and Hammerstein himself had just completed a successful collaboration with Romberg on *The Desert Song*, which opened just as work on *Show Boat* began. Romberg would repeat this story formula in *Cherry Blossoms* (1927). The difference in *Show Boat* was Joe and Queenie's son and Kim were—obviously—not a romantic pair. Instead, as products of the *Cotton Blossom* they lived similar showbiz lives—humble beginnings on the river, success in New York in their adulthood. Their paired stories offered tales of showbiz success as, perhaps, an acceptable replacement for romance as a musical comedy destiny.

Hammerstein's adaptation of a familiar romantic structure to nonromantic ends in service of a tale of popular music history suggests two conclusions. First, Ferber's Ravenal created real problems for anyone trying to adapt the novel to the musical stage, where happy endings were de rigueur. Hammerstein initially punted on the Ravenal problem, making no attempt to flesh out the central love story of Magnolia and Ravenal in a believable manner. (Later screenwriters, including Hammerstein, would try to do so.) His interest in act 2 never focused on reuniting the lovers, which seemed the most obvious way to approach the story if the conventions of operetta were being followed. Instead, Hammerstein was more interested in the show business story of Magnolia and Kim's success, precisely the tale Ferber had focused on in her novel.

Second, Hammerstein was inspired by the possibilities for making *Show Boat* a history of the present expressed in song and dance, an object lesson in the power of black music and a celebration of a moment in popular culture history when black music and musicians were breaking into mainstream white culture with undeniable force. That story was implicit in Ferber's novel, but she was uninterested in telling it. Hammerstein leapt on it, shaping *Show Boat*'s entire second act around the story, which had the obvious advantage of featuring Robeson but also gave the historical trajectory of Ferber's tale a new, positive twist. Hammerstein and Kern's *Show Boat* was always going to be a compendium of black and white Broadway in the 1920s. What the Robeson-Kim plot did was to name it as such, emphasizing the origin of the black elements by not only bringing black performers and a black star into the cast but building an entire sequence for a white star and the white ensemble around a demonstration of how black music was informing white musical comedy. In Hammerstein's plan, Kim has a black voice but so does everyone on the white musical comedy stage in the final contemporary scenes.

The Robeson recital and Kim's party remained in the works until well into the rehearsal process. Both appear in the August draft, with the added note "(If Robeson is not engaged, this recital comes out)." Clearly, the production team was still in negotiation with Robeson at this point. It would not do to have just any black singer do the recital. Only Robeson could fill this star spot dependent on his charisma, reputation, and name recognition. Both scenes also appear in the October script dating to the start of rehearsals. In that source, an unknown hand crossed out Andy's lead in to the Robeson recital and added "cue into reprise" in the margins. The handwriting may be Kern's, and the reference is to Ravenal's reprise of "You Are Love," which was used to end the Andy-Ravenal scene from the tryout opening. The October script was typed before Charles Winninger was announced for the role of Andy on October 16.[58] Two days earlier, Robeson and Brown sailed for Europe for a recital at the Salle Gaveau in Paris.[59] Only Robeson's departure on a transatlantic voyage seems to have convinced the makers of *Show Boat* that the "Robeson Recital" would not be part of the show. Kim's party may have remained for a while after Robeson's recital was cut. Just days before the tryout opening on November 15, the *Washington Post* listed "a gay party in modern-day New York" set "in a New York apartment" among the many scenes in the production.[60]

The draft scripts suggest that Hammerstein, Kern, and Ziegfeld were still hoping that Robeson would agree to play Joe as late as mid-October 1927. Media accounts only hint at the negotiation process between Robeson and the Broadway triumvirate. As early as December 13, 1926, Ziegfeld's press office was planting the news that Robeson would play Joe.[61] Woollcott provided a glimpse of the approach to Robeson in a 1928 column reprinted with relish by the *Pittsburgh Courier*, a black newspaper with national reach: "Mr. Kern, with the lovely melody of 'Old Man River' already in his head, stood hat in hand on a doorstep in Harlem. He wanted Paul Robeson to sing that song. When rehearsals were finally called, that dusky giant was entangled elsewhere."[62] Robeson's reservations about *Show Boat* were made public early on. On January 26, 1927, *Variety* reported that Robeson was holding out for more money. (Bledsoe was already being mentioned as a second choice.) Two weeks later, Ziegfeld shelved *Show Boat* until the fall, and Robeson's resistance may have been a factor in the postponement.[63] Few other rumors leaked out over the coming months as Robeson was in New York or traveling with Eslanda, so there are few letters from this period to open the window on private negotiations (Eslanda's frequently revealing diaries are missing for 1927). Gwendolyn Brooks reported in the March issue of *Opportunity*, "It is now a fact that Paul Robeson is going to play in the coming production of *Show Boat* . . . he will have a part in which he may sing. To me it bespeaks the type of artistry for which Mr. Robeson is striving that he has just refused splendid offers for vaudeville production."[64] An insider in Harlem artistic circles, Brooks may have been working with dated information or perhaps her reference to

Robeson and vaudeville reveals an ongoing discussion with Ziegfeld about the recital specialty. (The bit about how he "may sing" has an odd ring to it given the fact *Show Boat* was to be a musical. Perhaps by "sing" Brooks meant the Robeson-Brown recital specialty.) The August script note "if Robeson refuses" suggests negotiations were ongoing into the summer. 1927 was not a great year for Robeson's career. He spent the first half of the year on a sporadic and contentious concert tour with Brown and managed by Eslanda, which left the trio "profoundly discouraged."[65] From June to October, Robeson was in New York, his recital notoriety exhausted for the time being and no dramatic opportunities in the offing. He and Eslanda spent August in the black bourgeois enclave of Oak Bluffs on Martha's Vineyard, where Robeson sang a few local concerts.[66] To top things off, Eslanda was pregnant, and Robeson was not entirely pleased about it.[67] He ended up signing a contract with producer Caroline Dudley to appear in a black-cast revue the following year in exchange for a $500 advance, money spent on his and Brown's passage to France for the concert in Paris, which was part of a deal with the impresario Walter K. Varney to organize concerts in Europe for Robeson and Brown. The Dudley contract would come to haunt Robeson (see chap. 6), and the arrangement with Varney would fail to yield much in the way of income. Robeson and Brown sailed on October 14, at which point the Robeson recital was definitively cut from *Show Boat*. Bledsoe's hiring to play Joe was announced barely two weeks before the tryout opening night. The October draft script and late hiring of Bledsoe provide strong evidence that Hammerstein, Kern, and Ziegfeld held out for Robeson until the singer actually got on the boat for Europe.

Given what he sailed toward—initially a single Paris concert engagement—and left behind—the chance to star in a Ziegfeld book show—Robeson's resistance to *Show Boat* was powerful, likely backed by strong convictions as the opportunity offered much in the way of practical benefits to a performer whose career appeared to have stalled. Indeed, there were few prospects for Robeson in New York in 1927 other than *Show Boat*. When Robeson sailed in October, he left his pregnant wife near to full term. Paul Robeson Jr. was born in Brooklyn on November 2, 1927. Eslanda experienced complications after giving birth, and Robeson ended up returning to the United States immediately. He arrived back in New York the day before *Show Boat* opened on Broadway. Perhaps he attended opening night. Had he chosen not to sail, Robeson would have been nearby for the birth of his son while in rehearsal and tryouts for a starring role in the biggest production that had ever come his way—all he had to do was say yes to *Show Boat*.

But Robeson said no. Why? Eslanda Robeson's 1930 book *Paul Robeson, Negro* provides insight into Robeson's goals as an artist in the late 1920s. She presents him as a talent nurtured in Greenwich Village. Robeson enjoyed the intellectual aura of bohemia, seeking to re-create this world in Chelsea during his various periods in London. In these confines, Robeson developed a firm belief in artistic expression over commercial compromise, a position that buttressed his conviction that the black artist had a particular burden to show the full humanity of his race to the white public. As described by Eslanda, Robeson's spiritual concerts were "artistic experiments," "just the sort of thing [the Greenwich Village types] enjoyed doing," and "something about which they all could be honestly enthusiastic."[68] Eslanda quotes Robeson in a long passage where he articulated how *Emperor Jones* and *All God's Chillun* had served specific purposes in bringing the race before the white audience. Clearly, Robeson valued how his Provincetown allies had allowed him to forge a career on the mainstream stage while also fulfilling personal goals. The fact that these shows did not generate consistent work or income for the Robeson family went unremarked. (Eslanda's version left out Robeson's own concerns about the effect his career strategy was having on the family's finances. In a letter to Eslanda sent from France on December 12, 1927—the chance to be in *Show Boat* now lost—Robeson reflected on the choices he had made for the sake of his "*art*." "There are so many things I would have done to make us money if I had not been afraid of my '*art*.' *Black Boy*—Vaudeville—Picture houses—*Show Boat*—Hammerstein, etc. . . . and it really hasn't been so much '*art*' as thinking what people would say—which of course is silly."[69]) In her biography of Robeson, Eslanda also called attention to the historic roles played by Roland Hayes in the concert hall, and writers now associated with the Harlem Renaissance in literary culture bringing the attention of the white public to "another class of Negro," initiating a "mixed social life" filled with "interesting and intelligent Negro writers, artists, musicians" and others. She stated categorically, "This 'mixing' is the best thing that could happen to help solve the Negro problem in America. When white people come to know the Negro as he really is, whether or not they decide to like him, become bosom friends with him, or marry him, the greatest single barrier will be broken down."[70] Eslanda's biography of her husband articulates a classic case of the New Negro as a man of talent breaking down racism by way of artistic excellence.

It is difficult to imagine Robeson and Eslanda looking at "Ol' Man River" and the draft librettos for *Show Boat* as vehicles that would support their very intentional view of his career. After the commercial failure of *Black Boy*—his first show outside the orbit of Provincetown with a plot roundly ridiculed by most all critics (but especially black ones)—the Ziegfeld *Show Boat* with its twisted biography of Robeson as Joe and Queenie's pickaninny could hardly have been an appealing offer. Robeson had avoided all-black musical shows for years; it was never his ambition to appear as a featured player in a musical. And Robeson may have had a general resistance to Broadway as well. Eslanda recorded in detail in her diary the couple's humiliating experience at a 1926 performance of *Bride of the Lamb* at the Henry Miller Theatre. The usher and box office staff refused to seat Paul in their orchestra seats and the pair left in disgust.[71] In her biography of Paul, Eslanda pointedly observed that in New York Robeson found it "a great practical inconvenience" that he couldn't eat at a restaurant between Tenth and 130th Streets (in other words, outside of Harlem and the Village). He loved living in London precisely because he could eat across the street from the theater where he performed. As Eslanda noted, "This was important for his general well-being."[72]

Of course, these objections fell away months, even weeks, after *Show Boat* opened to great success on Broadway. Robeson was invited to play Joe in London by Sir Alfred Butt, a producer he knew and trusted in a town he loved. He sailed in April 1928 for a May opening at Drury Lane, which proved a major success, launching Robeson's public identification with the role of Joe and "Ol' Man River." He would play the role for more than a decade, appearing on Broadway in 1932, in the 1936 film, and finally in a Los Angeles production in 1940.

3

THE MORGAN PLAN

• • •

Helen Morgan was the only performer ever associated with the role of Julie in the press. In early May 1927, the *New York Times* reported the "nightclub entertainer" was crossing the Atlantic for appearances in London and Paris, then added that Morgan "may appear in *Show Boat* upon her return in the Fall."[1] Also in May, *Variety* noted, "An acute shortage of principals and suitable talent in every department bids fair toward elevating any number of vaudevillians and nightclub entertainers into the musical comedy and revue fields."[2] Morgan's return to the United States in early September was heralded with the news that she would, indeed, be playing Julie.[3]

The role of Julie in the January and August scripts made no concessions to any planned performer. "Can't Help Lovin' Dat Man," among the first tunes Kern and Hammerstein wrote, was not written with Morgan—or anyone else—in mind. In these scripts, Julie does not even sing in act 2 but appears instead in a dramatic scene straight out of Ferber where Magnolia encounters her long-lost friend as a secretary at Hetty Chilson's high-class brothel. Magnolia's audition at the Trocadero follows without Julie or the song "Bill." In the October script, written after Morgan was signed, the Chilson scene is cut, and Julie is now the star attraction at the Trocadero. She rehearses a song with piano accompaniment in a semi-drunken state then retreats to her dressing room, only to reappear while Magnolia sings her audition. Recognizing the girl from her show boat days, Julie silently flees the scene, opening up a spot for Magnolia to get her chance. Julie's departure nicely echoes her forced removal from the *Cotton Blossom* in act 1. The *Show Boat* scholar Katherine Axtell described these changes in broad terms: "The brilliant re-visioning of Julie as the prima donna of the Trocadero Restaurant who sacrifices her job, unbeknownst to Magnolia, for her old friend's sake first appears in [the October draft]. Save, perhaps, for the composition of "Ol' Man River," no other single creative impulse so profoundly affected the course of *Show Boat*."[4] What Axtell fails to note is that part, perhaps all, of the impetus behind this "creative impulse" was the casting of Helen Morgan as Julie. For this reason, Julie's inclusion in the Trocadero scene, which elegantly replaced a long dramatic scene requiring a separate set and two additional characters with one page of dialogue and a song, counts as a major adjustment of *Show Boat* to a performer. Furthermore, the alterations to Julie's part in act 2 had a sizable effect on the show's reception, warranting my characterization of these changes as "the Morgan plan." Kern, Hammerstein, and Ziegfeld took a chance on an up-and-coming star, a risk that yielded tangible returns to the original production and redounded to the benefit of many Julies and *Show Boats* in the ensuing decades. Always less ambitious than the Robeson plan, the Morgan plan had unintended, serendipitous consequences, highlighting the role of sheer good luck in the success of even so accomplished a musical as Hammerstein, Kern, and Ziegfeld's *Show Boat*.

In the October script, Hammerstein defined Julie's Trocadero song as "a popular sentimental ballad characteristic of the time." By the tryout opening, "Bill" had been chosen to fill this slot. (The title is penciled into the November script.) Morgan's performance of the song would emerge as an unlikely signature moment for the overstuffed show. Cut from Kern's *Oh Lady! Lady!!* (1918), "Bill" is a complete anachronism in the Trocadero scene, which is set around 1904. Neither well-known, sentimental (in the traditional sense), nor a ballad of the time, it meets none of Hammerstein's criteria. Understanding why "Bill" worked and how Morgan approached "Can't Help Lovin' Dat Man," Julie's other song, requires knowledge of Morgan's unique persona, which was emerging before *Show Boat* and grew in tandem with the success of the show during its two-year run, a period when Morgan was famous not only for her singing but also for ongoing legal problems relating to Prohibition. The nightly display of this woman with her name in the papers singing a weepy tune while half-drunk then exiting to go "off on a tear" was publicity made in heaven for both *Show Boat* and La Morgan.

Helen Morgan was born in Canada but raised in Illinois, living on the wrong side of the tracks in both places. Arriving in New York in the early 1920s, Morgan started out in a specific kind of venue: the Prohibition-era, barely legal, usually quite intimate nightclub. Her talents and persona were ill suited to vaudeville, and so she pursued a spot in a Broadway show. (Once she was famous, vaudeville would welcome her.) Morgan's first Broadway show was *George White's Scandals* of 1925, a piece of "summer fluff" in which she sang in two numbers and did some sketch comedy.[5] Her part was so small the *Times* reviewer didn't bother to mention her.

Morgan's big break came a year later in another summer revue titled *Americana*, which opened in July 1926 and ran for 244 performances. *Americana* played the Belmont Theatre, a small house seating only five hundred, ideal for Morgan's peculiar talents. The *Wall Street Journal* noted the importance of the venue: "intimacy is a help to an entertainment that successfully stands very close scrutiny."[6] Morgan started out in the small vocal ensemble and had a few featured duets.[7] The last week of August, Betty Compton, a featured performer in the show, departed for a role in the Gershwins's *Oh, Kay!* In the ensuing reshuffling, Morgan kept what features she had and picked up the small group number "Why D'ya Roll Those Eyes?" In the middle of September, Morgan got her chance for a solo, singing "Nobody Wants Me" midway through act 2. Within a month she was relieved of her duties singing backup, and her duets were given to others. Morgan's impact singing "Nobody Wants Me" was judged great enough to warrant saving her for that spot alone. And so, the story goes, Kern saw Morgan in *Americana* and cast her as Julie.[8] Hammerstein, writing in 1957, credited Ziegfeld with choosing Morgan: "He was a bold caster. For what Jerry and I considered a small but effective part Ziegfeld persuaded us to take Helen Morgan, who had just appeared in an intimate revue and had attracted attention as a singer with a personality that was very much her own. Could she act? We did not know. She had had no experience."[9]

What was it about Morgan's "Nobody Wants Me," sung seated on a piano in the orchestra pit, that suggested Julie to the makers of *Show Boat?* Morrie Ryskind's lyric to the song provides the first clue, for the connection between the content of "Nobody Wants Me" and the half-caste Julie was surprisingly direct. The second line of the verse—"I got the lonesome misery"—marks the singer as black within the codes of popular song lingo. Caught in a world of hurt, the singer appeals to "the Lord" and moans a bit on the repeated word "Oh," further reinforcing the song's presumptive blackness at the outset. The refrain mostly consists of repetitions of the line "I got those Nobody Wants Me, nobody likes me, nobody loves me blues," a construction recalling Ira Gershwin's 1924 lyric "(I've Got the) You Don't Know the Half of it, Dearie, Blues," written for Fred Astaire. But Ryskind's bridge lyric finally identifies the source of the singer's blues: the lack of a "yaller boy" to kiss and cuddle.

"Nobody Wants Me" offered a 1920s take on the coon song. The lyric presumes a black singing subject—as coon songs did—but the tone is serious rather than comic. Current, still rather new Broadway stereotypes of the tragic high yaller—a stereotypical oversexed, light-skinned, black woman doomed to unhappiness, powerfully captured in Lenore Ulric's blacked-up performance in *Lulu Belle* (1926)—are evoked in a simultaneously sympathetic and titillating vein. Marked "quasi spiritual," Henry Souvaine's syncopated tune—filled with chromatic touches—rode above complex, bluesy harmonies, flirting with the minor mode throughout, creating a dark, sophisticated mood. Similar songs expressing the romantic predicament of a sexy black woman would follow on Broadway, among them Thomas "Fats" Waller and Andy Razaf's "(What Did I Do to Be So) Black and Blue" from *Connie's Hot Chocolates*, the lament of a black woman too dark-skinned to attract a "yaller boy," and Howard Dietz and Ralph Rainger's "Moanin' Low," performed by Libby Holman in high-yaller makeup to great acclaim in *The Little Show* (both 1929). (Holman would be considered an alternative for Morgan as Julie in the 1930s.) Morgan never recorded "Nobody Wants Me," and she was never known for embodying the high-yaller racial type in her later career. But for the makers of *Show Boat* who encountered her in *Americana*, Morgan offered a charismatic new personality articulating a racial predicament that could be mapped on to the character of Julie. Julie, of course, would never sing a song like "Nobody Wants Me." The keynote to her character at this point in *Show Boat* history was the concealing of her blackness.

"Nobody Wants Me" was Morgan's signature song while *Show Boat* was being cast, and Kern or Ziegfeld could easily have heard her sing it in any number of places besides *Americana* at the Belmont. By January 1927, Morgan had expanded into all facets of Manhattan entertainment. Featured in a Broadway show, she could occasionally be heard on the radio. But what really got her name in the paper was the opening of Helen Morgan's Fifty-fourth Street Club in mid-November 1926. Advertisements plastered her name everywhere. Not only was the club named after the "Inimitable Star Featured in *Americana*" but music at the club was by Helen Morgan's Syncopating Six. On New Year's Eve 1926, the biggest night of the year when clubs charged inflated covers, entrance to Morgan's cost $15, just $10 below the cover at Texas Guinan's establishment. Morgan and Guinan's names would be increasingly linked in the press over the next three years as poster girls for Prohibition-resisting New York. Not open two months, Morgan's club received its first attention from the police when a summons was filed because the lights were still on at 4:30 a.m., well past the 3:00 a.m. curfew.[10] Morgan and her various clubs—all financed by shady figures with Morgan as a public front—would perform an Apache dance with the law for the entire time *Show Boat* was in rehearsal and on the boards. In January 1927, Morgan added a third job: headliner at the Palace. She started at the top of the vaudeville world. As one paper noted, "This week she will be earning three incomes, which may just about equal the amount of the taxi bills she will run up dashing from place to place."[11] An early description of her act captured

Morgan's persona in the making: "Helen Morgan, a highly individualized chantress of not particularly consequential songs . . . possesses a somnolent, smoldering personality, with overtones of pathos which give her numbers, even the most banal of them, a certain charm and distinction."[12] The song title "Just Like A Butterfly (That's Caught in the Rain)," recorded by Morgan in 1927, aptly describes her emerging persona.

Before departing for Europe in May 1927, Morgan appeared in a trio of short plays under the title *American Grand Guignol*. Burns Mantle's review captures Morgan just nine months before Julie would make her a genuine Broadway star:

> Between plays a grand piano was wheeled onto the stage and one of those slightly emaciated young men who always brings his music sat down to it. A second later a pretty girl in black velvet walked in and hopped up on the piano. Sitting there, swinging her shapely legs, she sang three or four songs rather well. . . . It was quite Parisian and rather diverting. The young woman was Helen Morgan, whose late evenings are given over to a night club in the Fifties, where she acts as hostess and probably sings her songs again.[13]

Mantle declined to characterize her performance in one of the plays beyond noting she was "looking at least swell in a picture hat." If the makers of *Show Boat* saw this production they had a chance to see Morgan in period costume. The young man at the piano sounds similar to the character of Jake in *Show Boat*, who provides sympathetic accompaniment to Julie's song in the Trocadero rehearsal scene and almost always uses music.

Whenever and wherever she might be encountered, Morgan's audiences expected certain things would happen. She would sing with piano accompaniment and would sit on the piano itself, an affectation explained as originally a necessity. Her job at the tiny Backstage Club had required it or she wouldn't have been seen. Nothing cemented Morgan's identity as a piano-sitting singer like *Show Boat*, which exposed her to a far larger New York audience than nightclub singing alone ever could. Her songs would be slightly Continental, pleasingly ephemeral, usually about undying, ill-fated, grown-up love, and she would perform with palpable conviction. As one profiler wrote in 1932, "She refuses to sing anything she doesn't feel. When she sings lachrymose songs she cries because she actually feels the emotion she is uttering. That is why she has sung only some thirty different selections in the past five years."[14] Morgan drew her listeners in and made them cry; she communicated feeling above all else, anticipating by a few years the rise of the microphone-based singing style that took the nation by storm in the crooner craze of the early

1930s. Morgan's repertoire and physical stance while singing became as important as anything else about her and expressed a key aspect of her persona: its sameness. Unlike other singers of the 1920s also categorized as torch singers, Morgan rarely ventured beyond a narrow stylistic and emotional range. Fanny Brice and Ruth Etting used the "torch" pose as one of several ways to put over a song. Morgan embraced torch singing like few others and managed, with the help of *Show Boat*, to build a career lasting about a decade on this Johnny-One-Note approach.

Hammerstein and Kern reshaped Julie for Morgan only in act 2. (The character's scenes in act 1 went unchanged, and Morgan was expected to play the part as written.) The rewritten Trocadero scene in act 2 did not call for Julie to deliver a lot of dialogue: setting up Morgan's song was the priority. But Julie did need to do some acting in the scene—bidding a silent farewell to Magnolia—and Morgan's abilities as a physical performer were quickly developed and effectively used. Indeed, Zeke Colvan, the credited director of *Show Boat*, used Morgan's performance in the scene as a model for aspiring actors:

> An unusually fine piece of pantomime, expressed almost entirely by the hands, was done by Helen Morgan as Julie in the original production of *Show Boat*. In directing later companies of the play I was never able to get another actress to duplicate the move with the same precision. . . . Attracted by the song, Julie reentered, unseen by Magnolia, whose back was turned to her. Julie, delighted, put out her hands as though to embrace Magnolia. Then, as she realized that Magnolia was badly dressed and obviously in need of the job, she backed away, drawing her hands inward. With one hand she groped for her hat and bag on the top of the piano. Her other hand reached out once more, tenderly. Then slowly she drew it to her mouth as though to stifle the words. Hastily, Julie backed away. In this scene, without any spoken word, Helen Morgan conveyed joy, the hopelessness of her own condition, and the fact that she was sacrificing her job.[15]

This sequence is astonishingly efficient. Not only does Magnolia sing "Can't Help Lovin' Dat Man"—nicely plugging an anticipated hit tune once again— but Julie compounds the moment with an added layer of complex emotion. Morgan rose to the occasion, likely after being intensively coached.

Julie's added song was the key to the role as transformed for Morgan, and "Bill" emerged as a stand-out moment in *Show Boat* that had no roots in Ferber, no precedent in Hammerstein's drafts, and no connection to Ziegfeld's brand of showmanship. It was all Morgan, the force of her persona overcoming a somewhat odd choice of interpolated song and the challenge of a huge theater like the Ziegfeld.

The original lyric for "Bill" was by P. G. Wodehouse, known for his clever, brittle approach to character. In *Oh, Lady! Lady!!*, "Bill" was sung in act 1 by the youthful female lead Molly about her fiancé Willoughby Finch. In an early version, Molly celebrated Finch as the perfect male, sharing the number—set to a different Kern tune—with the ladies of the chorus.[16] At some point, Molly's celebration of Bill's perfection was inverted by Wodehouse for comic effect, with a new lyric describing a rather disappointing young man of 1918, who doesn't have a car, can't dance, dresses poorly, can't play any upper-class sports (golf, tennis, polo), and is positively homely (not handsome, tall, straight, or slim). And yet, Molly still loves "old Bill." Sung at a healthy *Allegretto* clip, Wodehouse's "Bill" is a musically modest, lyrically overstated complaint that the singer—herself young and inexperienced—isn't in love with someone more suitable by all the fashionable standards of the day. In changing the song for Morgan's purposes and a scene set in 1894, Hammerstein left most of Wodehouse's lyric untouched, removing only the most egregiously anachronistic references to Bill's "motor car" and poor skills as a dancer (a reference to the ongoing dance craze of the late 1910s). Tellingly, Wodehouse's uses of "boy" were changed to "man," implicitly elevating the age and life experience of the singer as well. In *Show Boat*, "Bill" becomes a song for a woman to sing. Kern revised two bars of his tune, improving the song's flow, and the tempo mark was slowed to *Andante moderato*. But the musical text was hardly transformed, and on the face of it "Bill" appears an unpromising candidate for an existential meditation on the mysteries of love. Yet this is precisely what Morgan made of it.

What made "Bill" work in *Show Boat* was Morgan's contribution of both vocal skill—she was an effective if idiosyncratic singer—and perceived personal connections between her and her audience. White Broadway audiences identified with Morgan and through that identification were able to read "Bill" as a deeper song than the text itself would suggest. This connection was enhanced by events that kept Morgan in the public eye as the show continued its run. Reviewers of *Show Boat* did not have the space to analyze Morgan's persona. However, the reviews for *Sweet Adeline*, the period show Kern and Hammerstein created for her after *Show Boat*, offer several descriptions of Morgan that are applicable to "Bill." (She sat on a piano in *Sweet Adeline*, too.) Morgan's voice was described as "not large" but "clear and agreeable."[17] (Recordings reveal a singer with a sure sense of pitch and impeccable diction but little to no power. It's difficult to believe Morgan was not assisted by a microphone when singing in the Ziegfeld Theatre.) Burns Mantle wrote, "as a sort of superballadist of the nightclubs[,] Helen affects an olive gray complexion and sings autobiographical laments wondering why she was ever born. As no one seems to know, everybody feels a little sad about it and applauds gen-erously in the hope of cheering Helen."[18] "Bill" typifies her repertoire in its direct address of the listener as the singer's confidant outside any specific context. Morgan was, in essence, a singer of soliloquies, ready to spill her guts in song to anyone who might be listening. In the words of one critic, this stance encouraged "nightclub cynics to see into their napkins and resolve to lead better, nobler lives. . . . Miss Morgan is a winsome lady with a pleasant little voice and a quavering way of singing sob ballads with emotional sim-plicity and reticence. In an unaffected way she has decided charm."[19]

Central to that charm was alcohol—the cultural obsession of the day. After describing Julie's disheveled physical state at the Trocadero in the October script, Hammerstein put a "pint flask" in her hand from which she "furtively takes a drink." (Ferber's Julie—and Hammerstein's in the January and August scripts—was a quiet, modest, efficient bookkeeper, a woman in con-trol of herself.) Making Julie a drunk after casting Morgan played directly into the late 1920s moment. Hammerstein might have been describing a fig-ure seen regularly around Manhattan by this point, almost ten years into the social experiment of Prohibition: men and women ruined by drink, sipping from flasks, ordering glasses of ice to which they added their own booze in a manner that fooled no one. Morgan's professional origins in speakeasies and prominence as a nightclub hostess worked together in the Trocadero scene to point the audience toward the present. The tacit assumption, never aired in the press until the 1930s, that Morgan herself was an alcoholic added to the connection. "Bill" as performed by Julie in the Trocadero rehearsal scene was sufficiently generic to let Morgan's 1920s persona shine through in an almost entirely unmediated fashion. The narrative context of Julie's life was never the issue. Audiences didn't care what the circumstances of Julie's fall had been or what had happened to Steve. As a drunken torch singer singing songs of hopeless devotion, Morgan embodied an impossible position in an absurd situation, her persona a good stand-in for the predicament faced by wets in Prohibition Manhattan, otherwise law-abiding citizens who lived part of their life in the bizarre alternative public sphere of speakeasies and bootleg-gers. Morgan, "the sad eyed crooner of blues songs who sang her way . . . right into the slightly alcoholic heart of Broadway," effectively carried the burden of the moment for her white audience both at the time and in popular memory for decades after.[20] (In the 1950s, a decade fairly obsessed with pro-cessing the experience of the 1920s, both a television drama and a film wrote the history of Prohibition through the story of Morgan's alcoholism.[21])

Julie's single scene in act 2 was tailored to Morgan's skills and persona, but Julie's scenes and songs in act 1 had already been written when Morgan was hired. Here, Julie was not visibly dissolute; she was a woman with a secret. She didn't just sit and sing; she had to move and show a variety of feelings. Julie's big vocal moment came in a context filled with tension. In the supposed safety of the *Cotton Blossom* kitchen, Queenie expresses surprise that Julie knows "Can't Help Lovin' Dat Man," a song only "colored folks sing" according to the cook. The November script has each word of Queenie's query "How come y'all know dat song?" underlined separately in dark pencil, evidence Hammerstein and Colvan wanted an emphatic, deadly serious reading of the line. The black cook's questioning of Julie's relationship to the musical color line was not to be dismissed as a casual observation, and Julie's reply, both spoken and sung, had potentially meaningful consequences. Eager not to deny her knowledge of the song in front of her beloved "little sister" Magnolia, Julie proceeds to sing verse and chorus. Hammerstein and Kern invented this scene—it has no precedent in Ferber—which puts Julie in a dramatic and musical bind. A mixed-race woman passing as white, Julie's knowledge of the song raises suspicions about her racial identity. Furthermore, the stakes are high for her performance of the song. *How* Julie sings "Can't Help Lovin' Dat Man" will either calm or further awaken Queenie's evident suspicions. Magnolia, still nominally a child and thoroughly immersed in black culture, as her shuffle dance later in the number demonstrates, is oblivious to the issue. And *how* Julie sings "Can't Help Lovin' Dat Man" remained a crucial performance decision across the history of *Show Boat*, marking larger shifts in how the work was understood and where the sympathies of the audience were directed.

Judging from her 1932 recording and the 1936 film, Morgan sang "Can't Help Lovin' Dat Man" in a thoroughly white fashion. Hammerstein wrote blackness into the song, dropping final g's throughout. The verse's opening exhortation—"Oh listen, sister"—suggests a black voice hailing a black listener. Kern, likewise and uncharacteristically, built musical markers of blackness into the tune, which incorporates many blue notes and has a verse built on the twelve-bar blues realized in the full-voice quarter-note chords typical of bluesy Broadway songs at the time. The blackness of the musical text is overdetermined, one reason "Can't Help Lovin' Dat Man" works so well when Queenie, Joe, and the black chorus take over after Julie sings it. But Morgan consistently kept the song's black elements at arm's length. Her "can't" carried a hint of "*cah*n't"—an affectation that crops up regularly in her recordings of other songs—and she persisted in putting the final g's back in, even if it spoiled Hammerstein's rhyme scheme. Morgan sang squarely on the beat, didn't lean on the blue notes, and stuck with a light soprano tone.

The decided whiteness of Morgan's performance choices are put in perspective when compared with Tess Gardella's recording of "Can't Help Lovin'

Dat Man" from 1928.[22] Gardella originated the role of Queenie from within her blackface stage persona Aunt Jemima. On her recording, Gardella swings from the start. She leans on, scoops up to, and freely bends Kern's blue notes, coloring her voice expressively and subtly in an easy manner. Gardella plays with both the time and the tune, and cornet commentary throughout adds to the jazzy quality of her recording (see chap. 5 for more on Gardella's position as a white woman in blackface playing a demanding black singing role in *Show Boat*). Gardella's recording puts Morgan's torch singer persona into racial perspective. Morgan's vocal style was resolutely white. Like the flapper, the torch singer as cultural icon in the 1920s was raced as white. Morgan, unsurprisingly, maintained Julie's attempt to "pass" throughout, even to the way she sang "Can't Help Lovin' Dat Man." In effect, Morgan's Julie sang the song without revealing that she knew how to sing it right, how to sing it black. She knows the text but not the proper performance style. Queenie steps in and sings it black, immediately taking the pressure off Julie. Morgan's approach would persist until the 1970s.

In the October script, Hammerstein detailed Julie's inner concerns at being caught by Queenie singing a black song. Julie's face should show "swift terror . . . succeeded by an expression of stolid caution" at Queenie's initial question about Julie's knowledge of "Can't Help Lovin' Dat Man." When Queenie asks, "Can you sing the whole thing?" Julie's performance of verse and chorus is described this way: "She starts to sing in an attitude of defiance, then lapsing into the 'Blue' spirit of the song." In the Broadway script, the description of Julie's lapse into a blacker "'Blue' spirit" was removed, leaving only the initial "attitude of defiance," a revision of stage directions likely made in response to the manner in which Morgan was approaching the song.[23] Post-1970 Julies would unknowingly follow Hammerstein's initial direction that Julie give evidence for her black identity by way of specific performance choices (see chap. 9).

How Morgan moved while singing "Can't Help Lovin' Dat Man" remains somewhat up in the air. In the 1936 film, directed by James Whale and discussed in chapter 6, Morgan holds completely still while singing her verse and chorus, hanging on to a nearby by bannister or chair for dear life. When following the shuffling Joe, Queenie, and Magnolia out the door of the kitchen at the close of the number, Morgan moves stiffly and without commitment. The only surviving still from Morgan's performance of the song out of context for the musical prologue of the 1929 *Show Boat* film suggests a quite different approach (see fig. 3.1). Here, surrounded by members of the black chorus from the Broadway cast, Morgan raises her hands in an ecstatic gesture that at the time would have signaled knowledge of black performance on Julie's part.

3.1. *Helen Morgan and members of Will Vodery's Jubilee Singers perform "Can't Help Lovin' Dat Man," one of four excerpts from the 1927 Broadway production featured in the musical prologue to the 1929* Show Boat *film. (Courtesy of the Margaret Herrick Library, The Academy of Motion Picture Arts and Sciences)*

Morgan was a hit from the start. Walter Winchell noted in his opening night column that she was "handsomely appreciated (stopping the proceedings once),"and she did not disappoint as a source of publicity for *Show Boat*.[24] In fact, while Morgan played Julie onstage, her offstage life began to resemble the plot of *Chicago*, Maurine Watkins's sensational play, which ran for the first five months of 1927. (*Chicago* is better known today in Kander and Ebb's musical adaptation from 1975, which prospered in a long-running revival opening in 1996 when the 1994 *Show Boat* revival was still playing.) Virtually always paired with fellow nightclub hostess Texas Guinan in the press, Morgan played Velma Kelly to Guinan's Roxie Hart. As the *Chicago Tribune* reported, "Miss Morgan had a different courtroom manner than that of Miss Guinan. The latter was volatile, chummy with the prosecution and even with the judge, there in person and in character, shooting her remarks fast and snappy. Miss Morgan was in the opposite feminine role, scared, wet eyed, and almost fainting."[25] Morgan's visibility as a standard bearer for wet forces in the city couldn't help but reflect on her role as the drunk but sympathetic Julie.

Morgan was arrested on December 30, 1927, forty-eight hours after *Show Boat* opened at the Ziegfeld, in "one of the most spectacular nightclub raids in the history of metropolitan prohibition enforcement" (reported the *New York Times* breathlessly).[26] Morgan and eight others were taken into police custody just after 1:30 a.m. and held on $1,000 bail. Morgan was released at 5:30 a.m. The Helen Morgan Club was completely wrecked, fixtures literally ripped out of the walls and carted away. The government agents raiding the club were greeted by onlookers on the street with "hisses and boos and the sound of many automobile horns." There was no doubt whose side the fashionable Broadway public was on. The Prohibition administrator Maurice Campbell had chosen his target well. (In good *Chicago* fashion, Campbell regularly declared he deplored publicity.) Striking at Morgan served notice on the entire Midtown charade of Prohibition enforcement. At the end of February, all charges against Morgan were dropped and the fixtures ordered returned. In the midst of the controversy, Morgan sang for the annual Catholic Actors' Guild of America benefit.[27] In May, she stood beside columnist Robert Benchley as hostess for a benefit for the American Women's Association, a society charity group led by Mrs. Pierpont Morgan Hamilton.[28] Gathered in the Crystal Room of the luxury liner *Ile de France*, the elites of Manhattan society yielded symbolic leadership to a nightclub torch singer from humble circumstances who defied Prohibition with a silk scarf in hand: a better tableau of the odd cultural logic of late 1920s Manhattan would be hard to find.

Happily for her continuing notoriety, Morgan's legal troubles were not over. Her new club, Helen Morgan's Summer Home, was among eleven raided by well-dressed Prohibition agents in June 1928, just in time for the summer slump in Broadway ticket sales. This time the agents were not wanton in their destruction. The *New York Times* had the good sense to mention that besides presiding over her club, Morgan was "a principal in the Ziegfeld production of *The Show Boat* [sic]."[29] This raid was masterminded by Mabel Walker Willebrandt, a Parthy-esque figure who pursued Broadway drinkers from her post in Washington. Both Morgan and Guinan escaped arrest on the night, and the papers speculated they had been tipped off, reporting Morgan slipped out after "changing costumes with her cloakroom girl."[30] None of Morgan's scenes in *Show Boat* were quite so dramatic. The next morning, in a stunt worthy of musical treatment, Guinan and Morgan together trekked down to the Manhattan Federal Building to surrender. Initially unable to find anyone who would book them, several hours elapsed before Morgan and Guinan could be properly arrested, after which Morgan's lawyer "angrily and repeatedly" told reporters the only reason his client had been charged was "Publicity." Morgan was conspicuously absent at the mass arraignment of those arrested on June

28. Guinan showed up and played the scene to the hilt, calling the charges "bologna."[31] When Morgan appeared in court the next day beside Guinan, she gave a good show in her own fashion. Walter Winchell painted the scene for *Life* magazine's national readership: "Dear old Tex keeps making flip remarks about the Government agents and her alleged best friends are hoping she will shut up. Everybody seems to think that her competitor, Helen Morgan, played her part better down at the courthouse, for Helen removed all rouge and mascara, put on the weep act, got coy, and hung her head as though she really was sorry. If that stuff fails to win the jury, Helen probably will go into her baby talk routine."[32] While not completely analogous, the miscegenation scene Morgan played nightly required weeping and outward expressions of shame. It would be difficult for Broadway audiences to separate Morgan as Julie being arrested onstage from Morgan herself moving tearfully through the legal system. Through it all, Morgan received reporters in her dressing room at the Ziegfeld.[33]

And the saga went on as *Show Boat* continued its run, only now it was Ziegfeld's turn to play a role in the tabloid drama surrounding his star. On August 6, Ziegfeld announced that Morgan had "ended the cabaret chapter of her career" in a decision to "conserve all her energies for her work as a featured artist of the legitimate stage." "Featured" is a key word here: Morgan's quirky image made her a tough fit for standard leading roles on stage. As a film actress, she found a niche playing various dissolute types in lowlife dramas. Ziegfeld said Morgan was moving to Great Neck, giving up "late hours and overwork" for a "country home."[34] The declaration was, in fact, a bit disingenuous given that Morgan's club had been padlocked, and she was under indictment. But Ziegfeld didn't want her to stop appearing in nightclubs entirely: he wanted her for *his* nightclub. In September 1928, Ziegfeld announced the reopening the New Amsterdam Roof Garden, a mainstay of pre-Prohibition nightlife shuttered eight years earlier. On New Year's Eve, Ziegfeld's legendary *Midnight Frolic* would be resurrected with Eddie Cantor as host, Paul Whiteman's band, and La Morgan presiding on top of the piano. Ziegfeld must not have minded her staying up late to sing at his establishment, and Morgan probably appreciated working her second shift at a spot that was unlikely to be raided. In the meantime, the case against Morgan was in limbo, and she kept on singing "in her characteristic style" the songs from *Show Boat* that everyone wanted to hear.[35] By now Morgan was a national figure, known across the country and because of her Broadway credentials able to take an honored place among elites that would have been inaccessible to the likes of Guinan. A *Life* caricature pictured her among a small group of Broadway and Washington notables greeting the arrival of President Coolidge and the First

Lady at the New Amsterdam Roof Garden.[36] That party would have likely been inaccessible to Robeson even if he had chosen to be in *Show Boat*.

As *Show Boat* reached the end of its run, the drama of Morgan and the Prohibition enforcer Mabel Willebrandt reached its conclusion. Morgan was cleared of all charges on April 19, 1929. One headline read "Helen Morgan Free; In Tears at Verdict." "Miss Morgan was pale and trembling when the jury came in. When she heard the verdict she seemed about to faint. She regained partial control of herself and then, beginning to cry softly, she was soon weeping unrestrainedly. Her only comment was: 'I don't want to think any more about it.'"[37] And as she had done for the entire run, Morgan put aside her legal difficulties and went to the Ziegfeld that night to play Julie and sing "Bill" yet once more. *Show Boat* closed less than two weeks later on May 4.

Morgan's offstage notoriety was an important—and commercial— element of *Show Boat*'s initial Broadway run. For some in the audience, the show wasn't the principal attraction: Morgan was. Bernard Sobel, the Ziegfeld press agent, summed up her effect on ticket sales: "Again, after *Show Boat* had run more than a year and the interest of the public was presumably exhausted, the box office took a sudden spurt up as a result of the automatic publicity from the trial of Helen Morgan, a member of the cast. Patrons walked up to the window and asked definitely if she were in the cast, and, finding that she was, they bought tickets to see her."[38]

Morgan was a professional. She apparently never missed a show because of her legal troubles. Indeed, her only reported absences were a four-day bout with the flu and a short trip to Florida to make a personal appearance at the premiere of Universal's *Show Boat* film, which featured Morgan singing both her signature songs in its musical prologue. Ziegfeld, with a financial interest in the film, graciously permitted her absence.

4

A ZIEGFELD SOPRANO AND
A SHUBERT TENOR

* * *

Who were the leads in Ziegfeld's *Show Boat*? Advertisements provide one set of answers. The first *New York Times* ad offered caricatures of nine actors in their parts on an elaborately drawn boat: four couples and Julie.[1] Overlarge heads on tiny bodies transform the figures into dolls on display, the first of many *Show Boat* group portraits. Magnolia and Ravenal in wedding attire stand hand in hand at the prow; Julie rides alone at the stern: all three are drawn as full figures. The other six actors peek their comical heads from above the railings on the side of the boat. On the upper deck, Frank and Ellie frame a banner emblazoned with the words *Show Boat*, Frank's head cocked in a ballyhoo gesture that promises this couple will provide some fun. On the lower deck, Parthy looks in profile toward Andy while Queenie and Joe tilt their heads toward each other. Andy and Queenie smile broadly. Parthy looks angry; Joe, thoughtful. With *Cotton Blossom* lettered on its side, the boat rides a river called "Old Man River" [*sic*], shrewdly combining a familiar name from the novel with a catchy phrase that wasn't yet widely known as a song title. The names of the actors playing the nine pictured characters appear in all caps below the boat, suggesting a pecking order:

NORMA TERRIS	HOWARD MARSH
EVA PUCK	SAMMY WHITE
HELEN MORGAN	EDNA MAY OLIVER
AUNT JEMIMA	JULES BLEDSOE

AND
CHARLES WINNINGER

"150 Glorified Girls—Jubilee Singers" rounds out the ad's description of the cast. Black newspapers were quick to notice Bledsoe's billing, "featured heavy with the big 'Ofay' stars," and the black chorus being "played up" as well.[2]

Two weeks later, a Christmas Day ad offered *Show Boat* as a "Ziegfeld Christmas Gift to New York."[3] A bit of high-toned rhetoric presents the company as a "Cast of Distinguished American Players." Here, only eight names make the list, with Winninger again at the bottom in the largest type. (His contract likely called for such emphasis.) Removed from the list of leads was Bledsoe, whose name now appeared in smaller type with the black chorus: "JUBILEE SINGERS, DANCERS & JULES BLEDSOE." "150 GLORIFIED GIRLS" in type as large as Winninger's ended the list of players. The black members of the cast were effectively reduced to a single small line.

Ziegfeld's weekly ads in *Variety* were more modest. By January 1928, only the seven white leads were being named in the Broadway listings section. A good-sized ad across the page from the theater listings in the January 28, 1928, *Variety* stands out (see fig. 4.1). Performers often took out ads for themselves in *Variety*, a professional paper where those currently "at liberty" or experiencing big success could insert their names into industry chatter. Bledsoe was a prickly character, and the big ad seems entirely within his persona. He clearly understood his Joe to be "making theatrical history," correctly anticipating the lasting power of "Ol' Man River." Ziegfeld didn't see it that way, at least as evidenced by the way he sold the show. In hindsight, the visual counterpoint between a list of white leads and an ad taken out by a black featured singer graphically represents the gap *Show Boat* was bridging between a Ziegfeld show—one among many—and a show that broke new ground for black performers in particular.

Ziegfeld's and Bledsoe's ads speak to the tremendous importance of performers as the primary draw on Broadway at the time. This chapter, like the previous two, explores how individual performers shaped the original Broadway production and how performed racial types shaped the making of Ferber's novel into a musical. Here, the focus turns to the six white characters who carry the show's plot and have contended with each other across *Show Boat* history for the status of principal lead: Andy, Parthy, Magnolia, Ravenal, Ellie, and Frank. (Chapter 5 looks at the black chorus and the blackface role of Queenie.) Before looking closely at Norma Terris's Magnolia and Howard Marsh's Ravenal, a quick survey of the other four white leads offers insight into the genre politics of the show and the explicit and implicit questions of race *Show Boat* inevitably raised. As with Robeson and Morgan, understanding how these six performers shaped *Show Boat*'s white leads demands a look at their respective careers *before* 1927. What these performers brought to the show, what Broadway audiences expected of them, what Hammerstein, Kern, and Ziegfeld understood they could deliver, ended up defining both the content of *Show Boat* in 1927 and the parameters within which all subsequent

4.1. Ad from February 15, 1928, issue of Variety. *(Author's collection)*

Show Boats would be forced to work. Andy, Parthy, Frank, Ellie, Magnolia, and Ravenal cannot be understood without first assessing how much of Charles Winninger, Edna May Oliver, Sammy White, Eva Puck, Norma Terris, and Howard Marsh remains in each respective role (see fig. 4.2).

Charles Winninger was among the last principals signed for *Show Boat*. Only Bledsoe came aboard later. Winninger's Broadway career reached back to the war years. In 1927, his most recent success had been *No, No, Nanette*, where he famously executed a backflip during the song "I Want to Be Happy." (Newspaper caricatures of Winninger as Cap'n Andy hint he may have done the flip in *Show Boat* as well.)[4] When his 1927 show *Yes, Yes, Yvette* proved a flop, Winninger came into *Show Boat*. There's no indication that Hammerstein was thinking of Winninger when he wrote Andy's role. Most every element of the part—including the virtuoso one-man version of *The Parson's Bride*—was in the works well before Winninger was cast. The only enduring contribution Winninger made was playing the violin for the play-within-the-play. This detail appears only in scripts typed after Winninger was hired. The notes he played were entered into the published vocal score. Later Andys who mime playing the fiddle are ghosting a signature moment from Winninger's portrayal of the character.

Hammerstein used Andy to voice a sympathetic view of Julie that was not part of Ferber's original. In the novel, when Julie's racial status is revealed,

4.2. *Backstage at the Ziegfeld Theatre on Christmas Eve, 1928. One year into* Show Boat's *original Broadway run, the principals of the cast join the producer Florenz Ziegfeld for a group photo. At center, Helen Morgan, unlikely star of the show, stands beside Ziegfeld and the child Kim. Howard Marsh and Norma Terris frame this central trio on either side. Third from left stands Tess Gardella, who removed the blackface makeup she wore for the role of Queenie in time for the photo. At the right, Edna May Oliver stands between Charles Winninger and Jules Bledsoe (still in his Joe costume and old-age makeup). With her right arm around Winninger, Oliver links her left arm through Bledsoe's right, a pose they could not have repeated in a photo intended for public consumption. (Billy Rose Theatre Division, The New York Public Library for the Performing Arts, Astor, Lenox, and Tilden Foundations)*

Andy says to her—"kindly"—"Well, Julie, m'girl," a fragmentary remark that could be interpreted in several ways (even that he knew all along and was letting her pass last as long as possible).[5] In the musical, Andy makes a strong albeit indirect statement about racial tolerance. After Magnolia defies her mother and goes to Julie's dressing room to be with her disgraced friend, Parthy sets up a pair of lines with a sniff, "Well, Hawks, you see what the show boat has done to your daughter." Andy replies, cryptically, "I think the Show Boat's made a damn fine girl out of my daughter." This exchange appears in the January draft. From his first try at the scene, Hammerstein's advocacy of racial tolerance was in evidence, modulated to match the Broadway context where outright statements were unwelcome but more subtle expression of antiracist themes could be made.[6]

Like Winninger, Edna May Oliver was available for *Show Boat* because her most recent show had proved a flop. She ditched the Gershwins' *Strike Up the Band* after its Philadelphia opening night. (It ended up closing out of town.) Oliver was not a singer, which worked out fine as Parthy was never conceived as a singing role. Kern had worked Parthy into the fabric of the underscoring in act 1, scene 1 with a characteristic orchestral theme. This musical idea appears in the earliest continuity drafts from late 1926 and can be understood as an expression of Ferber's character. Parthy's first scene—a brief spat with Windy, the towboat pilot—exploited audience knowledge of the book: Ferber spent several pages developing a contentious Parthy-Windy subplot. Oliver was a dramatic actress, accustomed to playing a part as written. The role remained effectively unchanged after her hiring except for the elimination of the Parthy-centered trio "Cheer Up," which was cut and replaced by "Why Do I Love You?," where Oliver danced an unwilling fox trot with Winninger.

("Cheer Up" had been Hammerstein's attempt to insert a nostalgic reminiscence from his youth. The January draft has Andy playing an impromptu barker on the Midway, introducing Parthy as "Sober Sue" and challenging anyone in the crowd to make her smile. "Sober Sue" was a vaudeville novelty—a woman with nerve damage that made smiling impossible—who had played Hammerstein's grandfather Oscar I's Victoria Theatre. Like the change from Jopper's to the Trocadero, which inserted some of Ziegfeld's past into *Show Boat*, "Sober Sue" and "Cheer Up" had Hammerstein adding his lived experience of show business history into the musical. At the final chorus of "Cheer Up," Hammerstein imagined "the three principals and entire chorus down to footlights and right over at audience," an idea that prefigures the staging of the title number of *Oklahoma!*)

One addition to the show made after Oliver's casting is the exchange between Parthy and Kim in the final scene, a moment preserved in most subsequent versions. Dressing Parthy as a flapper, complete with long cigarette holder and bobbed hair, must have struck all concerned as a good visual joke. The potential for Parthy's stern character to soften, particularly under the influence of her stylish, grown-up granddaughter, dates to the November script, where Kim sums up her grandmother with the unlikely line, "O Parthy, you're wonderful!" The musical comedy desire to find cracks in Parthy's exterior—to let her in on the fun—proved irresistible, playing, as it did, into contemporary jokes about oldsters adopting the radical ways of the young, dancing the Charleston and the like. How Oliver played the moment remains unknown, but her capacity to pull it off and get the laugh can be assumed.

Eva Puck and Sammy White, the original Frank and Ellie, were experienced Broadway leads, a married couple who had carried Rodgers and Hart's *The Girl Friend*, a solid hit of the 1926 season. Puck had been a child star on vaudeville and did a double act with her brother prior to teaming with White in 1923. Her first Broadway role was a secondary lead in *Irene* (1919), one of the Cinderella shows that launched postwar musical comedy on a contemporary note. Reviewers compared Puck to Gertrude Lawrence and Adele Astaire, praising her as "comely, tuneful, agile, with a pleasantly weird mannerism . . . in herself sufficient to make a considerable attraction of *The Girl Friend*."[7] White also began in vaudeville, touring with a blackface duo that appeared on Broadway in the late 1910s in several editions of the Shuberts's *Passing Show*. Generally known for his eccentric dancing, in *The Girl Friend* White had again "unlimber[ed] his legs in his familiar dance specialty."

Puck and White were hired out of big-time vaudeville for *Show Boat* in October 1927. *Variety*'s review of *Show Boat* in tryouts singled out the pair, saying "They never overdo it for a minute."[8] Another review noted, "much of the evening's loudest applause followed [Puck and White's] dancing and comic moments."[9] The apparent necessity of their presence was commented upon as well: "Mr. Ziegfeld, who has studied the inevitable compromises with the public, must make room even on the banks of the Mississippi in the eighties, for the Broadwayish quips and antics of Eva Puck and Sammy White. (The audience, last evening, gave ample proof of insisting upon them.) . . . [They] make the most of their incongruous place."[10] That place was shaped around Puck and White's particular brand of showmanship grafted onto Hammerstein's initial plan to use Frank and Ellie to move *Show Boat*'s story forward.

Frank and Ellie play essential roles in the unfolding of *Show Boat*'s plot. They witness the crew member Pete telling the sheriff about Julie's racial identity, which allows Ellie to run ahead and warn Steve, setting up the blood-drinking scene. Frank has the idea to hire Ravenal as the boat's leading man. In a strained coincidence, the pair run into Magnolia at the very moment Ravenal deserts her. Ellie reads aloud Ravenal's farewell letter, and Frank helps Magnolia get the audition and the job at the Trocadero. And even though there is no rationale given for their presence, Frank and Ellie show up in the final scene flaunting their success in Hollywood. Hammerstein assumed audiences cared enough about Frank and Ellie to want to know how they came out in the end.

All these uses of Frank and Ellie to move the plot forward were in place in the January script. Changes in subsequent drafts involve the content and character of their dialogue and the addition of musical numbers. After the hiring of Puck and White, Ellie and Frank start to talk more and more like characters from contemporary musical comedy. One example typifies the sort of changes effected by the entrance of known quantities into the show-making process. In the January script, Frank and Ellie are revealed at the close to be frauds. Ellie struts about in a "very Ritz" manner, talking of Hollywood, their villa, and their "pretty swift" social life. After this display of ego, Frank draws Andy aside and asks for twenty bucks. Andy gives it to his old employee and says, sagely, as Frank and Ellie exit, "Those movin' pitcher people are wonderful." Hammerstein works off of Ferber here, giving Ellie, in particular, a less than sunny fate. (In the novel, the aged Elly ends the story back on the *Cotton Blossom* playing character roles after a disappointing career of failed attempts to make it big off the river.) The January script brings the Frank and Ellie subplot to a dark, even pathetic close. This was hardly the style of Puck and White. In the Broadway script, their final exchange with Andy revels in comic braggadocio, with the pair sharing in the surprise success of their adopted son, a Hollywood child star who makes a million a year.[11] Andy's line about "movin' pitcher people" remains, but now the joke is on Hollywood. Like most musical comedy types, Frank and Ellie end up in a pot of jam.

Several musical sketches in Kern's hand pull back the curtain on the making of Puck and White's musical numbers. Kern and Hammerstein promised the pair a certain number of featured moments and, when these were not forthcoming during rehearsals, tempers began to rise. Kern advised Hammerstein to pay some attention to the duo in a dummy lyric scribbled on a rejected musical sketch.

> Oscar, darling, won't you please get busy?
> Ev'ry time I see her Puck gets quizzy
> Evidently thinks we lie like bastards.
> True we do;
> But if you get a chance for Christ's sake block out
> Something they can dance to:
> (Not a knockout.)
> Just enough to keep our word.
> And then we're through.[12]

Puck effectively used some moodiness to ensure that her and White's roles were more than mere plot support, and Kern and Hammerstein clearly felt obliged to honor their pledge to give the pair a chance to dance. The pair ended up with two song-and-dance duets—"I Might Fall Back on You" (a book number at the midpoint of act 1) and "Goodbye, My Lady Love" (a performed number at the

Trocadero). In addition, Puck was given the charm solo "Life Upon the Wicked Stage" backed up by the ladies of the white chorus.

"I Might Fall Back on You" replaced two earlier attempts to enliven act 1 after the lengthy miscegenation scene (which did not include a musical number and still feels more like a dramatic playlet than a scene in a musical).[13] Frank and Ellie's all-too-cute song and dance introduces the essential contrast between the two: Frank is eager to marry; Ellie resists. The couple embodies a basic musical comedy trope: the "average lad" pursuing the coy girl. The number also complements the brief appearance of the backwoodsmen, an element dating to the January draft. Two undifferentiated caricatures of southern rural whiteness—hicks who've never seen a play—step up to the box office and pay for their tickets with Confederate money, then get so wrapped up in the performance of *The Parson's Bride* they pull their guns on Frank in his role as the villain. Frank, already afraid of the backwoodsmen, flees the stage in terror. The germ of this subplot can be found in Ferber's descriptions of "backwoods dwellers [who] had never witnessed a theatrical performance in all their lives—simple child-like credulous people to whom the make-believe villainies, heroics, loves, and adventures of the drama were so real as sometimes to cause the *Cotton Blossom* troupe actual embarrassment."[14] Ferber's backwoodsman becomes so absorbed in the drama he reaches for his gun. But the nameless, solitary figure never interrupts the play and sheepishly withdraws into his belligerent nature when the villain exits. In the musical, of course, the backwoodsmen shoot at the stage to great comic effect, stopping the show in a display of ignorance. Hammerstein turned Ferber's poignant portraits into Broadway caricatures, complicating *Show Boat's* presentation of southern whiteness. The backwoodsmen also anticipate the hillbilly stereotype in Depression-era comic strips such as *The Mountain Boys, Lil' Abner*, and the introduction of Snuffy Smith to *Barney Google*, which made the characters even funnier for later audiences (see fig. 4.3).[15] The backwoodsmen provided a foil for Frank—a conflation of two men from Ferber: Schultzy and Frank—setting in further relief his Broadway identity as a dancing wimp, victim of Ellie's jokes, a weakling in an era much concerned over a perceived masculinity crisis.

A newspaper caricature of Puck and White in *The Girl Friend* further captures the racial identity of the pair.[16] White plays a tense, narrow-chested suppliant, an Eddie Cantor knockoff who can dance. Puck plays the modern girl, elbows and knees all akimbo as if the Charleston has shaped her every move. Puck and White embodied a mid-1920s, white, jazzy, modernness in its harmless comic mode, their syncopated energy cleansed of any of the social pathologies associated with the popularity of jazz among white youth.

4.3. *Sammy White returned to Broadway as Frank Schultz in the 1946 Broadway revival. Frank's comical encounter with a pair of backwoodsmen (Jack Daley and Jerry Prosk) is seen here in front of the* Cotton Blossom's *separate entrances for white and "colored" patrons. (Author's collection)*

Broadway had absorbed enough black music and dance by this point to make jazz an unproblematic mark of white youthfulness. Syncopation was profitable, the sound of the day, the moral concerns of the immediate postwar years largely swallowed up in the accelerating energy of the Jazz Age. Perhaps in an ideal world, Fred and Adele Astaire, at the peak of their Broadway stardom when *Show Boat* was made, would have played the dancing pair. (The Astaires opened in *Funny Face* a month before *Show Boat* came to New York.) Frank and Ellie's relationship is comic and rather siblinglike. The notion of real romance between them is absurd: they are show business partners. They dance more than they sing, and the tone of their characters—except during the dramatic Ontario Street scene where they witness Magnolia's abandonment by Ravenal with real sensitivity—matches the good humor and up-to-date repartee for which the Astaires were known. Frank and Ellie as shaped by the

peculiar talents of Puck and White contributed this kind of Broadway whiteness to the 1927 *Show Boat*.

A final note on Puck's act 1 solo "Life Upon the Wicked Stage," which was
added during rehearsals. Despite its placement in the 1880s, Hammerstein's
lyric employs relatively recent notions of the life of an actress. Ellie sings of
"stage-door Johnnies," an American coinage from the early 1910s. The life
Ellie describes matches Jazz Age depictions of the chorus girl as gold digger—
pursued by (and pursuing) "wild old men" bearing "jewels and sables"—found
in plays (*The Gold Diggers*, 1919, and *Gentlemen Prefer Blondes*, 1926) and the
media. The lyric offers a veritable catalog of popular notions of the life of a
Ziegfeld girl but, set to Kern's schottische, the number comes off as at once
old-fashioned and ironic.[17] The gap between the tune and the text works
because Ellie, like everyone on Ferber's thoroughly respectable boat, is, mor-
ally speaking, above suspicion. "Life Upon the Wicked Stage" ends up being
just so much dress up. The number continued to work in later remakings of the
show, suggesting the enduring need for a lighthearted female lead to leaven
with some comic variety the rather serious trio of Magnolia, Parthy, and Julie.

On November 7, 1926, the "Rialto Gossip" column in the *New York Times*
included a historic scoop: "Elizabeth Hines, it is reported, will appear in the
musical version of Miss Ferber's *Show Boat*. A news announcement of the
week had it that Jerome Kern and Oscar Hammerstein 2d, respectively composer and adapter, were about to fare southward in search of local color.
Another way to find it, perhaps, would be to read *Show Boat*."[18] This tidbit is
the earliest published mention of the musical (yet found), predating Ziegfeld's hearing of the score by two-and-a-half weeks. Two days after Hammerstein and Kern auditioned their work-in-progress for Ziegfeld, the *Telegram*
reported that Hines would appear in the show, and about a week after that
her picture was in the *Times* as slated for *Show Boat*.[19] Hines was, indeed,
signed to play Magnolia for an anticipated opening in spring 1927. When
Show Boat was postponed, Hines sued. The case was settled in Ziegfeld's favor
in July, but Hines appealed.[20] In the meantime, she took the title role in
George White's *Manhattan Mary*. In September, while her show was in out-of-
town tryouts, Hines abruptly quit. She married a society banker in October
and never appeared on Broadway again.

Hines was one of many musical comedy ladies to enjoy short careers in the
1920s, when the sheer volume of shows demanded many actors. After diligent
training for the stage and an initial engagement as a dancer in a tour of Kern's
Oh, Boy at age sixteen, Hines won the title roles in two long-running shows for
George M. Cohan: *The O'Brien Girl* and *Little Nelly Kelly*. A further title role followed in 1924 with *Marjorie*, which featured a chorus of flappers. Hines

reminded reviewers of Irene Castle. In late 1926, her most recent in a string of ingénue roles was the lead in *June Days*. In short, Hines was a musical comedy performer through and through, an all-rounder equally comfortable singing popular songs, dancing up-to-date dances, and delivering snappy lines. She did not have a trained voice suitable for operetta and was an average talent. Never a big name, her theatrical biography reads like the fantasy tales of Ziegfeld girls who left the stage to marry wealthy society men. In Hines's case, she happened to play a few lead roles instead of just appearing in the chorus.

Two other names mentioned in the press as possible Magnolias were major musical comedy stars: Marilyn Miller and Gertrude Lawrence. Ziegfeld was negotiating a contract with Miller in February 1927, and the press leaked the possibility that she "might return to the Ziegfeld fold by September to play the leading role in [*Show Boat*]."[21] Miller signed that month, and Ziegfeld mounted the lavish *Rosalie*, which opened just days after *Show Boat*, in celebration of her return. Miller's Magnolia would, of necessity, have been a dancing lead. As late as June 27, Gertrude Lawrence was being publicly associated with *Show Boat*. Ziegfeld had reportedly offered the British star "the leading role in *Show Boat*," and her potential participation was framed as important enough to postpone the show yet again.[22] Lawrence was currently in London repeating her Broadway success in the title role of the Gershwins's *Oh, Kay!* More comedienne than singer or dancer, Lawrence would have brought an established persona to Magnolia that, like Marilyn Miller, was not about beautiful singing.

Finally, on August 21, Norma Terris was publicly announced as Ziegfeld's Magnolia.[23] Behind the scenes, Terris's name had come up much earlier. In the January draft, she was penciled in for the role of Ellie. Terris recalled the circumstances of her hiring in 1976:

> Flo [Ziegfeld] heard about my work for the Shuberts, in revues *A Night in Spain*, *A Night in Paris*. I did a walkoff with Phil Baker and his accordion to "Sam, the Accordion Man" which was the talk of Broadway. I'd been in vaudeville with my first husband, Max Hoffman, Jr., whose mother Gertrude was a variety star. When Max and I married, and it was a kid thing, his mother set us up in an act, Junior and Terris, so we could make our own living. After we separated Max replaced Clifton Webb in a show and I became a single. Ziegfeld sent for me and then sent me along to Kern and Hammerstein as a possible Magnolia. Jerry took me to his country place and played me the whole score, I was dazzled. He asked me why I thought I could play Magnolia. I told him I'd read Edna Ferber's novel and it was the story of my mother. I was born in Columbus, Kansas, and both grandfathers were Mississippi River oriented.[24]

Hammerstein knew Terris from his 1922 show *Queen O' Hearts*, in which she played a small role. Since that time, her credits were limited to vaudeville and two Broadway revues: *A Night in Paris* (1926) and its follow-up *A Night in Spain* (1927). Terris, best known for doing imitations of contemporary musical and dramatic stars, had played only one musical comedy character when she was hired for *Show Boat*.

No trained singer, no performer associated with operetta, was ever publicly considered for the role of Magnolia, and the performer who was cast—Norma Terris—put *Show Boat*'s romantic female lead squarely in the musical comedy column. By contrast, all the men considered for Ravenal were solidly in the operetta camp, and the singer hired to play opposite Terris—Howard Marsh, famous for his high notes—was, in the scale of things, a most extreme sort of operetta singer. This generic contrast, filtered through Terris and Marsh's individual talents and personas, would come to define Magnolia and Ravenal's musical roles in the show.

When Ziegfeld initially heard Kern and Hammerstein's score in progress, the first person he thought of was the tenor Harry Fender.[25] Fender had most recently played the lead in Ziegfeld's *Louie the 14th* (1925), a role that clearly demanded a tenor.[26] Prior to that, Fender had sung leads in *The Last Waltz* (1921) and a revival of *Florodora* (1920), both produced by the Shuberts, whose signature genre was operetta. Fender's name was quickly replaced in Ziegfeld press releases with that of Guy Robertson, a tenor who had appeared in three Hammerstein shows (*Daffy Dill, Wildflower, Song of the Flame*) and played operetta leads as well as parts in musical comedies. After *Show Boat* was postponed, Robertson went into *The Circus Princess*, a Shubert operetta with a score by Emmerich Kalman.

In June 1927, Ziegfeld signed Dennis King, a well-known Broadway leading man, to "star in a dramatic operetta which will open in October," which speculation suggested would either be the new Marilyn Miller vehicle or *Show Boat*.[27] King went into neither and instead played D'Artagnan in *The Three Musketeers*. D'Artagnan was similar to King's other major roles: Jim Kenyon in *Rose-Marie* (1924) and François Villon in *The Vagabond King* (1925). All three operettas had scores by Rudolf Friml. Hammerstein would have known King well from *Rose-Marie*. Vocally, all of King's roles are of a middling baritone quality; Villon, Jim, and D'Artagnan never rise to a tenor's high C. Indeed, Villon never goes above F (above middle C) and hands off all the vocal climaxes to his romantic opposite. Jim and D'Artagnan similarly defer to their respective leading ladies' top notes. King was more baritone than tenor, and vocal prowess was never central to his performances. The tessitura of King's roles falls in line with two other major operetta roles from the late 1920s:

Pierre in *The Desert Song* and Robert in *The New Moon* (Hammerstein shows made before and just after *Show Boat*).

Howard Marsh, announced for Ravenal on August 28, 1927, was a singer of an entirely different order than any previously considered for the role. The *Times* noted that "Mr. Marsh is the tenor who gave a good account of himself in *The Student Prince*."[28] The description of Marsh as a tenor—a designation more associated with opera than Broadway—was completely to the point. Marsh was an extraordinary singer on the 1920s Broadway stage, and his two previous credits locate his persona within a particular realm: the Shubert operetta.

Marsh introduced romantic tenor leads in two legendary Shubert operettas: *Blossom Time* (1921) and *The Student Prince* (1924). In the former, one of the signal hits of the decade, he played Baron Schober, the tenor who won the heart of the woman Franz Schubert (a baritone) loved. Schober's vocal range extended beyond a high A on several occasions and avoided the uncomfortable C below middle C.[29] The role of Karl Franz in *The Student Prince*, another phenomenally successful Shubert operetta, demanded extreme stamina and constant vocal display. The second pitch Marsh sang in the show was a high G, and the tessitura of the part remained in the upper reaches, again and again requiring Marsh to sustain that note, pushing him up to high A at the end of his long act 3 soliloquy, and going all the way up to tenor high C in the famous "Serenade." Karl Franz's love interest, the barmaid Kathie, matched him high note for high note in their duets. Perhaps this characterization of the central couple by way of repeated high notes contributed more than anything to the Shubert brothers's perception that *Student Prince* was excessively operatic.

Marsh was available for *Show Boat* because his most recent Shubert operetta *Cherry Blossoms* (music by Sigmund Romberg) had failed. In that score, Marsh as Ned Hamilton again climbed to vocal heights unusual for anyone but him on the Broadway operetta scene, and it seems that Kern attended closely to the melodic shapes Romberg created for the tenor. After *Show Boat*, Marsh appeared in one more original operetta—*The Well of Romance* (1930, a dismal flop opposite Terris)—before rounding out his Broadway career in limited-run revivals of Gilbert and Sullivan operettas and other operetta chestnuts produced by a company in which Marsh had a financial interest. Marsh's career and the parts he introduced—Schober, Karl Franz, Ned, Ravenal—express the successful incorporation of trained operatic singing onto the commercial stage in sentimental, lavishly produced shows that typified 1920s Broadway every bit as much as the jazzy insurgencies of musical comedy and revue.

When work on *Show Boat* recommenced at the end of summer 1927, an odd couple of sorts had been placed at the center of the story: a musical comedy-cum-vaudeville-ingénue opposite an extreme operetta tenor would embody Ferber's romantic couple (who had their own happy-ending challenges as characters). Terris and Marsh had a profound impact on their roles but not to the degree Robeson or Morgan did on theirs. Joe and Julie were sui generis, in part because both original performers hailed from outside the conventions of commercial, narrative musical theater. Magnolia and Ravenal stay within the generic expectations of lead singing characters, even if their respective genres of origin were different. Marsh's "trained voice," to use William Everett's term for operetta singing, and Terris's popular stage voice, could not help but conflict.[30] The expressive détente between Marsh and Terris—no personal or professional animosity was ever reported—was worked out during rehearsals and the start of the tryout period. Ravenal's part was basically set by the Washington opening. Magnolia's part required adjustment into the second tryout week, and late changes made at Terris's insistence directly impacted the surviving elements of Hammerstein's popular music plot.

Marsh's and Terris's reciprocal impact on the music for Ravenal and Magnolia kept questions of racial performance at the center. Operetta as a genre was defined by whiteness: there were no black-cast operettas. It was a style of performance and set of musical stage conventions reserved for whites, expressing emotions and structures of feeling read by white audiences as the province of white characters only. Appropriately, Ravenal remains consistently aloof from the black elements in *Show Boat*, quite a trick given the nature of the show. Magnolia, of course, could not be so sequestered and, thus, the tensions arising from cross-racial performance at the core of the show lodge particularly deeply in her part. In the end, Terris exercised her star power to shape the role's engagement with blackness.

"Where's the Mate for Me" and "Make Believe"—Ravenal's introductory solo and the pair's initial duet—were part of the larger musical and dramatic structure of act 1, scene 1, that Kern and Hammerstein labored over in fall of 1926.[31] This long musical scene was complete before the casting of *Show Boat* began, and Ziegfeld likely heard the whole in something like its final form at the audition that excited him so much. The form and structure of the sequence as it appears in the January libretto and earliest continuity drafts basically remained unchanged at the Broadway opening. In this part of the show, Terris and Marsh assumed their roles as written except for one subtle change. At some point after the scene had been orchestrated and recopied for the engraving of the vocal score, "Make Believe" was transposed up by a half step. Kern conceived of the tune in D-flat major—he notes the key explicitly on several sketches—which put the bottom of the song's range (for a male singer) at a sustained C below middle C.[32] This bottommost note is prominent in the first setting of the title phrase, which drops to its lowest note on the second syllable of "believe" (see ex. 4.1). In the original key scheme, the reprise of the refrain sung by both Magnolia and Ravenal was pitched a half step higher in D major, making C-sharp the bottommost note. Marsh would have thus sung "Make Believe" in both D-flat and D. At some point, likely during tryouts, the entire sequence was raised a half step, putting Ravenal's solo chorus into D and the shared chorus into E-flat. A copy of the vocal score prepared for the engraver effects the upward key change with a minimum of recopying, salvaging every bit of already copied music, suggesting the move was made quite late in the show-making process.[33] In the conductor's score, which has the D-flat to D major version, the change of key was never notated. Instead, a terse note advised that the music "changes key here" a few bars before the first chorus begins. The conductor's text apparently never matched the sounding pitch of either orchestra parts or singers.[34]

Raising "Make Believe" by a half step might seem insignificant, but this kind of change happens all the time with singers, for whom a slight up or down transposition can make a substantial difference in both vocal comfort and the potential to project. In this case, the shape of Kern's tune—its downward trajectory in the very first phrase—might have encouraged the making of a cost-effective concession to a singer's needs. Marsh was unused to doing more than touching the C at the bottom of his range. The first phrase of "Serenade" from *Student Prince*, a signature Marsh song, offers a contrasting case (see ex 4.1). Romberg's melody just touches the tenor's bottom C before leaping back up for the peak of the phrase on a sustained high F. Romberg's opening gesture—difficult to sing and wide of range—provides a showcase for the tenor voice. Kern's opening for "Make Believe" follows a similar contour but with different intentions. Kern's melody sits on the bottom C for a long time, requiring the singer to sustain the pitch, and doesn't rise nearly as high, peaking a fourth below Romberg's top note. Kern keeps the range

Example 4.1 The opening phrase of "Make Believe" compared to Sigmund Romberg's "Serenade" from The Student Prince *(1924).*

within modest proportions, making a musical comedy song the average singer can sing, a tune to be enjoyed around the parlor piano. "Make Believe" had to be transposed in the show to accommodate Marsh's voice, a sort of voice Kern did not have in mind when he wrote the song. The music Kern wrote for Ravenal after Marsh was hired is of a different order altogether.

Ravenal's importance as a star part built on vocal display is evident in the compositional history of act 1, scene 3, the waterfront scene. In the January draft, the scene opens with a fragmentary reprise of "Where's the Mate," sung by Ravenal from offstage while he gambles with a group of swells in a saloon. The sheriff Vallon, standing outside, comments to a bystander that Ravenal got into "a little fuss"—he killed a man—but proved it was self-defense, adding that "Nuthin' worries him." Pete enters and buttonholes Vallon, ready to reveal Julie's racial status. When Frank and Ellie appear, Pete brings Frank into his conversation with Vallon. As Pete, Vallon, and Frank enter the saloon, Ravenal comes out, accompanied by two male companions. Ellie tries to attract Ravenal's attention by dropping her handkerchief as she had done in scene 1, but Frank retrieves the token instead. Ravenal exits—his appearance in the scene little more than a crossover—and Ellie goes into a featured number called "Yes Ma'am" with the two men who had been with Ravenal. The scene remained unchanged in the August script, and Kern drafted a complete continuity sketch of the music.[35] Featuring the as yet uncast Ellie seems to have been the only idea Kern and Hammerstein had to insert a musical number into what was, in essence, a plot scene facilitating a scene change to the *Cotton Blossom* auditorium.

During the rehearsal period, Ellie was given a new waterfront solo "Life Upon the Wicked Stage" (with a women's chorus rather than two men) but lost her spot at the close of the scene. Ravenal, instead of moving through the waterfront as a shadow, was given a previously unplanned solo spotted in a position of strength at the end of the scene. The instrumental introduction to Ellie's cut "Yes, Ma'am" was recycled as the opening measures of Ravenal's "'Til Good Luck Comes My Way," which was added for Marsh. Indeed, the new goal of the waterfront scene was featuring Marsh vocally, as an analysis of this most extraordinary number demonstrates.

With a change of lyrics, Ravenal's "'Til Good Luck Comes My Way" could be transferred into *The Student Prince*. A prime feature of that operetta had been a large male chorus singing complicated parts. *Show Boat*'s waterfront gamblers acquired similarly advanced vocal skills once Marsh joined their company. The range of Ravenal's part in the number fits that of Karl Franz almost exactly. "'Til Good Luck" extends across almost two octaves, from the tenor bottom C to a high B-flat, putting the song outside the realm of sheet music for the public. Kern ingeniously constructed the verse around three successively higher melodic goals. Ravenal sustains successive high E and F on the repeated word "world." After a rollicking choral insertion that has two different texts being sung simultaneously—a nod toward the concerted choruses of operetta—Ravenal's top sustained note rises to G on the word "know," a bold declaration that this role requires a tenor to do it justice. (Romberg employed a similar progression of progressively higher sustained notes—D, E, F—in Marsh's "Tell Me, Cigarette" from *Cherry Blossoms*. Yet another example, from "Let Me Awake" in *Blossom Time*, had Marsh singing high G, A, and B in succession, several of these climaxes emphasized by fermatas.) To give "'Til Good Luck" a stunning vocal climax, Ravenal follows the example of Kathie in the similarly rousing "Come, Boys" from *The Student Prince*, where she sustains a soprano high C while the chorus sings lustily beneath her. Ravenal sustains a high F, which rises to G then A, the highest note he has sung so far. The passage demands superior breath control and power. At the song's closing phrase, Ravenal sings a stepwise rising melodic line that ascends to a final high B-flat. Held for five beats and cutting off with the orchestra, the marking *rallentando* allowed the conductor to extend this long, loud, high note a bit, adding to the thrill of the close, after which the stage went to black on what should have been big applause. Kern worked out this entire sequence, as evidenced by a holograph short score, which lines out all the vocal parts.[36] Perhaps he consulted with Marsh ahead of time, but surely Kern knew his singer's capacity to ascend to the heights, thereby allowing *Show Boat* to briefly push some operetta buttons. Few numbers express the power of performers to shape the musical content of a show as directly as "'Til Good Luck Comes My Way," which reflects Marsh rather than the Ravenal of "Make Believe."

Marsh's preferred range and style was again the driving force when Kern came up with a new duet for Magnolia and Ravenal to sing at the boat's iconic water barrel (the only place the couple can escape Parthy's watchful eye). In one of the few additions to the show appearing in the August draft, Kern and Hammerstein produced a duet called "Creole Love Song," which bears a more than passing resemblance to "Serenade Creole (When Your Eyes Looked Into Mine)" from Frank Harling and Lawrence Stalling's *Deep River*. Beyond the conceit of a Creole expressing his love in a serenade, both songs speak of a glow in the lover's eye as the true sign of love. Harling's tune is in duple meter, Kern's in triple, but both employ a patterned rhythmic accompaniment and an outward-directed mode of musical lovemaking. The problem with "Creole Love Song" was likely the song's range. Its tune sits heavily on that troublesome bottom C, never rises to a genuine high note, and simply doesn't require a tenor. Perhaps Marsh said outright it wasn't right for him, but anyone could have heard the mismatch of singer to song. (The operatic tenor Jerry Hadley as Ravenal darkens his sound appreciably on the 1988 John McGlinn recording, perhaps attempting to channel an inner baritone. By contrast, Fredericka Von Stade as Magnolia welcomes the opportunity to sing in her accustomed mezzo soprano range.)

As a replacement, Kern composed "You Are Love," one of several numbers that make their first appearance in the October draft in a form that does not reflect the Broadway version. In the October draft, there is no indication "You Are Love" was meant to be a duet. The text is not divided between the pair—Ravenal gets it all—and there's no mention of a repeat of the chorus. Stage directions focus on Magnolia's reaction to Ravenal's declaration of love: "of her own accord" she embraces and kisses him. The Broadway version would make the song into a sort of duet. Like "'Til Good Luck Comes My Way," the final version of "You Are Love" tapped into operetta style, which appears only in relation to music composed for Marsh. The verse has a broadly theatrical quality. Again, this is not the sort of vocal music designed to be transitioned from the stage to the home. Beginning with a *Tempo di Valse*, which includes large, relatively difficult leaps and rises to a high F, the second part of the verse, marked *Poco agitato*, grows more insistent and more technically difficult. Magnolia's single vocal line in the verse comes here, at a point when the forward motion of Ravenal's elaborately expressed love is already galloping along. It's hard for Magnolia to do much more than make her entrance on time under such circumstances. Ravenal's emotions and voice are featured above Magnolia's. The moment is not shared equally.

The chorus of "You Are Love" follows, sung once through by Ravenal. Kern divided his forty-eight-bar strain into three sixteen-measure phrases. Kern's opening bears a more than casual resemblance to the start of "Some Day," the lover's waltz from *Cherry Blossoms* (see ex. 4.2). Both tunes begin near the bottom of the tenor range and ascend to successively higher top notes by way of leaps in the same direction. Similarities of melodic contour and generic style alike suggest that Kern knew Marsh's most recent work and was now thinking of Ravenal in Rombergian terms. The second and third phrases of "You Are Love" transpose the initial three notes of the tune—those setting the title—up an octave, inviting a display of dynamic control by the singer, who is directed to sing the second phrase *piano* and the third *forte*. "You Are Love" is a tailored tour de force in operetta style. Magnolia is—finally—permitted to sing a second time in this "duet" on the repeat of the chorus. But Ravenal joins her at the third phrase and effectively takes over. On the final eight bars, the tune is recomposed to provide a big finish. Magnolia continues in her role as the vocally submissive partner while Ravenal blasts beyond her, singing his

Example 4.2 The opening phrase of "You are Love" compared to Sigmund Romberg's "Some Day" from Cherry Blossoms *(1927).*

But some day   Some fine day   All this will   be   Quite changed for   me.

You _____   are   love   Here in my   arms   Where you   be - long.

second high B-flat of the score as part of a predictable melodic formula. The pair holds the final note for an additional few bars while the orchestra plays *appassionato* and *fortissimo* beneath them. The effect is meant to be heart-stirring, passionate, epic. It was so effective Ravenal repeated the big, high, loud ending in act 2 without Magnolia in the reprise of "You Are Love" that replaced the Robeson recital. Three times during the show a high B-flat from Marsh sent *Show Boat* into a scene-changing blackout, a vocal special effect straight from operetta punctuating the show's large-scale form and sustaining audience participation by encouraging applause.

In the almost entirely thru-sung wedding scene that follows "You Are Love," Magnolia sings but Ravenal does not. The decision to keep the leading man silent on his wedding day has a specific history, which speaks to Ravenal's embodiment of a white, male, southern identity. Kern and Hammerstein completed the wedding scene as early as late 1926 so neither Marsh nor Terris were taken into account when it was made. Magnolia sings only one solo line at her wedding in the Broadway version. In the January draft and extant holograph scores she was to sing a second time, just before the curtain descended. The line Terris kept has Magnolia singing "Can't I share some of my happiness, dear friends, with you" as she greets the women of the black chorus, who "come forward enthusiastic, but a trifle diffident" after the white chorus sings their triple-meter tribute, "Happy, the Day." Magnolia's line, difficult to hear in (unmiked) performance, effectively bridged the gap between two contrasting sections, the shift from a generically white waltz chorus to a generically black buck-and-wing. Magnolia ascends by step to the vocal height of the entire role: in soprano terms, a modest high A. The "big levee shuffle dance" follows with the black chorus, Joe, Queenie, and Magnolia all singing "Can't Help Lovin' Dat Man." All scripts are careful to note that only the black characters and Magnolia sing during this public re-creation of the kitchen pantry shuffle.

To this point in all scripts through the October draft, Ravenal had not yet arrived at the wedding. He was absent while Magnolia shared one last song and dance with her black show boat family. Through October, Ravenal was to enter after the buck-and-wing, a reprise of "Happy, the Day" accompanying his ostentatious arrival and creating a white-black-white, ABA musical structure. Ravenal was to ride in "elegantly attired, seated languidly in an open barouche, drawn by two handsome chestnuts, with a liveried driver on the box." The text reads like a Ziegfeld press release—doubtless the horses would have impressive pedigrees—although in the center of it all was a man, and not a woman.

Immediately on the heels of Ravenal's arrival, Parthy makes her shrieking entrance with the shocking news that Ravenal is a murderer, to which Andy responds, in essence, *so am I*. Parthy faints, and the scene ends with the carriage carrying the bride and groom off to the chapel to cheers from the assembled crowd. Just before Parthy faints, Magnolia was to perform an operatic act of self-definition, singing to her mother "proudly—defiantly" in the stage directions, the pointedly altered lyric "Can't stop me now / There's no use to try / I've got to love my man till I die / Can't help lovin' that man of mine." Up until rehearsals began, this vocal statement from the leading lady was to bring down the curtain on act 1. But in the vocal score, the full company sings the regular lyric, the only time the white chorus sings this black song. Everyone onstage toasts the happy white couple by singing a black song with the words "Fish gotta swim, / and birds got to fly, / I got to love one man till I die. / Can't help lovin' that man of mine!" Only in this one, rather crucial moment do the specific categories of black and white music and performers break down. (Of course, heteronormative gender positions break down as well. Hammerstein had worked out alternative, gender-specific lyrics for the black men singing in the kitchen version of the song.)

Until they had an actual performer in front of them singing the role of Magnolia, Kern and Hammerstein imagined Magnolia as able to, in operatic fashion, put a sung button on the act, casting aside Parthy's objections with an act of vocal prowess. Ravenal as played by Marsh might have been able to do this—he had done so in *Student Prince*—but it was surely beyond Terris's capacity. Complex musical scenes like the act 1 finale were not being rewritten after rehearsals began; giving Ravenal a dramatic, vocal role at the wedding would have prolonged the scene (and act) and shifted attention from the bride to the groom (unseemly in any genre). And so Ravenal remained mute— a handsome man in a pretty carriage—and some in the company were put in the absurd position of singing about not being able to help loving their man. Spectacle and sheer exhaustion would hopefully dampen any strangeness felt among audience members to this choice.

Anyone who has seen *Show Boat* on stage knows the act ends with a good joke that pulls attention away from the bridal couple and toward the bride's parents. After Parthy faints at the news that her own husband is a murderer, Andy asks if she's "gone." With the assurance "she's gone," he shouts "Good—Now we can go on with the wedding." Laughter follows—it's delicious to hear Andy stand up to Parthy, even if she's lying down at the time—and hopefully no one notices the chorus sings words that make little sense in context. Andy's joke first appears in the very last layer of scripts. It's entirely likely the punch line was added during tryouts when someone on the production team thought the end of the act needing punching up. Returning to the Parthy and Andy relationship—and, for once, giving Andy the upper hand—endures as an effective way to remind the audience that they are indeed at a musical comedy. If Terris had had a voice to match Marsh, perhaps she would have sung the closing solo line as planned and act 1 would have gone out on a note of defiance from Magnolia rather than a joke at Parthy's expense. The original climax would have been vocal as in operetta rather than comic as in musical comedy. Casting a musical comedy rather than an operetta singer as Magnolia likely doomed Kern and Hammerstein's original plan. These kinds of subtle shifts in genre were dictated by the intersection of roles and performers. And, of course, all subsequent Andys have relished that funny final line.

Magnolia has relatively little to do on her own in act 1. Terris, a resilient professional prepared to take steps to better her role in a crowded field, apparently focused her efforts on enhancing Magnolia's part in act 2. Here, Magnolia comes to the fore, addressing Ravenal's abandonment like any good Ferber heroine does: by claiming center stage. Terris ended up with four musical numbers in act 2: three as Magnolia—"Why Do I Love You?" in the World's Fair scene; "Can't Help Lovin' Dat Man" sung in two styles (as a plaintive ballad and a ragtime rouser) as her audition for the Trocadero; and "After the Ball" performed as her Trocadero debut—plus the rousing production number performed by Terris as Kim on the levee circa 1927. Terris directly shaped three of these, and in the process Hammerstein's popular music plot was foiled yet again. The critic for the *World* wrote somewhat cryptically of Terris in *Show Boat:* "When Edna Ferber first wrote *Show Boat* it is reasonable to suppose that she didn't see her heroine as a Ziegfeld soprano."[37] Terris's pragmatic approach to reshaping Magnolia to her own desires suggests that the designation "Ziegfeld soprano" might be best understood as less a vocal type than a strategic ability on the part of a star performer to get Ziegfeld to present them at their best, regardless of the context. From this angle, Terris's Magnolia was a product of the revue.

In a 1976 interview, Terris claimed "Why Do I Love You?" was composed expressly for her. "At first the second act opened with Howard Marsh and I singing 'I Might Fall Back on You.' That was a comedy patter song and all wrong.

Jerry Kern was so dear and he listened when I said it was the wrong mood for lovers. The next day he and Oscar, smiling like cats who ate the canary, brought me a new song, 'Why Do I Love You?' and the patter song went to the comedy team, Sammy White and Eva Puck. I always felt 'Why Do I Love You?' was my song."[38] There's no archival evidence "I Might Fall Back on You" was initially intended for Marsh and Terris. Terris might be remembering an experiment that failed, although given how closely "I Might Fall Back on You" expressed Frank and Ellie's relationship, it's difficult to give credence to her memory. Still, Terris's claim that "Why Do I Love You?" was "my song" is borne out by the song and its staging, which met her needs as a star in several ways.

"Why Do I Love You?" is a tuneful fox trot with a modest range—just over an octave—entirely suitable for sheet music consumption, exactly the sort of theater song Kern was skilled at writing and Terris was accustomed to selling. The potential for "Why Do I Love You?" to be a hit was anticipated by its placement at the close of the overture. Indeed, it was the only tune from the score played in its entirety before the curtain went up.

Once Kern and Hammerstein had written "Why Do I Love You?," it had to be routined. The result highlighted Terris in specific ways. Somewhat like Marsh's "You Are Love," Terris's "Why Do I Love You?" is a solo (in this case, with chorus) masquerading as a duet. Terris took the portions of both verse and chorus that did not include sustained high notes, handing those moments off to Marsh. The dance scholar Frank W. D. Ries described the staging of "Why Do I Love You?" in a 1986 article drawing on a privately held source:

> The Sports and Ziegfeld Beauties frame the couple in a series of poses, and then Gaylord leaves and Magnolia performs what is marked in the score as a "skirt dance" to a light and charming waltz. Although not all her actions are notated, there are sequences that include her sweeping under the raised arms of the Sports and weaving in and out of the Ziegfeld Beauties' skirts. Magnolia disappears, and as the chorus poses, Captain Andy and Parthy Ann come on. The Captain sings the same song to her and then leads her in a comic two-step for sixteen bars that has Parthy Ann led around the stage until she is exhausted. They waltz offstage, and the chorus reprises the last chorus of the song while forming themselves into poses: eight chorus girls sitting on eight chorus boys' knees in a semicircle, eight more chorus girls standing with their boyfriends in the spaces between, and the sixteen Ziegfeld Beauties now posed on various platforms on the set (the sixteen Sports having left them to pose with the chorus girls for this final formation).[39]

Ries's source outlines a standard revue-style treatment of a potential hit tune: repeat the melody over and over while varying the performers and musical or dance style in a manner that keeps the audience engaged. The chorus of "Why Do I Love You?" was repeated eight times. Magnolia and Ravenal sang the first two, with the chorus of "girls" and "boys"—standard musical comedy designations—joining in on the second as if cueing a sing-along. Then a secondary verse explained Ravenal's exit to go and gamble. (Ravenal's solo line is pitched higher than Magnolia's.) With Ravenal gone, Magnolia/Terris finally had center stage to herself. She shared a third chorus with the chorus before going into her "skirt dance" (two choruses in waltz time), at the end of which Terris exited. The waltz concluded with a full stop in the music—a *ritardando* and fermata in the score—allowing, no doubt, for applause and likely a bow or scene call from Terris. Then, the chorus sang yet a sixth chorus marked "A la fox trot," anachronistically casting the tune in a 1920s dance rhythm and, hopefully, setting toes to tapping in the audience. The seventh chorus brought on the comics—Andy and Parthy—for a humorous reinterpretation of the lyric, and the eighth closed the number with a classic Ziegfeld pose, the white chorus arrayed about the stage in the hierarchy of showgirls, ponies, and chorus boys that expressed the fundamental values of Ziegfeld's art. This routine, lasting well over six minutes on McGlinn's recording and hardly a love duet, was a song-plugging extravaganza easily mounted during tryouts using the white chorus in existing costumes, effectively featuring Terris in a lovely and feminine dance, and giving Winninger and Oliver a comic turn as well.

Concealed within this marathon of "Why Do I Love You?" is the departure of Ravenal. He and Magnolia do not meet again onstage until the final moments of the show. Kern and Hammerstein made an effort to mark the moment and connect Ravenal musically to "Can't Help Lovin' Dat Man"—he sings a phrase to Magnolia just before he departs with the in retrospect ironic lyric about his wife being "good and patient with your man"—but the moment comes off as underplayed, more an excuse to get him offstage so Magnolia/Terris can do her dance than anything else. (The lyric "Darling, I have only just an hour to play" makes no sense: gamblers don't keep business hours, a point emphasized by Ferber.) The revue values of the sequence, which in its repetition of the chorus recalls nothing so much as Busby Berkeley's Hollywood extravaganzas made just a few years later, overwhelm the dramatic moment entirely. This, of course, could hardly have bothered Terris.

Magnolia and Ravenal never sing together after "Why Do I Love You?" Normal operetta lovers would. The ambivalent nature of Ravenal and Magnolia's reunion perhaps worked against their singing together at the close, and Hammerstein wanted to shift the focus from Ferber's (not very) romantic story to his own popular music plot. Magnolia's rise to musical stardom and Kim's success on Broadway were always more central to act 2 than any other element of the story. The Robeson plan was part of this. During rehearsals and tryouts, Terris brought her considerable influence to bear on Hammerstein's popular music plot, using her own star power to eliminate "It's Getting Hotter in the North," a major number conceived as a way to draw almost all the white main characters and the major themes together. In addition, Terris's choice of song for Magnolia's Trocadero debut marks a decided shift away from Magnolia's black voice, a pattern repeated in adjustments made to Frank and Ellie's act 2 number as well. A pattern emerges of the white musical comedy characters in act 2 shifting toward less-black, more-white personas as the show was adjusted during tryouts. These changes, of course, were frozen in the Broadway version and endured to exert a powerful influence on all subsequent remakings of *Show Boat*.

In retrospect, "It's Getting Hotter in the North" was a tremendously ambitious summing up of all that had come before. This lengthy eleven-o'-clock production number for almost the entire cast, was titled "No Mason Dixon Line" in the Kern papers. Contextualized as a sample of Kim's Broadway style performed for the folks on the levee, the modern musical comedy number conceived for the New York apartment scene was transferred to the river and performed with the electrified *Cotton Blossom*, rather than the Manhattan skyline, as the backdrop. Wherever she did her number, Kim embodied Hammerstein's notion of contemporary popular music and dance as linked to "old Southern tunes" and "Hotter in the North" drove the point home again and again.

Kern's tune for "Hotter in the North" drew directly on the piano melody used to introduce Magnolia in the show's opening scene. In that context, Ravenal heard the tune—played in a stuttering fashion by the as-yet-unseen Magnolia—and immediately incorporated it into his own "Where's the Mate for Me." Kern's use of the melody a second time as the basis for Kim's "Hotter in the North" speaks to his desire to construct a web of musical connections across the score.[40] But "Hotter in the North" was intended to make a popular music point about the present—about hot music and dancing. Kern was known to dislike dance-band arrangements of his music. He had declared in print that theater music was "so distorted by jazz orchestras as to be almost unrecognizable" and even refused to allow songs from his 1924 show *Sitting Pretty* to be recorded for that reason.[41] Once in Hollywood, Kern would have difficulty on several occasions producing syncopated tunes suited to the hot dancing of Fred Astaire.[42] "Hotter in the North" is not by nature a syncopated tune capturing the sound of 1927; perhaps this underlying lack of appropriateness to the dramatic moment contributed to the eventual decision to cut the number. In Hammerstein and Kern's creative practices, lyrics were added to finished tunes, and so the task of making "Hotter in the North" into a summation of the show's popular music plot fell largely to Hammerstein, the orchestrator Robert Russell Bennett, and the show's dance director Sammy Lee. And the performers, in the end, would have to sell it.

Hammerstein's lyric describes the transfer of southern "muddy-water-steps" northwards and a situation where "soon as they hear a band / ev'ry man's daughter" starts dancing. The specifically black origin of these steps is implicit in the dialect Hammerstein employs throughout, dropping every final *g* and using "'cause" and "ev'ry," as well as racially coded words like "gals" and "strut." In earlier scenes, these linguistic markers were only employed for songs "colored folks" sing, with "Can't Help Lovin' Dat Man" as the benchmark. But here, Hammerstein puts black dialect into the mouth of Magnolia and Ravenal's white daughter with no apparent disjunction: this is how white girls in the North are talking and singing now; this isn't a song for colored folks, it's how whites sing and dance, too. The final lines of the chorus lyric— "Up on the levees of Broadway / It's gettin' hotter ev'ry day"—reconfigure an earlier song making the same point. "It's Getting Dark on Old Broadway" was a major production number in the 1922 *Ziegfeld Follies*.

> It's getting very dark on old Broadway,
> You see the change in ev'ry cabaret;
> It's just like an eclipse of the moon,
> Ev'ry café now has the dancing coon.
> Pretty choc'late babies
> Shake and shimmie ev'rywhere,
> Real darktown entertainers hold the stage,
> You must black up to be the latest rage.
> Yes, the great white way is white no more,
> It's just like a street on the Swanee shore;
> It's getting very dark on old Broadway.[43]

This lyric describes a crossing of the color line: African Americans were, it seemed, suddenly to be seen everywhere in places that had been solidly white. The color line was being breached. What the song does not express is any real alarm at the phenomenon: it's simply the latest rage. Just five years later, Kern and Hammerstein could mine the same theme. "It's Getting Dark" and "It's Getting Hotter" both describe Broadway as now a southern locale: the former comments on the phenomenon of black performers; the latter on the pervasiveness of black style among whites. Kim is not in blackface: she's a big-time Broadway star doing what such cultural icons were expected to do, embodying the moment, which, in this case, meant dancing "the levee shuffle of the South" and "Doin' those neat low-down / Twistin' and turnin' steps."[44]

The linguistic shift from "dark" to "hot" permits whites to put on black style without calling it black, effectively appropriating the latest rage while only blacking up metaphorically.

Robert Russell Bennett's orchestration made the argument in musical terms. Early in the long dance sequence he calls for a "jazz solo" from the first clarinet, notating the scoops and slides of contemporary jazz practice.[45] Soon, the clarinet section switches to soprano saxophones, an instrument previously unheard in the orchestration. This change would transform the pit orchestra into something of a jazz orchestra, a sound 1920s audiences would have noted. And Bennett sets a seal on the stylistic shift to the present by quoting a fragment of Gershwin's *Rhapsody in Blue* in a break, lodging in the musical text a remnant of Kim's apartment scene. (Louis Armstrong inserted the same motto from Gershwin's well-known opus in his recording of "Ain't Misbehavin'" in 1929.) Within a few years, most notably with the pit orchestra for the Gershwins's *Girl Crazy* (1930), the Broadway sound would begin to lean toward jazz, a sax and brass-heavy sound that takes a short, thematically meaningful bow at just the right moment in *Show Boat.*

The dance to "Hotter in the North" was lengthy, like "Why Do I Love You?" built primarily on serial repetitions of the chorus. Bennett's score provides a few clues to the staging. Frank and Ellie were allotted a stop-time section ripe for some tap dancing. Winninger had a featured section as well, combining "Hotter in the North" and a bold statement of the Captain Andy theme. The two melodies clash delightfully at times, and the dance would have given Winninger one more moment in the spotlight. Perhaps he did his backflip. Then, just before the final repeat of the chorus, something extraordinary happened. All at once the orchestra started playing Eubie Blake and Nobel Sissle's "I'm Just Wild About Harry." Who danced during this interpolation of a hit song by a pair of African American songwriters? "I'm Just Wild About Harry" had very specific, and quite recent, connections to black female chorus lines. The song was the standout success from *Shuffle Along* (1921), which featured a black female dancing chorus exactly like that in *Show Boat* (see chap. 5). No Broadway denizen in 1927 could hear it without thinking immediately of star black performers like Florence Mills and Josephine Baker. Was the black dance chorus onstage during "Hotter in the North"? (The black chorus was present, but the librettos do not distinguish between the singers and the dancers.) If they were and didn't dance this bit, audiences would wonder why not. If they weren't already onstage, it would have been quite a *coup-de-theatre* to have them suddenly burst onto the stage near the close of a long dance number to—in essence—demonstrate how those "low-down" steps were meant to be done.

Terris didn't like "It's Getting Hotter in the North," and the number was cut in Washington. Terris remembered the circumstances:

> During rehearsals Jerry Kern wrote a completely new song for me to do when I came back—as Kim, my own daughter. . . . Somehow, it just did not seem right, so I went to Mr. Kern and said . . . "let me do my impersonations—pretend I'm a young Elsie Janis." . . . True to my vaudeville training, I went into my act—doing Ted Lewis, Ethel Barrymore, Bea Lille and Garbo. . . . We worked it out and my impersonations went into the show opening night in Philadelphia—and I modestly report "they stole the show at eleven o'clock."[46]

Terris's imitations follow the logic of specialty numbers that haunted the making of *Show Boat* from start to finish. After her imitations, two further specialties—a tap and an eccentric dance—were inserted before the perfunctory romantic reunion with Ravenal. The specialties provided time for Terris to get back into costume and makeup as Magnolia. The extended dance section after Terris's vocal in "Hotter in the North" served the same function but did not allow her to take a bow before exiting as the specialties did. Replacing "Hotter in the North" with imitations of current white Broadway stars had no impact on the larger goal of bringing *Show Boat* to a close in the present. Terris had performed similar imitations the previous season. But lost along the way was Hammerstein's popular music plot. Cutting "Hotter in the North" removed any explicit or implicit blackness from Kim's number: Terris did not do imitations of black performers. However, from the perspective of *Show Boat*'s production history, inserting Terris's idiosyncratic, unrepeatable specialty into so prominent a spot opened the door to many different final numbers, including several that returned to the fundamental themes of "Hotter in the North" (although the number itself was never revived onstage). In time, Kim's levee dance became a radically open element in *Show Boat*.

With the removal of "Hotter in the North," Hammerstein's popular music plot survived only in the Trocadero scenes. The compositional history of these scenes suggests a further effort to minimize the residual blackness in Magnolia's character as realized in musical terms for the Broadway stage. After "Bill," the focus shifted definitively to Magnolia, with a series of diegetic musical numbers: a slow audition song with guitar accompaniment, a quick, "ragged" version of the audition song, Frank and Ellie's Trocadero number, and finally Magnolia's successful debut performance. As is often the case, the January script reproduces the content of the novel. In this version, Magnolia sings "All God's Chillun Got Wings" for her initial audition in exactly the manner Jo/Joe had taught her. Hammerstein even incorporated Ferber's words into his stage directions: "She sits with the banjo across her knee, throws back her head, half closes her eyes and taps time with her foot smartly." After being questioned as to whether or not she's a "nigger," again following the book, Magnolia sings, "the song Ravenal sang to her at the water-barrel." This is the tune that gets ragged by Frank and the piano player Jake, who work together to transform Magnolia into an up-to-date singer. (Kern experimented with ragging "Creole Love Song" during the short period when it was the water barrel duet.[47]) In the October script—Julie now in the scene, the water barrel duet now the ragtime-averse waltz "You Are Love"—Magnolia's audition song was changed to "Can't Help Lovin' Dat Man," a tune that would attract Julie's attention and welcome a "raggy" beat. Hammerstein describes Magnolia's reaction to the ragtime treatment of her beloved Negro songs in telling fashion, directing the actress to walk away from the three men, sink into a chair, and cover her face with her hands. By contrast, the Broadway script ends with Magnolia joining in and Frank dancing "like mad." The blackout comes on the good news that Magnolia got the job. The Broadway Magnolia is more pragmatic than the sentimental, tearful woman from the pre-tryout drafts, and along the way Sammy White earned a short dance specialty that enlivens the middle of act 2 considerably as audiences predictably applaud his efforts.[48] Importantly, Magnolia embraces ragtime as a means to "get the job," as Frank shouts.

Having won a chance to sing onstage at the Trocadero, Magnolia now had to convince an audience of her worthiness, and here Hammerstein and Kern had to make concrete musical decisions about Magnolia's stage persona that Ferber avoided in her book. With little in the way of specifics offered by Ferber as to how Magnolia performed during her successful stage career, Hammerstein and Kern had to rely on their own knowledge of popular music and stage history. What vaudeville singer might they have known who could have had something like Magnolia's background? Ferber hints that Magnolia was a coon shouter but never broaches the issue of whether or not she performed in blackface. Among the female blackface singers still active in 1927 were Stella Mayhew and Tess Gardella.

Mayhew would enjoy a Broadway hit in 1927 singing "Hallelujah" in a featured blackface role in *Hit the Deck*. Gardella was hired to play Queenie in blackface. Another star who, like Magnolia, hit it big around 1905 was Sophie Tucker, who began in blackface but transitioned into big-time fame as a "Red Hot Mama," a sexualized and class-specific white persona that borrowed liberally from black blues queens. These sorts of performers generally matched the descriptions Ferber provided in terms of musical style, but Magnolia as romantic lead in *Show Boat* was never going to be of their ilk.

Further clues for how Hammerstein was thinking of Magnolia in the Trocadero scenes can be gleaned from the January script, which lists "In the Good Old Summertime" as a possible song for the Trocadero debut. This waltz-time tune from 1902 was associated with Blanche Ring, who often invited audiences to sing along—a common activity for turn-of-the-century audiences—just as Magnolia does. Magnolia gets the job at the Trocadero by demonstrating her ability to deliver "up to date numbers," to sing with a ragtime beat. Several female singers were famous for ragging tunes in similar fashion on vaudeville, among them Blossom Seeley and Ruth Royce, the so-called Princess of Ragtime who was famous for her smile (just like Magnolia). The October script has something called "the swing number" slated for Magnolia's debut. This might be Kern's "How'd You Like to Spoon With Me?," a hit song from his 1905 London show *The Earl and the Girl*. (Originally performed with a group of chorus girls on swings, this tune was given to Frank and Ellie in the London 1928 and 1971 *Show Boat*s.) Full of dotted rhythms but lacking any ragtime accents, "How'd You Like to Spoon With Me?" has a British music hall flair matching much of the music for the white chorus and Frank and Ellie.

A cut musical scene positioned between the Trocadero audition and debut scenes complicates the musical content of Magnolia's role as shaped for Terris. Set in the "Hall in front of Magnolia's dressing-room in the Trocadero," the scene does not appear in any surviving script. Only the Washington and Pittsburgh tryout programs list the scene and its two musical numbers, both interpolated popular songs. "My Coal Black Lady" was introduced by white blackface singer Lizzie C. Raymond in 1897. The sheet music includes the tune plus an alternate ragtime accompaniment for the chorus, capturing in print the contrast between straight and ragged versions of the same song demonstrated in the audition scene using "Can't Help Lovin' Dat Man." The second song was among the best-known coon songs of the 1890s: "The Bully Song," introduced by May Irwin in *The Widow Jones*. Both these interpolations used the word "nigger" as it commonly appeared in the coon-song era. The content of the hallway scene, likely played in front of a curtain, remains a mystery, and the inclusion then removal of well-known coon songs hints at a struggle over the racial implications of Magnolia's stage identity.

In the end, the song chosen for Magnolia's debut was "After the Ball," a Tin Pan Alley tune from 1892 and one of the best-selling songs in history to that point. This narrative waltz tells the story of a man who broke off his relationship with a woman he saw kissing another man at a ball, only to discover too late that the man was her brother (and hence no threat to the young woman's reputation). This cautionary tale about the perceived purity of white women of a certain class told in the voice of a regretful, now aged and "alone" male, was deeply invested in Victorian sexual mores and gender roles understood to be the province of white civilization. "After the Ball" was also introduced on the variety stage by May Irwin, who captures the contradictions at the core of Magnolia as a white singer with a black voice, but the song was such a hit that *Show Boat* audiences would not have associated it exclusively with Irwin. Sung in 1927, "After the Ball" carried echoes of a vastly different time, a completely other America before Prohibition, before the Great War, before the dance craze of the mid-1910s, before ragtime initiated the syncopated revolution in popular music. Terris claimed that she persuaded Hammerstein and Kern to use "After the Ball."[49]

What was the effect of having Magnolia sing a lily-white parlor song from 1892 to an onstage audience supposedly celebrating New Year's Eve 1905 for a Broadway audience in 1927? First, it injected a very familiar tune into the proceedings. The reviewer Willela Waldorf noted, "Of the music it may be said it was often spirited and pleasant, and that this reviewer came forth humming something which Mr. Kern did not write—'After the Ball Was Over.'"[50] Second, it may have encouraged a change in Frank and Ellie's Trocadero specialty, which occurred before the tryout week in Cleveland. The original choice had been the explicitly black-oriented "Hello Ma Baby" (1899), which hailed its object of affection as "my ragtime gal." The change to "Goodbye My Lady Love" (1904, the date of the scene) addressed the whiter "idol of my heart," although Puck and White still closed their routine with a cakewalk danced to "At a Georgia Camp Meeting."[51] Third, "After the Ball" pointed Magnolia's musical identity definitively in the white direction. A sentimental Victorian parlor waltz, by reputation the first to sell two million copies of sheet music, "After the Ball" was diametrically opposed to songs like "My Coal Black Lady" and "The Bully Song," which for a brief period preceded it in *Show Boat*. It was equally antithetical to the ragged "Can't Help Lovin' Dat Man" that gets Magnolia the job in the first place. Where did Magnolia's black voice go? What is her musical identity? The truth is, it really didn't matter. Musical theater audiences were (and remain) not that picky—they just want to be entertained. In 1927, an "After the Ball" sing-along apparently did the trick. It has had to work in later remakings of *Show Boat*, for this particular interpolation—Terris's choice—has always remained in place. Along the way, Magnolia's black voice and Hammerstein's popular music plot were written out of the story. In the musical, Magnolia triumphs as a white singer singing a white song.

5
COLORED CHORUS CURTAINS
• • •

Richard Watts, Jr., was assigned to review Show Boat, *and it turned out to be one of the memorable evenings of his playgoing career. It was during the intermission that the Southern-born managing editor of the* Herald Tribune . . . *walked up to Watts and gave his own extraordinary review of* Show Boat *in exactly three words: "Too many niggers."*
—*Ward Morehouse,* Matinee Tomorrow: Fifty Years of Our Theatre *(1949)*

From the earliest drafts, *Show Boat* began with the words "Niggers all work on de Mississippi / Niggers all work while de white folks play." These lyrics remain a touchstone of *Show Boat* history, an element that has demanded remaking, changed to "darkies all work," then "colored folk work," then "here we all work." Sometimes the chorus was cut entirely. What were the stakes of the initial word choice in 1927? Hammerstein noted of opening choruses in the 1920s, "There was always an opening chorus at the rise of the curtain, and it was never expected that the audience would understand the words."[1] Should this generalization made in 1949 be applied to *Show Boat*? Did Hammerstein use the word thinking the audience wouldn't catch it? No white critic in 1927 seems to have noticed the racial epithet offered by the black chorus as *Show Boat*'s opening salvo. This should surprise no one. White critics writing for white audiences—then and now—seldom raise racial issues. Black critics writing for black audiences definitely noticed the word, and reaction to its use was a topic of discussion in the black press in the weeks after *Show Boat* hit Broadway.

In his entertainment column for the *Pittsburgh Courier*, "Uncle Dud" described the black cast's role in *Show Boat* in detail, before turning to questions of content and compensation:

> I must admit that the word nigger is used quite often through the show, but the scenes are laid in the South and we must look for that; however, if we would only stop to think that the show was written to entertain and not to ridicule we could overlook the usage of the word. One thing sure we

have a chance to display our ability in the best theatres and that means much. I am informed by my old pal Wm. Vodery, who is responsible for the Colored end of the show, that the lowest salary paid is $50.00 per week and the highest is $500.00 per week. . . . I am sure that if this show makes good there will be other promoters producing shows that will open the doors to more Colored actors.[2]

Uncle Dud took a pragmatic approach, emphasizing the trade-off between an objectionable word and opportunities for black performers in the "best theatres." Most black commentators who covered show business felt the chance to work for Ziegfeld outweighed any objections to use of the "n-word," which was employed commonly in dramas at the time where the stakes apparently seemed higher. As Uncle Dud noted, *Show Boat* was entertainment and should be judged as such.

Ziegfeld's reputation played a role here as well—African Americans had not forgotten that Bert Williams's Broadway career occurred exclusively on the stage of the *Ziegfeld Follies*. Williams and *Show Boat* were explicitly linked by Floyd Snelson in a column for the *Courier* marking Ziegfeld's death: "Ziegfeld, the Glorifier (Negro Loses a Friend)." Snelson highlighted Ziegfeld's role as a taste maker—"his opinions were the master . . . his wishes were the decree of the Nation"—and his importance in a historical transformation that opened the highly visible, national space of the musical stage to all talent regardless of race. In the matter of promoting "talent, ability and artistic personality . . . regardless of color or state of being . . . [Ziegfeld] was supreme."[3]

But there were other voices in 1927 closer to the Ziegfeld Theatre who had a problem with the offensive word. Chappy Gardner twice reported on an ongoing backstage controversy

One of the opening lines of the Ziegfeld chorus offerings, in which more than 50 Negroes sing, is "We are the Niggers of the Show Boat." Some of the performers resent the use of the word "nigger." It hurts their pride—it cuts into their dignity. Yet they must work at their profession—and acting is their profession. When they come to the nasty word they stop singing. One night about 25 of them filed [???] out, stopped warbling. The stage manager, seeing this, asked in bold language: "What the h—is the matter with those N—lines?"

A rumor is going the rounds on the avenue that a gang of fellows with lots of Race pride is going down town to a certain theatre to kill off a few of those birds who continue to holler "Nigger" from the stage—and preach Race loyalty, manhood, unity on the street corners. Don't be foolish, dear mates, boys must work or starve. All they needed was a chance to show NY they have it. You can do wonders when you have a show.[4]

In an earlier column, Gardner counseled performers who objected to use of the n-word in *Show Boat* to stop using it in daily speech themselves, adding "It is hard to convince any sane person that Ziegfeld, the producer, hates you when he builds a show with you" and pays so well.[5] Gardner agreed with Uncle Dud: *Show Boat* was important because it gave a large group of black performers the chance to "show NY they have it." But Gardner didn't censure those in the chorus who refused to sing the n-word. Instead, he shared the delicious image of a white Broadway stage manager's confusion at the weird effect of black chorus members individually taking what steps they could to remove from *Show Boat* a word they did not care to sing. Resistance, Gardner suggests, could take many forms and marching out of the Ziegfeld stage door to protest one word in a show that featured so much black talent would be a step too far. (An entire black chorus would do just this over the n-word in 1988.) Gardner's showbiz column had only recently been renamed "Along the Rialto," a declaration that the number of black performers working in the Midtown area demanded consistent coverage in the black press. Blacks had a foothold on Broadway. That neighborhood was now part of their city, too.

The issue endured into the spring, when Salem Tutt Whitney, another black theatrical columnist, imagined a conversation between two black performers. Whitney's playlet is worth quoting in full as it captures an enduring ambivalence among black performers about *Show Boat*. The dialogue is set on Seventh Avenue, between Thirty-first and Thirty-second Streets—in other words, not in Harlem but just below the Midtown theater district where some blacks were finding good jobs:

"Have you seen *Show Boat*?
"They aint's lettin' 'em in fer nuthin' yet."
"They say it's a great show."
"Yeh, but the jigs ain't doin' nuthin', no one but Bledsoe, the rest is just atmosphere, whatever that is. I hear they got forty or more jigs down there singin' and tellin' the white folks what happy 'niggers' they are. Ha, ha, ha!"
"Yeh, and I'm one of them. I always said I wouldn't say it for nobody, but I'm sayin' and singin' it now. And I'm eatin' and sleepin' and don't have to play hide and seek with my landlady. To you jigs 'round here I was just an old has-been, down there I'm a bass singer and get paid regularly for being the same."

"They sent for me, but I couldn't see it."

"Where you workin' now?"

"Nowhere, but—"

"I thought you was loafin', I ain't never seen a loafin' actor that could see anything a working actor was doin'."

"Do you call what you're doin' work?"

"Beats panhandlin', and my stomach gets its regular exercise."

"I eat."

"Occasionally, when you're lucky."

"You ain't got more'n you need?"

"It wouldn't be sensible to say so 'round here if I had it?"

"Glad you're doin' so well. Say, can't you stake me—to—two bits?"

"I ain't got nutin' but a willin' disposition and the whole city of New York to cultivate it in. S'long! S'long!"[6]

Fall 1927 was a historic time for black performers in Midtown Manhattan, perhaps the all-time peak in performance opportunities. *Variety* said as much in a front-page article titled "Colored Show Folks' Best Season for White Stage Jobs" on October 12, 1927, just about the time *Show Boat* went into rehearsal and just about the time Ziegfeld, for the first time ever, hired a black chorus. Black choruses were becoming increasingly common, *Variety* reported, and the market for performers was tight. Beyond several high-profile shows on Broadway or touring—*Show Boat* listed among them, Bledsoe is mentioned playing *Emperor Jones* on the road—black performers were appearing in burlesque, on vaudeville, in dramas, and in the standard nightclub revues. "Picture house acts" had joined the "colored musical vogue" as well, mainly choral groups such as the Hall Johnson Jubilee Singers at the still-new Roxy. Unmentioned in the article was the upcoming opening of Universal's *Uncle Tom's Cabin*, which would deploy the Dixie Jubilee Singers singing spirituals from behind the screen. (Universal's next prestige picture would be the 1929 *Show Boat*.) A second unit of the Dixie Jubilee Singers was helping accompany the film *In Old Kentucky* at the Capitol.[7] *Show Boat's* black chorus would be christened Will Vodery's Jubilee Singers, in the words of the noted black poet and critic Alice Dunbar Nelson, writing for a black readership, "a delicate way of indicating to the patrons that some of the cast is colored."[8]

The inclusion of a large black chorus in *Show Boat* was completely within contemporary trends on Broadway and utterly foreign to Ferber's novel. Even more unusual, deeply disruptive of Broadway norms and challenging from the perspective of large-scale form and production costs, was the juxtaposition of this group with a white chorus on the generous Ziegfeld model. *Variety* broke down *Show Boat*'s chorus this way: "The Caucasian and Aframerican girls and boys of the ensemble number 96. The whites are in the majority with 52—36 girls and 16 boys. Jubilee Singers (colored) number 32, equally divided as to sex, and the Jubilee Dancers total 12 girls. In combination a great flash."[9] *Variety* neglected to divide the white chorus into categories but, as always in a Ziegfeld production, there was a (literal) hierarchy. Ries's source sorts the white women into two groups: twenty-four "Glorified Beauties"—tall show girls required only to sing, walk, and wear costumes well—and twelve dancing girls—the so-called ponies who danced with the boys of the chorus.[10]

The twelve Jubilee Dancers were the subject of interest early on, and their presence in a show also featuring "Glorified Beauties" and Ziegfeld ponies meant that *Show Boat* encompassed the full range of racially defined stage stereotypes of the sexualized female body. Segregated from each other in separate productions under normal circumstances, *Show Boat* allowed black and white female choruses to compete on the level playing field of the stage at the Ziegfeld Theatre. *Variety* reported in January 1927 that the "Negresses" for *Show Boat* would all be "dark brown" in an effort to avoid casting "light-skinned colored girls."[11] Was there concern that audiences would become confused if the black women weren't black enough? Colored chorus lines were famously light-skinned in the 1920s. Between September 1923 and July 1927 the black theater critic Theophilus Lewis devoted several of his regular columns in the *Messenger* to the phenomenon. *Variety*'s report suggests that Ziegfeld, Kern, and Hammerstein initially had precise notions about the appearance of the black chorus they were hiring. By casting "dark brown" women, the *Show Boat* "gals" would presumably not be confused with the "high yella" chorus lines seen on Broadway and in Harlem. But in the end, most of the women hired for the Jubilee Dancers came from predictable places: nightclub floor shows (the Club Alabam and Plantation Club in Midtown, Connie's Inn in Harlem) and stage shows (*Runnin' Wild* and *Deep River* on Broadway, *From Dixie to Dover* with Florence Mills in London).[12] Where else would black dancing talent come from? (In 1946, Hammerstein would be able to draw on quite different sources.) Their credentials suggest a certain kind of dancing and dancer normally associated with light-skinned individuals. Not to have used this group during the chorus of "I'm Just Wild About Harry" interpolated into "It's Getting Hotter in the North" would have been a positive waste of talent on hand.

In his book-length remembrance of the producer from 1934, Eddie Cantor made mention of the conceptual challenge *Show Boat*'s black chorus presented to Ziegfeld:

Only in one show were Zieggy's notions of color and costume disturbed. He wondered how he could glorify the colored people in *Show Boat*. He wanted fantastic costumes and typical *Follies* scenery, but both Jerome Kern, the composer of *Show Boat*, and Joseph Urban persuaded him to use realistic effects. It was the one show where Zieggy compromised and sacrificed his own ideas of glorification. The costumes of every period and locality were faithful historical reproductions and the scenery was as real and unpretentious as any legitimate show. It was a great sacrifice for Zieggy to make, but in the end the total effect of the production proved the wisdom of this move.[13]

Cantor highlights the "total effect of the production," and it is crucial to follow his lead. The black chorus was central to the success of *Show Boat*. The black chorus numbers would be subject to alteration and elimination in subsequent decades, but in 1927 the black chorus was an essential part of the whole. Black critics noted this again and again, taking white critics to task for neglecting to highlight audience reaction to the black numbers. Chappy Gardner in the Pittsburgh *Courier* made this a theme of his February 4 and July 14, 1928 columns. In the latter, Gardner explicitly contrasted New York critics' silence with London critics' generous praise of the black cast's importance to *Show Boat*'s success. The role of the black chorus deserves close consideration in any balanced historical assessment of *Show Boat*.

Searching the theatrical pages of black newspapers—just as black performers looking for work might have done—reveals how Ziegfeld went about assembling *Show Boat*'s black chorus. Always eager to spread the word about potential Broadway employment, Bob Slater mentioned *Show Boat* and Hammerstein's other 1927 show *Golden Dawn* in his "Theatrical Jottings" column in the *New York Age* in mid-September: "Bill Elkins is furnishing all the colored people for Arthur Hammerstein's new show, *The Dawn*. Twenty-six was the original number, but they have added some more. . . . Rogers and Roberts are furnishing the people for *The Show Boat* [sic], another new show to open on Broadway with a mixed cast."[14] Elkins, Rogers, and Roberts were African American show people with established careers in a position to help Ziegfeld and Hammerstein pull together black choruses for Broadway productions.

Bill, or William C., Elkins was an elder statesman among black theater and music professionals. His career stretched back to the Williams and Walker shows such as *In Dahomey* (1903) that first brought black casts to Broadway around the turn of the century. Elkins had a recent Broadway credit as one of ten black men billed as Jubilee Singers in the Al Jolson vehicle *Big Boy* (1925). He stayed with *Golden Dawn*, perhaps as a chorus member, in addition to being the manager-contractor of the chorus, and the *New York Age* continued to follow the show, courtesy of information Elkins sent to the paper. Working as a team on *Show Boat*, Alex C. Rogers was a lyricist and author with multiple performer credits, and C. Luckyeth ("Luckey") Roberts was a songwriter and ragtime pianist who influenced Duke Ellington, James P. Johnson, and George Gershwin. Like Elkins, Rogers was in *In Dahomey* and wrote part of the book and lyrics for the follow-up *Abyssinia* three years later.[15] He also wrote lyrics for the song "The Lee Family" (music by Will Vodery), included in the *Ziegfeld Follies of 1916*. Expanding opportunities for blacks in straight plays had brought Rogers some work as a dramatic actor. He appeared in the historic 1917 productions of *Simon the Cyrenian* and *The Rider of Dreams*, as well as *Taboo*, the play that indirectly launched Robeson's career singing spirituals. After *Taboo*, Rogers concentrated on writing the lyrics and books for musical shows, and in 1923 initiated a mid-1920s collaboration with Roberts. Together, Rogers and Roberts wrote the music, lyrics, and book for three shows produced on Broadway over the next four years: *Go-Go* (1923), *Sharlee* (1923), and the short-lived *My Magnolia* (1926), which starred Adelaide Hall, a major black revue star. None was particularly successful, but as a group these shows attest to expanded opportunities for blacks on Broadway and to Rogers and Roberts as experienced Midtown professionals.

Another approach to assembling a black chorus was the wholesale hiring of a preexisting black ensemble. Several such groups were working in New York, and the phenomenon of the professional black chorus, usually specializing in spirituals, would continue into the 1930s. The most notable such group was the Hall Johnson Singers featured in the 1930 hit play *The Green Pastures*; they went on to success in Hollywood as well. At least one established black chorus, the Kentucky Singers, auditioned for Ziegfeld as a group in early September 1926. Several others reportedly were preparing to audition as well.[16]

Leadership of the *Show Boat* black chorus passed to Will Vodery about a week before rehearsals began. Having just returned from London where he conducted a black-cast revue, Vodery was going straight to work "help[ing] on the musical score of *Show Boat* all set for its orchestration" (said *Variety*).[17] Vodery was a long-time Ziegfeld employee and among the most highly placed, technically skilled black musicians on the Broadway scene from the mid-1910s. Rogers and Vodery were colleagues, so it's likely Rogers and Roberts were acting as Vodery's proxies when the chorus was initially being hired.[18] Vodery's role orchestrating *Show Boat* is difficult to determine. All extant orchestral scores are in the hand of Robert Russell Bennett (except for "Bill," which was orchestrated by Hans Spialek). A choral arrangement for the black chorus number "In Dahomey" in an unidentified hand survives in the Kern papers, and this may be Vodery's work. He was credited in the program as the show's "choral director" and remained on the weekly payroll during the run.[19]

As the role of the black chorus expanded, Ziegfeld pulled in even more black theater professionals—in particular the choreographer Aaron Gates, who staged at least one additional number for the black ensemble during try-outs. The hiring of Vodery, Rogers, Roberts, and Gates demonstrates a recognition within Ziegfeld's organization—specifically on the part of Hammerstein, who was the de facto director—that white Broadway professionals did not have the connections to assemble a large black chorus of singers and dancers, especially in a competitive season. But even if African American professionals like Rogers, Roberts, Vodery, and Gates could be called upon to assemble and prepare a suitable black chorus, Kern and Hammerstein still had to write the music to which this chorus would sing and dance.

Putting the black chorus to good use forms a narrative of its own in the making of *Show Boat*. This tale, drawn mostly from draft scripts and tryout programs, reveals a pattern: white chorus numbers were cut while black chorus numbers were added. In their initial scripts (from January and August), Hammerstein and Kern found relatively little for the black chorus to do. Having written the group into the show in act 1, scene 1, few other places to use black singers and dancers suggested themselves. Ferber was no help on this score, and so the role of the black chorus would be shaped more by the musical and theatrical conventions of the day than anything else. In the end, *Show Boat* hosted examples of almost every kind of black musical show playing at the time. The October script differs in its use of the black chorus from the earlier versions in several, highly suggestive ways. Here, at the start of rehearsals, the seeds for several major numbers for the black chorus can be found. The most developed is "Mis'ry's Comin' Aroun'," a long choral scene featuring Queenie and Julie. After the tryout opening, "Mis'ry's Comin Aroun'" was cut, but Kern's haunting music survived as sung underscoring for the miscegenation scene and provided the bulk of an unorthodox overture. Two additional numbers for the black chorus—"Queenie's Ballyhoo" and "In Dahomey"—are present in embryonic form in the October script, where each appears as a compelling stage picture, a matter of image rather than music or dance. Both numbers developed their final form during rehearsals, likely in response to the black ensemble, a group that rapidly developed an identity of its own. As tryouts continued, a period when shortening *Show Boat* was the priority, an entirely new number for the black chorus was added: "Hey, Feller!," a 1920s number for Queenie and company.[20] The numbers for the white chorus unfolded in an almost exactly reverse pattern from those for the black chorus. Kern and Hammerstein thought up several numbers for the white chorus early on. The January script includes the lengthy "I Would Like to Play a Lover's Part," cut in Washington and replaced by Frank and Ellie's "I Might Fall Back on You." An elaborate opening chorus for the Trocadero scene was created during rehearsals, then summarily cut in Washington and replaced by an Apache dance by the Sidell Sisters (a specialty duo) and Frank and Ellie's "Goodbye, My Lady Love." In the end, the white chorus sang in predictable places. Their contribution fell in line with the conventions of operetta and musical comedy, where the chorus sets the scene, frames important occasions, or backs up a leading player's solo. The white chorus sang at the act 1 opening (in contrast to the black chorus); with Ellie during "Life Upon the Wicked Stage" (women only); with Ravenal during "'Til Good Luck Comes My Way" (men only); at the act 1 finale (again in contrast to the black chorus); at the act 2 opening at the World's Fair (arguably their only stand-alone feature); with Magnolia and Ravenal during "Why Do I Love You?"; as the onstage Trocadero audience during "After the Ball"; and at the close of the show, joining with the black chorus and Joe to bless the Ravenal family reunion with a phrase from "Ol' Man River." These numbers mainly used the white chorus as a frame for the leading white characters' stories. By contrast, the black chorus numbers stood alone as musical sequences with inherent entertainment value and often a practical function within the large-scale form and stagecraft requirements of the show.

Among the most surprising black-cast numbers made for *Show Boat* was "Mis'ry's Comin' Aroun,'" a lengthy musical sequence without a trace of glorification or minstrelsy in it: no grinning black faces or high-energy dancing; just solemn, even funereal singing of a kind white audiences were swooning over at the time. The precedents for "Mis'ry" are plentiful. Spirituals used in a dramatic context first appeared in the developing dramatic genre of the black folk play. By April 1927, Countee Cullen could remark of the play *Earth*, for which the black choirmaster Hall Johnson had composed the music, "It may sound blasphemous, but the way things are going we think a play about Negroes in which nary a spiritual was sung would be a huge success because of the sheer novelty of it."[21] When Cullen wrote this, the most important black folk play of the decade had yet to open. DuBose and Dorothy Heyward's *Porgy* took New York by storm in October 1927, opening just days before *Show Boat* went into rehearsal. It, too, used spirituals.

Alexander Woollcott offered extravagant praise for *Porgy*'s saucer-burial scene, calling it "one of the most exciting climaxes I have ever seen in the theatre," a reaction echoed by virtually all reviewers.[22] Brooks Atkinson noted the functional power of that scene:

But for the curtain of one of the early scenes [the direction] rises to splendid theatrical generalship. Serena's room in the tenement is crowded with negroes swaying and singing graveyard melodies beside the covered body of the murdered crapshooter. Gradually the singing becomes more and more preternatural. In the violence of the religious orgy the lights are deliberately turned down until the stage is illuminated only from the front, and the pale wall behind quickly swarms with a myriad of dancing, swirling, leaping shadows.[23]

Atkinson understood the saucer burial—a combination of music, movement, and dramatic spectacle—as a "curtain," a theatrical punctuation mark just before the scene came to a close. In a play like *Porgy*, with nine scenes and several complicated sets—reviewers complained about the slowness of the set changes—a crucial goal of overall pacing was to sustain the audience's interest by ending each scene with a memorable effect, whether dramatic, musical, or both. For *Show Boat*, an even more massive show with an almost unprecedented seventeen scenes, the importance of preparing each succes- sive "curtain" would be crucial to maintaining audience interest. (Most 1920s musicals had three to six scenes, but if *Show Boat* is understood under the rubric of the revue, the number of scene changes is less unusual.) As work on *Show Boat* progressed after August 1927, more and more "curtains" were entrusted to the black chorus. The expansion of their role in *Show Boat* can be dated to about the time the large, black cast of *Porgy* was taking Broadway by storm.

A tipping point of sorts, several white critics saw in *Porgy* the promise of a different kind of stage portrayal of black Americans. Frank Vreeland noted in the *Telegram*:

The advent of *Porgy* on the Theatre Guild stage the past week lends point to the fact that it is now the mode to take the Negro seriously. Until the war, whenever an author thought of a colored character he presented him as a jolly pickaninny, and vaudeville hasn't yet worked out of that carefree jocular stage. Then somebody—maybe it was Gilbert Seldes—discovered that the Negro has a soul and more wistfulness than you could crowd into one book.

Hence it has become the fashion to make a great, solemn sanctification of the Negro and to find that his race has a message. Not alone is he given a "theme" and a "motif" on the stage—the vogue of spirituals did that for him, almost raising him to operatic heights. . . .

The burden of [*Porgy's*] book rang again and again:—"It's mighty hard to be a nigger." There was little hint that these brown skinned people had ever given an excuse for minstrel frivolities. Teeth that were bared in broad grins of merriment in other books were here bared, primarily, in a snarl of resentment.[24]

By late 1927, the larger trend Vreeland describes had already underwritten Hammerstein's "Ol' Man River," the product of the previous year, and *Porgy* encouraged further exploration of this theme in the even darker "Mis'ry's Comin' Aroun'."

The October script, likely typed before October 15—*Porgy* opened on October 10—includes a version of "Mis'ry" for Queenie, Julie, and a few others. Joe, while present, is not assigned any sung lines. No musical sources for this version survive, so while Joe may have been understood to participate in the number, "Mis'ry" was not conceived as a chance to "feature Paul Robeson," as had been the case with "Can't Help Lovin' Dat Man" a year earlier. Hopes for Robeson's participation were surely declining by the time "Mis'ry" was first being laid out, and a shift toward other black characters—notably Queenie, already assigned to blackface performer Tess Gardella—was underway. Prominent in this version is a solo quatrain for Julie, sung to a relentless, minor mode melody (see ex. 5.1a):

Some poor nigger's been foun'
Some poor nigger's been foun'
De mis'ry's comin' aroun'
To make her blue

Except for this chorus, the "Mis'ry" lyrics are assigned to Queenie or "All," referring to Queenie and "two or three NEGRO HELPERS" cleaning the *Cotton Blossom* auditorium. The stage direction "All hum softly as they work, with a gloomy blue tone in their voices" indicates a brooding atmosphere. Kern would later add a second, more lyrical melody for "Mis'ry" (see ex. 5.1b), but the lyrics in the October script only fit the heavier, more fateful strain. The music continues behind brief dialogue exchanges for Joe and Queenie, Magnolia and Julie, and Julie and Queenie. The intent of the constant singing seems to be to get under Julie's skin. She responds to the music "in spite of herself," according to the stage directions. After her short solo, Julie brings the number to a halt mid-strain, shouting "Stop that rotten song. It's enough to bring misery to us all if you keep singing like that—." Julie's use of "us" telegraphs the revelation of her mixed-race identity to come just moments later. The October draft "Mis'ry" is a work in progress, more Hammerstein's than Kern's. Using a single melody at least seven times counting only the choruses with lyrics, the sequence would require much adjustment. The intent

Example 5.1a–c Opening measures of Kern's three melodies for "Mis'ry's Comin' Aroun'."

seems to be a continuation of the theme of "Can't Help Lovin' Dat Man" but in a darker vein. The same characters are present and, once again, Julie joins in on a song colored folk sing. Referring to herself as a "poor nigger" in this setting further deepens the context for Hammerstein's use of the contentious word in the opening chorus and elsewhere in all his *Show Boat* scripts. Hammerstein did not use that word lightly. He reached for it in his lyrics as a means to express what he understood to be serious expressions of the black experience, a new theme many white writers were working with at the time. Among musical theater lyricists and book writers, only Hammerstein seems to have had an interest in bringing this theme to the musical stage. Ferber's story—under constant alteration as it was made musical—offered a chance to do so.

Three musical sources for "Mis'ry" survive: a continuity draft of all of scene 4 (in both Kern's and Bennett's hands), Bennett's full score (which originally followed the sketch bar for bar but was altered before the orchestra parts were copied out), and a published version for piano and voices (included in the New York vocal score even though the number was cut from the show early on).[25] None of these match the October script or the slightly different version laid into the November script, and each differs subtly from the others. Sorting out the exact chronology of the "Mis'ry" materials is not possible, but some larger conclusions can be drawn. The recent success of *Porgy* surely influenced the revision of the originally modest "Mis'ry" into a lengthy, musically complex choral scene for the entire black chorus. The connection to *Porgy* is made plain in the new solo assigned to Julie as a replacement for the quatrain found in the October script. Here, using Kern's other, more lyrical melody (ex. 5.1b), Hammerstein makes explicit reference to a saucer burial:

When I dies, let me rest
With a dish on my breast.
Some give nickel, some give dime,
All dem folks is fren's o' mine.

The saucer burial as staged and explained within *Porgy* was a kind of wake where visitors helped pay for burial costs by leaving money in a dish on the corpse's chest. Collecting money in this way was part of the Gullah culture of Charleston portrayed in *Porgy*. Julie is from Mississippi, but in the syncretistic logic of the musical stage *Porgy*'s effective saucer burial installed the practice as a part of black American folk practice more generally (at least for the Broadway audience).

Beyond explicit reference to the saucer burial, the musical proportions of "Mis'ry" grew considerably. John McGlinn's 1988 recorded version—a conflation of the sources—exceeds six minutes in length. Added to Kern's two melodies was a third, never set to text by Hammerstein but only hummed by the chorus (see ex. 5.1c). This theme grants considerable seriousness to "Mis'ry" and lends itself to surprising harmonic shifts, a potential that Kern, working with Robert Russell Bennett, exploited throughout the number. The vocal parts as they appear in the vocal score are detailed, shifting, often featuring one or two individuals and thereby suggesting the presence of many strong solo singers within the black chorus. Black newspapers made sure to highlight the solo work of the soprano Henrietta Lovelace in *Show Boat*'s convent scene, which featured all sixteen female members of the Jubilee singers singing in Latin. Chappy Gardner assured his readers that if you sat to the front of the orchestra seats—where only whites and blacks able to pass could sit—your suspicions that the nuns' voices were so good they had to be black might be visually confirmed.[26] Just before Julie's "Mis'ry" solo, a solo bass voice descends to an unaccompanied low C, quieting the stage with a display of vocal control that is, in context, both operatic in its reliance on the power of the voice alone and evocative of black concert singers like Paul Robeson. Perhaps this note was sung by an individual similar to the one imagined in Whitney's dialogue on Seventh Avenue, who notes of his role in *Show Boat*, "I'm a bass singer and get paid regularly for being the same." "Mis'ry" was developed into a meditative choral number unlike any heretofore heard in a Broadway musical comedy. It was deeply serious, drawing on the dramatic genre of the black folk play rather than nightclub or black revue sources. In making the number, Hammerstein, Kern, and Bennett were exploring new territory, responding both to *Porgy* and the talents of the individuals in *Show Boat*'s own Jubilee Singers. "Mis'ry" can also be heard as a further step in the direction of "Ol' Man River." Kern and Hammerstein's engagement with recent trends in black music and performance only deepened as they worked on *Show Boat*.

"Mis'ry" was summarily cut sometime in Washington, but the creative team did not want it to go entirely unheard. During tryouts, the "Mis'ry" sequence was refashioned by Bennett with slight changes in the orchestration into an unusual overture. (As mentioned earlier, a chorus of "Why Do I Love You?" was tacked on to the end.) A sizable chunk of music and a choral version of the haunting strain associated with Julie (ex. 5.1b) survives as underscoring for the moment when Julie and Steve face the show boat company, who have just learned the couple's marriage is a case of miscegenation. Helen Morgan recorded the saucer burial strain as a prelude to her 1932 version of "Can't Help Lovin' Dat Man."[27] The strange inclusion of a fragment from a cut number hints at the affection those in the cast might have had for "Mis'ry's Comin' Aroun'."

How much of "Mis'ry's Comin' Aroun'" was created with Tess Gardella as Aunt Jemima playing Queenie in mind? Gardella was among the first principals hired for the show, her casting announced in May. The stage name "Aunt Jemima" reached back to the 1893 World's Fair Columbian Exposition in Chicago—an event re-created as the act 2 opener in *Show Boat* (although Queenie does not appear in the scene). At the actual World's Fair, a black woman named Nancy Green—born a slave in 1834—made personal appearances billed as Aunt Jemima selling pancakes. Green would play the part at public events for twenty years. In 1909, an aggressive advertising campaign launched the Aunt Jemima brand of pancake mix nationally. By the 1920s, the black figure was a fixture in women's magazines such as the *Woman's Home Companion* (where Ferber's novel was initially serialized).[28] Gardella appropriated the name for her blackface vaudeville act beginning in 1920 and eventually played the part on radio for General Foods, singing almost daily. Gardella sued General Foods and NBC for $200,000 in 1935 when a different, in her view inferior, Aunt Jemima took the role on the radio after salary talks with Gardella broke down. She won a financial award but lost her stage name.[29] Hiring an African American woman to play Aunt Jemima on the radio in the early 1930s—or Queenie in *Show Boat* in 1927—would have been extremely unusual. In getting both jobs, Gardella benefited from a decade of live appearances in a highly personalized sort of Jazz Age blackface and from the fact that she was white.

Of Italian descent, Gardella started out singing in church theatricals and amateur minstrel shows. As a 1924 profile put it, "When minstrel shows lost their popularity, Miss Gardella was broken-hearted, but decided to combine the delights of minstrelsy with the pleasures of jazz. . . . To hear her sing is to listen to the honeyed croonings of a 'N' Orleans Mammy. Aunt Jemima, barring brief vaudeville engagements, had never been south of South Ferry [the southernmost tip of Manhattan]!"[30] Tess Gardella began the 1920s in a strong position to reinterpret the stereotypes of minstrelsy for the Jazz Age. Dressing up in imitation of the Aunt Jemima advertising icon, success arrived quickly. Discovered by George White and featured in his *Scandals* of 1921, by 1923 Gardella was playing the Palace, where she regularly appeared through the 1930s. (Just prior to the 1932 *Show Boat* revival, Gardella and Terris headlined the same bill at the Palace.) In 1924 she was billed at the Hippodrome as a "comedienne of syncopation in character songs," reinforcing her dual strategy of delivering comedy and up-to-date musical stylings.[31] She often performed with a band and minus her Mammy persona would perhaps have been categorized as a blues queen or, out of blackface, as a red hot mama. Being Aunt Jemima set her apart, and later in the decade Gardella's embodiment of an old-fashioned black stereotype would recommend her for Queenie. Her *Show Boat* costume matched that of her vaudeville appearances. *Variety* noted "Aunt Jemima (white), doing her familiar mammy, was ideal for the assignment."[32] Alice Dunbar Nelson, a noted black poet, praised Gardella, whom Nelson was unfamiliar with from the vaudeville stage. "A mystery seems to surround 'Queenie.' On the program she is billed as 'Aunt Jemima,' and behind the famous pseudonym hides a very good actress, with a mellow, rich contralto, and a nimble foot in spite of her obvious two hundred pounds. 'Aunt Jemima' should come out in the open."[33] According to her *New York Times* obituary, Gardella had "a big voice" and "often sang her own arrangements though it was said she never had taken a singing lesson."[34] Gardella's re-cordings reveal a jazz-oriented singer, capable of doing much more than just singing the tune. On the flip side of her 1928 recording of "Can't Help Lovin' Dat Man" (see chap. 3), Gardella really swings on the novelty song "Didn't I Tell You (That You'd Come Back)," sounding something like Bing Crosby at the time in terms of her rhythmic sense.[35] She rewrites the tune in the final half-chorus, finding the blue notes and inserting three-note melismas, getting close to hot improvisation without imitating models such as Louis Armstrong. Gardella had formidable talent as a vocalist and should not be judged by photos alone.

The ambitious scale and tenor of "Mis'ry's Comin' Aroun'" speaks for Hammerstein and Kern's confidence in Gardella's talent. The stark difference between "Mis'ry" and her earlier turn in "Can't Help Lovin' Dat Man" hints at her expressive range. Further features added for Gardella during rehearsals and tryouts brought even more variety to the Queenie role, which emerges as a major part shaped around Gardella but amenable to transformation by later performers. "Queenie's Ballyhoo"—added during rehearsals—gave Gardella a third featured number in act 1 at the Washington opening. "Mis'ry" would be cut, but Gardella would get an act 2 number, "Hey, Feller!," during tryouts, leaving her with three features at the Broadway opening, two of which were solos with the black chorus as backup. Queenie was (and remains) a major singing role in *Show Boat*, its creation for Gardella closely tied into the development of numbers for the black chorus. Combining a white performer in blackface with a black singing and dancing chorus was no cause of embarrassment in the late 1920s.

"Queenie's Ballyhoo" closes the box office scene on the levee, which includes the arrival of the backwoodsmen, Ellie and Frank's "I Might Fall Back on You," and Parthy and Andy's conversation about Ravenal. With the white audience presumably aboard the boat already, Queenie steps forward to ballyhoo the colored audience, telling Andy he just doesn't know how to attract "my people" to the show. A fast 2/4 marked *Allegretto* begins with Queenie's first word: "Hey," the call of the vaudeville singer for an audience's attention. (Her act 2 feature uses the same direct address.) Kern's music for Gardella features ragtimey rhythms in 2/4 time and persistent leaping gestures. The vocal range is narrow and middling, almost never going above the C above middle C. Gardella was a belter, projecting words more than tune. A 1930 reviewer noted she "resoundingly fills the [Palace] with the sentiments common to popular ballads."[36] The only time Gardella went above that top note in *Show Boat* was an impassioned section of "Mis'ry" that has her raising the tune up by an octave, singing sustained E's (an octave and a third above middle C). She could not have belted this passage, and, again, the range of her vocal abilities must have been impressive.

"Queenie's Ballyhoo" served a practical function: it ended the scene with musical energy and facilitated a complex scene change. After convincing the black chorus to buy tickets for the balcony—"where the colored people sit" explains Queenie—the Jubilee Dancers entered and, according to Ries's source, "parod[ied] the white folk buying tickets, walking on the levee, and putting on fine airs. The music returns to the original tempo and they begin a faster dance with Queenie urging them on; some of the steps marked in the score include double spins, splits, cartwheels, and a 'relevé shuffle,' whatever that might have been."[37] During the dance, black velvet drapes closed in behind the chorus, now positioned downstage, allowing the complicated scene change to begin during the dance. Hammerstein had anticipated that the shift from the levee to the multilevel set inside the *Cotton Blossom* auditorium would take extra time, so in the October script he inserted an "Interlude" to be played downstage. The initial idea was to re-create the front cover of *Show Boat* the novel as a *tableau vivant*, assuming that the musical's original audiences were readers of Ferber's novel. To liven up the scene, Hammerstein added, "there can be developed, if desired, a spontaneous specialty of some sort—a Negro boy starts to dance—a crowd surrounds him, flings him pennies, others join, etc." (Ferber refers to just such a generic scene.[38]) Building on the talents of Gardella and the Jubilee Dancers, Hammerstein and Kern went a different route, setting aside the hackneyed trope of a pick-aninny dancing for pennies and instead created "Queenie's Ballyhoo," a number that established a bond between Queenie—played by a white woman in blackface—and the black chorus, and featured the Jubilee Dancers poking fun at the white chorus. This theme of the black chorus observing then parodying the white chorus appears more than once in the sources. The Broadway conductor's score has the women of the black chorus watching and imitating the mincing walk of the white women on the latter group's first entrance at the top of the show.

A second "curtain" provided by the black chorus began as a simple cross-over in novelty costumes. Like the historical event being re-created, *Show Boat*'s World's Fair extravaganza found little room for African Americans. In the October script, Hammerstein had the black chorus do a crossover as the "Dahomey Village troupe." Their appearance elicits a racist remark from Par-thy: "Niggers—see 'em every day of my life. What are they dressed up for?" The Dahomey Village was a famous attraction on the Midway Plaisance at the 1893 World's Fair Columbian Exposition where African "natives" could be viewed as at a zoo. (*Show Boat* neglects to visit the respectable White City, remaining in the sensational districts of the Fair, near where Ziegfeld got his start. A musical episode featuring La Belle Fatima and her coochie-coochie dance serves as the primary attraction for the white chorus men and source of revulsion for the white chorus women. Andy and Parthy articulate this contrast in dialogue.) During rehearsals, the black chorus's modest crossover as the Dahomey natives in the October draft grew into the scene-ending, tribal-themed, extended song and dance "In Dahomey." Andy, Parthy, and Magnolia were removed from the sequence, which instead became a confron-tation between the black and white choruses.

"In Dahomey" begins with a drumlike figure in the bass marked *Moderato (in barbaric manner)*. The orchestrator Robert Russell Bennett used tom-tom and solo tuba together with an edgy melodic banjo part. The timbres and textures at the outset are striking, different from anything heard to this point in the score, putting the audience on notice that something unusual was imminent. With the addition of the black chorus singing in a made-up tribal language, "In Dahomey" began with an operatic grandeur built on some of the same 2/4 rhythms heard in Queenie's music. The introduction prom-ised a number of some length with perhaps even a pretense to artistic stat-ure. The vocal arranging for the black chorus, in particular, was technically difficult, sitting at the top of the range for most of the voice parts. The white chorus responded with alarm, fleeing the stage in fear of being a "spearful," their homophonic statements difficult to understand as the black chorus continues to sing wailing lines above them. This was the only time in the score Kern and Hammerstein had the black and white choruses simultaneously sing different musical material expressing different racial perspectives. (In the opening of act 1, they sing racially specific lyrics to the same tune.) Once the whites had left, the blacks exalted, singing in unison octaves, "We're glad to see them go," getting more specific on the repeat, "We're glad to see those white folks go." Nothing in Kern's music insisted on the second, racially taunting line (which added two syllables and necessitated a slight change in the melody). Hammerstein must be the source for this unusually direct articulation of a black communal response to the departure of a group of whites. It answers—in a way—Parthy's dismissive line from the October script about seeing black folks every day: a line cut in favor of "In Dahomey," which handed the stage over to the black chorus on their own, without Joe or Queenie, for the first and only time.

With the whites gone, the blacks revealed who they really were. With the start of the chorus, the music abruptly shifted into a new rhythmic matrix: two-beat jazz. The banjo part shifted to a rhythm role—marking the off beats—and the frenetic, energetic sound of 1920s jungle numbers erupted onto the stage. It's one of the more striking musical transitions in the entire *Show Boat* score, and original audiences would have registered the change viscerally—overly dramatic jungle drums giving way to a jazz beat that immediately connected the dancing savages onstage to similar nightclub numbers seen regularly at places like the Cotton Club. Making the point in the music was important because the lyric is tough to hear. Hammerstein's black Africans were, in fact, African Americans from New York playing Dahomey Villagers at the Fair. Their costumes were just that: costumes for a paying gig. (Bert Williams and George Walker posed as Dahomey villagers at the San Francisco Midwinter Exposition of 1894 until actual tribesmen from Benin arrived.[39] Perhaps Hammerstein knew the story; Ziegfeld may have picked it up from Williams himself.) Hammerstein showed his knowledge of black history in and around New York by having these black New Yorkers in a scene set in 1893 sing of their longing for Avenue A (*way* downtown: blacks didn't move uptown to Harlem until after World War I).

Like "Queenie's Ballyhoo," "In Dahomey" provided the curtain for its scene, and the final dance choruses were performed downstage so the black velvet drapes could be drawn during the number, jump-starting the scene change. In the October script, Hammerstein planned a costume parade of "Forty Beauties from Forty Nations" to facilitate this set change. This all-too-predictable

Ziegfeldian display of white beauty—the all-white Glorified Beauties would militate against any diversity beyond exotic costumes—was nixed in favor of "In Dahomey," a jungle dance that deployed the black chorus in yet another set of black musical theater tropes, this time set within an ironic frame that allowed the chorus to drop and don their racial disguises with the changing rhythm. The dance was particularly vigorous, with the men of the singing chorus demonstrating some spear throwing, the singing women doing "some folk-dance steps in a spiral and traveling figure-eight formation," and the dancing women doing "jetés, running steps into a sliding fall onto the knees, and fast spins around the frightened crowd of white folk."[40] "In Dahomey" pushed the talents of the black chorus farther to the front, showing them off in a range of black masks and even pointing out that these poses were just that, stereotypes of the musical theater. "In Dahomey," a number that is easy to dismiss from the perspective of nearly a century later, was not cut from *Show Boat* until the 1960s. It would serve a new generation of black dancers in the 1940s and 1950s (see chap. 7).

Yet one more number, "Hey, Feller!" for the black chorus, was added to *Show Boat* during the show's tryout week in Cleveland. This song and dance for Queenie and the black chorus was the last major new element added to the show, and its making called for new talent to be brought onto the creative team. On December 3 Bob Slater, a reliable black showbiz columnist, reported that "Aaron Gates, who left here two weeks ago to stage some numbers for the *Show Boat* Co., is back and reports that the show is in fine working order. The show will open here Christmas week."[41] In Slater's and Gates's eyes, *Show Boat* was a race show: black readers should care about its success and be aware of the race talent on display. Slater's item is confirmed by a payment of $118.50 to Arrison Gates in a Ziegfeld financial statement for *Show Boat*. (The credited dance director for *Show Boat*, Sammy Lee, was paid $2,500.)[42]

In 1927 Aaron Gates was struggling to build a business: his brief engagement with Ziegfeld was surely a welcome source of income. In April and May, the Aaron Gates School of Stage Dancing, located in the heart of Harlem on 135th Street, was prominently advertised on the entertainment pages of the *New York Amsterdam News*. "Manager and Proprietor" Gates offered a range of dance services to the community. "Using the 'Billy Pierce System' of instruction, Black Bottom—Special Class for Children, Specializing in American Tap, Buck and Wing, Soft Shoe and Strut," the ads promised "If You Can Walk, We Can Make You Dance, Special Black Bottom Routines, Musical Comedies, Revues and Acts Staged, Special Rates and Classes for Adults."[43] As April turned to May, Gates's ads decreased in size, disappearing in mid-May. But just before Gates's trip to Cleveland to work on *Show Boat*, "Gates School of Stage and Ballroom Dancing" resurfaced in two small ads promoting the institution as "The best colored school in America, where you can get special attention."[44] Perhaps Gates's enterprise was struggling; maybe positive word-of-mouth had made advertising unnecessary. In any event, 1927 was an important year for Gates, who was receiving income from a variety of sources, following the lead of Buddy Bradley, a black choreographer who created stage and dance routines for Broadway and vaudeville performers, and worked out of a Midtown studio patronized mostly by whites.[45] *Show Boat* was not the only job Gates had on Broadway during the 1927 season. He also did the choreography for the short-lived *Bottomland*, which opened in late June for a twenty-one-performance run at the Princess Theatre. Gates's work on Broadway in 1927 may seem surprising in view of his prior credentials. In the early 1920s, he produced and co-starred in two traveling blues revues with performers such as Gertrude Saunders and Edith Wilson. In 1922 Gates was in the cast of *Go Get It*, produced by S. H. Dudley and featuring Oliver Blackwell's Jazz Orchestra. Such black-cast shows, with their blues queens and comic teams, were designed for black audiences and a far cry in prestige and style from Ziegfeld. Yet creative skills honed in these arenas was exactly what the *Show Boat* team felt was necessary to put the finishing touches on their massive musical. Gates got the call from Ziegfeld.

"Hey, Feller!" played a direct role in marking *Show Boat*'s arrival in the present. The vocal arrangement made reference to a contemporary popular music catchphrase. In the breaks, the black chorus sang "vo-de-oh-do, vo-de-oh-de-oh-do-do," evoking a pair of novelty songs from 1927: "Crazy Words, Crazy Tune" and "Vo-do-do-de-o Blues" (both with music by Milton Ager and words by Jack Yellen). Widely recorded by white bands and singers, both tunes played on the idea of a popular music fad being so all pervasive as to drive the listener crazy. Stop saying "vo-do-do-de-o" both songs pleaded, even as they repeated the phrase again and again. This nod to a recent popular music craze would surely elicit a reaction from white audience members . . . but why put it in the mouth of the black chorus? "Hey, Feller," like "It's Getting Hotter in the North" (which was cut by the time "Hey, Feller" was written), was intended to be ultra contemporary, an entirely of-the-moment song. Putting white catchphrases into black mouths hinted at the general racial confusion of the late 1920s. What was black? What was white? "Hey, Feller!" was judged so prominent an element of *Show Boat* that Gardella and the Jubilee Singers filmed the number for the prologue to the 1929 *Show Boat* film.

Will Vodery's Jubilee Singers and Dancers ended up with much to do in *Show Boat*, and in fact the group had an identity outside the show as well. A few weeks after *Show Boat* opened on Broadway, a group of Jubilee Dancers performed for the visiting composer Maurice Ravel at a party in a Madison Avenue mansion. In deference to Ravel's interests, the evening included "only negro artists," with the Hall Johnson Jubilee Singers, singer Abby Mitchell, and R. J. Huey from the cast of *Porgy* performing as well.[46] *Show Boat* was seen by the event's organizers as a valid source for black American artists who might please a visiting European. During *Show Boat*'s three-week Philadelphia tryout, the black chorus did an elaborate concert at the behest of their leader, appearing in a Sunday afternoon benefit for Mercy Hospital, a black institution supported by African American elites in the city. Among the founders of the hospital was Vodery's mother. The society page of the *Amsterdam News* reported, "We doubt that [Vodery] has ever brought us a more versatile group than the famous *Show Boat* chorus. It is virtually a host of talent—everyone of which is an artist within himself."[47] Bledsoe sang the "Volga Boat Song" and was favorably compared to the famous Russian bass Fyodor Chaliapin by the black opera singer Florence Cole Talbert, who was in attendance. Art songs, religious parlor songs, and spirituals were sung; piano and violin solos filled out the program. Bledsoe and the men offered "Ol' Man River," which "registered big." These two events—one for white society, the other for black—suggest the extent to which *Show Boat* was a cultural event which elites on either side of the color line could embrace.

The importance of *Show Boat* for professional black performers cannot be underestimated. In a busy season Ziegfeld provided some of the best jobs around, and individuals in *Show Boat*'s black cast became celebrated members of the race community. The women of the chorus, in particular, were feted in the black press as glamorous show business figures in every way analogous to Ziegfeld's "Glorified Beauties." (The June 4, 1932 *Pittsburgh Courier* printed glamour photos of eight black chorus girls under the headline "Galaxy of Scintillating Stage Stars Who Are Sailing On Ziegfeld's Famous Show Boat.") Several individuals from within the chorus began appearing regularly in black society columns, where theater parties to see *Show Boat* were noted as well. If, as Cantor claimed, Ziegfeld resisted glorifying *Show Boat*'s colored chorus along his standard lines, then these performers found their place in the light by different means. Hammerstein and Kern ended up using them in a variety of ways that called attention to their range of talents. The black press obligingly provided some of the missing glamour. As one white critic noted when *Show Boat* visited Cleveland, Ziegfeld had created "a girl show in which the majority of the beauties, the liveliest of the dancers and the most stirring of the singers are African. Thus our blackamoor brethren are recognized with a respectful flourish by the dean of American producers, by the most celebrated of the girl show impresarios."[48]

The 1927 *Show Boat* brought together on one stage virtually every aspect of mid-1920s New York entertainment—from white-cast operetta and musical comedy to black-cast folk dramas and revues, with trends in the concert hall and the nightclub also prominently represented. As one Chicago critic noted when *Show Boat* first played the Windy City in 1929, "*Show Boat* . . . strikes me as being what very few music shows are, and that is everybody's show. One need not be worldly to enjoy it intimately; one need not be Broadwise—as at a revue, say—in order to savor its fun. It is as open to the whole American world as was Miss Ferber's racy novel from which it was plotted—a book that sold like sodas in the drug stores last Summer. Children and old women and flappers and floorwalkers and legionnaires and critics and interior decorators will meet on a common basis of appreciation at *Show Boat*."[49]

This assessment of the show's broad appeal would remain true even after the 1920s audience *Show Boat* was created to please had disappeared. *Show Boat* would remain entertaining and relevant long after its original cohort of musical shows—whether white or black cast—had ceased to be commercially viable or politically acceptable. *Show Boat* would survive the Depression, World War II, the civil rights revolution of the 1950s and '60s, and the political correctness of the 1990s, finding an audience even as American popular culture was transformed several times over. It would be committed to film four times, each capturing a particular moment in Hollywood's depiction of the color line, and gain a firm foothold in Britain, where a vibrant production history in London's West End offers a valuable outside perspective on the show's depiction of American race relations. As the making of *Show Boat* told in part 1 demonstrates, performers such as Robeson, Morgan, Puck and White, Terris, Marsh, Gardella, and the 1927 black chorus fundamentally shaped *Show Boat* as Hammerstein, Kern, Ziegfeld, and others—black and white—created the show from behind the scenes. Part 2 considers the remaking of *Show Boat* from 1928 to the end of the twentieth century, a more far-flung story, once again involving a myriad of creative figures, among them producers, directors, writers, choreographers, and—most importantly—performers.

PART II

REMAKING

6

FEATURING ROBESON

• • •

1928–1940

After saying no to *Show Boat* in 1927, Paul Robeson reversed course in early 1928 and said yes. He would play Joe and sing "Ol' Man River" for more than a decade. This chapter looks at the twelve-year period during which Robeson was associated with *Show Boat*, from his first bow in the 1928 London production to his last appearance as Joe in Los Angeles in 1940. Between those two productions, Robeson played Joe on Broadway in the 1932 revival—Ziegfeld's final production—and on the big screen in the 1936 Universal film. Robeson's attitude toward the show, how it was adjusted for him, and how he managed to use the show for his own professional purposes serve as a central thread in the story of *Show Boat*'s first generation of remaking. Other performer-centered stories emerged in these years as well: Helen Morgan's continued identification with Julie, Alberta Hunter and Hattie McDaniel's claiming of Queenie for African American actresses, adjustments made to Magnolia and Ravenal as other performers took on these roles, and how each version provided work for black performers. And Hammerstein's popular music plot made a notable if historically concealed return in these years as well. Universal Pictures made two cinematic *Show Boats*: a part-silent/part-talkie adaptation of Ferber's novel in 1929 and a lavish black-and-white version of the Kern/Hammerstein musical in 1936. After several changes of course, the 1929 version ended up incorporating music and performers from the musical and, for today's viewer, tells a frustratingly incomplete version of the popular music plot. The 1936 film, scripted by Hammerstein with three added songs by Hammerstein and Kern, was to tell the popular music plot in no uncertain terms. It ended up not doing so, but phantoms from the archives allow for a re-creation of how Hammerstein hoped to tell *Show Boat*'s tale of race and music on film.

Show Boat was the third Hammerstein operetta in a row to play Drury Lane, a historic theater in London's West End. Like their counterparts in New York, London audiences in the 1920s relished both jazzy modern musical comedies and sentimental operettas. Drury Lane was closely identified with the latter genre. *Rose-Marie* and *The Desert Song* preceded *Show Boat* at Drury Lane; *The New Moon*, another Hammerstein hit, followed it. Sir Alfred Butt produced each on a lavish scale that equaled that of Ziegfeld and the Shuberts, and Edith Day played the female lead in all four as well. London theatergoers, women in particular, were known to line up overnight to get opening-night tickets for the gallery.

Despite its position as the third Broadway import in a row at Drury Lane, most reviewers emphasized how unusual *Show Boat* was. One reviewer found the show's setting and content to be "utterly alien." He continued, "The house-boat on the Mississippi in which entertainments are given has no counterpart on the Thames. We have no colour question. Our sheriffs do not walk about in black frock coat, sombrero, gaiters, and an evening-dress waist-coat, and talk of arresting people. It is all rather bewildering."[1] There was no precedence for stories of miscegenation in West End musicals; the same could be said for Broadway, but New York audiences could be assumed to be famil-iar with southern "customs" and get the point of the scene. British audiences in the late 1920s, however, were well acquainted with black performers play-ing the full range of stereotypes from the American musical stage. Florence Mills had been a sensation in London, and issues of black Americans taking white Londoners' performing jobs were never far below the surface. During *Show Boat*'s run, two other musical shows exploring race played the West End. *Virginia* (opened October 1928) featured an interracial cast combining jazz-talking whites from New York come to England to marry aristocrats and a group of stereotypical black Americans—the whites' servants—who embodied minstrelsy and spiritual-singing stereotypes, which made *Show Boat* look positively restrained.[2] *Topsy and Eva* (also opened October) brought the Duncan Sisters' blackface vaudeville act to London in a retelling of *Uncle Tom's Cabin* and included a "big Specialty Charleston Dance."[3]

Drury Lane's leading lady Edith Day was a great favorite with audiences and reviewers, and Magnolia's character was inevitably understood through her persona, described by one reviewer in expansive terms: "[T]here is nothing that any musical comedy star could be asked to do, whether as actress, singer, or dancer, that she cannot do with complete accomplish-ment."[4] Day's performance of "After the Ball" turned up again and again as a highlight for reviewers. The baritone Howett Worster was cast as Ravenal. The combination of Day and Worster required adjustments to both roles preserved in the vocal score used by Drury Lane's chorus master and assistant conductor Frank Stamper.[5] "You Are Love" was lowered by a full step, and Day took the high notes at the close. The upward transposition of "Make Believe" was eliminated as well. Magnolia's single sung line in the wedding scene was crossed out in Stamper's score. Stamper's granddaughter remembered him telling her that keys were often changed for Day, who had trouble hitting high notes. Thus the delicate balance between musical comedy and operetta, which had been struck for Terris and Marsh in New York, required reworking in *Show Boat*'s first remaking.

Taking the role of Julie was Marie Burke, a "light operatic artist of rare distinction" and fashionable London figure credited with reviving the feather boa.[6] Burke's 1928 recording of "Can't Help Lovin' Dat Man"—made inside Drury Lane in conjunction with the production—reveals a vocal approach on the white side. Like Morgan, Burke didn't hint at Julie's racial identity in sonic terms, although Burke leans on the blue notes a bit more than Morgan ever did on record and sounds like a stage performer creating a role rather than a popular singer applying her general approach to the part.[7] The surprise comes in the second half of Burke's recording, which uses the arrangement from the show. Here, Burke takes on the role of Queenie. She darkens her sound at the bottom of the range and exaggerates the dialect elements in the lyric. Burke does not, however, play with the rhythm or reveal a working knowledge of black vocal style such as Gardella does on her recording. Burke's Julie was the first test of the role without Morgan's personality to carry it. One critic remarked Burke "sang her first song perfectly," adding "The second one, which she sang sitting on a piano, was not worth listening to. . . . 'Bill' has been replaced."[8] Without Morgan to sing it, the song did not impress London audiences.

Butt assembled a chorus roughly equal in size to Ziegfeld's: thirty-seven women and twenty men in the white chorus; fifteen women and fifteen men in the black singing chorus, and "an imported chorus of thirteen American race girls" rounded out the black ensemble, billed as the Mississippi Singers and Dancers.[9] The black American baritone John C. Payne, still resident in London, served as vocal coach for the Mississippi Singers. Once again, white producers called upon established black professionals to prepare the black-cast elements of the production. Some in the London theatrical community were up in arms over the appearance of blacks, and particularly black Americans, on the Drury Lane stage. The theater had earlier been known as the National Theatre, and there was some outrage at blacks taking white choristers' jobs.[10] Race was never very far from the surface in stories about *Show Boat*, with one paper noting Day's willingness not only to attend but to appear "on the stage with the coloured performers" at an "all-black matinee for the London flood fund" in the weeks prior to opening.[11] The general strangeness of an interracial cast attended *Show Boat* wherever it played in the late 1920s.

The perceived distance between British theater professionals and *Show Boat*'s thoroughly American characters was articulated by Cedric Hardwicke, a character actor who took the role of Andy. Hammerstein cast Hardwicke based on his performance as a crusty old codger in the hit play *Yellow Sands*. (Virtually every London reviewer evoked this earlier role as a reference point for Hardwicke's Andy.) When Hardwicke—age thirty-five—arrived for rehearsal *without* aging makeup, Hammerstein was taken aback. In his 1932 memoir *Let's Pretend*, Hardwicke expressed how foreign *Show Boat* felt to him. "Most of the things I had to say seemed pointless—the humour being American."[12] Hardwicke, who became good friends with Robeson, also related backstage anecdotes from Drury Lane, which speak to the cultural divide separating the New York and London stages as expressed in the performance of racial types:

> A troupe of coloured girls representing Mississippi villagers had been brought to Drury Lane from New York at great trouble and expense. They distinguished themselves at the dress rehearsal by appearing with white make-ups! Oscar Hammerstein's consternation can be imagined. Later, when performances had actually started, I noticed several of them standing in the wings and holding their arms high in the air. They had seen the English girls of the chorus doing this before they went on, but did not realize that the object was to drain the blood from the arms and thus make them look whiter.[13]

Some London critics articulated how the American story limited black performers already known to the audience. A contributor to *The Bystander* writing under the pseudonym "Jingle" also pointed out how even in a story of the color line, talent could win out:

> Negroes, as we know, take their choruses with something like religious fervor, and the whole-hearted opening of the Mississippi singers is an entrancing performance. Indeed, when the lovely young ladies of the usual chorus take up the running they seem commonplace by comparison. In the late Eighteen-eighties the colour-line on the Mississippi would naturally be drawn with some severity. . . . The sharp distinction of colour operates in the present instance a little quaintly, since the negro artists,

however distinguished, must necessarily represent persons of menial status in the play. For instance, that admirable actress, Miss Alberta Hunter, is no more than the native cook on the Show Boat; while even an actor of rare quality of Mr. Paul Robeson must not be regarded as the equal of 'white trash,' but may be nothing more than a Man with a Duster. It is a nice irony that Mr. Robeson takes the house by storm with his first appearance, and from that moment becomes the dominating personality of the Show.[14]

Alberta Hunter's role in the London *Show Boat* remains difficult to uncover. She described auditioning for Hammerstein and pretending she could dance when he asked, then quickly learning how.[15] She also praised Butt for helping her remain in London when her visa ran out.[16] Hunter appointed herself something of a welcoming committee for the *Show Boat* black cast, inviting the newly arrived ladies of the black dancing chorus to her house within minutes of their arrival in London.[17] But how Hunter played the role of Queenie remains a mystery. She wasn't part of the recording sessions that captured the Drury Lane cast, so her approach to "Can't Help Lovin' Dat Man" cannot be compared to recordings by Morgan, Gardella, and Burke. Archival evidence suggests Hunter didn't do much singing in the Drury Lane production. Her verse in "Can't Help Lovin' Dat Man" was given to Robeson. In fragmentary reminiscences preserved in her private papers, Hunter wrote "Me and my chorus girls we [sic] doing a number in *Show Boat*, called 'C'mon Folks' ['Queenie's Ballyhoo'] and because it was such a big hit up high in the show the star had the number taken out."[18] "Hey, Feller" was also omitted, which effectively left Hunter with no musical role whatsoever, perhaps the reason reviewers hardly mentioned her. Hunter regularly sent open letters chronicling her European career to black newspapers back in the States. In one of these missives, reprinted in the *Pittsburgh Courier*, Hunter touted her credentials as "the only colored woman who was ever signed to play a principal role in a Ziegfeld show."[19] A tireless self-promoter, she was unlikely to have admitted to the reduced size of Queenie's part. Hunter's achievement—the first black woman to play Queenie—appears to have been a symbolic victory.

The American black press took an interest in *Show Boat*'s London arrival. Ostensibly speaking for black American expatriates, the assertive critic J. A. Rogers dismissed the show as "a regrettable bit of American niggerism introduced into Europe" and took Robeson personally to task for "singing 'nigger, nigger' before all those white people."[20] But Rogers was in the minority. Most black newspapers followed *Show Boat* in London because black performers were always of interest to their readers. With Robeson as the star, *Show Boat* could, on occasion, reveal powerful whites in a position of need relative to famous blacks, a narrative with irresistible appeal. For example, the October 1928 *Opportunity* collated a series of newspaper articles about Robeson's recent suspension by Actor's Equity for breaking his contract with the producer Caroline Dudley to appear in an all-black revue. (Robeson used a $500 advance from Dudley to finance his and Brown's visit to France in October 1927, just when *Show Boat* went into rehearsal.)

The tale of Robeson's suspension adds detail to the singer's relationship with Ziegfeld, who, for a time, talked of opening a second *Show Boat* on Broadway. *Opportunity* quoted Ziegfeld (from the *New York World*):

> My only reason for producing a second company of *Show Boat* was the fact that I counted upon Paul Robeson as a tremendous attraction who would have made the twin company certain to play to capacity for a year at least. He was the first principal engaged for the original *Show Boat* company at the Ziegfeld Theatre and I let him go to London to sing for Sir Alfred Butt at Drury Lane. He was to return to me for the twin *Show Boat* company but now that Equity's suspension has eliminated him from my cast and prevents him from returning to this country to work under my contract I have to abandon my plan of another *Show Boat* production which would have given employment to 160 artists. I had already signed many principals all of whom feel that Equity's suspension of Paul Robeson has worked them a great injury.[21]

Butt made almost identical claims regarding Robeson's value to the London *Show Boat* when an injunction threatened to pull the singer from the show. Butt's lawyers argued, "the defendant took a leading part in the *Show Boat*, and if he were withdrawn there was a probability that the piece might have to be taken off, causing large numbers of persons to be thrown out of employment."[22] Ziegfeld and Butt shared a confidence in Robeson's ability to carry *Show Boat* by attracting the white audience in sizable numbers. Of course, Ziegfeld and Butt may just have been making producer's arguments against union intervention—that's how Equity took it—but black readers would register that the grand plans of these white theatrical heavyweights rested on Robeson's participation.

Robeson had initially played coy with Ziegfeld, refusing the second company offer and signing on to play Crown in *Porgy* for the Theatre Guild instead. In a letter, Eslanda described the decision as an act of desperation that had an immediate positive impact on daily life: "He has had the job [in *Porgy*] just two weeks, and we are now beginning to eat again."[23] Once more, Robeson resisted Ziegfeld's *Show Boat* as a Broadway showcase for his unique talents.

Ziegfeld's second company never panned out; perhaps in the producer's mind it all rested on Robeson finally saying yes to Joe, which the singer did only when Butt, a trusted London producer, was involved. Ziegfeld sent Robeson a congratulatory telegram on the night of the London opening reading "Best Wishes for Great Success Regards Ziegfeld."[24] Figure 6.1 captures Robeson in London in 1928 striking a thoughtful, even brooding pose as Joe.

After quoting an Equity spokesman on the specifics of the case, revealing along the way that Robeson was the first black to be a senior member of the union, *Opportunity* turned to an African American source for an insider's perspective—Eslanda Robeson as quoted in the *New York Amsterdam News*. "In March [1928] Mr. Robeson took the role of Crown in *Porgy* [still running on Broadway], but found it too much of a strain on his voice to sing above the other singers in the storm scene. . . . The actor's vocal experience in *Porgy* caused a serious doubt to enter Mr. Robeson's mind in regard to his

6.1. *A brooding Paul Robeson as Joe in a studio shot taken during the run of the first London* Show Boat *in 1928. (Photofest)*

appearance in the revue where, it was now revealed, the singing of the blues song would probably injure his voice. Then, also, Mr. Robeson was most unhappy over the prospect of singing the spirituals in a revue and that to do so would react unfavorably upon his state of mind and thus deprive his audience of his best efforts." Eslanda defended Robeson's actions on practical and artistic grounds: the need to protect both his voice and the artistic seriousness of his spiritual singing. Without either he would be putting at risk the core elements of his attraction for audiences, fundamentally endangering his career. Robeson's resistance to Dudley's revue—his distaste for mixing spirituals with commercial entertainment—speaks to his unwillingness to take the role of Joe in 1927.

In correspondence, Robeson's laid out in practical terms why he was, finally, willing to play Joe. He accepted the role in London because of its light demands on his voice and because appearing in *Show Boat* would facilitate the concert work he was after. *Show Boat* in London had the potential to financially support the Robesons while Paul pursued other goals. In a series of letters attempting to lure his accompanist Lawrence Brown to London for a series of recitals, Eslanda and Paul both emphasized how after singing Joe eight times a week Robeson had plenty of voice left over for concerts. Eslanda wrote first, in March:

> Now we have thot [sic] out this European concert thing pretty thoroly [sic] and it seems it is beautifully solved: Ziegfeld wants Paul to sing the part of "Joe" in the London production of *Show Boat*, beginning the first part of May. Alfred Butts [sic] is putting the show on there. If Paul accepts this part, he will of course reserve his concert rights, and all the time the play is in London he doesn't see why [Walter K.] Varney [Robeson's impresario in Europe] can't put on Sunday night concerts, in a suitable *theatre*, not a concert hall, and also arrange for concerts Sunday in all the good towns in England. The part is [sic] *Show Boat* is a ridiculously easy one,—he would sing the song hit of the show, "Old Man River," and it wouldn't tax his voice as much as a rehearsal. Also, Butts wants to practically star him, and do a great deal of special publicity around him,—so you see the situation seems made to order. . . . And there is always the chance that if *Show Boat* is a hit, as it surely will be, and Paul is the favorite, you and he may easily and speedily become the vogue in London and clean up, not only on Sunday nights but also in private engagements; for Paul could do as many of those as Varney could get, after the show evenings. And the play is opening at the height of the season, when every one [sic] is in London,—Court and all. . . . There is the situation. It seems grand to me.[25]

After arriving in London, Robeson continued courting Brown, sending several letters echoing Eslanda's argument and promising "I'll guarantee you a livelihood out of my salary—which is only fair. But I took this job only because it brought me back to my concerts with you and at the same time will give us something to live on while things are taking shape. You see I am only singing in this play and not enough to tire me. It's really made to order."[26]

When the part of Joe finally met his criteria, Robeson was happy to play it. Refusing Ziegfeld's offer for the second company, even when in dire economic straits, the Robesons assented to *Show Boat* in a context they liked and when doing so served other ends. For the Robesons, *Show Boat* was always to be a short-term expedient. Eslanda wrote to Brown in February 1929—the Drury Lane run winding down after almost ten months—"Paul is sick to death of *Show Boat* and will kick up his heels with glee when its [sic] over."[27]

Eslanda's point about not wanting to mix spirituals and revues surfaces between the lines of these letters. The Robesons surely must have gone to see the original production of *Show Boat* at the Ziegfeld. (Eslanda, in particular, was an avid theatergoer.) They knew and socialized with Bledsoe and must have known many in the black chorus as well. In early 1928, the Robesons were able to assess *Show Boat* and the role of Joe in a way they could not have done in 1927 during the rehearsal and tryout process, when Robeson would have been beholden to others, expected to do whatever was needed to make the show succeed. He probably never saw a copy of the script that didn't include the Robeson recital: it was cut definitively only after he sailed for France. Looking at a finished show—one in which Bledsoe was garnering solid applause—Robeson felt able to say yes. Here was a role introduced by another black man that Robeson could take over and make his own, doing to Bledsoe what he had done to Gilpin in the analogous case of *Emperor Jones*. (Robeson later starred in film versions of both.) Robeson detailed the content of Joe for Brown this way: "I sing only one song—Ol' Man River—but it runs all thru the show and I get 3 good spots for it—I'll get a lot of publicity."[28] Robeson's assessment was prescient. Joe has never failed to be a standout part: those "3 good spots" have proven to be plenty of exposure for the black man singing the role.

In *Paul Robeson, Negro*, Eslanda reduced the London *Show Boat* to a short chapter and credited Butt alone with bringing Paul into the show. Butt, according to Eslanda, "built 'Ol' Man River,' which Jerome Kern had dedicated to [Paul], into the theme song of the play."[29] Eslanda tells a selective story, although she may have thought Kern dedicated the song to Robeson as the words "Dedicated to Paul Robeson" appear on the sheet music as published in London. (The U.S. edition lacks any dedication, with the words "Joe and Male Chorus" under the title.) All three uses of "Ol' Man River" and its deployment as the "theme song of the play" stem not from Butt but from Hammerstein's original Robeson plan (see chap. 2). Eslanda gives Hammerstein no credit for structuring *Show Boat* around Robeson's talents.

Some changes were made for Robeson at Drury Lane, again preserved in Stamper's vocal score. Robeson sang "Ol' Man River" in B-flat, a whole step lower than the printed key, and his act 2 reprise of the entire chorus of "Ol' Man River" is marked "Three Times." "Can't Help Lovin' Dat Man" is similarly marked "3rd rept. Encore," extending Robeson's time on stage by simple repetition. He was also given Queenie's solo verse in "Can't Help Lovin' Dat Man." Stamper carefully changed all the personal pronouns, turning Queenie's complaint "Mah man is shiftless" into Joe's declaration "Your man is shiftless," achieving the imperative to "feature Paul Robeson" in the number with dispatch.

Hammerstein also wanted to add a new solo for Robeson. His efforts did not meet with success, but the lyricist made certain his plan to articulate a different side of Joe's character survived in print. Hammerstein included a lyric titled "Me an' My Boss" in his 1949 collection *Lyrics*, noting that it had been written for Robeson and the London production some twenty years earlier, then set aside in favor of a reprise of "Ol' Man River."[30] No music survives. Perhaps Kern never composed a tune for Hammerstein's lyric: the pair normally worked in reverse order, with Kern providing a tune to which Hammerstein added words. "Me an' My Boss" is not a spiritual, and it does not fall within any other category of black musical theater songs. The lyric is a political statement—a polemic using effective rhetorical strategies to argue for racial equality based on the most basic of human attributes: both the singer and his boss are born and die. Like "Ol' Man River," the lyric addresses an undefined listener, although "Me an' My Boss" only makes sense if the implied audience is white. Joe declares that he and his boss are the same— "no different"—except for their taste in food and the reality of segregation faced by the black man. Hammerstein even incorporated the term "Jim Crows," a remarkable word choice that moved the song across an invisible line of sorts. "Me an' My Boss" gives Joe the voice of an activist for racial equality. Although written in black popular song dialect, the sentiments are striking, undeniably confrontational, and fully engaged in larger efforts to address endemic racial discrimination. Where Hammerstein imagined inserting "Me an' My Boss" into the fabric of *Show Boat* is difficult to tell. The preservation of the poem in *Lyrics* suggests this attempt to deepen Joe's character and complicate *Show Boat*'s political content was important to Hammerstein, whose vision for the show consistently pushed at the limits of the permissible performance of race on the musical stage. How Robeson felt about "Me an' My Boss"—if, indeed, he ever saw it—remains unknowable.

Robeson's impact in the role of Joe quickly became the stuff of legend. London critics hailed him as the star of the production: "[H]is stage personality has that aspect of bigness which makes him a friend despite the intervening footlights"; "[H]is performance is worth all the money you will pay for admission."[31] An elaborate caricature of the production printed in *The Sketch* (see fig. 6.2) put Robeson at the top, hovering over the show like a sorrowing angel. The impact of "Ol' Man River" was underwritten visually by putting the lyric on the show curtain that greeted audience members when they entered Drury Lane. James Agate in the *Sunday Times* wrote "It is typical of this piece that Mr. Robeson, magnificent actor, exquisite singer, and a man cut out in such pattern as Michael Angelo [*sic*] might have designed, should be given nothing whatever to do except dodder about with a duster." Agate continued, "Criticism should be constructive, so let me suggest that half an hour should be cut out of the show and filled in by Mr. Robeson with his 'Steal Away,' 'Water Boy,' and other negro spirituals."[32] Hammerstein and Ziegfeld's reaction to Agate's idea would be interesting to know: it sounds a lot like "A Paul Robeson Recital." Robeson surely registered something of the irony surrounding the remark as well.

And just as they had planned, Robeson and Brown began to give concerts in London during the run of *Show Boat*. The largest of these took over Drury Lane itself. Billed as "A Paul Robeson Afternoon," Robeson and Brown appeared with the Drury Lane Orchestra conducted by Hermann Finck. Everyone involved—excluding Brown—also appeared in *Show Boat*. The same Harry T. Burleigh text about the origins of the spiritual was reprinted in the program, along with an ad for—of course—*Show Boat*. The concert began with the orchestra playing the final movement of Dvořák's *New World Symphony* that includes the "Goin' Home" melody, followed by Robeson and Brown in two sets: the first, spirituals, the second, folk songs and spirituals. Part 2 opened with the orchestra playing Samuel Coleridge-Taylor's *Danse Negre*, followed by a "Selection of Melodies from *Show Boat*." Sometimes called the "African Mahler," Coleridge-Taylor was a well-known English-born composer of mixed racial heritage who had died in 1912 but still enjoyed a popular reputation. The "Selection" from *Show Boat* may have been the overture. If so, Kern's "Mis'ry" music would have made a nice pendant to the Dvořák that opened the concert, with Coleridge-Taylor's symphonic dance adding yet a third sort of orchestral music drawing on black themes. Robeson and Brown returned for two more groups of four spirituals each. An annotated copy of the program in the Victoria and Albert Museum Theatre Collection lists the encores, a central part of the Robeson-Brown recital experience.

6.2. *When Londoners thought of* Show Boat, *they chiefly thought of Robeson. This drawing by Bryan de Grineau for* The Sketch *(May 16, 1928) positions Robeson at the top as a saintlike presence bearing a musical message of truth—untouched by ragtime or jazz—from the heart of the black American experience. De Grineau annotated the drawing with references to the various theatrical genres* Show Boat *suggested: from the quasi-Shakespearean romance of Magnolia and Ravenal's balcony duet to the melodrama of Julie as "The Bloodsucker's Bride" to the farce of Andy's New Year's Eve. The history of entertainment is evoked in*

Seven encores were sprinkled throughout the concert. The last—closing the program—was "Ol' Man River."[33]

At least three "Paul Robeson Afternoons" were given.[34] The reaction of the London press was, if anything, more breathless than the American reviewers (see chap. 2). James Douglas in the *Daily Express* went farther than most, producing a narrative of his experience at the first concert that was reprinted in full in subsequent programs. Douglas fairly gushed:

> I went into Drury Lane Theatre to hear Paul Robeson singing negro spirituals. For nearly two hours he transfigured the packed house of worldlings with mystical emotion. We sat there in a trance of noiseless ecstasy as he touched our heart-strings with his marvelous voice.
>
> He is more than a great actor and a great singer. He is a great man, who creates the soul of a people in bondage, and shows you its true kinship with the fettered soul of man. We became like little children as we surrendered to his magical genius.
>
> We laughed and wept. He broke our hearts with beauty. As he wiped the tears from his eyes we wiped the tears from ours. He shook some of us into sobs. We applauded until we were weary, and we made him sing till he was weary. I have never seen a more unsated and unsatisfied audience.
>
> What is the secret of his mastery of all our highest moods and all our holiest emotions? He stands there in a plain tweed suit, holding a piece of paper in his two immobile hands. Not a gesture. He is a giant, an athlete, a Rugby player, and a man of culture. . . .
>
> His songs are the Bible as we heard it at our mother's knee. They are the mother-songs of mankind, the hidden songs that all men and women hear whispering in their buried memory. It is not only the dreaming negro soul that yearns in these cumulative refrains. It is the sad soul of humanity reaching out into the mystery of life and death. . . .
>
> I have heard all the great singers of our time. No voice has ever moved me so profoundly with so many passions of thought and emotion. The marvel is that there is no monotony in the spiritual spell. It is effortless enchantment moving through fluctuant states of thought and feeling.

---

references to vaudeville, music hall, and the "modern broadcast play." At the center of the image, de Grineau imagined how viewing the Cotton Blossom *play-within-the-play from Drury Lane's dress circle might carry the audience back to the glory days of the venerable old theater. (© Illustrated London News Ltd/Mary Evans)*

As the house was swept along the path of prophecy I knew that, as a people, we are mystical to the core, and that even the worldliest worldling is capable of being captured by the great, good simplicities of religious faith. . . .

Strange that a negro singer out of "Show Boat" should be able to fill a vast theatre with the divine witchery of Bunyan and Wesley, and reveal to astonished worldlings the world beyond their world.[35]

Douglas (and many others) experienced Robeson as a revelation, a black voice that could touch the white soul, a breath of spiritual authenticity in the secular confines of the theater and concert hall. Robeson's persona as a powerful black figure with the potential to impact white audiences in an almost spiritual manner is hardwired into *Show Boat*. Every African American bass who has taken the role has been—to some extent—impersonating Robeson, hopefully tapping into his peculiar effect on white audiences. The effect is not transcendent so much as historically grounded in a particular desire by white audiences to have an experience with blackness, mediated by a strong black man singing music of a certain kind. This desire would not abate and would help sustain *Show Boat* down to the present.

In an exchange of letters and telegrams discussing possible collaborations for the 1931–32 Broadway season, Ziegfeld suggested to Hammerstein and Kern that a *Show Boat* revival with Robeson and "an interesting cast" might succeed with the public.[36] This would come to fruition in spring 1932, but before settling on the expedient choice of simply reviving *Show Boat*—at the time a rather unusual decision—Kern and Hammerstein offered a new idea: a *Show Boat* sequel. Hammerstein wrote to Ziegfeld, "Jerry had, what I consider, a wonderful idea in writing a sequel to *Show Boat* with Kim playing the lead and Robeson playing old Joe's son, now a successful concert singer. I think this is a germ of a great idea and since Edna Ferber would have to come in on it any way, having created the character, I should think she might be interested in writing the book herself."[37] And so the old popular music plot from 1927 remained in Kern and Hammerstein's thoughts, their one-sentence summary sounding like nothing so much as the original plan for act 2. Ziegfeld replied two days later; he thought the idea was "terrific."[38]

BROADWAY, 1932

Robeson finally consented to play Joe on Broadway in the 1932 revival. He had played the role to tremendous, indeed historic acclaim in London from May 3, 1928, to March 2, 1929, the full length of the run. In New York,

Robeson would leave the production before it closed and would not go on tour with Morgan and several other returning original cast members. Robeson's acquiescence to *Show Boat* in New York was short and marked by a strategic use of "Ol' Man River" in his concertizing. Once again, Robeson made *Show Boat* work for him.

Robeson had followed the Drury Lane *Show Boat* with a personal triumph: he played the title role in *Othello* in the West End, the sort of project that met his criteria for high-quality theater that uplifted the race. One London critic called him "the greatest Negro living."[39] However, the American critic Burns Mantle attacked Robeson's *Othello*, saying he hoped it never came to the United States. (It wouldn't until 1943.) Indeed, *Show Boat* would be Robeson's sole Broadway credit between *Black Boy* (1926) and the ill-fated black-cast musical *John Henry* (1940), which lasted only seven performances.

Mantle's reaction to Robeson's Othello underlined the relative safety of Joe as a noncontroversial, musical role that American audiences would accept from Robeson. Joe was also a role that overlapped with Robeson's concert persona, which he and Brown cultivated with renewed energy in the States beginning in early 1931. One change in their concerts dating to this period was the addition of "Ol' Man River" to the printed program. At a Carnegie Hall appearance in January 1931, Robeson closed his official program with "Ol' Man River" for the first time.[40] It would remain part of his printed repertory—almost always programmed last—through the mid-1930s. The Robeson-Brown concerts were always understood to be a mix of programmed songs, requests, and announced encores. Listing "Ol' Man River" in the program granted the song legitimacy as an expression of Negro identity—every other song he regularly sang was a folk song or spiritual arrangement understood to be authentic.[41] A Philadelphia critic noted the importance of the song for Robeson's impact: "it was [with] the popular "Old Man River," [*sic*], which he sang in *The Show Boat* [*sic*], that he most noticeably moved his hearers. Tears were in many eyes as he ended the philosophical plaint of the slave who was 'tired of living' and scared of dyin',' and the house rang long with applause."[42] At another concert, Robeson was "compelled by the sheer force of a tremendous ovation to sing the famous classic of the Mississippi River, *Show Boat*, first as an encore and later in the program, a second time."[43] Any recital appearance by Robeson in the early 1930s —he sang to capacity crowds at Town Hall four times in the four months prior to the 1932 *Show Boat* opening—was certain to include "Ol' Man River."

When Robeson stepped forward as Joe to sing "Ol' Man River" in the Broadway revival at the Casino Theatre beginning on May 19, 1932, the New York audience had been well prepared. Their reaction, recalled by Ferber in

1939, validated Kern, Hammerstein, and Ziegfeld's instincts about using Robeson all along. Ferber wrote, "I witnessed a New York first-night audience, after Paul Robeson's singing of Ol' Man River, shout and cheer and behave generally as I've never seen an audience behave in any theatre in all my years of playgoing."[44] In the *New York Times* that day, Ziegfeld promoted the show with a very specific promise: "Hear Paul Robeson sing 'Ol' Man River.'" The contrast with Ziegfeld's (non)promotion of Bledsoe in 1927 is marked, but conditions had changed. Now, more than ever, *Show Boat* needed Robeson. *Variety* singled him out as the production's "ballyhooed feature."[45] Robeson, alone, was a reason to go see *Show Boat* again.

And Robeson sang on his off days, just as he had at Drury Lane. On a Sunday evening in July, he appeared at Lewisohn Stadium, splitting the program with Albert Coates and the New York Philharmonic-Symphony Orchestra. Robeson, accompanied by Brown, sang five songs, ending, of course, with "Ol' Man River," which was greeted with "great enthusiasm," leading to the inevitable fifteen minutes of encores and requests.[46]

With Prohibition winding down, press furor over Helen Morgan could not be relied upon to generate business as it had in 1928 and 1929. Still, Morgan remained a draw, and Ziegfeld promoted the show by highlighting Robeson and Morgan together in a "miniature likeness of the show" on his new radio program a few weeks before opening.[47] Figure 6.3 registers one newspaper cartoonist's sense for how the leads stacked up against each other: Morgan the most prominent; Robeson smaller but definitely at her level; Terris and the new Ravenal, Dennis King, competing for the bottom. Stirling Bowen of the *Wall Street Journal* greeted the show in no uncertain terms as belonging to Robeson and Morgan, beginning his review with a claim that two songs alone could redeem the desultory situation on Broadway in 1932: "No season could seem altogether lost with Paul Robeson singing 'Ole Man River,' and Helen Morgan singing 'Bill' again."[48] Burns Mantle noted how on opening night Robeson, "in grand voice, and modestly fine as usual, was forced to take the usual three or four encores with 'Ol' Man River' and follow these with a scene call."[49] Morgan also stopped the show, Mantle reported. Julie remained Morgan's property in the United States for the remainder of the 1930s, even though once Prohibition officially ended just months after the 1932 *Show Boat* closed, the resonance of her performance began to change.

Katherine Axtell has examined the revival in detail, situating it within a fragile Broadway context and arguing persuasively that for Ziegfeld "the 1932 *Show Boat* revival more nearly resembles a final bid for maintenance of the status quo than an exercise in nostalgia."[50] The decision to set the final scene in 1932 rather than 1927, which allowed Terris to make her imitations

6.3. Helen Morgan, looking positively chic and completely up-to-date, dominates this caricature of the 1932 Ziegfeld revival cast. Robeson, appearing in New York for the first and only time in the role of Joe, peeks in from the side, while the new Ravenal (Dennis King) and the original Magnolia (Norma Terris) make do with the bottom. The relative importance of each player for the Broadway audience is reflected in their respective sizes and position. (Author's collection)

completely up to date, supports this view. Ziegfeld died several months into the run. At the Saturday matinee after his death, *Show Boat* paused for a minute of silence midway through act 1, scene 1.[51] A symbolic lowering of the curtain and dimming of the house lights marked the beginning of the end for *Ziegfeld's Show Boat*. Ziegfeld's Broadway was largely gone but *Show Boat* would continue on, remade by other producers, few with Ziegfeld's priorities or resources.

Robeson left *Show Boat* six weeks before its October closing. The *Pittsburgh Courier* reported him sailing for Europe—his "purpose vague . . . in quest of material for a new show for the New York winter season, but it is not clear why he should go on such a quest while he is still in good standing with the producers of *Show Boat* and the future of the production is so promising."[52] He was also making a lot of money. At $1,500 a week Robeson was the highest paid cast member: Morgan made $1,250; Winninger and King $1,000 each; Puck and White shared $1,250; Terris and Gardella both $500.[53] The *Courier* speculated that domestic problems might be the reason Robeson was taking off in the middle of his triumph. Eslanda had remained in London, and rumors of Robeson's affair with the wealthy white socialite Nancy Cunard were everywhere. Robeson's understudy Robert Raines took over, and the producer A. C. Blumenthal, who assumed responsibility for the production after Ziegfeld's death, opened negotiations with Bledsoe, who was holding out for more money. Bledsoe returned to *Show Boat* for the tour and would later join Winninger and the Hall Johnson Choir on the initial season of the *Maxwell House Show Boat* radio variety show.[54] Bledsoe and the choir remained with the program through the following January, a rare permanent spot for black performers on a radio show.[55] With major triumphs as Joe in London and New York, Robeson had proven he could use *Show Boat* for his own purposes, but clearly he bored easily with the role. When he took the part in Hollywood some years later, he forced the production schedule to minimize his time on the set and, once again, took off as soon as he could.

By contrast, Morgan clung to *Show Boat*, staying with the tour long after all other principals from the Broadway cast had left. The tour began with two weeks in Boston, followed by one-week stands in Philadelphia, Washington, Baltimore, and Pittsburgh.[56] Bledsoe left the tour over salary issues after the week in Baltimore.[57] Then came Cincinnati, which saw profitability fall to the point where salary cuts were required and leading players such as Terris, Puck, and White departed. The *Chicago Defender* let black readers know that the Harlem cabaret entertainer Ethel Moses, part of the dancing chorus, had also left the show over salary cuts.[58] Morgan remained as the headliner. After a two-week hiatus, which saw a reduction of the black chorus from sixty to sixteen and similar cuts in the white chorus, *Show Boat* played Cleveland and Detroit for a week each, followed by three weeks at Chicago's Auditorium Theatre where astute discounting kept the show alive. A proposed swing through the South was always unlikely, mostly because finding housing and food would be a major difficulty for a large group of black performers. Black bands or vaudeville acts could slip in and out of southern cities, but a black chorus singing "Niggers all work on de Mississippi" at the largest theater in town would be a clear target. Morgan's biographer writes that the southern trip was aborted when *Show Boat*'s black cast members threatened to leave the show over the planned journey.[59] At this point, Hammerstein's assistant Leighton Brill arrived with instructions from the lyricist on how to turn *Show Boat* into a ninety-minute "tab" show, fit for playing between screenings of feature films at movie palaces in Chicago, Cleveland, Brooklyn, and, finally, at the Capitol Theatre in the heart of Times Square, one block from where it began at the Casino.

While the tour was in Cleveland, Morgan reportedly threw a party for the black chorus at a club where Louis Armstrong was appearing. (Morgan herself sang two weeks at Cleveland's Mounds Club.) Armstrong supposedly ordered in an upright piano for Morgan to sit on after she pointed out that he was using a grand.[60] This apocryphal story—told by Morgan's adoring but not altogether trustworthy biographer in the 1970s—hints at the interracial conviviality that was always possible behind the scenes in any production of *Show Boat*. For if black and white were mostly segregated onstage, in the liminal world of the wings and dressing rooms there were few such barriers. A photo of Edna May Oliver arm in arm with Jules Bledsoe backstage on Christmas Eve 1928 (see fig. 4.2, chap. 4) hints at how casts of *Show Boat* might have interacted in ways that could not be pictured onstage or in the papers. Such interactions are lost to history.

The stop in Chicago was greeted by the *Defender* in diffident terms: "*Show Boat*, written and staged as a sentimental romance with mixed cast settings, is now nothing more than a musical comedy with all save the 'Black and Tan' background missing."[61] But the *Defender* still found reasons for the black audience to go, principally a new Joe—Robert Raines, the Broadway understudy still hanging on to the part—and Angelica Lawson as Queenie. The *Defender* critic wondered "how the cast moved along without" Lawson, an acknowledgement of the importance of the role and, perhaps, the rightness of the character now that an African American was playing the part. The link between Gardella's Aunt Jemima persona and Queenie as a character was severed here. From Lawson on—with the exception of a wartime London *Show Boat* featuring the Australian variety star Lucille Benstead in blackface—Queenie would be adjusted to fit a range of black women performers, each of whom brought her own performing persona to the role while, inevitably, working within the possibilities and limitations set down around Gardella.

The *Defender* review of the 1933 tour on its last legs provides a sober alternative to the New York first-night reviewers who had hailed *Show Boat* as a classic the previous May. Here, the residual value of the show for black audiences is unsentimentally assessed. A good (new) Joe, a good (black) Queenie, a good dancing chorus (albeit with nothing "really worthwhile to perform"): these might be attraction enough for some. As for the substance of *Show Boat*'s story, the *Defender* offered a subtle position: take it or leave it depending on your stomach for such things but in the run of white-made race shows, *Show Boat* wasn't the worst and even had some human values worth appreciating:

> Truly *Show Boat* doesn't strike solidly as offensive to my Race as some will likely contend. What it does toward pointing out racial identity is cleverly put and artistically done. It has all of the cracks contained in *White Cargo* and the peculiar Southern customs of King Vidor's picture *Hallelujah*, but the producer was more human in his presentation of those angles that have to do with the Race. Our idea is if you liked *Hallelujah* or either of the *Cargoes* then see another piece that is more cleverly put and less offensive than those two, but similar in many respects.

Hammerstein deserves credit here as the "producer" of the elements given qualified praise. The phrase "racial identity" proves a striking anticipation of the ways *Show Boat* would be analyzed in later decades, showing yet again that the voices of black newspaper critics must be heard if a complete picture of how *Show Boat* was understood in the past is to be gained. Questions asked by scholars of the recent past and present about race and the musical stage were there all along for the African American audience who saw clearly the stake they had in *Show Boat*'s portrayal of the American racial landscape.

Morgan stayed with the *Show Boat* tour to the bitter end. She also played Julie in the 1936 film and 1940 Los Angeles production. Morgan died of alcoholism-related illnesses in 1941. Upon her death there was immediate interest in making a film of her life story. Morgan's mother and husband (of several months only at her passing) asked $100,000 for her name and story, but the sticking point was rights to the songs from *Show Boat*. MGM owned the cinematic rights to *Show Boat* and its score, and the studio wasn't about to release Morgan's signature tunes and a prestige name like *Show Boat* for a bio pic about a notorious if sympathetic figure from the Jazz Age who had never worked on their lot. Indeed, MGM had other plans for *Show Boat* that would do much to erase the memory of Morgan in the part.

When the nascent television industry took up Morgan's story, *Show Boat* was hardly mentioned, but Kern's music was everywhere. In a 1957 *Playhouse 90* drama called "Helen Morgan" starring Polly Bergen in the title role, Morgan's story was told as if by her mother, Lulu.[62] Drink is Morgan's escape and downfall in this maudlin tale of the father who abandoned her, the married lover who stole her best years only to break her heart, the immature younger man she married in a drunken stupor and wisely let go, and the baby she adopted only to have the child wrested from her. Only about half of these stories were even partly true. Morgan sings "Bill" to her married lover, but the most interesting use of music comes with the incorporation of the melancholy descending melody from "Mis'ry's Comin' Aroun'" (see ex. 5.1b). The melody returns whenever Morgan faces a choice between domestic love and stardom. A particularly poignant use comes when Morgan must give up the child she adopted. Talking to reporters, who circle her at every juncture, Morgan says "A Broadway star must make her choice between her art and domesticity" to the sad strains of the "Mis'ry" theme. The tune also plays at Morgan's death. Divorced of any associations with Julie's mixed-race predicament, Kern's haunting melody effectively underscores the cautionary teleplay of Morgan's life, counseling 1950s viewers of the perils of life on the wicked stage for a white icon of a lost era.

HOLLYWOOD, 1929 AND 1936

The uneven nature of the first *Show Boat* film reflects several shifts in strategy during its making. Carl Laemmle, chief of Universal Pictures, bought the rights to Ferber's novel in 1927. While preparing his cinematic *Show Boat*, Ziegfeld's *Show Boat* opened to wide acclaim, and all at once Laemmle had a problem. The novel, now confused in the public's mind with the Broadway musical, was no longer a stand-alone property. A *Show Boat* film without Kern and Hammerstein's score would be perceived as less than complete. Laemmle then negotiated a deal that allowed for Kern's tunes to be used by Joseph Cherniavsky in his orchestral score for the film, so "Ol' Man River" is heard prominently throughout. Laemmle also decided to accommodate the shift to synchronized sound dialogue. (*The Jazz Singer* opened in Times Square just weeks before *Show Boat* first played the Ziegfeld Theatre.) With shooting already well under way, Laemmle ordered "spoken passages" inserted into *Show Boat*.[63] This allowed for a further exploitation of the Ziegfeld connection: now Laemmle's Magnolia could sing songs by Hammerstein and Kern in the key scenes where she achieved stage success in Chicago. Building on the original application of synchronized sound as a means to present stage performers doing their specialties, Laemmle also added a musical prologue to his *Show Boat* featuring three original stars of the Broadway production: Helen Morgan singing "Bill" and "Can't Help Lovin' Dat Man" (the latter with a supporting black chorus), Jules Bledsoe singing "Ol' Man River" (with members of the black male chorus), and Tess Gardella singing "Hey, Feller!" (with men and women from the black singing chorus). These numbers were filmed in costume in New York during the original run in a presentational manner, with Ziegfeld himself introducing each performer. All but one number ("Bill") featured black performers, emphasizing the importance of the Jubilee Singers as a standout feature of the show. As noted earlier, Morgan's star power extended to her personal appearance at the film's gala premiere in Palm Beach.[64]

Seven years later, Universal made a second *Show Boat* film, this time an expensive movie musical produced by Carl Laemmle Jr. The screenwriter Zoe Akins wrote an initial script in 1934. She cut "Make Believe" and "You Are Love," incorporated "Creole Love Song," and had Ziegfeld appear at the close so that Kim could make her Broadway debut in *Show Boat* itself. Rejecting Akins's efforts, Laemmle hired Hammerstein to write a new screenplay.[65] The result, produced by Hammerstein in a rush during October and November 1935, preserved key elements of the original but departed from the stage version at the close. Kern and Hammerstein wrote three new songs as well. The chosen director James Whale was best known for making horror movies and had no background in musicals. Whale and Hammerstein consulted regularly by mail, and Leighton Brill, Hammerstein's assistant who had created Morgan's tab show version during the 1933 tour, went to Hollywood to work with the director during production. Brill received screen credit as "technical director." In chatty letters sent to Hammerstein just before shooting began, Brill referred to the studio as "the about-to-be-bankrupt-at-any-minute Universal."[66] Indeed, the Laemmles lost control of Universal just as shooting on *Show Boat* was closing. Whale's fifty-plus hours of footage were edited into the finished film under the new owners.

Morgan was signed for Julie but not without some second guessing: Hammerstein visited her in New York to make sure she looked all right.[67] Her contract required Morgan to reimburse the studio for the cost of a replacement should she prove unreliable.[68] When Morgan arrived in Hollywood, Brill wrote that he expected to see her soon, adding "I hope sober."[69] (Behind-the-scenes production stills show Morgan graciously sipping and serving tea.) Julie's role in the film is virtually unchanged from the stage version; Hammerstein gave Morgan the opportunity to commit her signature role to film in a sympathetic and accommodating context. Whale wanted to "elaborate [the] production" of "Bill." Hammerstein and Kern together counseled him to just let Morgan sing it "with that wistful, half-pathetic simplicity which is her virtue." But, they added, "Please whatever you do, please don't let her sit on the piano!"[70] She didn't. Whale gave Morgan an extreme close-up during the song and surrounded her with an in-film audience of folks from the Trocadero—including tearful scrubwomen—who witness her pouring out her soul in song. The care given "Bill" speaks to the song and the singer's iconic status.

Other elements of the show were, however, greatly altered by Hammerstein and Whale. Many changes had to do with the desire to emphasize the film's stars. Universal's budget sheets described the film as a vehicle for "Dunne-Jones-Robeson," the trio of Irene Dunne as Magnolia, Allan Jones as Ravenal, and Robeson as Joe.

Robeson was the cornerstone of the film aesthetically and practically (see fig. 6.4). Beyond expanding Joe's role and adding a song—the duet "Ah Still Suits Me" for Joe and Queenie—the entire production schedule was designed to accommodate Robeson's demands. Once again, Robeson demurred about taking the part of Joe. Under a headline that declared "Robeson Will Play Lead in *Show Boat*," the *Defender* delighted in reporting that Robeson had refused the role until Laemmle himself came to the phone on a transatlantic hookup.[71] Laemmle detailed "our Robeson obligation" to Hammerstein: "He reports here November 14th and on January 2nd he goes east by train to return to London for his engagement at Albert Hall."[72] Hammerstein, hurriedly writing the script, took the time to meet with Robeson to try to convince him to be more flexible on the dates. Robeson refused and Hammerstein wrote Laemmle he was "Working hard to get balance of script out to you."[73] The first half of the shooting schedule was effectively organized around Robeson's schedule. Robeson was paid $40,000 for ten weeks plus $3,000 travel expenses for himself and Eslanda to and from London.[74]

Once Robeson arrived and made a singing test, Brill told Hammerstein of a clamor to add more songs for him, "not alone Kern songs, but any and every Negro spiritual that has ever been heard."[75] Once again, finding a spot for Robeson to sing spirituals in *Show Boat* seemed the most obvious of obvious ideas. Laemmle offered Hammerstein advice on ending the film that also sounds familiar: "It seems to me that with such a terrific personality as Robeson and his magnificent voice it would [be] a very good ending to the picture to have Paul Robeson sing his new number possibly with a production chorus. Don't take this too literally but it just struck me that it might work in to

6.4. *Universal Pictures' effort to frame Robeson as a star posed challenges to the Hollywood system of racial separation. Here, Robeson's cross-racial sex appeal is made manifest in a posed publicity photo in which the singer offers himself to the ladies of the white chorus. A photo like this was genuinely unprintable in the American press. Why it was taken remains a mystery. (Photofest)*

the ending you already have in mind at the Ziegfeld theatre."[76] In the finished film, the white love story wraps up at a Broadway theater with the reunited Magnolia and Ravenal singing "You Are Love," then cuts to a shot of the Mississippi in the moonlight accompanied by Robeson's voice singing the final phrase of "Ol' Man River."

Irene Dunne's Hollywood career was initiated by her successful appearance as Magnolia in the 1929 tour. She went straight from forty weeks in *Show Boat* to RKO and quickly became a star of melodramatic women's pictures. Dunne was slated for the Universal *Show Boat* from 1933. Just after *Show Boat*, her career would turn toward screwball comedy, a move perhaps anticipated by the insertion of a blackface number for Magnolia and her shuffle dancing in "Can't Help Lovin' Dat Man," sequences of unrestrained racial caricature that, to this day, provoke reactions of surprise and resistance from many viewers. Dunne made a flat $100,000 for playing Magnolia—standard star salary in the 1930s.

Finding the right Ravenal proved difficult. After looking at an initial draft screenplay, Whale telegraphed Hammerstein with advice that hinted at anxiety about the way Ravenal might be presented as a suitably attractive singing leading man. Whale wrote, "SUGGEST RAVENAL HAS SINGING ENTRANCE WHICH WOULD SELL RAVENAL ON HIS VOICE BEFORE AUDIENCE CAN DISLIKE HIS FACE OR ACTING ABILITY."[77] Names suggested for the part included three handsome leading men who would require dubbing—Robert Taylor (Kern's suggestion), Frederic March (Dunne's idea), and Walter Pidgeon—and Nelson Eddy, the baritone on the cusp of his cycle with Jeanette MacDonald at MGM.[78] The tenor Allan Jones was engaged literally days before shooting began, his tests with Dunne showing he could look "very manly" in costume, according to Brill.[79] And, he was cheap at $20,000 for ten weeks. Dunne and Jones proved a winning combination. Kern and Hammerstein produced "I Have the Room Above Her" for the pair, a charming new duet spotted between "Make Believe" and "You Are Love." (Plans for a similar courtship duet had been in the works in 1927 but never came to fruition.[80]) "I Have the Room Above Her" reappeared on a few *Show Boat* studio-cast albums in the 1950s and, finally, onstage in the 1994 revival when state-of-the-art Broadway stagecraft allowed for the theatrical translation of the duet's cinematic, two-story concept. ("Why Do I Love You?," sung by the couple while driving in a newfangled motor car during their Chicago glory days, was shot then cut in the editing phase, when minimizing the film's overall length was the overarching priority.)

Filling out the cast was Charles Winninger as Andy and Helen Westley as Parthy. Winninger enlisted Whale's support, and the two prevailed upon Hammerstein to put Andy's lines about Parthy being "gone" at the climax of the wedding back into the script (which had originally not included the joke).[81] Shrewd character actors like Winninger knew where the substance of a part lay. Universal wanted Edna May Oliver, now a well-known film actress, to reprise Parthy, but she was slated to play the Nurse in MGM's *Romeo and Juliet*. Both Oliver and Westley had appeared as an elder figure to Dunne in earlier films: Oliver in *Cimarron* (1931) and *Ann Vickers* (1933); Westley in *The Age of Innocence* (1934) and *Roberta* (1935). While always a tough old bird unafraid to throw her weight around, Westley projected a good humor and ability to enjoy herself that was foreign to Oliver's snooty, superior, humorless persona. Hammerstein rewrote Parthy to Westley's more generous spirit, and the result had lasting utility. When Harold Prince wanted to develop Parthy emotionally for Elaine Stritch in 1994, he incorporated several dialogue sequences written with Westley in mind.

Universal briefly floated the idea of using Tess Gardella as Queenie and took the idea to the Production Code Authority (PCA). The issues were racial and sexual, as the Code enforcer Joseph Breen wrote to Universal: "I think you should be extremely careful, however, not to indicate any physical contact between the white woman and the negro man for the reason that many people know Aunt Jemima is a white woman and might be repulsed by the sight of her being fondled by a man who is a negro."[82] Instead of Gardella, Universal went with Hattie McDaniel, who had played Queenie onstage in Los Angeles in 1933.

The effort to expand the size of Joe's part led to an enlargement of Queenie's as well: McDaniel benefited from the desire to feature Robeson. Hammerstein added a dialogue scene for the pair just before "Ol' Man River," establishing a bickering relationship where a physically robust, hectoring Queenie accuses Joe of laziness. In the tradition of black vaudeville couples such as Butterbeans and Suzie, this relationship was implicit in Queenie's verse from "Can't Help Lovin' Dat Man," but Hammerstein and Kern made laziness fundamental to Joe's character with the addition of the duet "Ah Still Suits Me." This tune—in which Joe declares his comfort in his own skin—was put to use later in the film when Joe challenges the elements, singing it at the top of his lungs while rowing a doctor across a stormy Mississippi to attend at Kim's birth. Production stills preserve a cut scene for the now aged Joe and Queenie—McDaniel contentedly smoking a pipe—which featured a reprise of "Ol' Man River."

McDaniel played many mammy roles in Hollywood; both her later 1939 role in *Gone with the Wind* and Queenie in *Show Boat* stand out. In *Show Boat*, though, she has a husband—no less than Robeson—with whom she sings a duet that for all its bickering ends on a note of affection. Joe and Queenie's status as a functional married black couple, to some extent echoing Andy and Parthy's equally contentious but committed relationship, was unusual in the 1930s. And too, McDaniel's Queenie embodies a range of expression seldom granted Hollywood mammies. More than a mere servant, McDaniel participates in the drama, most crucially when Whale's camera seeks out the suspicion in her eyes when she walks in on Julie singing "Can't Help Lovin' Dat Man" (see fig. 6.5). Julie's precarious position concealing her racial identity from blacks as well as whites is highlighted, and along the way Queenie, a black servant, judges an outwardly white woman in a way few Hollywood stories allowed. But Queenie's look of suspicion is undercut later in the song, when a cut to McDaniel rolling her eyes in time to the song conjures up the worst of Hollywood's preservation of minstrel tropes in the 1930s.

With Robeson and McDaniel in the cast, *Show Boat* was already guaranteed to be a major event for black audiences. But Universal hoped to add another black star to the film: the tap dancer Bill "Bojangles" Robinson. Hammerstein's script included two dance features for Robinson. First, he would dance on the shores of the Mississippi among a group of "Negroes gathered by a fire in front

6.5. *Hattie McDaniel as Queenie looks with suspicion at Helen Morgan as Julie in a production still from the 1936 Universal Pictures* Show Boat, *a rare Hollywood scene where a black character openly judged a white. (Photofest)*

of tumbledown shacks, softly singing 'Got My Eye On You.'"[83] Spotted just before Magnolia and Ravenal meet at the water barrel and decide to get married, the sequence was described as "Dance number (if we have Bill Robinson)." Without Robinson, this feature would not survive, making the idea similar to the "Paul Robeson Recital" back in 1927. A second feature for Robinson followed shortly after, with him leading the levee dance "buck-and-wing" during the wedding. This idea to insert Robinson into *Show Boat* suggests once again how central black performance was to Hammerstein's conception of the story and the eagerness of Universal to load *Show Boat* up with black stars and styles. Robinson had danced in two period films set in the South to this point in his career, *The Little Colonel* (1935) and *The Littlest Rebel* (1935), both with Shirley Temple. In both films, Robinson played a house servant, bringing him nearer to genteel paradigms of white southern life; his upright tap style, a sophisticated idiom created in urban vaudeville houses and normally performed by Robinson in formal dress, anachronistically cast back in time. Hammerstein's proposed use of the dancer in *Show Boat* would have taken Robinson into a more low-down context—down along the river—where his signature style would have made even less sense. Robinson was hardly a buck-and-wing sort of dancer. But had Robinson appeared in the 1936 *Show Boat*, it's safe to say subsequent reception of the film would have been altered.

Hammerstein's script used the word "nigger" throughout: at the opening chorus (which was almost entirely cut in the final print), in descriptions of action, and in dialogue during the miscegenation scene as in the play text. The PCA recommended deleting all uses of the word, as Breen noted: "As you know, the expression 'nigger' has proven offensive to the colored race, and we have consistently avoided using it on the screen."[84] But Universal wasn't quite ready to cut every instance and replied to Breen, "The word, 'nigger,' will not be used in dialogue, but will have to be used in one or two of the songs where it comes in naturally."[85] This can only be a reference to "Ol' Man River." In the film, Robeson sings "darkies" instead of "niggers," his standard practice on recordings of the tune, although on one occasion he had recorded the original version.[86] With no objections raised by the PCA and Universal clearly wanting to preserve the word "niggers" in the lyrics, the force behind the change to "darkies" was perhaps Robeson himself.

Hammerstein, Whale, and Robeson all contributed to the film's high concept visualization of "Ol' Man River," a number all surely recognized had the potential to be the film's signature sequence. (Whale would write to Robeson after the first preview, "It seemed you were really there, and the spine-chilling effect of that one song I shall never forget."[87]) Robeson's first appearance in the film comes just before "Ol' Man River." Framed carrying a sack of flour, Whale moved the camera in on Robeson in a bold manner, anointing him the star of the film in the same way John Ford would visually emphasize John Wayne's first appearance in *Stagecoach* a few years later. This sudden camera movement is typical of Whale's *Show Boat*, which employs a sometimes overheated visual rhetoric. Extreme close-ups are frequently used, with Robeson, Morgan in "Bill," a profusely sweating Donald Cook as Steve in the miscegenation scene, and even an exasperated Mrs. O'Brien in the Ontario Street rooming house all getting the treatment.

When Robeson begins singing the verse of "Ol' Man River" while seated on a wharf and whittling, Whale swings the camera around him in a circular crane shot that captures Robeson's body as if the actor were a statue. (In fact, Robeson had been somewhat scandalously immortalized in a life-sized bronze nude by Salemme in the 1920s. The statue was lost during World War II.) The elaborate camera move is timed to the length of the verse, pulling in for a close-up just when the chorus begins and staying on Robeson to the midpoint of the first chorus. The idea for this visual treatment stems from Hammerstein's script, which describes the camera movement quite specifically: "During first eight measures of refrain swing camera around slowly to face Joe. Stay on him for balance of refrain." At the close of the number, Hammerstein advises Whale as to the scale of the image and Robeson as to the content of Joe's emotional state: "CLOSEUP JOE'S FACE Covering the entire screen, takes on a look of grim, but resigned suffering." Whale followed these instructions but Robeson did not. The singer undercuts the final seconds of "Ol' Man River" in two ways. First, he stops singing visually—alters the shape of his mouth—before his voice cuts off on the soundtrack (to which he was lip-synching). Second, he begins to smile, indeed to grin, utterly ignoring Hammerstein's suggestion Joe's face bear "a look of grim, but resigned suffering." Robeson sunders the illusion of Hollywood's sound/image relationship and steps out of character at the end of his big number. A publicity still showed Robeson and Whale posed together, looking intently at the script. If Robeson read the script closely, he elected to end "Ol' Man River" with a very different look than Hammerstein intended.[88]

It was Hammerstein's idea to cut away from Robeson singing "Ol' Man River" to images illustrating the lyrics, a highly unusual choice within the practices of Hollywood musical film. Whale liked the idea but substantially altered the content of the images spelled out in the script. Hammerstein called for "LONG SHOT BOATS Through Joe's face," "A Simon Legree figure. . . . Black mustache, thin, cruel lips, pale face. A whip swings casually from his wrist," and "Pickaninnies playing on the shore," as well as images of the river, and "tater" and cotton fields seen through superimposed images of Robeson's face. Whale wanted to focus more on Robeson himself, and Hammerstein agreed that "making him the central figure of the illustrative shots is ever so much better."[89] Whale exposed Robeson's naked torso, posing him carrying an impossibly large cotton bale—other men are seen rolling these in later shots—and flexing his muscles in a brief moment that resembles nothing so much as a beefcake pose. In the midst of "Ol' Man River," Whale—a gay man whose sexuality and class background have been explored by recent biographers—presents Robeson's half-naked body as an erotic emblem.[90] Bare-chested men were indeed rare in 1930s film. Johnny Weissmuller's Tarzan series had just begun in 1935 when Whale created this sequence, which features not only Robeson but other black men similarly shirtless in stylized compositions hoeing fields and rolling bales. No other film set in the South made the spectacle of black male bodies part of the imagery of African Americans doing heavy labor. Stories of African tribesmen did, however, normally include black men in partial undress as Robeson appeared in the British film

Sanders of the River from 1935. Whale eliminated Hammerstein's images of cruel white authority, the "Simon Legree figure" evoking *Uncle Tom's Cabin*, and any sense of the "agitated protest" called for in the script. Even generic images of the river were not included. Whale's illustrative shots primarily focus on black male bodies, emphasizing the "man" in "Ol' Man River," the excess of exposed flesh strongly suggesting that Whale saw the number as a chance to introduce a certain kind of male nudity, which under different circumstances the Production Code would not have allowed. Race certainly played a part in permitting Whale's choices, but also crucial was Robeson's readiness to take off his shirt and flex his muscles at Whale's direction, just as he had posed nude in Salemme's Greenwich Village studio in the 1920s.

The 1929 *Show Boat* inadvertently demonstrated how tangential the Julie-Steve miscegenation plot was to Ferber's novel. The screenwriter Charles Kenyon removed Steve, eliminated Julie's mixed-race identity, and made Parthy's jealousy the sole motivation for Julie's ejection from the *Cotton Blossom*. Parthy's stunted maternal affection, repressed feelings, and power to simply kick Julie off the boat make her the central and strongest character in the film—Andy is a weak figure. Kenyon enhanced the cinematic possibilities of Magnolia's visit to Hetty Chilson's brothel by casting Julie as Hetty herself. Stepping from a ballroom bacchanal covered in glittering jewels, Julie denies she knows Magnolia, then retreats to her boudoir and cries bitter tears while looking at a photo of Magnolia as a girl, which she still keeps on her dresser. The stigma of blackness is entirely removed from Julie in the 1929 film, replaced with gender-specific white tropes—Parthy's jealousy, Julie's lapse into prostitution—that served equally well (perhaps better as without Steve on the boat there's no need account for his disappearance in Chicago).

The race plot in Ferber's novel that did not prove dispensable to Kenyon and Universal was the story of Magnolia's black voice. Independent of Hammerstein and Kern, Kenyon created his own version of *Show Boat*'s popular music plot. Telling this tale in a sound film forced the question of what Jo, Queenie, and Magnolia sounded like and what Magnolia's stage career was built on. The film audience got to see and, in the end, hear Universal's decisions regarding all these aesthetic choices. The popular music plot appeared in both the all-silent and silent-sound hybrid, with important differences. Complicating the situation, the soundtrack for select reels of the final version, produced in a sound on disc format that stored sound and image in separate media, have been lost. As a result, how Universal solved the issue of Magnolia's black voice remains something of a mystery.

Only one copy of Kenyon's script for *Show Boat* survives in the major film archive collections.[91] This "Sixth Draft" typescript includes pencil edits comprising a "Seventh Draft," and many of the changes relate to the use of music in the film. By April 1928, when the source was typed and edited, Laemmle had acquired select elements from Ziegfeld's *Show Boat* for use in what was to be a silent film. "Ol' Man River" turns up in three important places in this script that predates the decision to make *Show Boat* a part-talkie.

Near the start of the film, Kenyon re-created the *Cotton Blossom* kitchen where Jo and Queenie taught Magnolia how to sing Negro spirituals. Originally, the song they sang at Magnolia's request was "I Got Shoes," following the novel. In the script, this song was replaced with "Ole Man Ribber" [*sic*], the lyrics for which would appear as a title card, effectively forcing the composer Cherniavsky to use Kern's tune at this spot. The song was to develop into a dance for Joe and Magnolia, a high-spirited romp suggesting that Kenyon was familiar with how "Can't Help Lovin' Dat Man" was routined in the analogous scene in the stage musical. Parthy's arrival brings the music and merriment to a halt. This scene of a white child learning black music preceded the arrival of the *Cotton Blossom* at a Mississippi landing that opened the film as released. Kenyon took care to initiate the narrative with interracial scenes that established Magnolia's black music credentials. Kenyon returned to the kitchen at the close of the film, where the aged Parthy—estranged from Magnolia for many years—thinks back in sorrow on the past, the film flashing back to the child Magnolia singing and dancing with Joe and Queenie. In a third usage in Kenyon's script, "Ol' Man River" replaced the spiritual "Deep River" in a scene developing Magnolia and Ravenal's romance. It is evening, and Joe and Queenie are below in the kitchen, singing (as always). Magnolia, on the top deck, lying on a hammock and strumming her banjo, listens to the music by way of a ventilation shaft, which pipes Joe and Queenie's voices directly to her. Ravenal watches Magnolia "in admiring silence" from the shadows, the sequence ending with a return to Joe and Queenie still singing below. Kenyon notes that "Ol' Man River" should continue behind the entire scene, complementing images of the river in the moonlight. Kenyon's plan echoes the underscoring for a similar moment in the stage musical, when the black chorus hums "Ol' Man River" from the wings just before "You Are Love." Once again, the stage musical seems to be informing Kenyon's use of music.

None of the above three uses of "Ol' Man River" survived in the finished film. All were cut in favor of synchronized dialogue scenes, some of which also included singing. "Ol' Man River" was spotlighted at the crucial moment when Magnolia shows she can hold a Chicago audience. Kenyon set the scene at Jopper's, taking a cue from Ferber, and had Schultzy play the role of long-lost friend who arrives at just the right moment to help Magnolia get her chance—this taken from Hammerstein. The silent version of the scene contrasts Magnolia's musical choices in no uncertain terms. She is introduced as "Magnolia Hawks—Coon Shouter" and in previous scenes is shown practicing a song that begins, "Coon, coon, coon, I wish my color would fade, etc." But Magnolia is not confident in this new identity and says, in a title card, "Oh, I wish I could sing one of the old time darky songs." Shultzy reacts in horror: this boisterous urban crowd wants a coon song. But a visibly nervous Magnolia proves unable to pull off her prepared coon song, and the crowd rejects her soundly. She flees back to the wings. Angry at the audience's reaction, Schultzy tells Magnolia in a title, "Go out there and sing your own nigger songs like you sung 'em on the Show Boat. . . . You've got to. Remember your father—and Julie—and Gay and SING!" Kenyon's description of what happens next should, by now, be quite familiar:

> In dead silence. Magnolia enters [the stage] to a chair which has been placed for her. She is like one apart from her surroundings. She now has poise, purpose. She sits and throwing back her head as Joe and Queenie had taught her, she half closes her eyes and tapping time with her right foot begins singing with the soft husky negro tones she had learned from the negroes on the Show Boat so many years before.

Kenyon, like Hammerstein in his early drafts, was captivated by Ferber's image of a white girl, head thrown back, eyes half closed, immersed in black music making. During the song, Kenyon imagined special effects that would clarify the meaning of Magnolia's performance.

> A BEAUTIFUL STRETCH OF THE MISSISSIPPI RIVER.
> Which seems to fill the entire stage, flowing out over the orchestra pit. Through the water clear and distinct can be seen the figure of Magnolia in her white gown. Over the water on one side double expose darkies singing in a cotton field. On the other side of the stage double expose darkies dancing in front of a cabin with little children playing around. Then double in Jo and Queenie in the kitchen of the Show Boat singing.
> LAP DISSOLVE INTO
> AUDIENCE
> Sitting spellbound. . . .
> STAGE. CLOSEUP.
> Magnolia singing quietly, with a far-away expression on her face. There are tears in her eyes, but she is smiling.

These superimposed images simultaneously take the entranced Magnolia back to the origins of her musical self and visualize associations the in-film audience makes upon hearing Magnolia sing. Several in the crowd—men and women alike—are moved to tears.

Once it was decided that Magnolia would actually sing in the film, the songs chosen for her Jopper's debut became songs from Kern and Hammerstein's score. In the sound remaking of the scene, Laura LaPlante as Magnolia sings "Ol' Man River" and quiets the noisy crowd, again bringing some to tears. In a promotional newsletter to exhibitors, Laemmle claimed LaPlante's performance had a similar effect on the film's audiences during *Show Boat*'s premiere engagement, claiming "The expression on their faces is one of rapt ecstasy."[92] A short montage of her career leads to a second performance for Magnolia, this time on a richly adorned stage in a fancy gown. Here, LaPlante sings "Can't Help Lovin' Dat Man." It bears repeating that Universal had LaPlante sing "Ol' Man River" and "Can't Help Lovin' Dat Man" in the same narrative juncture where Norma Terris sang "After the Ball" in the stage musical version.

What LaPlante—or more precisely her voice double Eva Olivotti—sounded like remains, unfortunately, a mystery.[93] The soundtrack discs for both her sung numbers have been lost, leaving only the visual evidence and denying later viewers the chance to hear Magnolia's black performance style as it was voiced in this particular instance. But Magnolia's black voice remained central to the story as Kenyon read it and retold it, and this popular music plot survived the radical restructuring of the 1929 *Show Boat* into a part-talkie.

Magnolia's black voice was a key element of Hammerstein's script for the 1936 film as well. Three slightly different versions of Hammerstein's script survive. As noted above, he worked under pressure, first writing the dialogue—needed for pre-production budgeting and planning—and then turning to the making of three new songs with Kern: a duet for Magnolia and Ravenal, a duet for Joe and Queenie, and a performed number meant to serve both Magnolia on the show boat and Kim on Broadway. The earliest draft, located in the Robeson papers at Howard University, spots all three new numbers without providing lyrics or titles.[94] The next draft, in the Hammerstein collection at the Library of Congress, includes complete lyrics for the two new duets and a first attempt at a number for Magnolia and Kim.[95]

From early on, the Magnolia/Kim song was conceived as a blackface routine for Irene Dunne, an idea enthusiastically embraced by all. As Hammerstein wrote to Whale in mid-November, "I hope you will agree that a naïve, old-fashioned 'coon number' production is just the thing for the Show Boat, and it seems to us that having Irene Dunne doing a number in blackface is novel and different from anything she's ever done. It 'loosens her up.' She herself is most enthusiastic about the idea. I think it is one of those things that is sure to be talked about by those who see the picture, and is all in all a good stroke of showmanship."[96] The first try at what Andy introduces as "a little Southern song—solo with banjo by Miss Magnolia Hawks . . ." was titled "Got My Eye On You."

verse

Magnolia: My high-fallutin' lover,
        Yo' heart is under cover . . .
        Dat only makes me want yo' more!
FRANK (spoken): Keep right on wantin'!
MAGNOLIA: You better make yo' mind up
        Dat in de end Ah'll wind up
        By findin' what Ah'm lookin' for.
FRANK (spoken): Ah'll keep mah door locked.
MAGNOLIA: Won't do no good to lock yo door!

refrain

Got my eye on you
Look out for me
Look out for me
Got my eye on you
You better beware
All de tea leaves in my teacup
Tell me love will sneak up
On you; afore you know it's dere . . .
Got my eye on you
Look out for me
No use tryin', you
Can't git away free
Got my heart all set upon you
I won't let up on you
Till you
Got yo' eye on me.

interlude

Does yo remember
Ah seemed to want you
De very day we met
Ah had a feelin'
Ah'd always want you
Ah got dat feelin' yet.

As the text suggests, "Got My Eye on You" was conceived as a duet for Dunne and Sammy White as Frank, performed in blackface as a cleaned-up coon song lacking the grossly offensive elements that marked the genre in its day. Hammerstein noted the strangeness of having Magnolia appear in blackface in the set up for the scene, which gauges the *Cotton Blossom* audience reaction as "Applause, cheers, screams of delight greet her. Their romantic leading lady is going to do a blackface song! 'If this don't beat all!'" Kern's manuscript suggested the song "be sung as if arranged by Cap'n Andy for his troupe, not the Hall Johnson choir."[97]

The plan for "Got My Eye On You" included two other uses of the song. Bill Robinson's solo on the levee was to use the tune—situating it as genuine black material—and Kim was to reprise the song at the close of the film, which put her literally on a Broadway stage. Hammerstein returned to his original 1927 idea of having Kim perform a contemporary Broadway number in a New York setting, shifting the locale from her apartment to an actual stage. Hammerstein described how "Got My Eye On You" would be routined in detail—unusual for musical scripts—using a set featuring a "Southern mansion with long white columned portico" with Kim as a hoop-skirted belle telling a scary story to a group of "four or five picaninnies." Hammerstein even included "a fat Negro mammy" in the scene. During the number, Ravenal, who has secretly obtained a job as the doorman of the theater, sneaks into a box to watch his daughter's big opening. While watching Kim, Ravenal flashes back to Magnolia singing "Got My Eye On You" on the *Cotton Blossom*. Hammerstein recommends a crossfade to images of the earlier number, working a theme found also in Kenyon's 1929 script, that had a crossfade taking Parthy back in time to the idyllic days on the boat. In both scenes, musical performance unlocks personal memories. Ravenal's reverie is interrupted when Magnolia, Parthy, and Andy—arriving late for the show—enter the box. Magnolia instantly recognizes him and insists he stay. Dunne had played similar scenes of reconciliation after years of absence in several previous films: it was a melodramatic specialty for her.[98] When Ravenal says they have nothing in common, Magnolia points to Kim, still singing on the stage. Hammerstein wrapped up the film by having Magnolia sing the interlude lyric from "Got My Eye on You" to Ravenal, then give him a kiss on the cheek. Their reconciliation is private, gentle, even comic, and, importantly, sung in black dialect. Magnolia and Ravenal come together by way of a genteel coon song remade for a 1920s Broadway show.

"Got My Eye on You" did not satisfy the 1936 *Show Boat* team. Dunne joined the *Show Boat* shoot already in progress in December, having just finished *Magnificent Obsession*. Perhaps she didn't like sharing her adventurous blackface turn with White and demanded a solo instead. So Kern and Hammerstein quickly came up with "Gallivantin' Aroun'," which was incorporated into the third surviving draft of the script (copies in Hollywood and New York).[99] The routining was largely the same: a blackface banjo number on the *Cotton Blossom* for Magnolia and a Broadway production number for Kim that evoked the mythical southern past of plantations and slaves (a surprising element foreign to Ferber's post–Civil War story). And again, Magnolia was to use a bit of the tune in a private moment with Ravenal at the close of the picture. But given the chance to rethink this crucial number, Hammerstein went farther and revived the popular music plot in an explicit way in both production numbers using "Gallivantin' Aroun'." These ideas did not survive in the film as released but were judged good enough to warrant shooting.

Dunne's blackface "Gallivantin' Aroun" remains a troubling moment in the 1936 *Show Boat*, an instance of extreme racial caricature that, together with Dunne's physically uninhibited shuffle in "Can't Help Lovin' Dat Man," marks this version of *Show Boat* with an embarrassing and extreme instance of Hollywood's depiction of blackness. Unlike the 1951 MGM version, which largely sublimates or eliminates questions of race and performance, the 1936 film remains a document in racist caricature demanding careful historical explanation. (It has never been released on DVD in the United States, a pessimistic commentary on the film's perceived commercial potential in later times.)[100] Hammerstein's original plan for "Gallivantin' Aroun'" attempted to bring the film audience explicitly into the scene. During Magnolia's performance, Andy was to sneak up behind Parthy standing in the wings—"Smiling contentedly for the first time this evening"—grab her around the waist, and pull her onstage, "swinging her gaily around the stage in a polka step." The expectation that Parthy would respond positively to Andy's overtures demonstrates just how completely the character had been rethought for Helen Westley. (A shot of Westley "contentedly" watching Magnolia from the wings remains in the final print.) After their impromptu polka, Andy stepped to the footlights and invited the show boat audience to sing along on a reprise of "Gallivantin' Aroun'," the lyrics for which were projected using lantern slides. After this, Hammerstein scripted an audience participation scenario, which in retrospect would have been a stunning, perhaps disturbing addition to the history of *Show Boat*'s remaking:

BIG CLOSEUP . . . ANDY'S HEAD
    Presumably addressing show boat audience, but actually talking right at real audience in motion picture theatre.

ANDY

That was pretty good, but I think we can do better.

Now this time everybody sing—an' I mean everybody!

(pointing his finger) You and you and you!

BIG CLOSEUP . . . MAGNOLIA'S HEAD

MAGNOLIA

Come on, folks!

CLOSEUP . . . WORDS ON SCREEN

Nothing else in shot. HOLD this shot long enough for first two lines to be sung.

QUICK FLASH CLOSEUP . . . MAGNOLIA

MAGNOLIA

You'll have to do better than that.

MED. CLOSE . . . WORDS ON SCREEN

Magnolia's head down in right hand corner of shot, singing the words, encouraging the audience.

Dub in voices of show boat audience to support real audience if they are singing, or to keep song alive if they are bashful. Finish refrain loud and strong.

At end of refrain

CLOSEUP TWO HEAD SHOT . . . ANDY AND MAGNOLIA

Facing audience cheek to cheek

ANDY

Just one big happy family!

DISSOLVE

Production stills suggest this entire sequence was shot and that everyone in the *Cotton Blossom* troupe—including Ravenal—came onstage for the sing-along to "Gallivantin' Aroun'." The sing-along Hammerstein imagined for the movie theater audience takes the historical white audience for *Show Boat* to an interesting extreme of response. *Show Boat* already included a sing-along for the Trocadero patrons to "After the Ball." Theater audiences may have joined in a bit as well, perhaps just humming along. Indeed, many reviewers described leaving the show with the tune stuck in their head. But with "Gallivantin' Aroun'," Hammerstein was betting on the willingness of the film's audience to not only learn a new song in an old-fashioned popular music idiom but to sing it in a spirit of fun with Winninger and Dunne. The sequence banks on the tune, the star power of the pair leading it, and the memories of those in the film audience who would recall singing along with illustrated song slides or shorts in the pre-synchronized sound era when the practice was relatively common. From the perspective of race, the appeal here is resolutely white. Black audiences had long before rejected blackface, which was nearing its historical demise. The practice largely disappeared from Hollywood musicals after about 1942 but not before an early 1940s resurgence best captured in the Mickey Rooney–Judy Garland films that, like *Show Boat*, explicitly revived earlier popular entertainment regimes such as minstrelsy. Actual black audiences—unlike the fictional one pictured enjoying Magnolia's number from the *Cotton Blossom*'s blacks-only balcony—would likely have rejected the invitation to sing along with Andy and the blacked-up Magnolia.

But the plan to engage the audience with "Gallivantin' Aroun'" didn't end on the show boat. The routining of the song for Kim's big number also included a sing-along, this time with the Broadway audience. Having completed the production number, Kim was to approach the footlights and address the audience:

> KIM
> My mother could always get the show boat audience
> to join in with her. I wonder if I can make you do
> the same for me. Come on, everybody!
> She starts refrain. Nobody sings.

> KIM
> Come on. Forget you have stiff shirts on. Make believe
> you're on the show boat.
> A few start to sing. Others follow and soon the whole audience is singing
> lustily.
> TWO HEAD SHOT . . . ANDY AND PARTHY

> ANDY
> She's got 'em! She give 'em the smile!

Andy attributes the success of the song to Kim's ability—inherited from Magnolia—to dazzle audiences with her smile. What worked with the simple folks on the river also succeeds with the "stiff shirts" of New York. This version of popular entertainment history again rewrites Ferber's more pessimistic view of contemporary, urban audiences. Hammerstein wants continuity, and with the power of the screenwriter he can command audiences to respond.

Supporting Kim's success was a return to the popular music plot that haunts virtually every version of *Show Boat* Hammerstein worked on. Still mining the vein first opened up in the January 1927 script, Kim's "Gallivantin' Aroun'" is introduced by her manager as "an old number her mother used to do. We're going to do it the way it was done on the show boat years ago." After an initial sequence using Deep South scenes evoking the 1860s—a remnant of

"Got My Eye On You"—the "stage turns and on other side is fashionable night club of to-day, with another chorus doing same melody to rumba rhythm and rumba dance routine." The rumba was a mid-1930s phenomenon. Hammerstein was clinging to the notion that *Show Boat* docked in the present even though the chronological reach of the story was already absurd in 1927.

Production stills from this very elaborate number bring a level of detail to the sequence only suggested by the script and the fragmentary glimpses that survived in the finished film.[101] The 1860s sequence featured two large dance choruses: white belles and beaux in stylized plantation finery and black slaves in rags, the men bare-chested. The whites floated about while the blacks did a shuffle dance. The contemporary sequence used a divided stage: one half suggesting Midtown, the other with a sign reading "heart of Harlem." The entrance to a subway station far upstage connected the two. Judging from the production stills, the white chorus—arrayed in futuristic, black costumes—remained on the Midtown side of the stage. The black chorus—dressed in sexy white versions of 1930s fashions—stayed on the Harlem side, with Kim in futuristic white and carrying a banjo bridging the gap at center. This staging of "Gallivantin' Aroun'" made the same equation attempted by "It's Getting Hotter in the North," except the inclusion of the black chorus on equal terms is manifest. With the rise of the lindy hop and swing, black music and dance had assumed an even higher profile nine years after *Show Boat* had first dramatized the connection between those old southern songs and contemporary trends in mass culture (now the province of Hollywood rather than Broadway).

Had it stayed in, Kim's "Gallivantin' Aroun'" would have made this point explicitly. But just as "It's Getting Hotter in the North" didn't survive, the huge investment in Kim's big number was largely lost. In the end, the makers of the 1936 *Show Boat* opted for an operetta close, attending more to the white love story than the popular music plot. In a new closing sequence, hastily assembled after the film's initial preview under pressure from Universal's new owners, Kim's debut was reduced to a short dance punctuated by shots of Andy, Parthy, and Magnolia racing to the theater. All traces of the modern half of Kim's "Gallivantin' Aroun'," as well as the sing-along, were removed. Accepting applause in her 1860s costume, Kim hands off her encore to Magnolia, who begins to sing "You Are Love." Ravenal, who has left the box at this point, begins to sing along in the hallway. Magnolia hears him and brings him into the scene for the climax of the song. (Dunne and Jones both take the high B-flat.) Kim looks on wide eyed and, after a quick return to the Mississippi in the moonlight, accompanied by the voice of Robeson singing "Ol' Man River," the film concludes. "You Are Love" had never been planned for the Universal *Show Boat*, and its insertion at the close necessitated adding it in earlier as well, with Dunne and Jones sharing a single chorus during the water barrel scene (where, again, they both take the high B-flat). Use of "You Are Love" in this way brought *Show Boat* in line with Dunne's weepy dramas; the white love story—central to all studio-era product—becoming the primary reason for the whole film. In the process, Hammerstein's perhaps untellable popular music plot was lost yet again.

LOS ANGELES, 1940

The Los Angeles Civic Light Opera (LACLO) opened its third season with a production of *Show Boat* that marked the end of one era in the life of the show. Terris, Robeson, and Morgan reprised their roles a final time. Zeke Colvan directed. Kern was in attendance opening night and took a bow from his box before act 2. Lacking its own black chorus, the LACLO hired the Hall Johnson Singers and assembled a troupe of black dancers. Opening night reviewers were generally underwhelmed with the singing, faulting rehearsal fatigue and the cavernous Philharmonic Auditorium. But Robeson and the black chorus came in for typical praise: "The Negro performers, both singers and dancers, had it all over their white co-workers last night."[102] Robeson stopped the show twice, with "Ol' Man River" and "Ah Still Suits Me," the latter marking the first insertion of a number made for a *Show Boat* film into a stage production. *Show Boat* proved a festive selection for the LACLO: "it's the music we all love to hear" noted the *Los Angeles Times* society reporter.[103]

For black critics, Robeson's bow in *Show Boat* was reason to celebrate yet again. The black columnist and film actor Clarence Muse enthused about Robeson's arrival in Hollywood, pairing him with Duke Ellington, also in town at the time:

> THE fact that both ELLINGTON and ROBESON have consistently portrayed the NEGRO in his own IDIOM down through the years, is in my opinion the REASON there is so much commotion when they come this way. . . . HOLLYWOOD "learns" when [Robeson] arrives. PAUL ROBESON lifts their souls as he follows the steady purposeful melody of THE SPIRITUAL. THE OLE MAN or "OLE MAN RIVER" stands up in the water, and waves NORTHWARD, past CAIRO and on and on—until some day he will arrive in the SUN. HOLLYWOOD is fortunate when these great SOULS ARRIVE, FRIENDS. I AM happy too. AREN'T YOU proud of THEM?[104]

In his coverage of opening night, Muse made sure that the reaction to Robeson was put down in black and white. The audience "acted as if it was a Paul Robeson folk concert and that he should sing and sing, regardless of lyrics and story. Such was the reception of this great international artist in Hollywood."[105] Muse praised John Boles as Ravenal and Terris as Magnolia, but reserved special mention for Morgan as Julie. During "Can't Help Lovin' Dat Man," Muse wrote, "You sit in the audience and suffer with her. But when she returns later in the show and sings while seated on an upright piano in that same 'Red dress' (I believe) 'My Bill' art again rises above the material and floats into the spiritual. Her great soul stirs you and you forget that her voice is merely adequate. You are privileged to hear and see a rare artist." Muse knew Morgan; he played a poignant added scene with her in the 1936 *Show Boat* where Julie articulates to Muse, as the Trocadero doorman, her long-ago friendship with Magnolia who is auditioning with "Can't Help Lovin' Dat Man" on the adjacent stage. It's a tender, friendly exchange between a white woman and a black man, echoing once again the undocumentable offstage world of the entertainment industry where *Show Boat*'s interracial cast could build cross-racial relationships.

The 1940 LACLO production was the final bow for almost all the members of *Show Boat*'s original cast.[106] Never again would the show be a vehicle for legendary personalities, a tailor-made setting for Robeson and Morgan's distinctive musical personas and personal histories. In the case of Joe, this featured role for a black bass had already proven its viability without Robeson. Todd Duncan, the original Porgy in Gershwin's *Porgy and Bess*, would play Joe in the next LACLO *Show Boat* in 1944, initiating a line of black baritones and basses that would include Kenneth Spencer, William C. Smith, William Warfield, Willard White, Bruce Hubbard, and Michel Bell. But without Robeson, something would be lost in the nature of *Show Boat* as an expression of a particular moment in popular culture when the concert spiritual as presented by Robeson touched the white audience with special power. Audience response to later Joes, however enthusiastic, must be heard as but an echo of the reception Robeson received every time he stepped to the footlights to sing "Ol' Man River." By contrast, Morgan's Julie would change markedly over the years, almost immediately transformed musically, dramatically, and racially as women who had little in common with Morgan assumed the role. Julie would endure apart from Morgan, this most personality-driven role showing an astonishing flexibility that helped keep *Show Boat* current.

7

BROADWAY BLACK, HOLLYWOOD WHITE
• • •
1943–1957

Show Boat came to London for the second time in the middle of World War II, and for the only time in a major professional production, Joe was sung by a white man in blackface: the Australian bass Malcolm McEachern billed as "Mr. Jetsam." Possessing an extremely deep bass voice, McEachern choose not to build his career on opera but instead met broader British tastes by appearing in Gilbert and Sullivan operettas and singing oratorios. His recordings reveal a flexibility and range well suited to the vocal demands of Handel. McEachern's career took a decidedly popular turn in 1926, when he teamed up with the pianist and tenor Bentley Collingwood Hilliam. Performing as Mr. Flotsam and Mr. Jetsam on the variety stage, records, and radio, the pair was resolutely British, singing without a trace of irony songs like "Polonaise in the Mall," which told "a story of love, tradition and loyalty" about the British royal family to the pleasing strains of a light classical favorite by Chopin. Flotsam and Jetsam's songs, most of which were penned by Hilliam, often spoke to the gap between traditional British entertainments, such as pantomime, and the ongoing invasion of American jazz. The team stood firmly for the old ways, offering in a line from "Only a Few of Us Left," "grammatical words to a British tune." "Who wants a mammy down in Alabamy" they rhetorically asked later in the song, replying for themselves and their listeners, "I don't— I don't." But Flotsam and Jetsam's comic personas raised racial questions, particularly when apprehended only on records or radio. Flotsam acknowledged the confusion when he had an imagined questioner comment, "I thought you chaps were certainly men of color," and Jetsam's "trademark" laugh, often used at the end of their records, could be heard as stereotypically black in an American context.

McEachern's performance of "Ol' Man River" was inevitably compared to Robeson's, marking the first in a series of reviews from the 1940s that brought critics' memories of earlier performers into the assessment of a *Show Boat* revival, a pervasive practice that, again, suggests the importance of performers to this show. Midcentury audiences wanted to know how new performers stacked up to well-remembered originals. "This production is fortunate in that in 'Mr. Jetsam' it has a singer who can follow Mr. Paul Robeson and survive the comparison. 'Mr. Jetsam' has not Mr. Robeson's presence and power of domination, but he has a voice which can cope with 'Ol' Man River,' and that, for the present purposes, is enough."[1] "Though burnt cork (or its modern substitute) leaves Mr. Jetsam looking somewhat less plausibly sun-kissed than Mr. Paul Robeson, . . . his rich, bassoon-like bass does sonorous justice to the negro's simple philosophy, and compels the encores which are Old Man River's tribute."[2] Others saw *Show Boat* anew in the absence of Robeson's overwhelming presence. "For most London theatergoers, *Show Boat* means Paul Robeson and the shock of delight we felt when fifteen years ago 'Ol' Man River' thundered first round the walls of Drury Lane and subsequently round almost every bathroom in England. And so it is surprising to find . . . that the part of 'Joe' has only a few words of dialogue and the song."[3]

McEachern as Mr. Jetsam playing Joe recalls Gardella as Aunt Jemima playing Queenie, except that McEachern did not come into the show with an established blackface persona. Racial impersonation was not part of his career. McEachern's ability to step into the part of Joe suggests the extent to which Robeson was judged through his repertory alone and not through any "black" performance style. A suitably powerful singer—in McEachern's case, one accustomed to singing classical, light classical, and popular fare— made up as black proved sufficient. The location of the production outside the United States, where the casting of a white man as Joe would have surely raised objections from black critics and general audiences alike, permitted McEachern to take on the role. Perhaps Londoners viewed his casting as an example of wartime "making do," a concession to the "present purposes" referred to by the above reviewer. McEachern's successful turn as Joe suggests that the musical and lyrical content of "Ol' Man River" and the performer's skin color define Joe as black. A white concert singer with no experience in racial mimicry was judged capable of delivering the song in satisfactory fashion.

Mr. Jetsam's *Show Boat* played the Stoll Theatre, a massive house seating almost 2,500 and originally erected for Oscar Hammerstein I in 1911 as the

London Opera House. (Intending to compete with Covent Garden, Hammerstein gave up after one season.[4]) After serving as a home for revue, variety, and motion pictures, the Stoll reopened in 1941 with a series of pantomimes and musical revivals produced by Prince Littler, an important West End figure who went on to control multiple theaters and bring many American shows to London. *Rose-Marie* and *Lilac Time* (the London version of *Blossom Time*) preceded *Show Boat* at the Stoll; *The Student Prince* played there briefly in 1944. Productions of *The Vagabond King* and *The Desert Song* were mounted elsewhere in London in 1943. In familiar company, *Show Boat* played more performances than any of the other 1920s operettas receiving wartime revivals. Littler managed *Show Boat* like a pantomime, giving two shows daily; the five-month run racked up 264 performances.

Like its fellow operetta survivors from the 1920s, *Show Boat* was understood by London critics as a solid show worth seeing again. "In these difficult days, when so much theatre talent is otherwise engaged or unavailable, it is no doubt convenient for theatre managers to have on hand—like tinned delicacies in the larder—old favorites that have proved their worth and established their popularity."[5] These "tinned delicacies," a group of commercially successful 1920s operettas, would survive together for another fifteen years or so to be remade as Technicolor musicals and studio-cast LPs. Only *Show Boat*, with its always topical investment in the color line, would retain its relevance beyond the 1950s.

Show Boat's survival in the 1940s and 1950s illustrates a period when challenges to prewar modes of racial representation and stereotype were heating up but before the advent of rock and roll and the social revolutions of the 1960s had registered their powerful impact. The high-profile postwar *Show Boats* were marked by fairly radical remakings that often went in opposite directions. New York stage productions—the 1946 "new production" under the direction of Hammerstein, and the 1956 and 1957 outdoor productions at Jones Beach—attempted to retain by way of significant revision the show's major black musical numbers. In the process, these productions provided jobs for black performers, dancers in particular, that helped sustain fledgling careers. Out in Hollywood, this time at Metro-Goldwyn-Mayer, *Show Boat* would appear on the big screen in two versions: an extended sequence in the 1946 Jerome Kern biopic *Till the Clouds Roll By* and a third *Show Boat* feature film released in 1951. These MGM remakings used *Show Boat* chiefly as a platform for the studio's stars, among them Lena Horne, Frank Sinatra, and Ava Gardner. The 1951 film subjected *Show Boat* to the most radical remaking it would ever see, truncating the story's chronological reach and eliminating issues of race as much as possible while still retaining "Ol' Man River." But, as with the Universal films, phantoms from the archive preserve glimpses of quite different MGM *Show Boats* that didn't get made.

BROADWAY, 1946

In January 1946, *Show Boat* returned to Broadway after an absence of four-teen years. The revival, heralded as a "new production" by producers Richard Rodgers and Oscar Hammerstein, was at once an accidental memorial to Jerome Kern (who had died unexpectedly in November 1945), conclusive evidence that *Show Boat* had a postwar audience, and the first Broadway revisal. Hammerstein, who revised the script and directed in addition to co-producing, described the effort as "a 1945 approach to a musical show of 1927," providing a terse description of the revisal strategy, where the raw materials of a dated hit are reshaped to match whatever is new on Broadway without sacrificing the qualities that made the show succeed in the first place.[6] *Show Boat* would be the first "classic" musical to get such treatment, predating by half a century the revisal trend of the 1990s (which would see yet another "new" *Show Boat*).

The original productions of *Oklahoma!* and *Carousel* were both still running when Hammerstein put together his "new production," and these hits factored into his choices. In casting the white singing leads, Hammerstein sought a con-tinuity of sound and style between *Show Boat* and his two successful 1940s musical plays. Jan Clayton went directly from *Carousel*, where she originated the role of Julie Jordan, into the *Show Boat* revival as Magnolia. Clayton's light soprano voice as heard on the cast recording—thin on the top, wearing its training lightly, pointing the listener toward the words and not the beauty of the voice—gave the role a fresh, earnest quality echoed by later Magnolias like Barbara Cook (1962 and 1966) and Rebecca Luker (1994) also captured on cast recordings.[7] Clayton was the first to bring this postwar singing-actress ap-proach to the part.

Remaking the male half of the central romantic pair, Hammerstein cut the waterfront scene and with it "'Til Good Luck Comes My Way," lessening Ravenal's position as the vocally dominant partner and reshaping the role to match the new breed of Rodgers and Hammerstein leading men, none of whom insist on their singing prowess. *Oklahoma!*'s Curley tops out at a high F-sharp and cedes the show's only vocal climax to Laurey's high A at the reprise of "People Will Say We're in Love." Billy Bigelow's top note in *Carousel* is also F-sharp, putting both roles in the Broadway baritone category. The only genuine tenor role in Rodgers and Hammerstein's musical plays, and the only part analogous in terms of range to Ravenal, is the prim but boastful character role Mister Snow in *Carousel*. Snow's top note—a sustained high A, still a half-step below Howard Marsh's signature B-flat—is used for character-building rather than voice-displaying purposes.[8] One of the only changes made in the re-engraved *Show Boat* vocal score from 1946 was a lowering of "Make Believe" by a full step from the 1927 original, reversing the changes made for Marsh and pushing the lowest note for the role down to a sustained B, anathema for typical tenors. The 1946 score was, until the mid-1990s, the only version available for rental. On the cast recording, Charles Fredericks as Ravenal ceded the high notes at the close of "You Are Love" to Clayton, tilting the number toward Magnolia.

A letter from Kern to Hammerstein discussing possible casting for the Broadway revival hints at how the composer was rethinking Ravenal. Kern framed the character's trained voice as a dramatic problem: "Not only are singers lousy actors congenitally, but the better Ravenal sings, the less we believe in his having to resort to pawning *the* ring and *the* walking-stick. If that audiences weren't intoxicated with our entrancing words and music (a detonation from the Bronx) they would say, why doesn't the son-of-a-bitch get a job as a singer, to keep his daughter in that beautiful Urbanesque [referring to Ziegfeld set designer Joseph Urban] convent, just as does poor, drab Magnolia, with much inferior singing equipment."[9] Kern implies that as a role Magnolia called for less of a singer than Ravenal and that if Ravenal sang too well the dramatic credibility of the story might suffer. A shift in vocal masculinities had occurred, with the new Rodgers and Hammerstein male lead not cut from operetta cloth but instead singing in a register closer to the speaking voice and bursting into song in a dramatically convincing manner, which didn't call attention to itself as singing. Ravenal—a remnant of the 1920s—could never be completely remade to fit this new mold, although casting baritones in the part would succeed in making the role more manly in midcentury terms.

Range also played a part in the remaking of Julie. The stakes were high for Carol Bruce, who stepped into the role and the shadow of Helen Morgan, which was still fresh historically but already legendary. Richard Watts, pushing his hyperbole only a bit relative to other critics, wrote that Morgan's "memory is everyone's greatest personal recollection of *Show Boat*," but one measure of how different reception of *Show Boat* had been in London, where, of course, Robeson dominated memories of the show. Watts continued, "Certainly there were people in that first-night audience who would have been capable of homicide if [Bruce] had seemed in any way unworthy of their memories."[10] No wonder Bruce confessed to being "haunted nightly by the specter of Helen Morgan."[11] She had little to fear: audiences and critics embraced her new take on Julie, which altered the role by dropping the register of the part from soprano to alto. The original keys for both "Can't Help Lovin' Dat Man" and "Bill" were lowered substantially—a full fifth—on Bruce's recordings for the cast album, and both numbers also featured up-to-date jazzy accompaniments specially made for the record market.[12] In the case of "Can't Help Lovin' Dat Man," stylistic choices made by both the singers and the arranger reinforced in aural terms the racial distance between Julie's and Queenie's versions of the song. A cool mix of pop strings and saxophones accompanied Bruce's articulate, almost arch Julie, anticipating the classic pop sound of the 1950s. Slurred clarinet solos and blaring "dirty" brass in the breaks blackened the effect of Helen Dowdy as Queenie. Dowdy heightened Hammerstein's dialect considerably, singing "chimbley" as no subsequent Queenie would.

Bruce's "Bill" remains the slowest on record—in 1946 marking a radical departure from the way Morgan sang it—and ends with an almost complete breakdown of rhythm, vocal control, and emotional equilibrium. At the line "I love him / Because he's—I don't know," Bruce loses composure, speaking the words "I don't know" and taking Julie's desperation to a depth exceeded on record only by Lonette McKee, the Broadway Julie of choice in the 1980s and '90s (see chap. 9). Bruce, who sings in a white manner at all times, with perfect diction and a square rhythmic approach, ended her recording of "Bill" softly, retreating into private pain just as Morgan had.

Much like Morgan, Bruce launched her career in nightclubs and featured spots in Broadway shows. She broke onto Broadway in a featured role in *Louisiana Purchase* (1940)—described by one wag as "the musical show that has Carol Bruce in it"—singing the title song and the pseudo-spiritual "The Lord Done Fixed Up My Soul."[13] While appearing in *Louisiana Purchase*, Bruce doubled as a chanteuse in two hotel lounges, the Pierre and the Waldorf-Astoria, and could be heard on the radio with Ben Bernie. Bruce, who must have had a terrific press agent, even landed on the cover of *Life*.[14] She headed off to Hollywood but success did not follow. By 1946, her season of notoriety was forgotten. Julie was a perfect fit for the still young Bruce who already had plenty of life experience. A tall and robust figure—physically unlike the fragile, petite Morgan—Bruce effectively began the process that effaced Morgan's approach to the role from historical memory.

A standout feature of both *Oklahoma!* and *Carousel* was their use of ballet and modern dance–inspired movement to further the story, amplify characterization, and add a note of artistic seriousness to the whole. While it is difficult to imagine adding a dream ballet to *Show Boat*—Susan Stroman would do so in the 1994 revival—Hammerstein took steps to include serious dancing in his "new production," hiring Helen Tamiris, a choreographer long associated with modern dance, and featuring Pearl Primus, a current star of the small but vibrant New York Negro concert dance scene. In the process, "Queenie's Ballyhoo" and "In Dahomey" were remade, extending the life of these two black chorus numbers for another generation.

Helen Tamiris's career as both choreographer and dancer reached back to the late 1920s, when she mined the very same vogue for spirituals that launched Robeson and *Show Boat*. An early Tamiris solo concert included two dances set to spirituals, of which Tamiris remembered in her autobiography, "They [the audience] liked best of all the Negro Spirituals—I said to myself as I came off stage . . . I will make many Negro dances—I understand the Negro people so well!—their yearnings—I was happy that they liked these dances."[15] She was the only white American modern dancer to make the experience of black Americans a consistent theme. Tamiris's best-known work, *How Long, Brethren?* (1937) was the most performed modern dance work of the 1930s, a signature product of the dance wing of the Federal Theatre Project (FTP).[16] Set to Negro spirituals sung by a black chorus and danced by Tamiris and a company of white women, *How Long, Brethren?* was intended to express the contemporary predicament of southern blacks. Tamiris made no effort to include black dancers available in the FTP, but her use of black singers accompanying white dancers was an unusual instance of interracial performance. In a sign of changing times that made a similar mark on the text of *Show Boat*, Tamiris changed "niggers" to "darkies" in the song texts sung by the black chorus. After the war, Tamiris shifted to commercial work on Broadway. Her acclaimed dances for *Up in Central Park* (1945) likely recommended the choreographer to Hammerstein. After the success of *Show Boat*, Rodgers and Hammerstein hired her for *Annie Get Your Gun*. All of Tamiris's mid-1940s Broadway work involved the vogue for Americana sweeping the theater at the time and stemming from *Oklahoma!*; *Show Boat* was easily assimilated into this trend.

Show Boat required Tamiris to work with black dancers for the first time, and among those cast in a featured role was a young African American woman named Pearl Primus.[17] Born in Trinidad but raised in New York, Primus was one of several anthropologist-cum-dancers doing innovative work. Like Katherine Dunham, Primus "transferred [her] knowledge and experience of African diasporan culture to an African American setting and, in this process, rejuvenated notions of blackness."[18] Primus's precocious concert stage debut—she had been training for a career in medicine and only dancing for a short while—came in February 1943 in a program of works she both choreographed and danced. Primus opened with "African Ceremonial" and included dances about racial injustice in the South. A solo dance to a recitation of the lyrics to "Strange Fruit," a song about lynching made famous by Billie Holiday, helped take her small company into Café Society Downtown, a leftist interracial venue. That same year, Primus was featured in the Negro Freedom Rally at Madison Square Garden alongside Duke Ellington, Langston Hughes, and Robeson, and appeared at Carnegie Hall with Asadata Forata, the African concert dancer who first brought tribal dancing to the New York stage in the 1930s. Primus spent the summer of 1944 in the South gathering dance ideas at black churches. Her Broadway debut concert again opened with "African Ceremonial." Dances to spirituals and poems by Hughes, including "The Negro Speaks of Rivers," followed. The finale was a solo to music by John Cage, who accompanied Primus on prepared piano. Then came *Show Boat*, her first appearance in a Broadway show.

In the words of the dance historian Julia Foulkes:

> Primus's body more broadly conformed to the stereotypical male or female "Negroid": broad nose, large expressive eyes, dark pigmentation, and muscular thighs and buttocks. Although only five feet two inches tall, she was described as strong and sturdy rather than petite. Perhaps largely due to her distinguishable physical characteristics, descriptions of her dancing generally pointed to how well she performed the "primitive rhythms." White reviewers described the muscular and barefooted Priums as a "strong, rhythmical, wild creature," a "young filly" romping over the pasture, showing all the signs of being a "thorough-bred," and looking out from "jungle distances" as, in Martha Graham's phrase, a "panther." Identifying Primus as a member of the animal kingdom reinforced prejudices about African Americans' sexual nature and their place on the evolutionary scale. Put a different way, one audience member of the 1940s I spoke to said she did not know until she saw Primus that women could move with such weight, strength, and masculinity.[19]

How did Tamiris and Primus put their mark on *Show Boat*? Tamiris was the choreographer of record; Primus, still a new talent, entered *Show Boat* as a featured dancer known for innovative, racially engaged, self-choreographed dances performed on the concert stage. A *New York Times* announcement at the start of rehearsals listed Primus as "Fatima," the coochie-coochie dancer at the World's Fair, hinting that originally Hammerstein assumed the dancer might fill this small body-oriented but not necessarily dance-centered role.[20] If she was ever considered for the part, Primus was all wrong for Fatima's exotic stereotype of the veiled Middle Eastern dancer. Indeed, there was no existing role in *Show Boat* for her to play and so new named characters were created for her as Primus commandeered two black chorus numbers for her own purposes. Tamiris was certainly involved in the making of these numbers: backstage stills depict her working with the black dance chorus. But Primus's reputation had been built as a self-choreographing soloist. Unlike many modern dance pioneers, Tamiris had no codified technique, instead working with her dancers to craft specific movements for specific occasions, always with a commitment to expressing social truths in compelling ways.[21] (Tamiris had worked with Primus in a studio context several years earlier at the New Dance Group, a New York collective founded with the intention to "actively welcome all regardless of race."[22] In 1940, Primus was the first black dancer to receive a scholarship to the collective.) Tamiris was perhaps an ideal collaborator for Primus: the former helping the latter shape her concert dance persona to the commercial stage. However managed in practice, the collaboration between Tamiris and Primus worked to remake "Queenie's Ballyhoo" and "In Dahomey" into memorable moments open to further alteration by later dancers and choreographers.

Virtually all the lyrics for "Queenie's Ballyhoo" were cut. (Like Alberta Hunter before her but for different reasons, Helen Dowdy lost this particular skirmish in the ongoing struggle over Queenie's musical numbers.) In the place of Queenie's breathless description of a stage melodrama, Primus and Tamiris inserted a dance titled "No Shoes." Primus as Sal and LaVerne French as Sam played two shoeless blacks on the levee. Dancing with flexed feet and jutting elbows, Sam and Sal joined a group of better-dressed, well-heeled black patrons, all entering the *Cotton Blossom* for the show. Despite Lucinda Ballard's stylized costuming, Primus and Tamiris used "No Shoes" to inject some class contrast—not conflict—into the black chorus of *Show Boat*, creating a little narrative of diversity within the black ensemble, adding subtlety to the usually homogeneous Broadway chorus.

The best fit for Primus, and likely the number that gave Hammerstein the idea of hiring her, was "In Dahomey." Judging from the published score, Tamiris and Primus did not change the vocal or dance music from 1927. (Hammerstein's lyric for the black chorus "we're glad to see those white folks go" was, however, softened to "those people.") But the program and reviews suggest the original ironic reading of "In Dahomey," building on Hammerstein's lyric, was jettisoned in favor of a narrative tribal dance, utterly sincere in its content. Four new named characters were invented for the scene and added to the cast list in the program. Primus played the Dahomey Queen (see fig. 7.1). Alma Sutton, who had appeared in the breakthrough African narrative dance production *Kykunkor* in 1934, played Ata. Claude Marchant and Talley Beatty, both associated with Dunham's well-known company, danced Mala and Bora. Beatty had played the Fugitive in Dunham's antilynching work *Tropic Death* (1937) and would choreograph *Southern Landscape*, a breakthrough work featuring a new kind of black male dance virtuosity, shortly after *Show Boat* closed. He worked again on Broadway with Tamiris in the revue *Inside U.S.A.* (1948). *Show Boat* offered all these black dancers consistent employment that supported concert dance projects, which they pursued concurrently, appearing, as Primus did, in dance concerts on Sundays when *Show Boat* was dark. Indeed, the 1946 revival marked the beginning of a twenty-year period when *Show Boat* played a role in the careers of black concert dancers, providing well-paying jobs in the commercial theater that could support even less stable

7.1. *Pearl Primus as the Dahomey Queen. This photo—along with similar posed images of Magnolia and Andy and Frank and Ellie—was likely on display in the lobby of the Ziegfeld Theatre, where* Show Boat *played in 1946.(Photo by Vandamm Studio © Billy Rose Theatre Division, The New York Public Library for the Performing Arts)*

(and less remunerative) work on the concert stage, revisiting in the domain of dance the strategy Robeson had used to build his concert career in London in 1928.

Primus and the other black dancers made a strong impact on reviewers, most of whom wrote about the new dance sequences. *Life* described "In Dahomey" as "A new-style dance, not in the original production, . . . executed with stunning vigor by a troupe of 36 negroes."[23] Walter Terry allotted a sizable portion of his *Herald Tribune* review to the black dancers:

> The primitive African dance which occurs in the World's Fair scene has the intensity of an incantation as the pounding feet and vibrating bodies generate rhythmical magic. Pearl Primus, the star of the [Negro] unit, centers both rhythm and action in the crescendos of her body pulsations, the brilliant Talley Beatty gives visual verity to the song lyric "I'm walking on the air," LaVerne French describes arenas of action with great sweeps of the leg, while Alma Sutton, Claude Marchant and the others contribute individual bits to the enrichment of the whole. In the levee dance and in other dance interludes, the Negro group in *Show Boat* accounts for many of the high-spots in this distinguished revival, and that is something of a tribute when one pauses long enough to realize that they are competing with a brace of the best loved tunes in America.[24]

Writing for the leftist *Daily Worker*, Samuel Sillen praised the work of the black performers and the production itself but found the content of *Show Boat* wanting, anticipating later and louder protests, "The Negro artists account for a good part of the evening's success. . . . Pearl Primus does two especially fine dances, 'No Shoes' and 'Dance of the Dahomeys' in different moods. . . . The entire Negro ensemble does a brilliant job. . . . It is good to find this production attempting to avoid stereotypes, within the framework of the Jim Crow locale for the story; but the story-pattern is by no means altogether satisfactory as a vehicle for a mixed company."[25] More satisfactory mixed-race musicals would be a long time coming, but when they did arrive *Show Boat* would still be around (see epilogue).

The Dahomey tribal dance in particular proved a flexible and lasting part of *Show Boat* for a generation. When Primus left the cast, LaVerne French took over as the Dahomey King (see fig. 7.2). French danced the role on the national tour, and nearly every review collected by co-producer Richard Rodgers's national clipping service highlighted his contribution to the show.[26] Descriptions of French's dancing by white theater (not dance) critics recorded his impact on audiences across the nation. These critics struggled to find the right language to describe French and the black dancers' evident technical skill while also registering the meaning of their dancing in racial terms, mixing notions of the primitive (black) body with classical (white) ballet. "Last night the colored members of the company, though their roles are lesser, brought the best moments to the performance for the most part. They contributed zest and a kind of glee which gave the show flashes of warmth which it very much needs. The choreography provided for them in the dances is certainly nothing very imaginative but their vigour and fervor made the dancing the most zingful spots of the evening."[27] "To end this review without mention of the superb dancing of the Negro corps of dancers would disregard a great portion of the enjoyment of the show. The dancing could almost be classed as ballet and in many of the leaps exceeded the best we have seen in the classical field."[28] Critics described French as "nimble as a cat," "superbly lithe and rhythmic in movement and strikingly dramatic in pantomime," his barefoot "splendid acrobatic dancing" was "astounding," his "prodigious leaps" and

7.2. *LaVerne French as the Dahomey King. (Author's collection)*

"spinning gracefulness" "demanding an agility and classical understanding that is rarely combined."[29] Performed in scarlet costumes against a red African art-inspired backdrop by Howard Bay, which contrasted strongly with the Victorian gingerbread of the rest of the set, "In Dahomey" was categorized as a "native sketch," "torrid," "a really galvanic Negro ritual dance," "a pagan ballet [and] a wild orgy."[30] The critic for the *Denver Post* brought these strains together: "Bounding onto the stage like a thunderbolt, a dancer, LaVerne French, made a tremendous impression. A dance of primitive force which worked into a magnificent frenzy was given meaning by the brilliantly projected force of his dancing."[31]

French embodied stereotypes of black tribal culture by way of undeniable technical control, which challenged easy notions of "natural" black rhythm or sensuality. This type of dancing—particularly by a black male—was new to national audiences, especially those who attended Broadway touring companies and who were not necessarily a sophisticated dance crowd. The technical control of the black dancers in the 1946 *Show Boat* was undeniable to all who saw them, and French was anointed a star of the revival tour. Others in the cast, such as Beatty, would put this technical prowess to expressive work in concert dances like the male solo "Mourner's Bench" from *Southern Landscape*, which remains a signal early example of the combination of extreme virtuoso control and forthright emotional expression of the black experience that would come to global prominence in the work of Alvin Ailey.[32] Within the history of black concert dance, French's "In Dahomey," building as it did on Primus's original, participated in the historic innovation of new, danced, black masculinities that would emerge with great power in the late 1950s.

Show Boat—like *Porgy and Bess* for singers—played a practical role in the careers of black dancers for as long as Negro modern dance was part of the show. The Jones Beach *Show Boats* of 1956 and 1957 were massive summer productions playing a waterfront outdoor amphitheater located a short drive from New York City. Included among the cast were Albert Popwell, Geoffrey Holder, and Alvin Ailey. The power of the Dahomey sequence at Jones Beach was dramatized by Al Hirschfeld in a caricature from 1956 (see frontispiece). Popwell (as the King) and company take over from the right. Sam and Sal from "Queenie's Ballyhoo" appear in the middle ground. Andy looks on impassively at the left. The massive *Cotton Blossom*, a barge that literally sailed into the scene, provides the background. Hirschfeld suggests a chief attraction of *Show Boat* at Jones Beach was the dancing of skilled (and nearly naked) black dancers. For many audiences in the immediate postwar decades, this was indeed the case. Popwell had danced with Primus in 1943 and appeared in the mixed-cast shows *Beggar's Holiday* (1946) and *Finian's Rainbow* (1947), and the black-cast *House of Flowers* (1954). After *Show Boat*, he joined Ailey's company. Holder, who danced the King at Jones Beach in 1957, had danced in and created a *banda* dance for *House of Flowers*, and would stage and dance a tribal king-centered ballet in *Aida* at the Met in the early 1960s. (The *Aida* ballet had been conceived for Holder's wife, black ballerina Carmen DeLavallade. When she took ill, he stepped into the part, a further example of the gender flexibility of tribal-themed dance in this era.) Alvin Ailey, another alumnus of *House of Flowers*, would emerge shortly after appearing in the chorus of the 1957 Jones Beach *Show Boat* as the premier African American modern dancer and choreographer of his generation. Ailey's international reputation was built on works like *Revelations* (1960), a dance to Negro spirituals, which was exported around the world by the U.S. State Department. *Revelations* became the most seen modern dance work of the Cold War era, harkening back to Tamiris's *How Long, Brethren?* only this time created by a black choreographer and danced by a (mostly) black company.[33] Between these two concert dances set to spirituals, *Show Boat*'s postwar black concert dance numbers—created for Primus, built upon by later dancers, effectively remaking the strong contribution of 1920s black dance to the success of the show—provided a connecting bridge.

The opportunity for a black modern dancer to create and perform in *Show Boat* would last until the late 1960s. Carlton Johnson, a versatile dancer who had worked in theater, film, and television, was the assistant choreographer and danced the added character Outcast in the Los Angeles Civic Light Opera's 1960 and 1967 productions. A witch doctor and Petro-Drummer rounded out the featured dancers in these last vestiges of the Tamiris-Primus "In Dahomey."

HOLLYWOOD, 1944–1951

Hammerstein had nothing to do with *Show Boat* at MGM, and the studio's use of the property for its own purposes produced an extreme remaking without historical precedent or subsequent influence: the Technicolor version of 1951. But prior to this commercially successful film, MGM toyed with *Show Boat* for almost a decade.

MGM acquired the movie rights to *Show Boat* in 1938, and the screenwriter George Wells produced a completely new script in 1944.[34] Wells gave Magnolia the role of voice-over narrator and filled out Ravenal's southern identity by creating a plantation for him to visit with Magnolia and Andy. Wells's Ravenal is the black sheep of a respectable southern family rather than Hammerstein's "way-farer along the river." Wells added "an ancient, grizzled negro—a house servant" to the story as Ravenal's faithful retainer, taking *Show Boat* closer than it had ever gone to what Karen Cox has dubbed the "moonlight and magnolias" strain of the South as imagined in popular culture.[35] When the aged Magnolia learns Ravenal has quit gambling and is living out his days at the old plantation, she and Kim and the entire *Cotton Blossom* go there to bring him back into the fold. This unused remaking of *Show Boat* emphasized the southern aspects of Ferber's tale, anticipating the 1951 film that would similarly play down Chicago and eliminate New York as important locales.

Interested in keeping the valuable property alive without investing in a full-blown cinematic version, MGM simultaneously put up 75 percent of the capital for the 1946 stage revival—Rodgers and Hammerstein supplied the rest—and made use of *Show Boat* in the Jerome Kern biopic *Till the Clouds Roll By*.[36] Produced by the Arthur Freed Unit, one of three musical-making units at the studio, *Till the Clouds* was in production from late 1945 to May 1946, exactly the period when Hammerstein's revival was rehearsing and running.

Till the Clouds Roll By opens with a seventeen-minute version of *Show Boat* presented as the triumph of Kern's creative life. This mini-*Show Boat* features Lena Horne—MGM, indeed Hollywood's, only black contract star—costumed as Julie and singing "Can't Help Lovin' Dat Man" as a solo out of any story context. The sequence begins with the opening chorus from act 1, using separate black and white choruses, the latter given greater prominence. An abbreviated ballyhoo for Andy follows, during which Horne appears for a few seconds only: a concession to the lyric that mentions Julie by name. By contrast, Virginia O'Brien as Ellie and Bruce Cowling as Steve (uncredited on the print) are featured in short comic bits with adoring white males and females respectively. In this version, an obviously black Julie cannot stand next to Steve for a moment. The opening segues into Tony Martin as Ravenal offering a bit of "Where's the Mate for Me," with Kathryn Grayson as Magnolia joining him for "Make Believe" (prefaced by a bit of dialogue). Both songs were taken at soporifically slow tempos, an approach to *Show Boat* which consistently marked MGM's treatment of the score, perhaps the musical expression of the studio's idea that *Show Boat* was "immortal." Next, O'Brien sings "Life Upon the Wicked Stage" in her signature deadpan manner. Horne's "Can't Help Lovin' Dat Man" follows. The black bass Caleb Peterson singing "Ol' Man River" with a mixed chorus of blacks and whites all swaying behind him brings down the curtain. Peterson and the black chorus move down to the footlights on the song's final phrase: their swaying walk effectively turned to a physical expression of weariness; their raised hands at the close recalling the *Porgy* saucer burial. The white chorus and principals—including Horne—remain on the *Cotton Blossom* at the back of the stage, observing—together with the in-film audience—the black cast deliver *Show Boat*'s signature musical moment in a way they never would have done in an actual production.

In a rush to put the sequence together, MGM sent the original 1927 lyrics for the opening black chorus to the Production Code Authority, which advised, as it had in 1936, elimination of the word "nigger," which MGM did forthwith, using the racially inspecific "here we all work" instead.[37] Roger Edens, Freed's musical director, created the *Show Boat* sequence, which at one point may also have included Horne singing "Bill."[38] This quickly made mini-version of *Show Boat* was the first to explore the notion that Julie might best be played by an actress of color. Horne would not be visually convincing in a "passing" role—particularly in a color film—and she had never sought to pass professionally, building her career as a trailblazing black star on talent that defied racial limits. By the 1990s, though, African American actresses with darker skin than Horne's were playing the role on stage (see chap. 9).

Show Boat as remade in *Till the Clouds Roll By* must be read in a specific production context. Edens pulled the sequence together in January and early February 1946, tacking the result on to the beginning of a weak script that went through multiple revisions.[39] Quick decisions on a film designed to showcase as many MGM stars as possible led to Horne—briefly and incompletely—taking the role of Julie in a context where *Show Boat*'s place in Kern's career trumped all other concerns. *Till the Clouds* uses *Show Boat* to point to Kern. The show's characters, songs, and stage pictures are abstracted rather than fleshed out and put to two mutually compatible purposes: insisting on Kern's preeminent place in Broadway history while also providing characteristic vehicles for MGM's stable of stars. O'Brien's "Life Upon the Wicked Stage" offers a case in point. As in all her MGM films, O'Brien remained almost completely expressionless while singing. And while she moves more in this number than most, the bright smiles and graceful moves of the white ladies of the chorus backing her up make O'Brien look dull by comparison. The contrast was, indeed, the joke. But the role of Ellie was built on physical and emotional exuberance: a dancing and singing part, which requires broad comic delivery and a spirit of generosity that reaches out to the audience, engaging directly in the spirit of vaudeville and musical comedy (the generic roots of the role and Eva Puck, its original interpreter). O'Brien's blank-face persona, crafted and platformed by MGM in the early 1940s, effectively threw a wet blanket on "Life Upon the Wicked Stage," offering a one-dimensional Ellie that would never work in a complete version of *Show Boat*. Horne's appearance as Julie is best understood in the same light: as the expression of an

MGM persona briefly grafted onto a *Show Boat* costume and song. Horne sings "Can't Help Lovin' Dat Man" in a vaguely southern but otherwise indeterminate location. She is not in Queenie's kitchen, and Queenie is not around to question Julie's knowledge of a song only colored folks sing. Horne's extremely slow and emotionally deliberate approach, on the edge of mannered, would be difficult to insert into the kitchen scene but would have a demonstrable impact on later MGM renderings of *Show Boat.*

MGM's Kern biopic had been in development since 1940 with active work on the script ongoing from 1943 involving many writers and several complete revisions of the story. A lengthy shooting schedule coupled with a period of retakes stretched production out over eight months—highly inefficient by studio standards.[40] Kern's death just as filming began necessitated further revisions. This was a troublesome project, and Kern was part of the problem, as screenwriter George Wells noted: "The main difficulty of this story seems to be the lack of colorful episodes in the career of the leading character."[41] Still, Kern had crossed paths with many famous, more interesting individuals, and this aspect was developed to draw favorable comparisons between famous theatrical names and MGM stars (for example, Judy Garland impersonated the Ziegfeld star Marilyn Miller).

Guy Bolton, a friend and collaborator of Kern's in the 1910s, was initially hired to write the film. He completed a treatment in January 1943 and delivered a script that July.[42] Bolton touched on *Show Boat* very little, but any story of Kern's life was going to have to incorporate "Ol' Man River," which Bolton took as an opportunity to include Paul Robeson in the film. The scene Bolton paints cannot be taken for fact, but he likely knew some version of the story from Kern. Treatment and script offer slightly different takes on the songwriter's encounter with a black singing star. In the treatment, Kern and Ziegfeld have a conversation about hiring Robeson—misspelled as "Robson" throughout—to play "the old Negro in *Show Boat*." Ziegfeld thinks Robeson can be gotten but, he notes, "It depends on how much he likes the part." The film dissolves to Kern at the piano, introducing "Ol' Man River" to Robeson in Ziegfeld's office. Robeson likes the song but says he cannot get out of his concert engagements and recommends his "friend" Bledsoe, who will "be just as good for you as I'd be." Robeson then sings "Ol' Man River," initiating a montage of songs from *Show Boat.* Bolton effectively elided the fact that Robeson did not, in fact, introduce "Ol' Man River." He also gave Robeson the opportunity to do on screen what he had done in real life—say no to Kern and Ziegfeld. The treatment clearly hinged on Robeson appearing in the film. In the script, Bolton eliminated Robeson and emphasized "Ol' Man River" as Kern's achievement. The scene begins with an unnamed "artist" singing "Ol'

Man River." In a bid to influence the musical content of the film, Bolton advised, "If the artist engaged does not make obligatory the singing of this number in full I suggest we pick it up at the end." Robeson alone would have been the artist of the stature to demand a complete singing of the song. The feasibility of bringing Robeson into the film—never very likely—was perhaps dictating the script's equivocal wording. During the song, the camera trucks back to reveal Kern conducting and Ziegfeld watching admiringly. When the number ends, Kern's wife Eva appears—"She is deeply stirred."—and kisses Kern across the orchestra rail. Having written Robeson out of the film, Bolton turns "Ol' Man River" into a token of Kern and Eva's marriage, an altogether typical approach in the postwar songwriter biopic cycle.

In the final film, which abandoned virtually every idea in the Bolton version, two "artists" sang "Ol' Man River": Caleb Peterson in the opening sequence in costume as Joe, and Frank Sinatra in the closing "Land Where the Good Songs Go" medley. "Ol' Man River" entered Sinatra's repertoire in 1945, when he recorded the song on a V-disc version of his radio show and sang it at a Hollywood Bowl salute to Kern.[43] An early script has *Till the Clouds* open with Sinatra singing the song as part of a radio broadcast.[44] With the insertion of the *Show Boat* sequence, Sinatra's "Ol' Man River" was bumped to the very end of the film, where it was routined in a grand manner with a full orchestra visible and Sinatra elevated to absurd heights, standing atop a white classical pillar, attired in a white tuxedo. Central to Sinatra's interpretation of "Ol' Man River" and played out to maximum effect in the film was a display of breath control between the end of the bridge and the start of the final phrase: "land in jail" and "I get's weary" connected by a downwards slide to a low note sustained for a very long time. (This added vocal flourish would be taken up by the black bass Michel Bell in the 1990s revivals of *Show Boat*.) The production history of *Till the Clouds* suggests again and again how the Freed Unit saw Kern's most famous score and song as tools to be deployed in the promotion of MGM stars. At Metro, "Ol' Man River" was, first and foremost, a chance to feature Frank Sinatra.

The Freed Unit finally made a full-scale, color *Show Boat* in 1951. The film proved a great success at the box office, touted in the exhibitor trade press as a "mortgage-lifter."[45] According to *Variety*'s summary of 1951, only the epic *David and Bathsheba* with its $7,000,000 take exceeded *Show Boat*'s return of $5,200,000. Freed's critically acclaimed *An American in Paris* and *The Great Caruso* (a tenor-centered musical produced by one of MGM's other musical units) tied for third at $4,500,000 each.[46] *Show Boat* was, appropriately, spelled $*how Boat* on one box office summary prepared for Freed.[47]

The press celebrated the pictorial beauty of Freed's *Show Boat* and the scale of the *Cotton Blossom* itself, a three-story paddle wheeler floating majestically down a three-quarter mile stand-in for the Mississippi—a leftover Tarzan set on Metro's back lot. The director George Sidney shot the exterior scenes outside, a costly choice that at times slowed production. Liberated from the claustrophobic soundstage environments that typified studio films and supplemented with footage taken on the actual Mississippi that was seamlessly blended with shots taken on the lot, the visual authenticity of this *Show Boat* renewed the impact of a story and score most reviewers noted was old hat by this point.

The MGM *Show Boat* was all about Julie, or, more accurately, all about Ava Gardner, who played the role as a variant of her previous portrayals of sexually loose women whose stories ended either badly or sadly. Producer Freed reportedly told squeaky-clean singer Dinah Shore, who was tested for the part, she couldn't play Julie "Because you're not a whore . . . Ava is."[48] Making Julie a "whore" was nothing new—Universal's 1929 Julie had been presented as one—but the difference here was Gardner, who redefined the role in Hammerstein and Kern's version, bringing the allure of screen sex—early 1950s style—to the part. In this way, *Show Boat* allowed MGM to effectively advance Gardner's emerging persona as a sexually aware white leading woman whose place in film narratives (and real-life behavior) had the capacity to titillate the white film audience for whom MGM created its product. And while Julie was still being described by some reviewers using words like "octoroon" and "mulatto," the racial drama of the character's plight could be downplayed so that race hardly mattered. As one reviewer euphemistically outlined the story, "complications force [Julie] to withdraw from the cast" of the *Cotton Blossom*.[49] At a time when social-problem films addressing race were on the rise, MGM soft-pedaled *Show Boat*'s miscegenation plot almost entirely.

MGM simultaneously reshaped *Show Boat* to conform to the studio's historic emphasis on family entertainment. Here, Ravenal emerged as the central character. Filling out his troubled journey away from, then back to, his place at the head of a nuclear family became the studio's solution to the perennial question of what to do with the character after he abandoned Magnolia and Kim. To further minimize Ravenal's decision to leave and also make his return more plausible, in the MGM version he is only gone for five or so years. He leaves before Kim is born—eliminating his reprise of "Make Believe" sung as a farewell to the uncomprehending girl—and returns to the bosom of the *Cotton Blossom* family when Kim is still a young child.

Both strategies—emphasizing Julie's sexual nature by way of Gardner's persona and tracing Ravenal's journey to responsible manhood so the story could end with a convincing happy ending—led to a radical paring down of the black characters and numbers that had always characterized *Show Boat* as a musical narrative in a period setting. MGM turned *Show Boat* into the story of a respectable white family—sundered, then restored—and the fascinating, hardly respectable but sympathetic woman who played a key role in their lives, all set in a picturesque premodern past and including just the right number of subservient black figures providing local color. Removing black characters and black musical performance from the story as much as possible and truncating the historical reach of the narrative effectively eliminated all traces of the popular music plot Hammerstein had explored over his twenty years making and remaking *Show Boat*. In fact, this version never even reaches the twentieth century. If *Show Boat* in the broadest sense is understood as Hammerstein's effort to bring black and white into a story that traces larger social changes by means of music and dance, then MGM's version marks the nadir of the original vision for the work, departing from the maker's concept and the show's production history to an unprecedented degree. After attending a preview of the film, Hammerstein telegraphed Freed, "I THINK SHOW BOAT WILL BE A DAZZLING SUCCESS I AM GOING TO PHONE YOU SOON AND TALK TO YOU ABOUT IT CONGRATULATIONS."[50] Hardly a ringing endorsement, Hammerstein acknowledged that MGM had made of *Show Boat* something that would sell very well. Tellingly, the MGM *Show Boat* had little impact on subsequent stage versions, which brought a more balanced approach in racial terms and further explored Hammerstein's popular music plot.

Ava Gardner was emerging as a big star when she was cast as Julie. *Show Boat* marked her first appearance in color and her first entrance—arrayed in hot pink satin with yellow trim—celebrated Gardner's arrival at the top of the Hollywood heap. But there were other reasons audiences wanted to catch a glimpse of Gardner in 1951. She arrived at *Show Boat*'s Hollywood premiere on the arm of Frank Sinatra, a married man, and a Catholic, seeking a divorce from his wife. Anyone paying attention to popular culture knew that Frank and Ava were having an affair, but the *Show Boat* premiere marked their first public appearance as a couple, an act that just a few years earlier would have been considered brazen and, among insiders, bad for Hollywood. The gossip columnist Hedda Hopper reprinted one reader's comment on the inherent irony in Gardner singing "Can't Help Lovin' Dat Man," Julie's song of devotion to her husband, Steve: "How untypical of Ava that would be."[51] The box office success of MGM's *Show Boat* cannot be easily separated from the frenzy of public interest in Hollywood's latest adulterous couple. Fortunately for MGM, Gardner's very public personal life was working in historically innovative ways, as *Time* noted in a cover story about her just weeks after the premiere. "Ava's open affair with a married man—following Ingrid Bergman's escapade with Roberto Rossellini and Rita Hayworth's fling with Aly Khan—has inevitably reawakened in some quarters the ancient question about Hollywood morals. It has brought her some censure (one letter writer habitually addresses her as 'Bitch-Jezebel-Gardner'). Yet it actually seems to be helping, rather than hurting, her earning power. Reports columnist Sidney Skolsky solemnly: 'Ava worried. She lost weight. But now she has found that scandal can't hurt her.'"[52]

Once again, public scandal in a star's personal life helped *Show Boat* succeed. And as with Helen Morgan and Prohibition, Ava Gardner and the Sinatra affair would play off each other in the 1951 *Show Boat* in a way that bracketed Julie's racial problem. Morgan and Gardner alike played Julie as a mixed-race woman who was physically capable of passing with ease and who lived a white life without much inner turmoil over her blackness. The shame of getting caught in the miscegenation scene was the only personal drama in being black borne by Julie in this approach to the role. How individual Julies say the line "Yes, that's right" in response to the sheriff's accusation "your pa was white, your mammy black" provides one key to how each actress taking the part understands Julie's blackness. Late in the century, Lonette McKee would say the line with a note of defiance. Morgan and Gardner admit the fact of Julie's blackness quietly, looking down, telegraphing nothing more than shame at being found out. Neither Morgan nor Gardner (who was dubbed in the film but could be heard singing on the cast album) brought Julie's blackness into the way they sang the part. (Mixed-race performers singing Julie in later decades would inject Julie's voice with clear notes of blackness.) What might be called the "white" approach to Julie allows for other pathologies to fill the void, such as alcohol in Morgan's case. In Gardner's case, her earlier roles prepared the ground for a sexual interpretation of Julie's character: the loss of Steve and the *Cotton Blossom* lead her down the path of sexual licentiousness. Julie becomes one of Hollywood's (and Gardner's) lost white women. An additional dialogue scene for Julie and Ravenal late in the story reinforced this interpretation and effectively remade Julie into a pitiable figure, a loose woman who belonged in the shadows but had a heart of gold. But before looking closely at Gardner's Julie, archival evidence affords a glimpse at an interpretation of the role that, had Freed's original plans come to fruition, might of turned the performance history of Julie in a very different direction.

While the MGM Julie would seem to be custom made for Gardner, the part as written by the screenwriter John Lee Mahin was originally intended for Judy Garland. Mahin's first script was completed just as Garland was coming off suspension for habitual tardiness and absences, which had disrupted production on several films.[53] Gardner was announced for the role just weeks before shooting began, right around the time Garland was definitively cut loose by MGM.[54] In the waning days of Garland's time at MGM, Julie—like Annie Oakley in *Annie Get Your Gun*—was understood to be a natural opportunity for the musical star. Two new songs were added for Garland's Julie. A reworked "Queenie's Ballyhoo" gave her an up-tempo number. A farewell song on the *Cotton Blossom* stage, to be sung just after the miscegenation scene but before Julie and Steve leave the boat, provided yet another emotionally fraught opportunity for vocal expression. Kern's "Nobody Else But Me" and "Why Was I Born?," the latter written for Morgan in *Sweet Adeline*, were both under consideration. The effort to expand Julie's part vocally for Garland—allowing for an extra song performed for an onscreen audience unaware of the character's predicament—explains why Mahin put the revelation of Julie's mixed-race identity backstage during the hurly-burly of a performance on the *Cotton Blossom* rather than during the quiet of a rehearsal (where Ferber and Hammerstein put the confrontation with the sheriff).

Garland's Julie would have been a very different creature from Gardner's, even with the same lines. Changing descriptions of the character mark this shift. Mahin described Julie as "sweet and warm" in 1949—when the role was Garland's: a reader's report from early 1951, responding to Gardner's casting, pegged Julie as "beautiful, brooding."[55] Essential to the difference would have been Garland's embodiment of Julie as a woman with a voice, first and foremost a performer who moved the audience by pouring out her heart in song. Garland's approach would have brought a forceful interpretation to Julie's songs that might have remade the character in substantial ways for later versions. Garland would certainly have dominated *Show Boat* in a different way than Gardner did. Gardner was not a musical star, and when she sang onscreen in previous films her voice had been dubbed. She had no vocal or, indeed, performance identity, but she did have a beautiful face and figure, which in the ways of movie stars elicited audience reaction in an almost alchemical fashion. Critics amenable to her charms called her "arrestingly beautiful" and "pictorially exciting."[56] Gardner was not a movie star who *did* things, like singing or dancing as Garland did with almost desperate commitment, but rather a screen image who simply *was*, the opportunity to look at her, to spend some time in her celluloid presence, enough to sustain a film and her career. This magical aspect of Gardner's persona, shared by all Hollywood beauties, is expressed by her "performance" as a dancer at the start of *The Barefoot Contessa* (1954). Gardner herself never appears onscreen during the number. Instead, the rapt faces of her audience—men, women, young, old—offer a variety of extreme responses to a dancing woman who remains stubbornly outside the frame. Gardner brought this magic to the role of Julie as written for Garland. The two songs added for Garland were no longer necessary or perhaps even doable without a singing star, and both were jettisoned. It was enough to gaze on Gardner in period costumes, to revel in her Technicolor presence, and to see her sing (while another voice sang) the two memorable songs that Helen Morgan had made famous. The *New Yorker* critic sarcastically wrote that Gardner was "subjected to such close scrutiny by the camera that her handsome face often takes on the attributes of a relief map of Yugoslavia, and when she opens her mouth in song, she and the invisible contralto who is doing the real work synchronize so rarely that she might as well be reciting Burke on the Colonies as doing lip service to 'Why Was I Born?'"[57]

Gardner's "arresting" beauty and alluring cinematic persona had been developed steadily in the five years prior to her Julie, and her interpretation of the role is best understood within this intertextual context. In her breakthrough role opposite Burt Lancaster in *The Killers* (1946), Gardner demonstrated the ability to play a duplicitous film noir femme fatale. But her talents were immediately put to more expansive use in *The Hucksters* (1947) opposite Clark Gable. Gardner played a nightclub singer and likeable if loose girl who loses Gable to the superior charms of Deborah Kerr, a proper English war widow who is unwilling to have an affair and, by virtue of her virtue, elevates Gable's sense of both himself and his place in the postwar world. Gardner makes an honest play for Gable—even simulating a happy home by making dinner for him at her apartment—but she's savvy enough to see that Gable wants more from life than the huckster's game they both can play with ease. She exits the film on a long fade-out, raising a snifter of brandy to her much-praised mouth. She would survive but at a cost regularly exacted of Gardner's characters: the price of loneliness. (Gable plays against type in *The Hucksters*, and the Gardner-Gable combination would score big at the box office with *Mogambo* in 1953, where they wisely chose each other.) Early in *The Hucksters*, Gardner sings a torchy nightclub solo with piano accompaniment. She's an effective lip-synching performer whose beauty onscreen is revelatory even here, before her iconic "face" had been defined by MGM's makeup department. In *The Bribe* (1949), Gardner again played a sultry singer, and in *The Great Sinner* (1949), opposite Gregory Peck, she donned period dress for a Dostoyevsky-inspired spiritual melodrama. The latter film forged a connection between Gardner's beauty and the superficial attractions of moral turpitude, showing her as able to internally overcome the perhaps inherent corruption that comes from being beautiful even as she remained always distant from respectability. This equation would be applied to her Julie as well. Gardner's film just prior to *Show Boat* was the melodrama *East Side, West Side* (1949), where she played an oversexed woman who breaks up Barbara

Stanwyck and James Mason's marriage not once but twice before being killed by the girlfriend of another man. In a stingingly sexual scene, Gardner lounges on a sofa, offering her body to Mason who says, "Aren't you being a little bit obvious." Gardner replies, "I always was. That's what you like." She provokes him to slap her, visibly enjoys the pain, then adds, "What you really want is to be a little rotten like me." All these performances, together with the Sinatra saga, provided context for Gardner's Julie.

Both of Gardner's songs revise Morgan's approach to crucial *Show Boat* moments. "Bill" is slightly shortened (one verse is cut), and Gardner takes a casual approach, lounging around in a relaxed manner in generally high spirits. Gardner's Julie is a happy drunk surrounded, as always, by men; Morgan's Julie was a solitary drinker. From his earliest drafts, Mahin remade "Can't Help Lovin' Dat Man" so as to entirely remove the race question from Hammerstein and Kern's song "only colored folks sing." Mahin's Julie never exchanges a single word with Queenie, whose role is reduced to almost nothing. "Can't Help Lovin' Dat Man" is sung on the top deck, not in the kitchen. The only remnant of the song's racial identity is a few black musicians on the levee—literally three floors down from where Magnolia and Julie are—who provide accompaniment for a short dance chorus. Julie demonstrates a few shuffle steps as done "down on the levee" by "the gals." Magnolia copies her; both are presented as imitating blacks who are, like the musicians playing, invisible. (Morgan's Julie didn't participate in the dancing; later Julies on stage would.) When Parthy arrives, the song peters out—the tune unfinished, unresolved. The power of black song and dance expressed by black characters in an unrestrained manner, heretofore central to every version of *Show Boat*, is summarily eliminated, a strategy that perhaps originated with the notion that Garland as Julie would not want to share the number with Joe and Queenie, no matter who played the roles and there were no obvious choices.

"Can't Help Lovin' Dat Man" is preceded by a relatively hot kissing scene for Julie and Steve witnessed by the fascinated Magnolia played by Kathryn Grayson (the only casting continuity with *Till the Clouds*). Grayson's physically mature form and 1950s silhouette makes her declared wonder at the sight of men and women kissing a bit strange, but the crucial distinction between the virginal Magnolia and the experienced Julie is made. Steve's exit was to include Gardner delivering the come-hither line, "Going to make me come and get it?," the kind of sexy retort Gardner was known for (and odd when imagined as spoken by Garland). Julie and Magnolia's conversation preceding the song is still about love and men, but lacking Queenie's presence the subtext becomes entirely sexual. Gardner sings the song (dubbed in the film by Annette Warren's smoky voice) at Lena Horne's very slow tempo from

Till the Clouds, taking even more energy out of the entire number. The style and subtext can hardly be read as a big sister's advice to a younger girl about love. Gardner's Julie is lost in a reverie about Steve, who she describes as "all man" in the song cue. Posed by Sidney against a blue sky and green hills—both beautifully real rather than soundstage simulacra—Gardner's long, slow "Can't Help Lovin' Dat Man" becomes a hymn to Gardner's beauty more than anything else. Horne's version at the same tempo in *Till the Clouds* produced a similar effect. The viewer gets a good long look at both stars: beautiful women—black and white—singing the same song in a similar manner but in different contexts that express the difficulty Hollywood had digesting the racial complexities at the heart of *Show Boat*. The mismatch between *Show Boat* and MGM was so great in this instance that an essential element—"Can't Help Lovin' Dat Man's" celebration of black vernacular song and dance—demanded extreme revision.

Mahin's focus on Julie extended to a radical redeployment of "Ol' Man River," tying the song to Julie rather than letting it stand alone as Joe's articulation of the historical predicament of African Americans. The musical introduction to "Ol' Man River" makes this connection explicit. The descending "Mis'ry" theme (ex. 5.1b) is heard for the first time in the film when Steve and Julie exit the boat. The haunting melody—sung by stereotypical "white" Hollywood voices—segues into a bit of "Can't Help Lovin' Dat Man," which serves in turn as the introduction to "Ol' Man River" (sung by William Warfield as Joe). This is the only version of *Show Boat* to make a connection between these three melodies. The underscoring accompanies Julie and Steve's encounter with Joe on the gangplank where, in Mahin's words, "She faces Joe as a Negress for the first time."

JULIE (WITH A FORCED GAIETY): Well—ride the river, Joe!
Joe bends over her hand, taking it with great reverence in both of his.
JOE (BROKENLY): Miss Julie. . . . oh, Miss Julie . . .
JULIE: Keep ridin' the ole river, Joe, boy . . .
She tousles his head and walks on. Joe looks after her.

Julie addresses Joe with the diminutive "boy," typical of white southerners' speech toward black men, hardly the manner a woman cognizant that she is now a known "Negress" might use. "Ol' Man River" follows, punctuated visually by images of Joe, the *Cotton Blossom* floating down the river in the fog, and Julie and Steve riding along on the shore: all shot outdoors, all with an atmospheric beauty, making the sequence a virtuoso visual achievement for the time. Shooting the sequence took several extra days due to weather problems and difficulty controlling the fog: from the studio's perspective, the number was a costly investment in cinematic verisimilitude.[58]

The counterpoint between the world on the boat—a respectable realm of contentment, interracial to the extent that mostly silent blacks are welcome—and the world on the shore, where those such as Julie are fated to live, is repeated at the close of the film. There, Joe reprises "Ol' Man River" while Julie looks on from the levee, longingly but with joy, as the reunited Magnolia and Ravenal kiss against the setting sun. Mahin's repositioning of "Ol' Man River," effectively tying the song to the *Cotton Blossom* as an idealized realm and Julie as a sympathetic figure fated to life onshore, erases the racially specific, more resonant use of the song by Hammerstein in both his stage and screen versions. There, "Ol' Man River" stood on its own in a position of strength that initiated historic audience reaction to a charismatic black singer leading a group of black men raising their voices. Subsequent reprises marked the passage of time or particular moments—such as Magnolia and Ravenal's first kiss—and were unconnected to Julie. At MGM, the meanings of "Ol' Man River" were narrowed and, as in the finale to *Till the Clouds Roll By*, focused relentlessly on the star being spotlighted, ironically now Gardner instead of her current lover Sinatra.

But condemning the MGM *Show Boat* for foreclosing on "Ol' Man River" as an expression of the black experience is not so easy to do when Mahin's early drafts are examined closely. Contrary to the whitening impulse that operated over the film in production, in pre-production Mahin imagined amplifying Hammerstein and Kern's historic racially divided opening chorus. While drafting his script, Mahin had access to a virtually complete archive of *Show Boat* scripts assembled by the MGM script department, including unproduced film versions, a treasure trove of *Show Boat* remakings.[59] Mahin literally cut and pasted Hammerstein's lyrics into his first typed draft.[60] Mahin wanted to expand the opening black chorus—"Colored folks work on de Mississippi"—in a manner completely in sympathy with Hammerstein's intent to give as realistic a presentation of black laborers as the genre of the musical allowed. Mahin's description of the film's opening begins, "FULL SHOT— EXPANSE OF BOTTOM LAND BY MISSISSIPPI RIVER. Negro field hands, men and women, are working, picking cotton. To the left, a small cluster of shacks and warehouses complement the wharf. Stevedores are working here."[61] Mahin revised the musical structure of the opening chorus so that the stevedores loading cotton bales could sing back and forth with the field hands picking cotton and even rewrote a couplet of Hammerstein's lyric so the field laborers could express the "back-breakin' . . . fingers all achin'" nature of their work. Mahin opened the film with an altogether subtle (for Hollywood) presentation of the rural black labor force, calling for two distinct black choruses, which Mahin wanted to use a second time during "Ol' Man River." In that sequence, Mahin envisioned intercutting images of Julie and Steve leaving with Joe singing, and the field hands and stevedores doing their respective labors, revisiting the opening imagery, this time with Julie added to the mix. But Mahin's field hands and stevedores didn't make it into the film. The opening chorus was cut, and the black chorus heard singing with Joe goes largely unpictured. Even African American extras are hard to spot.

In the oddest of *Show Boat* publicity stills, MGM took staged shots of Gardner in a low-cut gown in the arms of Howard Keel, the film's Ravenal and Metro's resident romantic baritone. (Keel's primary concerns on being cast were Ravenal's weak character and vocal range. He wrote in his 2005 memoir *Only Make Believe*, "I'm a bass baritone and the part had usually been played by a tenor."[62]) In foreign markets, the photos of Gardner and Keel showed up on posters for *Show Boat*. Why was Ravenal embracing Julie? Figure 7.3 reproduces another odd MGM publicity still that telegraphs nothing about the nature of the story, further evidence MGM conceived of *Show Boat* above all as a vehicle for its stars. These photos misled in their construction of a romantic entanglement between Julie and Ravenal but did point toward an encounter between the two added by Mahin. MGM inserted an unprecedented task for Julie in the story: *she* leads Ravenal back to Magnolia. Having abandoned wife and child, Ravenal returns to riverboat gambling, where Julie encounters him while herself in the company of an unattractive, abusive "sport"—not Steve, just someone else. Julie is a woman for hire, a "slack-lipped and red-eyed" lush who apparently hangs on anyone with the price of a drink.[63] When the "sport" hits her, Ravenal has the chance to play the hero for a moment. (The Garland version had Julie reprise "Can't Help Lovin' Dat Man" at this point, with Ravenal's knowledge of the song by way of Magnolia initiating his encounter with Julie. In the film, Gardner plays a few notes on the piano, all that remains of what could have been a new, emotionally resonant take on "Can't Help Lovin' Dat Man" had Garland played the role.) After figuring out who Ravenal is, Julie approaches him and proceeds to pour out her heart, revealing how much she still loves Magnolia and inadvertently revealing to Ravenal that he has a five-year-old daughter. Reviews made much of the fact that knowing he had a child restored Ravenal to his senses, motivating him to take his place at the head of a new nuclear family. Julie's role is—therefore— essential in bringing the Ravenal family back together.

Mahin invested a lot in Ravenal's journey, scripting a lengthy sequence, drawing on Ferber, to flesh out his and Magnolia's marriage in Chicago. The rise and fall of their fortunes was to climax when Magnolia, finally losing patience with Ravenal's gambling, shouts at him, "You're a weak man! You're weak—You're weak.—You're weak—!," adding, for good measure, "Take your

7.3. *Which woman will Howard Keel as Ravenal choose? His wife, Magnolia (Kathryn Grayson), to the left or the alluring Julie (Ava Gardner), to the right. Keel played scenes with both in the 1951 MGM* Show Boat. *(Author's collection)*

hands off me! Take them off, Gay Ravenal, before I *hate* you!" The final bit about Magnolia hating Ravenal was cut in the editing phase. Keel remembered walking out of the premiere at this point, disgusted that the editor and Grayson—who didn't want to say the line in the first place—had made "Ravenal appear pretty weak."[64] A chastened Ravenal leaves, and the boardinghouse scene from Hammerstein, where Ellie and Frank appear at the moment when Magnolia receives Ravenal's goodbye letter, follows. The Trocadero scenes unfold as usual, but unlike all previous versions, Magnolia's success singing "After the Ball" does not initiate a successful career. Instead, she goes back to the *Cotton Blossom* with her father, with whom she shares the news she's pregnant. Like a good postwar wife, the MGM Magnolia returns to the home to raise her child. A less Ferberesque heroine is hard to imagine.

In all other versions of *Show Boat*, the story ends in the 1920s (or 1930s), taking in a total of at least forty years of history. The journey toward modernity was essential not only to Ferber's tale but also to Hammerstein and Kern's conception of the show. At MGM the story takes less than a decade. When Magnolia and Ravenal reunite, Kim is still a small child who will probably not even remember her parents' brief separation. This change has momentous effects. First, *Show Boat* becomes a generic melodrama with a predictable happy ending. In most such films, Gardner would be Magnolia's rival. Here, she's a force for reconciliation, although it's tempting to imagine Gardner meeting Keel on the packet boat and seducing him rather than sending him back to Grayson. (The scene could also be understood ironically as Gardner acting against type, pleading with Ravenal as a Sinatra stand-in to go back to his wife.) MGM clearly saw some chemistry between Gardner and Keel: the pair played married ranchers battling Mexicans and Indians in the western *Ride, Vaquero!* (1953).

Second, a *Show Boat* that never leaves the nineteenth century finds itself anchored in a mythic past. The lived historical transformation evident in characters who grow old dissolves into a tableau-like family portrait beside an eternal river. Because Magnolia willingly returns to the river after Ravenal abandons her, life on the *Cotton Blossom* assumes a static quality, making this version an untroubling journey back to an earlier, supposedly gentler time. All that's required is Ravenal taking his manly place. Ferber's book, both previous film versions, and all stage productions dealt with historical change as a primary theme. The MGM *Show Boat*—an outlier—traffics in the fantasy of an eternal, genteel, post–Civil War South. Indeed, the southern aspect of the MGM *Show Boat* was made explicit at the film's Hollywood premiere, where a sun-tanned Joan Crawford posed for the paparazzi on prop cotton bales with an old black banjo player hired to give local color to the event. No flappers were in evidence.

This static world, untouched by musical or technological innovation, was a familiar one at MGM, which produced a string of premodern musicals in the late forties and early fifties: Technicolor films set before about 1910—safely pre–World War I—with all-white casts sporting fancy, old-fashioned clothes and riding horse-drawn carriages, except for the eccentric types who drove new-fangled automobiles that always seem to break down. Films like *In the Good Old Summertime* (1949), *Take Me Out to the Ball Game* (1949), *Two Weeks with Love* (1950), and *Excuse My Dust* (1951) typify this cycle. Set on the cusp of modern history, these films offered a mythic American past, free of the anxiety and problems of the unfolding postwar/Cold War present. Ragtime occasionally intrudes but always as performed by whites (see, for example, Jane Powell's "The Oceana Roll" in *Two Weeks with Love*). The MGM *Show Boat* fits easily in this category of nostalgic musicals, as one reviewer noted. "Except for some wistful photography taking in the boat, the river and the hazy bank, there is little to distinguish this *Show Boat* from the average run of summer extravaganzas dressing up old song hits in a Technicolor décor."[65]

The MGM *Show Boat* had an affinity with another Cold War dreamscape: Disneyland. Walt Disney spoke of Disneyland, which opened in 1955, as essentially a movie set and named recent films, which inspired specific features of the park. The Golden Horseshoe Saloon was designed by the same designer who had created the saloon for *Calamity Jane* (1953), and the jungle cruise ride was modeled on *The African Queen* (1951).[66] The MGM *Show Boat* was among the highest-grossing films of 1951, exactly the period when Disney was creating Disneyland. It's hard not to see MGM's *Cotton Blossom* in Disneyland's Mark Twain riverboat, one of the park's original attractions. Disneyland's opening day was broadcast live on television. Ronald Reagan hosted and various special guests appeared as well. The Mark Twain riverboat and entire Rivers of America area of the park was launched by Irene Dunne, whose movie career was well over in 1955 but was surely remembered by many as Magnolia in the 1936 *Show Boat*. It's otherwise hard to account for why this particular star turns up at this particular moment. Disney did what no Broadway or Hollywood *Show Boat* could do: he created, in the words of J. P. Telotte, an "inhabitable text," one that allowed audiences to enter a mythic river world much like MGM's *Show Boat*.[67] Just across from the Mark Twain's landing—on Disney's version of a Mississippi levee—visitors could enjoy a meal at Aunt Jemima's Pancake House, which retained the Jemima name until 1970, when the restaurant was rechristened the Magnolia Tree Terrace before assuming its current name, the River Belle Terrace a year later. Into the late 1960s, Aunt Jemima as portrayed by Aylene Lewis welcomed and sang to guests and posed for pictures like any Disney character. Visitors could be forgiven for thinking they had stumbled into a scene from *Show Boat* act 1.

Broadway and Hollywood remade *Show Boat* in strikingly different ways in the decade after World War II. The musical stage welcomed new black performance modes while the musical screen found little room for black performers or black themes at all. These differences highlight the extreme flexibility of *Show Boat* as a work open to radically different interpretations. The postwar *Show Boat*s also highlight in contrasting ways aspects of the show that made it unique in the 1920s. *Show Boat* forced a confrontation with issues of race and national memory like no other survivor of Broadway's Jazz Age heyday. After about 1960, *Show Boat* would be the only 1920s operetta or musical comedy to remain part of the active musical theater repertory, the only old show to consistently win new audiences. The story of *Show Boat*'s remarkable survival in the second half of the twentieth century is taken up in the remaining two chapters.

8

LANDMARK STATUS

• • •

1954–1989

Show Boat outlived the mid-century civil rights transformations and even thrived in an altered cultural landscape where prewar Jim Crow stereotypes came increasingly under fire and new ways of performing blackness developed on the musical stage. Hollywood was done with the property, but theater producers and directors consistently believed *Show Boat* could still command an audience. One strategy for sustaining *Show Boat*'s relevance in the theater was reconceiving the show as an opera, an approach where the roles requiring "big" voices took center stage. Two concurrent trends supported the bid to remake *Show Boat* as a masterpiece worthy of the treatment accorded high-status European works. Along one line, American opera companies began to embrace so-called classic stage works from the commercial theater as opportunities to expand the American opera audience. Simultaneously, an artistically self-conscious effort to resurrect the authentic sound of classic Broadway scores was abetted by unexpected archival discoveries and the willingness of major record labels to invest in lavish studio recordings. *Show Boat*'s strong name recognition put it in the top tier of this new category of classics, and the show's inclusion of black characters and performers tacitly enhanced the perception that this particular work was particularly American. Recasting *Show Boat* as an opera put old questions in a new light, and the controversies that arose around the show in the late 1980s for the first time led white critics to discover what black critics had known all along—that *Show Boat* was all about race.

NEW YORK, 1954

William Hammerstein's 1954 *Show Boat* launched a new production unit at New York's City Center. The 2,750-seat auditorium on Fifty-fifth Street, built in 1923 as a lodge hall, had been salvaged by Mayor Fiorello LaGuardia as a center for the arts in 1943. City Center offerings were affordably priced, providing access to the performing arts for as wide an audience as possible. William Hammerstein (Oscar II's son) was leading the creation of the New York City Light Opera Company (NYCLOC), drawing leads and chorus members from the New York City Opera (NYCO), which had been founded when the City Center opened and was known from its first decade for novel programming, investment in young singers, and willingness to cast African American singers in lead roles.[1] Also in residence at the City Center were George Balanchine's New York City Ballet and a theater production unit. Under Jean Dalrymple's direction, NYCLOC would mount *Show Boat* again at City Center in 1961. The ballet and opera companies would move to the New York State Theater in Lincoln Center in the early 1960s, where Music Theater of Lincoln Center (under producer Richard Rodgers) would present *Show Boat* in 1966, taking the production on an unsuccessful tour. The 1954 *Show Boat* was the precursor to these later productions.

The declared mission of the NYCLOC was to "present a repertory of the finest works in the field of musical theater and operetta."[2] *Show Boat*, directed by Hammerstein *fils* and conducted by NYCO maestro Julius Rudel, played fifteen performances in repertory with *Die Fledermaus* (sung in English to less than full houses) and *Carousel* (the hit of the season; lasting eight weeks beyond its intended two).

Before the May opening of the NYCLOC's inaugural season, William Hammerstein's *Show Boat* played three performances on the NYCO regular season, alternating with *Tosca, Don Giovanni, Carmen, La Traviata*, and *Salome*. It was listed as a new spring production along with Verdi's *Falstaff*. Rudel claimed he added *Show Boat* to the NYCO repertory based on an audience poll, which ranked the show second after *The Magic Flute*.[3] Rudel made much of restoring the 1927 orchestrations, using the original overture, and bringing back lost numbers ("Queenie's Ballyhoo" and "I Might Fall Back on You," respectively reduced and cut in 1946). These claims make the Rudel and William Hammerstein production the first to authenticate a new version of *Show Boat* by claiming a return to the original. That this happened as early as 1954 suggests that Oscar Hammerstein's "new production" of 1946 failed to solidify the text of the show. Unlike any other canonic musical, *Show Boat* remained open to remaking. Rudel also claimed he was striving to avoid "little cheap habits" in an effort to do the show "with a certain amount of taste." The comment smacks of a certain superiority toward *Show Boat*, but Rudel's role as an advocate for American musical stage works with artistic ambitions, yet designed for a broad audience, should not be underestimated. Rudel would keep *Show Boat* in the repertory for the fall 1954 season, further enhancing the musical's cultural cachet in the opera house.

Still in the loop as part owner of the rights to the musical, Ferber was, in her own words, "baffled" by young Hammerstein's approach, wondering in a letter to Oscar what an "operatic performance of *Show Boat*" might be.[4] Hammerstein II wrote Ferber that his son's plan boiled down to casting: "The 'operatic' performance of *Show Boat* will be no different from the usual version except that the cast will favor singing rather than acting, since some of them are in the opera troupe."[5] As so often in the past, the size and makeup of the cast was the defining element of this production.

Above-the-title billing went to Burl Ives as Andy and Robert Rounesville as Ravenal. Ives was described in the program as "one of America's best-known singers of folk songs." His wide-ranging career had only recently survived an appearance before the House Un-American Activities Committee, where he alienated many in the folk music movement. The choice of Ives initiated a long-standing practice of casting Andys who had name recognition from outside musical theater or opera. Many aged film stars—among them Andy Devine (Jones Beach, 1956), Pat O'Brien (Los Angeles, 1967), Donald O'Connor (Houston Grand Opera, 1982; Broadway, 1983), Eddie Bracken (Houston Grand Opera and Paper Mill Playhouse, 1989) and Van Johnson—would turn Andy into the above-the-title star in major productions of *Show Boat*.

The NYCO proved an ideal company from which to cast *Show Boat* conceived as a singer-centered show. Rounesville had sung tenor leads with the company since 1948 and originated the role of Tom Rakewell in Stravinsky's *The Rake's Progress* in 1951. His marquee value drew on an unusually wide range of appearances outside the opera house: on the big screen as the title character in Michael Powell and Emeric Pressberger's *Tales of Hoffmann* (1951); on television as Don Jose in *Carmen* (1953). Like Howard Marsh, Rounesville was an experienced lead in Gilbert and Sullivan revivals. After the 1954 *Show Boat*, he would play Enoch Snow, the highest male role in the Rodgers and Hammerstein canon, in the film version of *Carousel* (1956) and introduce the title role in Bernstein's *Candide* (1956), another higher-than-average part. With the casting of Rounesville, Ravenal moved back in the direction of the operetta tenor sound for which the role was conceived. Rounesville's Magnolia was Laurel Hurley, a young but experienced opera singer who had played Kathie in *The Student Prince* on Broadway (at age sixteen) and a number of leads in other operettas from the 1920s, as well as operatic leads for NYCO over the previous three seasons. Hurley had a light soprano voice, suited to roles such as Zerlina in *Don Giovanni* and Oscar in *Un Ballo in maschera*. Hurley's casting marks a departure from earlier New York Magnolias, who tended to come from musical comedy backgrounds. Julie was taken by Helena Bliss, a soprano with a long career in light opera on both East and West Coasts. Perhaps her portrayal of Claire, the mulatto empress, in NYCO's 1949 production of William Grant Still's *Troubled Island* suggested Bliss to Hammerstein as a possibility for Julie. All three of these singing leads came from mixed operatic and musical theater backgrounds, but, importantly, all were opera singers by training. The cavernous City Center auditorium could only have encouraged Rounesville, Hurley, and Bliss to sing in a manner that maximized volume and power.[6]

Joe and Queenie proved easy to cast from the rising ranks of a generation of black opera singers who would soon transform the postwar opera stage. The NYCO had from its start been a friendly place for this trailblazing cohort. Lawrence Winters first gained fame singing "Red Ball Express" in the 1946 Broadway revue *Call Me Mister*, a long-running salute to returning GIs, which had a slightly integrated cast. Since 1949, Winters had been singing lead roles with the NYCO. In the same season where he sang Joe, he appeared as Count Almaviva in *The Marriage of Figaro*. This mix of racially specific and color-blind casting was still quite new, a harbinger of things to come for black opera singers. Helen Phillips sang Queenie. Phillips had integrated the ranks of the Metropolitan Opera chorus in 1947, when she was called as a last minute replacement and was allowed to go on by a stage manager who chose not to draw the color line.[7] Phillips had sung a Town Hall recital in 1953 and spent much of her career singing concert tours in West Germany and Austria for the State Department. As was customary in a repertory company, various other singers took these roles in the 1954 NYCO spring and fall performances.

William C. Smith sang Joe in both seasons. He had understudied Joe in the 1946 revival, eventually replacing Kenneth Spencer on Broadway and during the tour. Smith went on to play Joe across the country in the late 1940s and 1950s, including Atlanta, where *Show Boat* stopped in a Deep South city for the first time in 1949, and at Jones Beach in 1956 and 1957.[8] A 1954 profile claimed Smith had played Joe 2,000 times, singing "Ol' Man River" "at least 10,000 times on stage as he sings this number five times in each performance" (see fig. 8.1).[9] With degrees from the Hampton Institute (a historically black college) and Juilliard (which generally welcomed black students), Smith was celebrated in the black press as "no Uncle Tom" and credited with giving "dignity and perspective to a stage era when the Negro was often a buffoon." Smith began his career as a soloist in Eva Jessye's spiritual choir, where he learned to sing in dialect, and found a spot in the 1942 revival of *Porgy and Bess*. Smith frequently appeared opposite Helen Dowdy as Queenie. Dowdy was the original Strawberry Woman in *Porgy and Bess*, a tiny role that nonetheless makes an impression late in the show. Smith and Dowdy were held up as "Examples of Negro Perseverance in the Theatre" in a shared 1960 profile in the *Pittsburgh Courier*.[10] *Show Boat* and *Porgy and Bess* served both singers well, and the two shows would continue to find a place in American opera houses, supporting the careers of black performers along the way.

William Hammerstein's ensemble was divided into three groups. Four white girls formed a modest Congress of Beauties. (The 1927 scripts called for forty.) Thirty-seven individuals are listed in the NYCLOC choral ensemble, which for the first time in *Show Boat* history was not divided into black and white in the program. Seven children were listed separately. The dancing chorus was eliminated. The racial makeup of the singing group is tricky to sort

8.1. *The black bass playing Joe has always had the capacity to bestride* Show Boat, *overwhelming attempts by any other players in the cast to dominate the production. William C. Smith—a midcentury Joe who reportedly played the part more than 2,000 times—makes the white leads look like miniature talents in this caricature from 1952. (Author's collection)*

out. Seven of the thirty-seven singers appeared in both *Fledermaus* and *Carousel*: these must have been white (or white enough to pass); eleven (maybe twelve) can be identified as black, based on their appearance in black-cast shows on Broadway.

William Hammerstein streamlined the story from a technical perspective, in some cases altering the function of musical numbers. "Can't Help Lovin' Dat Man" was played in the *Cotton Blossom* auditorium rather than the kitchen, allowing for a direct segue into the miscegenation scene (Oscar had cut the waterfront scene in 1946). "Why Do I Love You?" closed the World's Fair, eliminating "In Dahomey" for the first time, likely for practical reasons due to the lack of a black dancing chorus. No attempt was made to reinforce the show's arrival in the 1920s by way of a jazzy number for Kim. Hammerstein crammed three musical numbers into the box office scene, bringing back "I Might Fall Back on You" and using "Life Upon the Wicked Stage" as the scene's curtain. "Queenie's Ballyhoo" played in between these two white-cast numbers, eliminating the structural "curtain" role this number had formerly played. Hammerstein's remaking emphasized musical numbers for the white characters in a manner that was genuinely new.

Critics—both musical and dramatic—embraced *Show Boat*'s new operatic location wholeheartedly. Reviewing the NYCO performances, the *Christian Science Monitor* concluded, "Putting [*Show Boat*] into the opera house has heightened the quality of vocal performance and increased the poignancy of Edna Ferber's original story."[11] The *New York Times* focused on the music, noting "the thought occurred (and not for the first time) that Mr. Kern is one of the most underrated American composers of this century."[12] Robert Coleman, after the obligatory nod to the original cast, wrote, "Let's face it: [*Show Boat*] was intended to be sung as an opera."[13] This was, to put it mildly, a bit of revisionist history. Nothing about the previous life of the show, except perhaps for Marsh's Ravenal, suggested the opera stage as the obvious destination for *Show Boat*. Walter Kerr described the acting as "the sort that normally afflicts people who are proud of their singing voices," but found this dramatic lack redounded to the credit of Kern's music, the orchestration ("exhilarating in its perpetual inventiveness"), and the abundance of underscoring. "The scene may be woodenly played; the stealthy music makes it seem moving and wonderful. Or maybe nostalgia has got me."[14] Few New York reviewers fully trusted their reactions to *Show Boat* even in the 1950s. John Chapman in the *Daily News* wrote his review as a letter to a photo of Helen Morgan he kept on the wall in his office. Helena Bliss had not exceeded her, he assured Morgan, but she "was a good singer and a good actress doing 'Bill' the way she thought it should be done."[15]

Others noticed a decline in the number of laughs and—significantly—Frank and Ellie were entirely ignored (even though the pair had been given all three of their original 1927 numbers). Reviews of *Show Boat* as an opera or operetta zeroed in on praise for Kern and the assessment of the voices of a group of leads who would coalesce as central to the work's reputation as a singer's piece: Magnolia, Ravenal, Julie, and Joe. In fact, this quartet, augmented by a chorus, performed a shortened concert version of *Show Boat* at Lewisohn Stadium in July 1954.[16]

HOUSTON, NEW YORK, CAIRO, 1982–83 AND 1989

The bicentennial decade saw a resurgence of interest in American works for the opera stage, and no company invested in this movement like the Houston Grand Opera (HGO) under the leadership of David Gockley. Brought on as associate director in 1971, Gockley immediately hinted at the expansion of the repertory to come when he brokered HGO support for a touring company of *Jesus Christ Superstar*. In the words of HGO's official history, the ensuing controversy "gave Houston a foretaste of the eclectic Gockley point of view. This attitude was not necessarily an asset in the eyes of the more conservative among HGO's audience; a few had minor strokes at the mere announcement that HGO would produce *Show Boat* alongside 'real' operas. However, [Gockley's] broad view gave Houston audiences a chance to see *Treemonisha*, *Porgy and Bess*, *Hello, Dolly!* and the best of Lehár and Offenbach."[17]

HGO's *Treemonisha*, the first fully staged production of Scott Joplin's 1910 opera with restored orchestrations by Gunther Schuller (who also conducted), proved a tremendous success. The black-cast production took over HGO's Spring Opera Festival in 1975 and went on to a national tour, a short Broadway run (at the Uris Theatre, where *Show Boat* would play in the 1980s and '90s), a recording on Deutsche Grammophon, and a videotaped version of the stage production telecast on PBS and released commercially on the Kultur label. The success of *Treemonisha* encouraged Gockley to program a second black-cast American opera in 1976: *Porgy and Bess*. Not seen onstage in a major production for almost twenty-five years, HGO opened a restored, thoroughly operatic *Porgy and Bess* as a special production, which toured nationally and internationally, visiting eighteen cities in the United States—including a healthy run on Broadway, again at the Uris—as well as La Scala in Milan, Paris, Tokyo, Osaka, and Nagoya.[18] Similar tours followed in 1986–87 and 1995. HGO effectively inserted *Porgy and Bess* into the operatic canon where it continues to thrive.

HGO's first *Show Boat* opened in 1982, and Gockley followed the pattern of *Treemonisha* and *Porgy and Bess* in both production and exploitation of this third HGO show in seven years that required a black chorus and principals. *Show Boat* opened as a special summer production, giving fourteen performances in ten days before embarking on a national tour, which visited Broadway, playing the Uris for a disappointing seventy-three performances (*Porgy and Bess* was running at Radio City Music Hall at the time). Gockley brought *Show Boat* back in 1989 as part of HGO's regular season of European operas sung in their original languages. Programmed beside *Carmen, The Marriage of Figaro*, and *Otello* (with Plácido Domingo)—each of which played six to eight performances—*Show Boat* was presented fourteen times, exceeded only by the fifteen-performance run of the family Christmas opera *Hansel and Gretel*. Gockley's faith in *Show Boat*'s ability to draw a much larger audience than even warhorses like *Carmen* speaks to his cultivation of the larger Houston audience and the continued viability of *Show Boat*.

Another motivation for the 1989 revival was a one-stop tour to Cairo, where HGO enjoyed the distinction of being the only American company invited to appear in the opening season of the Cairo National Cultural Center, a performing arts complex situated on an island in the Nile. A Kabuki troupe from Japan, ballet companies from London and Paris, and a German orchestra rounded out the visitors, all of whom had to secure outside support for their visits, to the tune of $1.25 million in the case of *Show Boat*. HGO had long been supported by the Houston oil industry, and connections with Middle Eastern corporations were a natural. The U.S. Embassy played a part as well: publicizing the production, encouraging American companies in Cairo to support the effort, and brokering a deal with the Egyptian government that two-thirds of the seats would be sold to the general public. *Show Boat* turned out to be a tremendous draw. Cairo audiences reportedly stormed the box office causing "a near riot."[19] Even the dress rehearsal sold out. Cairo was "infected with *Show Boat* fever," wrote the *Houston Chronicle*, noting that the various *Show Boat* films were even being shown on television.[20]

The HGO *Show Boat* continued earlier claims to restore the work to Kern and Hammerstein's original intentions. The conductor and show music historian John McGlinn consulted with HGO's music director John DeMain and stage director Michael Kahn on the production, which used the original overture drawing on "Mis'ry's Comin' Aroun'" and generally brought back the 1927 orchestrations—or at least made the claim to do so. Queenie's "Hey, Feller," not heard since 1932, was added back in as well. As one critic noted, "According to all involved, this song greatly helps the continuity of the show by helping to bridge the story's final leap into the 1920s. In recent productions there was no up-to-date music to put the new times solidly in the audience's ears. 'Hey, Feller' does so."[21] Kim had no final number, so HGO appears to be the only major revival to put the entire burden of representing the 1920s on the shoulders of Queenie and the black chorus.

Several African American basses took the role of Joe in HGO's various productions. Donnie Ray Albert, an alumnus of *Treemonisha* and one of two Porgys in the original HGO *Porgy and Bess*, sang Joe in 1982, demonstrating the continuity of work for black singers these three productions allowed. Michel Bell sang Joe in 1989 and would be the singer of choice for Harold Prince's *Show Boat* revival in the 1990s. The operatically trained Bruce Hubbard played Joe at the Uris in 1983. He came to Broadway in 1976 for Bernstein's ill-fated interracial musical *1600 Pennsylvania Avenue*, stepping out of a voice program at Indiana University before graduation to do so. Eagerly sought for the *Porgy and Bess* running at Radio City, Hubbard held out for *Show Boat*: "I said no to *Porgy* because there were so many casts, and they couldn't guarantee that I'd get reviewed. I was trying to make a big career move."[22] Hubbard described singing "Ol' Man River" in familiar terms: "In the 1936 movie of *Show Boat*, Paul Robeson sang the hell out of 'Ol' Man River.' His spirit is with me. He sat on a log and sang plain and simple. I, too, try to be very still on stage. It is the hardest thing to do, but very powerful, to sit there and let the words do it for you." Stillness and the power of the black male voice—here grounded in operatic training—had lost none of their power. Hubbard banked on Joe to launch his career, but Gershwin's opera continued to be important. He appeared as Jake in *Porgy and Bess* at the Met in 1985—the only time that company has staged the opera—and at Glyndebourne. The latter production was captured on record by EMI-Angel under the baton of Simon Rattle in 1986. Hubbard sang Joe on McGlinn's omnibus recording of *Show Boat* in 1988, an analogous recording also for EMI-Angel. Gershwin's restored opera and Kern and Hammerstein's musical-comedy-turned-opera followed parallel paths in the 1970s and 1980s, and African American singers such as Hubbard benefited from the popularity of these American shows in the opera house and on Broadway. Hubbard, however, did not have much of a career outside these two revivable works with high name recognition. He died prematurely in 1991, shortly after playing Joe one last time in the Opera North/Royal Shakespeare Company *Show Boat* (see chap. 9). In that production, one critic praised Hubbard's "Ol' Man River" for evoking "real racial anger," making the anthem "a passionate shout of protest against a lifetime of economic slavery."[23] Perceiving Joe in this way was at once in the tradition of London critics, always quick to point out *Show Boat*'s critique of American racism, and a harbinger of the way *Show Boat* would be read by scholars and critics in the 1990s.

New York critics generally praised HGO's *Show Boat* for its musical achievement, bringing a score all recognized as historic back to the commercial stage with voices that sold it effectively as a high-quality work of the American musical stage. "Fundamentally, it has been staged with the same kind of reverence—using that word in the loosest sense—as if it were an opera."[24] "It boasts many fine trained voices (though the amplification essential to this ungrateful auditorium [the Uris Theatre] makes it difficult to assess their true value)."[25] Critics were just coming to terms with increased amplification in the mid-1980s, and the transition was particularly felt with regard to *Show Boat* at the cavernous Uris, the largest house on Broadway. The set—dismissed by *Variety* as "a series of gaudy drops . . . obviously built for touring"—came in for much criticism.[26] "The immitigable taints of any road-company show are to be detected in the flimsy, garish settings and costumes and in the generally coarse and self-indulgent performances given by the cast."[27] Finding a middle ground, Frank Rich built his review around the disjuncture between "crudely lighted sets" and "glorious voices." Read in retrospect, Rich longed for a director like Harold Prince to rescue *Show Boat* from pedestrian operetta staging, calling for "the cinematic flow that the writing invites." (Prince would articulate his vision of *Show Boat* as explicitly cinematic.) Making *Show Boat* cinematic would require an investment in state-of-the-art stagecraft no opera company likely to mount *Show Boat* would make, and the operatic, singer-centered approach alone was unlikely to make *Show Boat* succeed again on Broadway.

LONDON, 1988

In 1987, the distinguished classical music label EMI-Angel engaged John McGlinn to lead a series of expensively produced studio-cast albums of classic Broadway scores from the 1920s, '30s and '40s. Still comparatively new on the scene, McGlinn was described in the pages of the classical music audiophile magazine *Gramophone* as having "more or less cornered the market on 'authentic Broadway.'"[28] A self-styled musical theater scholar with classical training and experience in opera, McGlinn made a name for himself conducting concert versions of restored early Kern shows at Carnegie Hall during the centenary of the songwriter's birth in 1985. McGlinn requested the EMI series begin with *Show Boat* and, as the press pack for the four-hour, three-disc result noted, "McGlinn felt it was imperative to record every note."[29] This ambitious effort was facilitated by the conjunction of three elements: the discovery of a cache of *Show Boat* materials in a Secaucus, New Jersey, warehouse in 1984; a still-developing cycle of studio recordings of Broadway scores using opera singers initiated by Leonard Bernstein's well-promoted 1985 *West Side Story* on Deutsche Grammophon (featuring Kiri Te Kanawa and José Carerras); and the prosperity of the music industry riding the recent introduction of the compact disc. The McGlinn-EMI *Show Boat* marked the beginning of a short but productive burst of expensively produced "complete" recordings of Broadway shows.[30]

McGlinn's choice of *Show Boat* was shrewd. The show enjoyed high name recognition and had been recently revived by HGO (with input from McGlinn). The sheer length of the show, especially with the inclusion of all the cut material and items added by Kern and Hammerstein for later versions, gave *Show Boat* a scale that made it look important. No other musical could fill out three discs and look so "operatic"—save *Porgy and Bess*, which, as noted above, EMI had recently recorded in a "complete" operatic version conducted by Simon Rattle. Both box sets were honored by *Gramophone* as the best recordings of 1989 in their respective categories: musical theater (new to *Gramophone*) in the case of *Show Boat*; and opera, in the case of *Porgy and Bess* (a significant anointing of the restored version).

William Hammerstein, alone among the Hammerstein, Kern, and Ferber heirs who now controlled the rights to *Show Boat*, initially resisted McGlinn's insistence on completeness, arguing that some numbers had been cut for a reason. The differing aesthetic priorities informing a successful production versus a successful audio argument for *Show Boat*'s artistic stature—only the most important works have their cut numbers recorded—were at issue. *Gramophone*'s critic echoed Hammerstein's concerns, comparing the importance of McGlinn's recording to Georg Solti's epic complete recording of Wagner's *Ring* cycle but wondering if *Show Boat*'s cut numbers would be of interest to "the less specialized listener. Would he not prefer an absolutely complete and balanced *Show Boat* at the expense of these variants?"[31] But the desire to consecrate *Show Boat* and thereby secure the foundation for elevating the status of the Broadway musical lay behind McGlinn's project (and career). Ironically, William Hammerstein's own 1954 production, the first to move *Show Boat* into the opera repertory, had marked the first step along this road.

McGlinn made expansive claims for the value of restoring *Show Boat*'s original orchestrations. "When I turned to 'Ol' Man River,' it was like cleaning off an old painting and finding the original colors. Originally it wasn't a huge bombastic number but a simple folk song with sustained strings, a little oboe and bells."[32] Similar claims had been made by Rudel for the 1954 NYCO production, which had used the same argument that *Show Boat* could be made new by way of a return to the work's lost past. McGlinn's approach was contextualized within the concurrent historical performance movement transforming Baroque and Classical music performance and recordings, a rhetorical parallel that made old Broadway shows—usually called American musicals in the press—seem like stable works of art analogous to the European operatic canon. But the claim of authenticity and the need to anoint the Broadway musical as worthy of such attention and expense by a classical label was bound to generate aesthetic conflicts. As had so often been the case with *Show Boat*, it came down to practical questions of casting. For even as he made bold claims for the old orchestrations, McGlinn did not seek to re-create the 1920s singing styles these arrangements were designed to support. In the vocal department, the EMI *Show Boat* sat squarely in the opera house. (See fig. 8.2.)

The operatic connection was made explicit in the casting of the three principal white singing roles: North American–born opera singers who were young enough to be convincing but established enough to immediately give the recording stature were chosen. All were regulars at the Met. This trio's names-above-the-title sold *Show Boat* as worthy of opera-like packaging. Fredericka von Stade as Magnolia was the best known of the three. A tremendously successful, widely recorded mezzo soprano with a distinctive voice, von Stade had an ingratiating persona that brought a certain seriousness to the role. She was not a musical comedy or even operetta type. Magnolia was well outside von Stade's accustomed expressive register but fit her vocal range well enough; her casting suggests McGlinn understood Magnolia is not, by nature, a soprano role. Whether the role fits a light operatic mezzo remains in question. McGlinn included all the 1927 underscoring with the dialogue spoken over it, giving portions of the recording the quality of a radio drama. Playing Magnolia on record required von Stade to deliver spoken dialogue for the first time in her career. The tenor Jerry Hadley was a solid choice for Ravenal given the vocal requirements of the part: using the 1927 original, Ravenal was again a tenor. One English critic parsed the romantic pair in nationalistic terms: Von Stade and Hadley "radiate an aristocratic Volksoper style, adding American warmth and candour."[33] Given their voice types, von Stade and Hadley would seldom be a romantic couple in any musical theater genre as tenors and mezzos don't normally fall in love.[34] Hadley sounds comfortable throughout (except in "Creole Love Song"): he and Howard Marsh are of a type. Von Stade sounds ill at ease in the jazzier numbers such as "It's Getting Hotter in the North" and "Gallivantin' Aroun'." In these numbers, casting an opera singer worked against the contrast between a musical comedy personality and an operetta tenor written into the roles as shaped for Norma Terris and Marsh. Like good late-twentieth-century opera singers, von Stade and Hadley respected the text: Hadley sang the high B-flats in "You Are Love." (Given her voice type, von Stade likely wouldn't have wanted to anyway.) Teresa Stratas as Julie brought her characteristic dramatic intensity to the part, and being an opera singer, she sang the role in a manner Helen Morgan simply could not. Stratas's approach fits well into the tradition of brooding sung Julies initiated by Carol Bruce in 1946 and brought into the opera house by Helena Bliss in 1954, Anita Darian in 1961, and Constance Towers in 1966 (Darian and Towers can be heard on studio recordings[35]). In interviews, McGlinn went on and on about the intensity of Stratas's approach to the role and how much he learned from her. Their initial rehearsal of "Bill" supposedly lasted four hours.[36] While Hadley fit well within the original sound of the 1927 *Show Boat*, von Stade and Stratas differed in almost every respect from the original performers around whom the roles of Magnolia and Julie were made. McGlinn's interest in authenticity was, therefore, selective. Casting big-name opera singers may have been a practical decision—EMI would have needed names on which to sell the set—but *Show Boat*'s long identification with the opera house as a singer's show seems to have influenced how far McGlinn was willing to go toward recovering the show's "original colors."

8.2. *Fredericka von Stade (Magnolia) and Teresa Stratas (Julie) join Bruce Hubbard (Joe) for a publicity photo that expresses the energy and enthusiasm conductor John McGlinn brought to the landmark 1988 EMI-Angel recording. (Clive Barda/ ArenaPAL)*

The McGlinn *Show Boat* was a resounding success with record buyers and classical critics, topping the "crossover" charts and winning more than one record-of-the-year award.[37] *Newsweek* endorsed the use of opera singers because, as McGlinn had convincingly argued, *Show Boat* was different. "Musicals swooped on by opera stars usually fail because the singers tend to have no sense of the idiom's style: what's pretty is often vapid. Classical training can trip up artists. Much of *Show Boat*, however, is inherently better suited to such singers because of its technical demands: its complexities, as McGlinn points out, can verge on the Verdian."[38] Terris, Morgan, and Robeson were hardly opera singers, and even the demands put upon Ravenal as shaped for Marsh were modest compared to almost anything in the European operatic canon. The facile notion, attributed to McGlinn, that something resembling Verdi can be found in Kern's *Show Boat* echoes responses to William Hammerstein's 1954 production, when critics all at once heard the show as always intended for the opera house. This is wishful thinking. For all the scholarly claims made by McGlinn, neither he nor EMI had the desire to approximate the original voices for this recording that self-importantly proclaimed the revelatory nature of the restored orchestrations. The realities of record making—different in their specifics but analogous in their impact to the realities of show making—inevitably left a mark on McGlinn's recording, which is not scholarly in the strict sense but, like every other remade *Show Boat*, the product of a particular place and time.

The politics of race that had always provided the context for *Show Boat* returned to haunt McGlinn and EMI shortly before the first recording sessions at London's Abbey Road studios. The London Sinfonietta and Ambrosian Chorus had been engaged as orchestra and white chorus respectively, but plans to hire a black chorus faltered. The producer John Fraser described the issue in euphemistic terms in the press pack: "With only days to go [before recording began], our black chorus and our Joe withdrew on the grounds that certain textual references were offensive. Our pleading was to no avail. We tried to convince them that the references in the text were deliberately there to underline the heinous treatment of many blacks in the 1880s, and that the whole point of the drama was to demonstrate the extent of the prevailing sickening prejudice. Alas, we failed to convince. Imagine our joy when we discovered that Bruce Hubbard was free for our, by now, firmly booked recording sessions."[39] At issue, yet again, was Hammerstein's use of the n-word. Hubbard was willing to sing the original text, and McGlinn settled on the expedient of having the Ambrosian Chorus—also willing to sing the text as put in front of them—sing the black chorus numbers as well the white.

McGlinn's first-choice Joe was Willard White, a Jamaican-born British opera singer who had recorded Porgy on a complete version of the Gershwin opera conducted by Loren Maazel in 1976 (too early to benefit from the rise in *Porgy and Bess*'s fortunes initiated by HGO).[40] White would record Joe for a 1993 "complete" *Show Boat* based on Hammerstein's 1946 version conducted by John Owen Edwards.[41] Hammerstein had already changed "niggers" to "colored folk" for that version.

The black chorus who walked out on EMI was a group assembled by Glyndebourne for their *Porgy and Bess* production and recording. This group of trained black singers clearly did not see Gershwin's opera and Kern's show in the same light. McGlinn had a history of trying to restore the 1927 reading of the opening chorus lyric, advocating for its use in the 1982 HGO production. His effort there had been similarly "overruled by indignant chorus members," according to the *New York Times*, which foregrounded the controversy in a feature article on the recording.[42] As happened so often in *Show Boat* history, the black press had a different take on the issue. In an article titled "Angel Records restores 'niggers' to *Show Boat*," Raoul Abdul located the label's decision to support McGlinn in the political context of the 1980s. "Now—in the Ronald Reagan era—Angel (EMI) Records has just released a 'historic' recording which seeks to restore *Show Boat* to its original form. The famous English Ambrosian Chorus have smeared its faces with burnt cork and we hear that 'Niggers all work on de Mississippi.'"[43] Abdul reprises arguments stretching back to 1927, but with the income from a handful of recording sessions all that the black chorus members stood to lose economically, the old argument that *Show Boat* provided jobs for black performers didn't hold much sway. (The 1927 option of not singing the offending word was, obviously, off the table in this context.)

Hubbard explained his participation in a one-page statement in the press pack. He was the only singer required to formally articulate his relationship to the project. "When I sang 'Ol' Man River' on Broadway [in 1983], my performance was controversial because I made the song defiant, not submissive. But the important thing to remember is that 'Ol' Man River' is failsafe if done with honesty. I was not scared of its fame. It is always new. It is a new day and a new age, and we can shed new light on the number, which tells its story in black terms *and* universal terms. I do not feel it necessary, unlike some of my colleagues, to make any apologies for this song. I don't simply present this number, it has to be *experienced*. . . . This song is still relevant today as history repeats itself."[44] The resonance of that word *experienced*—harkening back unknowingly to Robeson's concert persona—suggests the continuing power of Joe as a rare figure on the American musical stage. Hubbard, who had tied his career to Joe, was willing to trust in the impact of "Ol' Man River" on the listener and look past Hammerstein's still controversial use of the offensive word.

And so, despite efforts to cast *Show Boat* as a "landmark" enduring racial controversies arising from the simple fact that Hammerstein and Kern had used an interracial cast ended up impacting McGlinn's final product. And even as EMI tried to situate the show in a particular way—restoring, in Miles Kreuger's words, "the grit and power of the drama" which had been lost in a generation of operetta-like productions—*Show Boat* after Black Power and during the age of Reagan was not going to be an uncontroversial classic nor could its racial content be easily explained away to a group of black professionals.[45] Behind these controversies was the ironic fact that one reason *Show Boat* had survived at all, one reason HGO had revived it so prominently in the 1980s, was the show's very inclusion of blacks, a point in its and *Porgy and Bess*'s favor at a time when opera companies wanted to present more diverse works and expand their audiences. Significantly, in the coverage of McGlinn's recording race finally asserted itself in discourse about *Show Boat* in the *white* press in the United States. Critics could not simply praise the black-cast contributions as they always had in the past but this time had to explain why the producers of the recording, able to engage famous white opera singers, could not find a black chorus willing to sing the show. This was news—to some. For African American performers, press, and audiences, *Show Boat* had been controversial from the beginning.

9

QUEENIE'S LAUGH
• • •
1966–1998

In 1948 Lee Newton, theater critic for the leftist newspaper the *Daily Worker*, wrote an open letter to Rodgers and Hammerstein, producers of the *Show Boat* running at the City Center, the final stop for the 1946 tour. After praising *Show Boat* as "a permanent institution in the American theatre," Newton projected his own discomfort with the show onto Rodgers and Hammerstein, while also noting the potency of musical theater stereotypes in society. Newton believed that how *Show Boat* presented blacks mattered for the health of American democracy.

> I have a hunch that you would be happier about *Show Boat* if it was changed just a bit. I'm not talking about your theme, your fundamental story-line, the songs, etc.: the changes I'm referring to would not in any way affect the structure of *Show Boat*. They would, in most cases, be a simple matter of omission. I mean omitting all the Uncle Tom business, the Negro as a shiftless, lazy good-for-nothing—the Negro as the object of patronizing ridicule. Why retain these blemishes in a show which will be seen by many more Americans in the years to come—including impressionable youngsters—who will more easily absorb the patronizing attitude toward Negroes simply because of the memorable songs that go with it. I don't believe that either of you are consciously propagandizing Jimcrow. To the contrary, those who should know, say you're on the liberal side of the fence. . . . As a matter of fact, I got the impression from watching the City Center production, that many of those involved were conscious of, and uneasy with, the Uncle Tom business. They, and I'm sure that you as well, know that Jimcrow has always been a bad actor. So how about those changes? It'd be nice if they were made before *Show Boat* sails much further.[1]

Rodgers and Hammerstein's response—likely penned by the latter—was unequivocal: "We believe that the Negro in *Show Boat* emerges with honor and respect and affection and that this play has always been good for the Negro." Hammerstein then began searching for exactly what might qualify as "Jim Crow" in the City Center *Show Boat*. It could not be "Ol' Man River," as "that has become acknowledged as one of the best in American light opera." Nor could it be the miscegenation plot, as "the sympathies of the authors are so clearly with Julie and against the sheriff." Indeed, Hammerstein had revised Ferber's scene to produce just this effect. Nor could it be the depiction of separate entrances for white and blacks on the *Cotton Blossom* stage set, as that is "an honest presentation of conditions in the South and far from carrying with it an implicit endorsement." The text of the show, Hammerstein argued, was above reproach. The only element Hammerstein could find that smacked of Jim Crowism was a matter of performance, specifically Queenie's laugh. "Queenie, [Joe's] wife, is an industrious woman and a useful citizen on the *Show Boat*. The only thing we can think of in her character to which you might object is a loud 'Yak-yak' laugh which she emits as she is making an exit. This, we urge you to believe, is in performance rather than characterization. In directing this scene, we have many times tried to tone this laugh down but the various artists who play the role are always tempted by the audience response to build up the laugh and there seems no way of stopping this." Hammerstein offered a defense of *Show Boat* as a text, deflecting the blame for any racial offense the show might engender onto a (black) actress—Helen Dowdy, in this case—trying to connect with her (predominantly white) audience. While offering a revealing snapshot of himself as director—striving for a particular effect, sensitive to the resonance of even something so minor as a laugh—Hammerstein argued that performers had the power to shape the way *Show Boat* dealt with race.

This final chapter considers how late twentieth-century stage productions balanced *Show Boat*'s text—or characterization, to use Hammerstein's term—and the possibilities of performance as imagined by directors and practiced by performers. Text and performance alike remained unusually open in the case of *Show Boat*. McGlinn's recording effectively laid out all the musical options from across the long history of the show's text. The rise of powerful directors and choreographers facilitated remakings of the show as a whole. And performers who, as always, made the show happen, continued to influence how *Show Boat* was remade, drawing, as so often in the past, on new ways to perform blackness and whiteness on the musical stage. In the process, *Show Boat* came into creative dialogue with unfolding Broadway history, itself subject to transformations in popular music. Beginning in the 1980s and gaining steam in the first decade of the twenty-first century, a small crop of interracial shows that followed *Show Boat*'s example and used popular music to explore the American experience of race began to appear on Broadway. These radical remakings of Hammerstein's popular music plot were *Show Boat*'s grandchildren, and *Show Boat* itself survived in revivals to see this new generation of musicals take their place on Broadway.

No commercial Broadway producer placed a bet on *Show Boat* from 1948 to 1994. *Show Boat* played New York in those decades, but it did so in repertory, as a special summer production, or as part of a tour (brought into town to perhaps predictable responses from the critics). And yet, under the right circumstances *Show Boat* once again found a big Broadway audience in 1994 when the producer Garth Drabinsky—a latter-day Ziegfeld—and the director Harold Prince—a formative creative figure in the post-Hammerstein decades—remade the old chestnut. Susan Stroman, a rising-star choreographer, contributed fundamentally to the revival as well. The Drabinsky-Prince-Stroman production effectively reinserted *Show Boat* into the theatrical mainstream: their version is licensed for rental by Rodgers and Hammerstein Theatricals and continues to be produced regionally. The 1994 *Show Boat* benefited from a crush of other revivals of classic musicals, which reached a critical mass in the mid-1990s, leading to the creation of a Tony Award for Best Revival of a Musical in 1994. (The Drabinsky-Prince-Stroman *Show Boat* won in 1995.) And once again, *Show Boat*'s interracial content made the show stand out from its historical peers, allowing it to become a cultural lightning rod in ways no other revived musical (except for *Porgy and Bess*) could. Hammerstein and Kern's interracial musical continued to be relevant and controversial almost seventy years later.

Prince's *Show Boat* began as Drabinsky's idea. The Canadian media mogul saw the 1989 version produced by Opera North and the Royal Shakespeare Company in Britain and determined that if *Show Boat* was ever going to return to Broadway in a commercial revival, it would have to be on a Ziegfeldian scale: both massive and new. The Prince-Stroman *Show Boat* would have been impossible without Drabinsky's deep pockets. Drabinsky's innovative, publicly traded production company Livent, Inc. brought the show in on a huge scale: over seventy in the cast, thirty musicians in the pit, a production cost of $7.5 million.[2] As it had in 1983, *Show Boat* played the Uris—now renamed the George Gershwin Theatre—where it sported a new top ticket price of $75. The production lasted more than two years, racking up 947 performances, making it the longest-running *Show Boat* in Broadway or West End history. The New York production recouped its investment thirteen months into the run, and Drabinsky sent out multiple touring companies.[3]

But the Drabinsky-Prince-Stroman version did not conquer London. A 1998 West End engagement at the Prince Edward Theatre closed after less than five months just as *Chicago* and *The Lion King*, other recent Broadway imports, opened to seemingly endless runs.

The failure of the 1998 *Show Boat* was surprising given the welcome the show had generally received in London. In 1971 the producer Harold Fielding, a postwar, West End Ziegfeld, mounted a production that ran at the Adelphi Theatre for 910 performances. Geoffrey Block described the Fielding *Show Boat* as "an unmistakeable example of the triumph of accessibility over authenticity."[4] The importance of Cleo Laine in the role of Julie will be covered later, but another featured performer deserves mention here. Miguel Godreau, like LaVerne French before him, was given featured dancing bits, which garnered loud approval from audience and critics alike. Similarities with French's reviews are striking. "The Puerto Rican dancer Miguel Godreau dazzles us with his precision and elevation."[5] "The dancers, led by a tiny pulsating dynamo called Miguel Godreau who has the attack and vivacity of the New York City Centre Ballet at its best, really dance."[6] "The dancer, Miguel Godreau, formerly dancer-choreographer with the Alvin Ailey Company, brings a classical yet elastic elegance to his technical mastery and exciting showmanship."[7] Judging from production photos and programs, the director/choreographer Wendy Toye used him prominently in the wedding buck-and-wing where a barefoot Godreau led a group of white dancers (see fig. 9.1); at the World's Fair as an exotic "Knife Thrower"; and in an added dance called "Time Lapse," which brought the story into the 1920s. For this last sequence, Godreau and "the Boy Dancers" were listed in the program as "The Jazz Dancers" and costumed in tight-fitting gangsterish outfits. The light-skinned Godreau apparently did not dance in "Can't Help Lovin' Dat Man" or "Queenie's Ballyhoo." "In Dahomey" was out. Godreau's turn as *Show Boat*'s "principal dancer"—reinterpreted in terms of where and when he danced and not necessarily a black dance role—marked the end of this particular added part.[8]

In 1989 a co-production of *Show Boat* by Opera North and the Royal Shakespeare Company (ON/RSC) toured England, with two stops at the London Palladium, to great acclaim.[9] Directed by Ian Judge, the ON/RSC production was the first to benefit from McGlinn's recording. Judge put "Mis'ry's Comin' Aroun'" back into the show, as well as "Ah Still Suits Me," (which had been added for the 1936 film and used onstage as early as 1940 for Robeson), and "Hey, Feller!" (previously reinstated by HGO). "Mis'ry" hadn't been part of *Show Boat* since the Washington, D.C. tryout some sixty years earlier. Prince would follow Judge in restoring "Mis'ry" but would not use "Hey, Feller!" or

9.1. *Miguel Godreau, costumed as a shoeless boy on the levee, leads members of the white chorus in the spirited dance celebrating Magnolia and Ravenal's wedding. Hammerstein and Kern assigned this buck-and-wing dance music to the black chorus. (Author's collection)*

"Ah Still Suits Me," two numbers that emphasize the comic sides of Queenie and Joe. Prince said the latter "diminishes the character of the man who sings 'Ol' Man River.'"[10] London critics embraced the ON/RSC *Show Boat* at a time when the West End was dominated by megamusicals. "At last, a musical with some real tunes in it," one magazine thrilled.[11] Another noted, "It is a pleasure to see a classic musical handled so well—and without millions being spent on gimmicks to help it along."[12] For Rupert Christiansen, the melodic power of Kern's score alone was enough "to throw into cruel relief the febrile tricksiness of a Sondheim or the screaming cliches of a Lloyd Webber."[13] The quality of the singing was consistently praised as well, and there were elements in the reviews to suggest some old *Show Boat* verities persisted. "Bruce Hubbard's 'Ol' Man River' has to be worth the ticket price itself."[14] "Some of the dancing—though not that of the black performers—is a trifle dusty."[15] A new tone also crept into the reviews. "Here is a chronicle not simply of individual destinies, but of a nation. That gave Kern and Hammerstein the courage and vision to nail the Big Lie at the cotton-pickin' heart of the Deep South. Negro aspirations, negro grievances, negro humiliation: these are not exactly central to *Show Boat*'s course, but they are at least treated with dignity and humility by the white authors."[16] *Show Boat* had not been parsed in these historical terms by white theater critics in the previous decades. In the 1990s this view of the show increasingly entered critical vocabularies, first in Britain, then in the United States.

The 1994 *Show Boat* was shaped in its making and reception by unprecedented and intense public protests. The controversy was largely limited to the production's opening engagement in Toronto in 1993, where the Coalition to Stop Show Boat—an ad hoc group of mostly Afro-Caribbean activists—battled against the production in the media and staged protests opening night. The scholar and activist M. Nourbese Philips's *Showing Grit: Showboating Above the 44th Parallel* (1993)—a short book dedicated to Robeson—recounted the protests and attempted to take the entire history of *Show Boat* into account. Philips objected to reviving the show under any circumstances, taking the view that *Show Boat* was dangerously dated. "Whites must ask themselves the following question: Why are they being served up entertainment whose function is to assuage their deep-seated and often unacknowledged anxieties about race and class; why are they being encouraged to believe that everything is in its place and the 'Ol' Man River' of racism runs as usual? *Nothing and no one* is in their place any longer."[17] Philips's point is well taken. Remaking *Show Boat* so that it could speak about race to contemporary audiences formed a central challenge faced by anyone who would mount the work at the end of the twentieth and into the twenty-first century. The appearance of new musicals that picked up themes of race and music explored in *Show Boat*—many mining rock and roll and soul, popular musics with black origins that would be anachronistic in *Show Boat*—made the challenge even greater.

Drabinsky and Prince met with the Coalition but refused their requests to see the script in advance of the opening. Drabinsky did, however, let the well-known Harvard professor Henry Louis Gates Jr. preview the script and invited the African American scholar to give a lecture on *Show Boat* in Toronto in the newly established Drabinsky Lecture Series. Drabinsky is surely the first *Show Boat* producer to establish an academic lecture as part of the show's promotion. Gates declared the production "a victory for tolerance and sensitivity," and framed the controversy as an issue of censorship.[18] The opening night gala, which marked the opening of the publicly funded North York Performing Arts Centre, saw picket lines, police, and a gaggle of New York critics. Drabinsky noted, "In a curious kind of way, the history of controversy and protest helped us. . . . It put pressure on the critics. It wasn't just another review they would be writing." Critics generally hailed the production, discounted opposition to the show, and praised *Show Boat* as historically important for its exploration of race in America.

A master of marketing, Drabinsky advertised heavily in the early weeks of the Toronto and New York runs, hiring the distinguished black actor James Earl Jones to be the "voice" of the show in television and radio spots. Drabinsky said of Jones, "we needed to establish a major image with a voice that would become synonymous with *Show Boat* . . . he has the quintessential voice for a great musical."[19] Jones brought Robeson slyly back into the mix. Jones had filled a Robeson-like niche in theater and film for decades, finding initial stardom in *The Great White Hope* (like Robeson's *Black Boy*, a boxing story based on Jack Johnson). Jones had even played Robeson in a one-man show on Broadway in 1978. Drabinsky's choice of a recognizably black voice belonging to a famous dramatic actor as the "quintessential voice" of *Show Boat* was a not-so-subliminal argument for Kern and Hammerstein's classic as a musical that dealt seriously with questions of race. Would Jones have been the "quintessential voice" of just any "great musical"? Would Drabinsky have chosen him to be the voice of *Kiss of the Spider Woman* (the producer's previous triumph) or a revival of a show such as *Guys and Dolls* or *South Pacific*? Jones as the voice of *Show Boat* simultaneously pointed toward the show's defining blackness and calmed concerns about its appropriateness in an era of political correctness.

Ironically, Prince and Stroman had from the start endeavored to highlight the racial questions implicit in *Show Boat*, but it is essential to evaluate their choices by comparison with other late twentieth-century *Show Boats*, for they were not alone in bringing the *Cotton Blossom* back to the stage. In addition to the ON/RSC production, the Paper Mill Playhouse—a nonprofit repertory company founded in 1938 in Millburn, New Jersey—also mounted a major production in 1989. The Paper Mill *Show Boat* was broadcast nationally on the PBS series *Great Performances*, the only time a complete stage version of the show has aired on U.S. television. Both the Paper Mill and Drabinsky productions were captured live on video, allowing them to be assessed with a level of detail missing for earlier stage *Show Boats*.[20]

Directed by Robert Johanson, the Paper Mill production solved the problem of Ravenal's return at the close of act 2 by shifting the reprise of "You Are Love" to after Kim's 1920s number instead of before it. This allowed Magnolia to join Ravenal in the reprise, converting it from a regretful solo to a duet of reconciliation. By adding her voice to Ravenal's in their old water barrel duet, Magnolia effectively forgave her husband for the lost years. The moment, built on the dramatic power of song, was poignant and convincing. For once, a stage production of *Show Boat* came to a close like an operetta. When Kim appeared, Magnolia's final line—"Look Gay. Here's Kim"—was followed by a credible embrace for the little family to the strains of "Ol' Man River." Prince did not follow Johanson's lead when it came to Magnolia and Ravenal's reconciliation.

Both Johanson and Prince inserted numbers from the 1936 film: Johanson, the duet "Ah Still Suits Me" for Queenie and Joe; Prince, the duet "I Have the Room Above Her" for Magnolia and Ravenal, which had never been used on stage. These choices aptly express the fundamental difference between these two productions. Johanson relied on charismatic individual performances, delivered old-fashioned musical comedy effects that welcomed applause throughout the long show, and brought humor into the story whenever possible. Prince privileged a cinematic smoothness of transitions facilitated by an impressive (and expensive) set, which made the two-story "I Have the Room Above Her" into a display of stagecraft worthy of the contemporary *Sunset Boulevard*, and thus cast an air of seriousness over the entire production. Prince seldom sought to elicit laughter from the audience and generally suppressed applause in favor of seamlessness, at times altering the musical fabric of the score to achieve this goal. Both directors altered the text: Prince freely combined dialogue from Hammerstein's 1927 stage and 1936 screen versions; Johanson went farther, adding entirely new lines, some with significant consequences for how the color line was presented.

All of the above productions, with special attention to Johanson and Prince, can be fruitfully considered through the complementary prisms of three key female roles: Queenie, Julie, and Kim. Queenie endures as the last surviving "mammy" of the 1920s still negotiated by contemporary performers. What Queenie says and sings (her text) and how she talks, sounds, and moves (her performance) has required much remaking. Prince succeeded in silencing Queenie's laugh almost completely, and his Queenie walked off with a Tony Award. Queenie's multiple transformations serve as touchstones for the representation of black women and the careers of black female performers on the musical stage. Julie was remade by tapping into the black singing voice, a transformative force in American popular culture that inevitably touched Broadway singing and played a part in the continued relevance of *Show Boat*. The casting of two mixed-race singers in the role—Cleo Laine in London, Lonette McKee in the States—remade Julie's relationship to the other black characters in the story and to her own identity as a black woman seeking to "pass." The strong return of Kim's levee dance provides a third point of entry into these productions. Dance has always been a flexible element in *Show Boat*—a nonverbal text in the hands of choreographers. The ways in which Kim's levee dance was used to evoke the 1920s provides an important indicator for how post–1970 productions understood the questions of racial performance and popular culture history lodged within the story *Show Boat* tells.

The late twentieth-century remakings of this rousing production number at the close of act 2 staged the strong return of Hammerstein's popular music plot, along the way marking the limits of how much *Show Boat* could tell a contemporary audience about the American experience of the color line.

QUEENIE

Tensions between text and performance proved central in the effort to adjust Queenie to changing racial sensibilities. Substantial changes to the text— beyond simply cutting numbers—began as early as the mid-1960s, when the lyrics for Queenie's verse in the unremovable "Can't Help Lovin' Dat Man" underwent the first of two revisions. In the 1966 Music Theater of Lincoln Center production, Rosetta Le Noire sang lyrics designed to eliminate Hammerstein's descriptions of Joe as lazy and prone to drink, while also redesigning the couple's relationship on more generic (white) romantic terms.[21] Hammerstein, who died in 1960, was not the author of the new lyrics. Le Noire's Joe was a "dreamer" rather than "shiftless." All references to gin were removed, as was the line about Joe's kisses. Except for Le Noire's mature voice, her Queenie sounded like a dreamy girl with an absentminded boyfriend, her solo ending with the sentimental line "Oh how I love him when he's looking at me." In 1994 Prince dispensed entirely with the text of Queenie's verse and had Joe and Queenie sing a variant of Julie's verse, which begins "Oh, listen sister" and describes love as planned by angels. Repeating lines and rhymes, the logic of Hammerstein's imagery was undone by Prince's revision, but once again Joe was shielded from the accusation that he was a "shiftless" gin drinker. Both these approaches demonstrated discomfort with Hammerstein's original text and saw no way to salvage the verse by way of performance choices.

Johanson's solution retained Hammerstein's original 1927 text and called upon a new kind of black female persona to transform the moment for contemporary tastes. Ellia English and P. L. Brown, the Paper Mill Queenie and Joe, approached the verse like comedians with the glint of sex in their eyes the entire time. The shared line "He's never roun' me / yo' when dere's workin' to do" was performed by both in a caricature of a spousal scold, face to face with exaggerated voices and gestures. One reference for this approach is George and Louise Jefferson from the 1970s television sitcom *The Jeffersons*. (English would play Aunt Helen on *The Jamie Foxx Show* beginning in 1996, bringing the variety, generosity, sharpness of comic timing, and slyly sexual humor seen in her portrayal of Queenie to a contemporary, mostly black-cast television comedy.) The Paper Mill Queenie and Joe had each other's number and clearly liked to spar as a prelude to expressions of affection and attraction. They were—above all else—husband and wife. English sang the final line—"Ah even loves him when his kisses got gin"—while being embraced from behind by her Joe. They swayed together, sharing their enjoyment of the music, and just for a moment the spirit of *Ain't Misbehavin'* sneaked into *Show Boat*.

Winning a Tony for Best Musical in 1978 and running for almost four years, *Ain't Misbehavin'* was the most successful example of the late 1970s resurgence of black musical theater rooted in the music and energy of the 1920s and '30s but revised to meet post–civil rights sensibilities. Re-energizing the still commercial black-cast show, *Bubblin' Brown Sugar* (1976, based on a concept by Le Noire), *Ain't Misbehavin'*, *Eubie* (1978), and *Sophisticated Ladies* (1981) brought the style and high spirits of prewar black entertainment to the Broadway stage in non-narrative contexts, which celebrated the past and, for most viewers and critics, rehabilitated the difficult historical position of black performers and creators whose careers were shaped by segregation. There were no "mammy" or "Uncle Tom" figures in these shows, which instead presented sophisticated, sassy, sexy, and funny black men and women. This development on the musical stage opened the door for English and Brown as Queenie and Joe to recast Hammerstein's unchanged lyric as if it were a scene from *Ain't Misbehavin'*. In fact, English had been a standby during *Ain't Misbehavin'*'s Broadway run.

The approach also breathed new life into "Ah Still Suits Me," which Johanson inserted into act 2 just after Magnolia's triumph at the Trocadero. In one of many innovative directorial choices, Johanson brilliantly reinterpreted the aftermath of "After the Ball" as a sad moment—Magnolia and Andy exiting very slowly in a spotlight, she still absorbing the shock of Ravenal's departure while the crowd celebrates New Year's Eve in the shadows. On the heels of this serious moment, English and Brown's "Ah Still Suits Me" brought the story back to the *Cotton Blossom*'s kitchen where "Can't Help Lovin' Dat Man" had been sung. Changes in Joe and Queenie's makeup and hair—both now gray-headed—revealed that a substantial period of time had elapsed. English's short cotton dress shifted the time frame to post–World War I. "Ah Still Suits Me," written for the always dignified Robeson, was played entirely for laughs. Throughout the number, Brown, the most relaxed of Joes, sat and whittled while English literally made biscuits. Complicated stage business with dough, rolling pins, and other utensils added a rhythmic accompaniment to the song, complementing the banjo in the orchestration. Along the way, the physical labor of black women workers such as Queenie was highlighted in a manner that had little in common with old-style mammies—English was no smiling Aunt Jemima. Whatever universality there was in a bickering married couple—plenty to be sure—was made concrete in historical terms by Joe and Queenie's position as black workers on the *Cotton Blossom*. In Johanson's version, the pair did not pause to do a song and dance; their feature had to be performed while also performing necessary labors to feed the white folks still running the boat. The Paper Mill audience witnessed how Queenie's famous biscuits were made.

Johanson clearly recognized that he had something both special and timely in Ellia English, and flashes of the new black Broadway woman were sprinkled throughout the Paper Mill production. At the close of "Can't Help Lovin' Dat Man," English's voice and chemistry with Brown were again emphasized. In the playoff, Magnolia and Julie exited together while Queenie and Joe remained onstage to embrace in a blue spotlight all their own. In a special arrangement of the music that let her set the pace, English belted out the final lyric one last time—"Can't help lovin dat man of mi-i-ine."—with just a bit of gospel-derived flair, adding yet another touch of contemporary black musical performance. The blackout followed after a lingering kiss on the cheek from Joe. Another blackout on English closed "Queenie's Ballyhoo," which featured her as a dancer as well as singer. While singing the song's complicated lyric, English used the resource of the wireless microphone to color the lyrics with maximum variety: she didn't shout the whole number. Indeed, a bit of sexy innuendo broke in on the line "Is you or ain't you dyin' to know," which English performed with all the implied naughtiness of Mae West. English departed definitively from the desexualized, maternal mammy: she played Queenie as a vibrant black woman, effectively inserting racial performance modes innovated in the 1970s and '80s into a period show set many decades earlier. Correctly anticipating that the audience would adore her, Johanson used English several times as a "curtain," adapting Hammerstein's similar use of the black chorus in 1927 to the presence of a charismatic featured performer in 1989.

Ellia English was not the only "hot" Queenie of the 1980s. Karla Burns appeared, by her own count, in eleven productions of *Show Boat*, including the HGO stops in New York and Cairo, before taking the role in the ON/RSC version in 1989. Burns proved a star sensation in London and was the first black actor awarded an Olivier Award, the West End equivalent of the Tony. She sang Queenie on McGlinn's recording as well, making Burns one of only two African American voices on the discs. An opera singer by training, Burns freely embraced the typecasting that came her way, saying "Size and color, the things that would seem my obstacles, haven't been."[22] She played Lily in the

Met's *Porgy and Bess*, Katisha in *The Mikado*, Bloody Mary in *South Pacific*, and Hattie McDaniel in a one-woman show. The London press took up the question of Burns's size directly, and she was quoted at length in a *Times Saturday Review* profile that transliterated her Oklahoma accent in a manner no American newspaper would likely have allowed itself: "Ah'm comfortable with mah body. . . . Ah've always been a round wumman."[23] Her impact on the British audience, Burns thought, was directly linked to her size. "I make my body the instrument of communication. People think, 'My goodness, she must weigh 20 stone.' Then I leap in the air and dance, and they say, 'How graceful she is,' and I feel infinitely in control" (see fig. 9.2). In another profile, Burns discussed the question of whether the original reading of *Show Boat*'s opening line should be used. "Each time I've come across a new production of *Show Boat* the song has been discussed in earnest. Sometimes the discussions are very painful. . . . I'm never offended, whether they decide to use the n-word or not. I've come to peace with myself."[24] Burns noted that Cairo audiences misread her character's role within the world of the show, assuming a character so important to the telling of the story had to have more power within the story. "But in Egypt they took her name Queenie for Queen. It did something to them culturally, made them feel good about having dark skins. When I was doing interviews there, they really wanted to hear that she was more than just a boat's cook. I was able to tell them, she certainly was."

Prince abandoned the hot, dancing Queenies of the 1980s, instead building the role around "Mis'ry's Comin' Aroun'" and the opera singer Gretha Boston,

9.2. *Karla Burns as Queenie the flapper leads black and white cast members from the 1989 Opera North/Royal Shakespeare Company* Show Boat *in a 1920s song-and-dance showstopper. (Author's Collection)*

who claimed she had never read Ferber nor seen *Show Boat* in any form. Boston drew her models from the real world rather than the precedents of the musical stage. "I used to see women going in the morning to clean white folks' houses. They left in the morning with dignity and returned home with dignity. That was all I needed."[25] Boston's interpretation drew upon yet another new musical stage persona open to African American women in the postwar period: the operatic diva. Boston played Queenie from within the tropes of dignity and reserve innovated by black female opera singers such as Leontyne Price. Price made a career out of embodying the princesses of European opera, who while often in peril always remained in control. Boston treated Queenie along these lines. This shift from hot and wild—English and Burns's approach—to cool and collected in no way lessened Queenie's potential to be a strong presence in *Show Boat*'s crowded field of main characters. When asked by a black newspaper why Queenie seemed "more significant in this production than in previous ones," Drabinsky responded, "Gretha Boston. . . . It's a hard part to cast. You need to have dimension to the character. A strong operatic voice. Someone feisty. . . . She takes the stage so strongly that you feel her presence quite effectively."[26]

Boston's voice was central. Despite wearing a wireless microphone, she sang in a supported, trained manner throughout—unlike the more varied English, who favored a musical comedy approach to the part vocally. Boston *sang* Queenie: blending chest and head registers into a smooth sound from top to bottom, distinctly presenting the consonants but building the sound on the vowels, respecting Kern's notes and rhythms, relying on the beauty and power of her instrument despite the fact that a sophisticated sound system projected her voice into the hall. This approach—applied to music written for a popular singer and performed in a context where such trained voices are rarely heard—altered the stature of Queenie's songs. They sounded weighty, less laden with the trappings of showbiz, musically more substantial.

Boston's approach to Queenie's speaking lines was also reserved and serious. Only once in the entire production did her Queenie laugh—at Magnolia's revelation that she's in love. Boston didn't even crack a smile at her own joke about Joe being so lazy he would put popcorn in flapjacks so they could flip themselves over. Her largely humorless but not unsmiling or ungenerous approach to the part gave Queenie the potential to play a particular role in the lives of the white folks on the boat. For example, Boston's Queenie forced Elaine Stritch's Parthy to take the infant Kim into her arms for the first time, initiating an abrupt change in the white woman's character. And contrary to all social conventions, Prince had Ravenal shake Queenie's hand when he, Magnolia, and Kim departed for Chicago. Boston's reserve and dignity opened the door to these added touches.

The contrast between Boston's reserve and English's good humor was made manifest from the moment each actress made her first entrance. In the first bit of dialogue in act 1, scene 1, Pete, the engineer, confronts Queenie about the brooch she is wearing. He recognizes the item as a gift he had given to Julie, who passed it on to Queenie in an effort to conceal the item from Steve. Brought up short by Pete's cruel question with its threatening epithet—"Hey nigger, where'd you get that brooch?"—Boston delivered a revised version of Hammerstein's original line: instead of the flamboyant "You mean dis scrumptious piece of jewelry!" she replied "You mean this?" in a tone that spoke to her inherent dignity and even a sense of hurt. Boston was offended but unafraid, and it's difficult to imagine her Queenie ever using a word like "scrumptious." No one else onstage witnessed this interracial confrontation, and Boston ended the dialogue with a reading of the reply "Ask me no questions, I'll tell you no lies" that did not look for a laugh. Prince removed the dialect from Hammerstein's original, which read "Ax me no questions 'n ah'll tell y' no lies!," and cut Queenie's exit line "Dat man! Axin' me where I get my jewelry" altogether. By contrast, English made a star's entrance from the show boat, calling a greeting to the black gals stage left with a friendly "Mornin' darlings"—they replied "Hi Queenie"—and delivering water to the black stevedores stage right, hard at work on the levee. She called one stevedore by name—"Here you are, Jason"—and warned the men, "Don't drink it all in one swallow." These are added lines with no precedents that introduced Queenie as a generous woman known to all the black chorus members. Matriarch of more than just the *Cotton Blossom* kitchen, she was also a pillar of the black community. English responded to Pete with a mix of genuine fear of physical harm (the Paper Mill Pete was truly scary) and impudent boldness. She spoke each line from within a different assessment of the color line in this exchange, which is more than just white threatening black but also black speaking to black about the realities of life under Jim Crow. After Pete's departure, Queenie addressed her line about "that man" asking her about the brooch not to the (white) audience in search of a laugh but to the black women onstage with her.

The context for Queenie and Pete's confrontation also spoke to the differing ways Johanson and Prince highlighted the reality of black oppression at the top of the show, where Hammerstein himself made it a major theme. For all his articulated desire to bring out themes of racial oppression, Prince's greatly remade opening focuses on an event: the arrival of the *Cotton Blossom*. Hammerstein and Kern's text assumes that the *Cotton Blossom* has already docked, and so Prince and his musical assistants had to substantially alter the opening chorus to accompany an event that fit into megamusical aesthetics:

their *Cotton Blossom* plays the role of the chandelier in *The Phantom of the Opera* or the helicopter in *Miss Saigon*, a marvel of modern stagecraft that rewarded late twentieth-century audiences' desire for technically sophisticated visual spectacle. The first stage production to invest in the arrival of the *Cotton Blossom* onstage was the 1966 Lincoln Center version, designed by Oliver Smith. The director Lawrence Kasha emphasized "smoothness" of transitions, anticipating Prince's approach. The boat also "sailed" onto the stage in the London 1971 production.[27] Eugene Lee's design for Prince's *Cotton Blossom* was complex in its functionality, moving both side to side and up and down, but Spartan in its decoration, eschewing entirely the Victorian gingerbread typical of Howard Bay's midcentury stage designs and MGM's wedding-cake paddle wheeler. Setting up the arrival of the boat disrupted Kern and Hammerstein's careful contrast of the black and white choruses. Indeed, the arch exchange between the white belles and their beaux "What a pretty bevy" was almost entirely eliminated by Prince, short-circuiting the musical contrast between blacks at work and whites at play that Hammerstein and Kern had created in late 1926. Prince chose scenic spectacle over musical expression, and the original power of the opening chorus was reduced considerably.

By contrast, Johanson built upon Hammerstein and Kern's musical architecture, leaving the musical text unchanged and enhancing its power with unusual performance choices. Johanson raised the curtain during a bit of "Ol' Man River" that closed the Paper Mill overture (a revision of the 1927 original). The stage was dimly lit and filled with fog. Shirtless, sweaty black men pulled the *Cotton Blossom*—a white, gingerbread confection mounted on a turntable—into position, straining at the ropes in an abstract expression of their role in the economy of the river. One black figure carried an enormous cotton bale on his back, a visual homage to Whale's use of the shirtless Robeson in 1936. Joe watched from above; the audience applauded; the opening chorus followed immediately, and the stage was entirely given to the black chorus, the "colored folks" who work on Mississippi. The women of the black chorus flirted openly with the men, some even tossing cotton balls from an open picking sack into the air. Then, all at once, the dynamic level of the singing dropped to almost nothing, and all physical action returned to working. Vallon the sheriff, played in a threatening, completely bigoted manner, had entered and every black character onstage reacted physically and vocally. The lowered dynamic level persisted until Vallon's slow crossover was complete, undercutting the musical climax of the chorus and abruptly inserting a palpable fear into the scene. This performance choice allowing dramatic staging (the added crossover for Vallon) to influence musical choices added new dimension to the power structure Hammerstein and

Kern had laid out without altering the musical forms themselves. The black community was initially shown as they were to each other: the Paper Mill *Show Boat* began as a black-cast musical. When Vallon entered, the need to adjust their public selves to white expectations, motivated by a realistic fear of white power, effected a sudden change of affect and dynamic in the black community. Black-cast energy gave way to a sudden drawing of the color line even as the music continued on. When the white belles and beaux entered—costumed and staged in a stereotypically musical comedy manner—the racial ground shifted yet again. All of this informed Queenie and Pete's first exchange, which, by virtue of the added lines for Queenie and English's subtle performance, continued themes of black solidarity and white threats of violence already established.

Johanson's reliance on Hammerstein and Kern's text, and trust in the efficacy of staging and performance choices alone to inflect new meanings more appropriate to the 1990s, is a powerful vote of confidence in *Show Boat*'s continued relevance. The way the words were sung, the way the performers embodied their roles, the power of the director to add subtlety to the stage picture by inserting new action (such as Vallon's crossover) all worked together in this remaking of the original text in performance. In addition, the Paper Mill opening chorus expressed the racial context of the river world in all its ugliness without recourse to the n-word, allowing contemporary audiences to get the point without causing controversy or offense.

JULIE

The post–civil rights transformation of Julie involved no alterations to the text but rather a fundamental revision of the way the character gave voice to her mixed-race identity. If Helen Morgan, Carol Bruce, and Teresa Stratas sang Julie "white," Cleo Laine and Lonette McKee sang her "black." This performance choice gains resonance when trends in Broadway singing provide the context.

A significant performer-centered trend of the post-1960s Broadway stage was the emergence of a new sort of voice: a black, usually female, gospel voice, arising in popular music from the late 1950s on, that proved to have tremendous dramatic potential, capable of carrying a black-cast show or being inserted into a white-cast show. Somewhat like the emergence of Paul Robeson and the concert spiritual in the ferment of the Harlem Renaissance, Mahalia Jackson and black gospel music attracted white audiences in the midst of the civil rights movement of the 1950s and '60s. Here was an American voice that was raced but called for justice in a way that welcomed all to sing along, like the spiritual singers of the 1920s offering a sung black identity that liberal white listeners could embrace. Both voices did historic work in the quest for racial equality, and both had potential for crossover into the commercial sphere. Singers like Sam Cooke and Aretha Franklin applied gospel style to secular love songs with great success. This new "soulful" voice came to Broadway in the 1970s: *Purlie* (1970), *Raisin* (1973), and the more pop-oriented *The Wiz* (1975) all used the sound. *Purlie* was nominated and *Raisin* and *The Wiz* won the Tony for Best New Musical.

In time, the gospel-inflected, soulful voice began to be heard in mixed-cast shows that narrativized raced popular music styles in a similar manner to what *Show Boat* had done in the 1920s. The differences with *Show Boat* were, however, great. The late twentieth and twenty-first century mixed-race shows invested more narrative interest in their black characters, developed explicitly liberal themes resonant with the civil rights movement, and presented race mixing as creative, positive, and defiantly musical. These shows—among them *Dreamgirls* (1981), *Big River* (1985), *Ragtime* (1998), *Hairspray* (2002), and *Memphis* (2009)—matter here because *Show Boat* played off these trends as it returned to Broadway, and all these shows reworked some of the basic strategies of racial performance initiated by Kern and Hammerstein in 1927. This crop of shows—a set of radical remakings, all except for *Ragtime* winning the Tony for Best New Musical—forms a major legacy of Hammerstein and Kern's *Show Boat* as a work that dealt directly with the color line.

Dreamgirls deployed a range of black and white popular music voices in a compelling narrative, focusing on the question of how black a voice could be and still "cross over." Almost all the professional tensions in the show circle on this question. The record producer Curtis Taylor Jr. replaces the assertive gospel stylings of Effie White with the less black, "smoother" pop sounds of Deena Jones, and the Dreams soar to the top of the charts. Effie responds by redoubling her commitment to her black sound in the defiant "I Am Changing." Curtis also forces the James Brown figure of James "Thunder" Early to cool down his style, leading to Early's defiant reassertion of his blacker style in "The Rap." To make its popular music point, *Dreamgirls* required a handful of whites: a small group sings a Pat Boone–style cover of "Cadillac Car"; Deena's backup dancers in act 2 included one white male; and Curtis and Effie both made use of white lawyers in act 2. The Pat Boone sequence nets a laugh and ironic cheers, but the question of racial performance and black access to the white market remains front and center. This one white-cast number sets the whole show in context. The difference with *Show Boat* is, of course, the centrality of the black main characters—no white character has a name in

Dreamgirls—and the investment in authenticity. Effie, as introduced by Jennifer Holliday, injected a gospel shouting style into the heart of Broadway. (Holliday won the Tony.) But neither the score nor the show punishes Deena or Curtis for their success at crossing over. *Dreamgirls* revels in many different raced styles all along the black side of the spectrum; Henry Kreiger and Tom Eyen's score tapped into popular music history in a way that remains clear to current audiences. Hammerstein and Kern did the same with *Show Boat* in 1927 but the passage of time has dulled audience awareness of the musical contrasts being drawn. In *Dreamgirls*, the issue of crossing over replaces that of passing and the search for artistic and personal integrity trumps mere commercial success. It's tempting to speculate that *Dreamgirls*'s plot would have pleased Ferber. All the women succeed on their own terms, transcending and jettisoning weak men, ending up sadder but wiser, just like any good Ferber heroine does.

Big River faithfully retold Mark Twain's novel *The Adventures of Huckleberry Finn* in a refreshingly low-key manner. With music by Roger Miller, a country songsmith from outside the Broadway mainstream, the score featured reedy country voices, traditional hymn singing, and pure gospel numbers. The funeral anthem "How Blest We Are" gets white and black treatment in succession. The relationship of Huck and the escaped slave Jim lay at the heart of the show, such that the actors playing these roles bowed together while holding hands at the curtain call.[28] Their interracial friendship—the show's only love story—developed across a series of duets where they met on shared musical ground: from the call-and-response arrangement of "Muddy Water" to the pop-country FM radio mix of "River in the Rain" to the soulful pop-gospel of the more emotionally effusive "Worlds Apart." The original Jim, Ron Richardson, regularly laced his singing with gospel touches. The musical climax was given to Jim in the song "Free at Last" that put civil rights tropes from Martin Luther King Jr. into the mouth of a slave in chains, who stood stock still and sang a rising vocal line filled with gospel melismas, supported by piano comping and a black choir. "Ol' Man River" is the clear precursor, only here the black man's anthem is the culminating musical-dramatic moment for the whole story—the emotionally climactic eleven o'clock number—rather than a featured number in a musical about white people. *Big River* is, in the end, about black and white people, and all the post-1960 mixed-cast shows have this great advantage over *Show Boat*. For while *Show Boat* might point to racial divisions, might put the color line onstage, it doesn't seek to remove the line nor does it use the utopian power of the musical stage to show how individuals in a world without the color line might sing and dance together. Mixed-race shows that came along after Prince's revival—*Ragtime*,

Hairspray, and *Memphis*—did this to great effect and are discussed in the epilogue.

Prince's *Show Boat* had only one competitor for the Tony for Best Revival of a Musical in 1995. The director Des McAnuff's production of *How to Succeed in Business Without Really Trying* injected a black gospel voice into the show, shrewdly casting Lillias White, who had played Effie in *Dreamgirls*, as Miss Jones. Audiences familiar with *How to Succeed* could anticipate the show's inspiring if ironic eleven o'clock number "Brotherhood of Man," which features Miss Jones, as the moment when White would take over. Remaking the original arrangement, which had a white Miss Jones singing operatic high notes, White gloried in some jazzy scatting and turned the company of all white executives into her own gospel choir. However, before they could support her they had to learn how to clap on the off beats—how to clap black—and how to hail White as a "sistah" in their fraternity. The historic role that black music, dance, and performers played in the making of white cool could hardly be more explicitly stated, except that the number was not presented as ironic. There might be a way to tacitly slip a black Miss Jones into the secretarial staff at World Wide Wicket, but there was no way to address the fact that everyone else was white, and the text of the show, like most all white-cast shows, admitted no insertion of questions of racial justice. Of course, *How to Succeed*, dating from 1961, similarly foreclosed on feminist questions and so could be taken as a quaint period piece, forever stuck in the bad (but funny) old days.

Unlike the use of White in *How to Succeed*, putting a black performer into *Show Boat* in a role previously reserved for whites and letting that performer sing black had meaningful results, demonstrating *Show Boat*'s capacity to remain relevant in greatly changed racial contexts. The role was Julie, a mixed-race role that had been the province of white performers until Cleo Laine took the part in London 1971 and Lonette McKee in New York in 1983 and 1994. Laine and McKee's careers and approaches to singing Julie raise key issues surrounding the meaning of race in *Show Boat* in the late twentieth century, and how those meanings were potentially different for London and New York audiences.

Cleo Laine was already famous when she played Julie in 1971. Laine had starred in dramas and musicals in the West End and was regularly hailed as one of the great singers of the age by the British press. The size of her reputation and talent forced unprecedented changes in *Show Boat*. Two songs were not enough for Laine, so a third was added, necessitating a new scene in act 1 wedged between "You Are Love" and Magnolia and Ravenal's wedding. Set in "A Bar in St. Louis"—a city *Show Boat* had never previously visited—Laine's

Julie sang a languorous version of "Nobody Else But Me," the song Kern had composed as Kim's up-tempo dance number for the 1946 revival. Laine made the added song a condition of her acceptance of the part. The Hammerstein-Kern-Ferber heirs agreed but only if Julie disappeared from the story for good after "Bill."[29]

Laine sang "Bill" a la Morgan—atop a piano—but applied her own approach to the song, only slightly toning down her idiosyncratic, somewhat mannered jazz pop style. Laine's version of "Bill" on her 1973 album *Live at Carnegie Hall* elaborates only slightly on her version recorded for the 1971 cast album. Laine approached Julie as a dramatic vehicle where she could insert her peculiar vocal persona with relatively minor adjustments. "Bill" had been shaped around Morgan's existing vocal persona in much the same way.

But Laine's Julie upset the balance of "Can't Help Lovin' Dat Man," the arrangement for which was substantially remade. Laine took her time on Julie's solo verse and chorus, which takes up more than half of the number on the cast album. After Queenie's verse, the focus returned to Laine, who "introduced that silver filigree of sound that is her personal signature" into the breaks where Joe had originally been featured.[30] The dance aspect of the number was minimized to make room for Laine, who took a long cadenza-like, out-of-time solo at the close as an opportunity to show off her huge vocal range. The imperative to feature Cleo Laine trumped any other priority in this Julie-centric visit to the kitchen pantry.

Assessing the way Laine sang Julie within the categories of black and white vocal style proves difficult, for Laine remains a truly unusual singer, and the categories of race operative in the United States cannot so easily be applied to her. In 2007 Laine described her background this way: "My father was a Jamaican who came to England to fight in the First World War and after-wards settled in Southall where he married my mother who was white from Swindon and therefore ostracized from then on by all her family. Anyway my father had all these records of Negro singers like Billie Holiday and I suppose they influenced me, though come to think of it the greatest influences on my childhood were Deanna Durbin and Judy Garland."[31] In the early 1950s, Laine began singing with the white British jazz leader John Dankworth, and the two married in 1958 (when interracial marriage was still illegal in parts of the United States). Laine and Dankworth forged successful careers together and apart. A mature performer in her mid-forties when she played Julie, Laine was known to be "deeply resentful of any attempt either by the press or man-agements to pigeon-hole her."[32] Her apparent indifference to questions of race as they touched on *Show Boat* cropped up in the press. When Michael Billington asked Laine about race in *Show Boat*, she deflected the issue, declining to put her own history into context beside that of her character. One of the few items to highlight the appropriateness of her casting quoted producer Fielding's publicist pointing out that Laine was "the first 'ethnically correct' actress to play the part." When the remark was repeated to Laine, she again deflected: "That's history at least, isn't it? . . . I'm sure Ava Gardner wasn't 'ethnically correct.'"[33] But in her 1994 autobiography, Laine made more of the breakthrough: "My gut feeling [was] that the record of white versus colour for the role should be put straight at last."[34]

Laine's Julie cannot be simply read as black. Her sound was her own, informed by a specific background and consistently unique, even strange, vocal identity. Nor was Laine's career a story of mixed-race identity setting limits or defining what parts she might play. Still, the approach Laine brought to Julie marked an important redefinition of the role. Laine sang Julie without shame. Her "Can't Help Lovin' Dat Man" is singularly jazz-oriented, full of slides, swung rhythms, colored vowels, and a general intensity of musical expression that typified "the skill with which she can transform any lyric into something reflecting her own personality."[35] Whether this made her singing "black" was not the issue. Julie isn't supposed to know "Can't Help Lovin Dat Man" or how to sing it: Laine gives absolutely no evidence of trying to conceal either. Laine, a singer first and foremost, wasn't about to take the dramatically credible—i.e., restrained—approach that most Julies had employed to this point. Instead, she took over, supported by a contemporary pop strings-heavy arrangement, and ran the song through all her tricks. Her Julie was confident, unafraid to raise her voice and lead the black ensemble in this song "only colored folks sing." During Laine's cadenza, a woman's voice can be heard whispering "sing the song, child."

From the beginning and across most *Show Boat* history, this song and scene had been about the celebration of black vernacular culture in unambiguous terms. Critics caught this spirit even when they did not articulate the racial content. For example, one critic noted, "I'm sure, though, that musical comedy has given us few arrangements as persuasively exciting, as giddily invigorating as the free-for-all second chorus of 'Can't Help Lovin' Dat Man.' Once the fragile Julie has finished her wistful version of the number, the rest of the company [the black cast] rides into the act. I kept wondering last evening why they weren't one and all transported into midair by the sounds that were coming from the orchestra. They weren't, exactly. But the music made such an irresistible stir in itself that the stage seemed to take off anyway."[36] In the London 1971 remaking, "Can't Help Lovin' Dat Man" was centered not on Magnolia's shuffle or the black characters singing but on Julie who, in Laine's performance, set aside the tradition of "wistful" performance and instead declared her blackness *in the context of the show* in unambiguous terms. Her full embrace of the song and the evident approval of the black characters onstage with her made Laine's Julie a leader among the show's black cast. This Julie's racial peers embrace and build on her version: in the past, Queenie's verse and Magnolia's shuffling had set things in motion. Featuring Laine and giving her the artistic authority to reshape the song so completely put Julie in complete solidarity with *Show Boat*'s black cast, which, in effect, altered Julie's relationship to her own black identity. The confidence and power Laine brought to her other songs—an ingrained aspect of her persona, perhaps something she could never act out of—further enhanced her strong Julie who took over the kitchen pantry with the power of her art. In an American context, a less vocally unique American mixed-race actress would similarly align a strong Julie with the black folks in the kitchen.

Lonette McKee described her parents this way on the occasion of her debut as the first black performer to play Julie on Broadway: "He is really, really black and she is real, real white. People weren't very tolerant about that," in the poor, mixed-race Detroit neighborhood where she grew up, McKee told the *Times*.[37] McKee's career began early. She scored a regional pop/R&B hit at age fourteen and left school to pursue show business. In 1983 McKee said of playing Julie "it's astonishing—I get to play what I am. The word is 'mulatto'—a word I hate."[38] In a busy career she would find herself frequently exploring roles that were somehow connected to her precise racial identity. McKee made an auspicious film debut in *Sparkle*, a 1976 film about a 1960s girl group in which she played the beautiful lead singer who fell into a life of drugs and abusive relationships. In the 1982 short film *Illusions*, McKee played a black woman passing as white in wartime Hollywood, who came to understand her role as an assistant to a studio mogul as important work in the struggle for democracy at home. Prior to playing Julie in 1983, McKee made her Broadway debut as the wife of Jackie Robinson in *The First* (1981), a failed musical about the integration of major league baseball. Between appearances in the HGO and Drabinsky *Show Boats*, McKee found success Off Broadway as Billie Holiday in the one-woman show *Lady Day at Emerson's Bar and Grill* (1986). The play allowed her to contextualize performances of Holiday's signature songs within the racism that plagued Holiday's life, presented by playwright Lanie Robertson as a force that deeply disfigured the singer's closest relationships. McKee also appeared in two contrasting jazz films: Francis Ford Coppola's *The Cotton Club* (1984) as a Lena Horne–type figure who successfully passes as white at a Midtown club only to return to her black lover Gregory Hines at the end; and Bertrand Tavernier's *'Round Midnight* (1986) as saxophonist Dexter Gordon's long-lost love, singing a duet with

Gordon in a Paris jazz club. Across these years McKee also had a cabaret and nightclub career, recorded several albums, and appeared in three films directed by Spike Lee.[39] McKee's stage and screen persona was consistently connected to issues of race and performance set within historical show business narratives exploring changing racial regimes from a female perspective.

McKee brought this background to her portrayal of Julie in Prince's *Show Boat*. She sang "Can't Help Lovin' Dat Man" in a confident manner, with vocal touches such as leaning on the blue notes, coloring her sound, and playing with the rhythm that—in a Broadway context—could only be heard as black. Her delivery of the line "Oh listen, sister" beckoned a black listener directly, in a historically unprecedented manner. And McKee's Julie didn't simply sing—she also danced, revealing racial knowledge not only in her voice but in her body (see fig. 9.3). McKee's Julie taught Magnolia to dance right along with Joe and Queenie. If Laine's solidarity with the black characters was implied, McKee's was direct and insistent. John Lahr praised her "terrific, swinging interpretation" in a kitchen scene that "dramatizes the blues corrupting the white world with pleasure."[40] These choices were explicit on McKee's part. Having played the role in 1983, she had new ideas about the part in 1994. "Actually, I wanted to make her a little blacker. . . . I wanted to play her more realistically. Not as Julie trying to pass as white but just plain Julie—as she is."[41] McKee's interpretation—taken from personal and professional experience as a mixed-race performer—remade Julie, taking the text constructed for Morgan and transforming the role for late twentieth-century audiences. With no desire to depict a woman hiding from her blackness, McKee freely expressed Julie's black identity in ways no previous Julie had.

And like Laine, McKee brought a new confident interpretation to "Bill." Both sang out loud and strong on the last five words—"Because he's just my Bill"—putting a mark of belief in the power of her love on the close instead of collapsing into the quiet self-pity that had marked Helen Morgan and Carol Bruce's performances. This ending has important consequences for recasting the torch singer as a figure of strength. Whatever Julie had suffered—and Prince spelled out her trials in both added lines and stage action—she still had reserves of strength that could be heard in the way she sang. (McKee honed this approach to singing in a dramatic context while playing Billie Holiday.) But Laine and McKee's strong endings to "Bill" also tap into the larger meanings of the blues as a vehicle for the transfiguration of suffering into a celebration of the human capacity to survive. In this sense, these two singers allowed Julie to sing the blues for the first time, doing more than just opening up the role to mixed-race performers but also letting a historically innovative black voice into *Show Boat* and rearticulating the musical impact of key songs

9.3. *Julie (Lonette McKee) joins Magnolia (Rebecca Luker), Joe (André Solomon-Glover), and Queenie (Gretha Boston) in the exuberant dance to "Can't Help Lovin' Dat Man" in the 1994 Broadway revival. (Author's collection)*

in a way that helped new audiences experience these scenes from within a different racial regime.

Hammerstein had anticipated the possibility of singing Julie in this way, and his cut stage direction from the October draft advising Julie to "[lapse] into the 'Blue' spirit of the song" while singing "Can't Help Lovin' Dat Man" gives evidence he understood something of the expressive resources banked within Julie's mixed-race character. Morgan didn't take Hammerstein's advice and subsequent white Julies didn't know he had made the suggestion.

Laine and McKee needed no such direction to tap into the resourcefulness of the blues while giving voice to Julie in a new, blacker key.

Drabinsky needed several Julies for Broadway, London, and his many touring companies, and he stuck with the practice of casting black women in the part. Singer Marilyn McCoo of The 5th Dimension took over for McKee on Broadway in late 1995.[42] Unlike McKee, whose career had been built in part on "passing" roles facilitated by her very light skin, McCoo was a well-known pop singer associated with an all-black pop group. McCoo's career and appearance raised questions as to whether she could credibly pass for white while playing Julie. (Some felt McKee was also "not fully credible as a character who passes."[43]) Indeed, the physical appearance of the women Drabinsky hired to play Julie (pictured in the tour's souvenir program) suggest that for this widely seen production, Julie's ability to pass physically took on a symbolic rather than literal value. Everyone—the characters onstage and the audience watching—was expected to participate in the charade that Julie could pass . . . despite her appearance. In exchange, the story of Julie and Steve was granted a visceral authenticity that no white Julie could hope to have and an audibly black voice could add to the experience of "Can't Help Lovin' Dat Man." This trade-off marks but one way Drabinsky's *Show Boat* made peace with its 1990s context.

KIM

How to end *Show Boat* like a musical remained a problem for Hammerstein and Kern, and for all who remade the show after them. Ferber imagined Magnolia taking Parthy's place as mistress of the *Cotton Blossom*, a "straight silent figure" standing on the top deck, "silhouetted against sunset sky and water— tall, erect, indomitable."[44] The image might have worked to end a film, especially with the resource of "Ol' Man River" to accompany it, but the perceived need to reunite Magnolia and Ravenal persisted. Audiences have generally accepted their perfunctory reconciliation at the close, facilitated as it is by Hammerstein's invention of the Old Lady on the Levee who reminds the couple (and the audience) of the romance of the wedding that closed act 1. Only in the 1936 film and the 1989 Paper Mill production did Magnolia and Ravenal sing together at the close, like any decent operetta couple must. "You Are Love" served different scenarios reasonably well in both cases.

But the majority of *Show Boats* have not invested much energy in the reunion of the now-aged lovers. Instead, the 1927 levee scene has been an occasion for the insertion of modern youthfulness. Kim—all grown up and a Broadway star—has been the predictable leader of the *Cotton Blossom's* climactic revels. After nixing "It's Getting Hotter in the North," Norma Terris offered imitations in 1927 and 1932. Edith Day sang the added number "Dance Away the Night" as Kim in London in 1928, and in the 1946 revival Jan Clayton as Kim sang "Nobody Else But Me," the last song Kern wrote. This final try by Hammerstein and Kern referred to the Charleston in its lyric and boogie-woogie in its dance arrangement.[45] In the 1950s and '60s, Kim's feature went into eclipse: the MGM film never made it to the 1920s; Jones Beach cut it (and the grown-up Kim) entirely; light opera productions in New York dispensed with dancers for the most part.[46] But pressure exerted by performers to adjust *Show Boat* to fit their talents soon began to bring it back. The 1967 Los Angeles Civic Light Opera production added a 1920s number for Frank as played by Eddie Foy Jr., who did a demonstration called "Dancing in the '20s" with Ellie and the ensemble. It's not clear what specific songs Foy used, but inserting some novelty dance moves—surely a lot of Charleston—into the final scene doubtless worked to the lengthy show's advantage. The London 1971 Frank took the 1920s levee number for himself, tapping away to "Dance Away the Night." The HGO *Show Boat* restored "Hey, Feller!" for Karla Burns, and the eleven-o'clock rouser passed to Queenie for a few years. The ON/RSC version doubled down, keeping Queenie's number and adding a further 1920s moment for Kim, Parthy, and company doing "Why Do I Love You?"

The 1920s production number in the Paper Mill production began with Kim doing an impersonation of Magnolia. (Rebecca Baxter played both roles.) Then, in a transition that reached back to Hammerstein's 1927 idea for a scene in Kim's apartment, Kim said, "Here's how we sing it today!," launching "Why Do I Love You?" as a hot Charleston—the dance late twentieth-century audiences most associate with the 1920s. In the ensuing dance, Frank and Ellie and even Parthy got into the act. After the whites' turn, Queenie and the black chorus took the stage. Attired in flapper style, Ellia English led the group in a medium-tempo grind done to a chorus of the blues. When "Why Do I Love You?" returned, everyone danced together—blacks and whites, principals and chorus—coming into an interracial group pose at the end. As the pose broke up to loud cheers from the audience, Frank and Ellie and Joe and Queenie all started to act their age: their old bodies worked fine while the music was playing but were now stiff and sore. The two couples exchanged verbal goodbyes—ad libs but still added lines—that reinforced the parallel comic roles these performers played in the production. The Paper Mill production, which so effectively expressed the climate of racial fear and resentment in its opening scene, collapsed into a utopian vision at the close. On the show's unlikely Mississippi levee circa 1927, everyone dances the Charleston, everyone dresses up. There's no sense of where these dance moves came from, no popular music plot implied, and the interracial final pose smoothed over the color line completely at the moment when the production asked for applause. This may be satisfying musical theater, but it's hardly a credible vision of the past. (In yet another interracial dance that flew in the face of history, Frank and Ellie's Trocadero feature ended with the pair being joined by a troupe of black dancers for an interracial version of "At a Georgia Camp Meeting" that revived cakewalk struts and beribboned minstrel show tambourines.)

The closing dance number in Prince's *Show Boat* was titled "Kim's Charleston." Stroman used "Why Do I Love You?" Parthy and Kim initially sang the tune together, then Kim started the dance by stamping out the Charleston rhythm, her first hot break directed toward a group of black men at the side of the stage who responded positively. But the long dance that followed employed only Kim and the white dance chorus. Indeed, Stroman had few black dancers to draw from. The breakdown of the ensemble given in Stroman's choreography, which can be licensed by companies wishing to re-create her work, lists four men and one woman as dancers among the twenty-two members of the black chorus.[47] By contrast, Stroman cast four men and four women in the white dance chorus. This group of eight was used most extensively in "Kim's Charleston," a lengthy dance number that drew heavily on Stroman's breakthrough show *Crazy for You* (1992).[48]

"Kim's Charleston" functioned as a synopsis of the most effective elements from Stroman's earlier show. Like most of the major dance numbers in *Crazy for You*, "Kim's Charleston" deployed shifting groups of dancers on a stage full of people with much hooting and hollering throughout the proceedings. Groupings changed for variety's sake and to feature different individuals, some doing acrobatic moves. Two of the white male dancers are listed as dancer/acrobats in Stroman's *Show Boat* choreography book. Stroman reused a "follow me" approach seen in *Crazy for You*'s "Slap that Bass," where one dancer initiates a pattern that others join. In *Show Boat*, Kim is the leader. Stroman also brought back the crowd-pleasing "big line" (her term), where all the dancers form a line far downstage and do simple moves that touch those next to them and gain visual power from sheer repetition. The frontwards orientation of the "big line" in "I Got Rhythm" was altered to a sideways version in "Kim's Charleston." Both moments garnered appreciative applause from the audience. The tossing about of girls from man to man used by Stroman in "Stiff Upper Lip" returned as the four male dancers threw Kim about the stage, and a gleaming period automobile as a dance prop (borrowed by Stroman from Busby Berkeley's *42nd Street* and used in *Crazy for You*'s "I Can't be Bothered Now") also served Kim and her friends. The dance music sounded similar as well: William David Brohn orchestrated both shows.

Crazy for You, touted as the "new Gershwin musical," was an original book show using the best-known Gershwin songs of the 1920s and '30s. Stroman's choreography self-consciously re-created tropes from 1930s film musicals and was hailed as a return to old-fashioned showbiz values. In this respect, Stroman's signature style fit perfectly into the final scene of *Show Boat*. Kim's number was always intended to be a sign of arrival in a different cultural milieu. In 1927, this was the present. As the decades passed, differing cultural memories of the 1920s took the stage. Stroman's successful 1990s re-creation of prewar entertainment values effectively signaled the shift for the contemporary Broadway audience. In the process, for the duration of "Kim's Charleston" *Show Boat* looked and sounded just like a hit from two years earlier that was still running at the Shubert Theatre, just a few blocks from the Gershwin.

But Stroman did more than just apply a new version of the old to the final scene of *Show Boat*. She also tried to make a connection between the still-segregated dance for Kim and her white friends, and historic cultural shifts led by blacks. In a large-scale effort, which substantially remade act 2, Stroman and Prince returned to Hammerstein's popular music plot, using the cinematic potential of Eugene Lee's sets to tell stories of cultural transformation in a pair of "Montages." The first portrayed Magnolia, Ravenal, and the young Kim's fortunes in Chicago, where they begin in the splendor of the Palmer House and end up in poverty on Ontario Street. In Stroman's words from her choreography book, "we see the folks down South fuse into the folks up North. We do this choreographically by having the folks on the levee move off in various patterns as the folks from the North dance on stage in other patterns. The Southerners have more of strut and hip undulations in their walk. The Northerners are more upright and move faster." Stroman assigned race and class identities to each chorus member individually. Among the whites were a "Middle Class Woman with umbrella," an "Upper Class Woman" with a parasol, and "A Belle" with "A real Beaux" in "prop hell," loaded down with souvenirs from the World's Fair. A sprinkling of white workers—a taxi driver, an organ grinder—filled out the scene. The blacks were mostly workers, but a pair of "Black Swells" were also out for a stroll: "They step together. They show off their Sunday best." One black character, played by a dancer, is listed as "Sportin' Life," a streetwise character from *Porgy and Bess*. He and Frank have an exchange of hats suggesting the influence of black style on Frank, who would demonstrate some "very eccentric" moves in his attempt to help Magnolia land the job at the Trocadero. Stroman's effort to complicate the class identity of the ensemble harkens back to Tamiris and Primus's 1946 "No Shoes."

"Montage II" had more conceptual work to do and addressed broad cultural changes, "a transition of 21 years (1900–1921)." Like the 1927 levee scene in Hammerstein's original, Stroman used newspaper headlines to mark the date, only here the headlines changed as posters were successively pasted onto walls at stage left and right. The revolving door of the Palmer House marked the passage of time, a theatrical version of the flipping calendar pages used in classical Hollywood films to make the same point. Joe sang "Ol' Man River" at the start and finish of the montage, his presence accounted for by Stroman through the cinematic metaphor of a "split screen." The primary content of "Montage II" was not Magnolia's brilliant career—as it had been in the 1936 film—but rather the role of African Americans in the transformation of popular music and dance. Stroman's summarized the story being told this way in her notes:

> The Montage has three different moments of "street buskers." The first one involves a black "one man band" that is shooed away by a white doorman. The second involves a pair of black "tap dancers" that are shooed away by a white doorman. As the years go by, the Palmer House doorman changes to a black doorman. The Montage ends with three black Charleston dancers doing a Charleston in front of the Palmer house. The black doorman allows them to stay. As they dance, Joe appears again and sings Old Man River. They continue to do the Charleston.
>
> There are white onlookers who try to pick up the Charleston steps. In the next scene we see Kim and her white friends doing many of the steps invented by the black Charleston dancers in Montage II.

Stroman traces the color line in precise detail here, even to the extent that a black doorman, having achieved a position of power open to African Americans at the time, allows the latest black dance innovators to show off on a prestigious, potentially influential spot on the sidewalk.

Stroman articulated her intention to deal with historical issues of black and white in interviews. "The Charleston was first created in the black community. . . . We couldn't state it outright but we can show it poetically. Otherwise the montage would have just been a fashion show. . . . You're seeing the black community's contribution to American dance, which wasn't previously in *Show Boat*."[49] Stroman's final claim here is debatable. Black dance had almost always been central to *Show Boat*. What she and Prince expanded on was the narrativizing of black influencing white that was in the show from Magnolia's shuffle to "Can't Help Lovin' Dat Man" on. (Stroman described her take on the kitchen pantry dance as "Mocking the white master's ballroom steps.") Hammerstein tried again and again—usually without success—to develop this theme in act 2. In a late twentieth-century context where a concept-driven production privileged the director and choreographer over individual performers, this story could finally be told, not through the existing characters but by the addition of a dance drama—a *Show Boat* dream ballet—that laid out a larger theme implicit in the show from the start.

The question is whether the point sticks. As instructive as Stroman's "Montage II" is, can a sequence like this hope to impress itself upon the viewer with the power of "Kim's Charleston," a set-piece production number that pulls out all the stops in the interests of sheer entertainment? The imbalance between the white and black dance choruses in Stroman's cast speaks to a bigger challenge. Can black dancers regain the prominence they had for much of *Show Boat*'s history if exotic numbers like "In Dahomey" are judged politically incorrect, if Queenie no longer dances, and if black dance is reduced to sidewalk snippets informing an all-white production number? Still, a primary virtue of Stroman and Prince's second act is their refusal to accept easy solutions. At the final curtain—and appropriately so—the signs of racial segregation are still prominently displayed.

EPILOGUE

* * *

The remaking of *Show Boat* continues in the twenty-first century. Raymond Gubbay produced a mammoth in-the-round version at London's Royal Albert Hall in 2006, complete with a stand-in for the Mississippi filled with actual water. A 2008 semi-staged performance in Carnegie Hall moved the show into yet another temple of art music. And in early 2012, the Chicago Lyric Opera mounted *Show Boat* as part of its regular season, advancing the show further into the American opera house. The opera and theater director Francesca Zambello led all three of these productions. Her version of *Show Boat* for Chicago will also play the Washington National Opera at the Kennedy Center in Washington, D.C., the Houston Grand Opera, and the San Francisco Opera in coming seasons. Scheduled for thirteen performances, Chicago counted on *Show Boat* to fill the house more times than even *The Magic Flute* and *Aida*.

In Chicago, Zambello cast Nathan Gunn, an operatic baritone, as Ravenal, and Ashley Brown, a Broadway ingénue who introduced the title role of *Mary Poppins* (2006), as Magnolia. The mixed-race operatic soprano Alyson Cambridge sang Julie. Everyone in the cast wore body microphones—despite the Lyric Opera's marketing tag line "Our Singers Don't Need Microphones." The sound designer Mark Grey and the microphone manufacturer Shure Inc. were credited in the program with "audio reinforcement." The juxtaposition of Gunn's traditional operatic sound and Brown's twenty-first century Broadway style re-created in different terms the contrast audiences likely heard in 1927 between Howard Marsh and Norma Terris. Cambridge sang Julie like an opera singer—without any audible blackness—but danced with abandon, wriggling her hips like Ellia English did as Queenie in the Paper Mill production. Indeed, even Gunn's Ravenal experimented with some shuffling during the wedding scene. A surprising amount of the script was new to this version, but some things remained the same. Morris Robinson sang Joe and received the out-sized ovation that continues to greet "Ol' Man River." Angela Renée Simpson, a radiant operatic soprano known for singing the title role in *Aida*, sang Queenie and delivered the 1920s rouser "Hey, Feller!" to great applause, supported by a black dance chorus whose contribution to the show was balanced by a similar-sized group of white dancers. The two ensembles bowed in racially mixed couples but otherwise didn't dance together. Zambello's version works well in the opera house, perhaps the only place left where *Show Boat* can still be mounted on a Ziegfeldian scale.

A 2009 production by Washington, D.C.'s Signature Theatre tried something unprecedented—a minimal *Show Boat* with a cast of twenty-four and no attempt at scenic splendor, literally "No Boat." Most critics dismissed the exercise but Julie Gilbert, grandniece of Edna Ferber, appreciated the effort as important for the survival of the show. "We don't want *Show Boat* to be extinct. We don't want it to be a big old boat that floats out there in history. The object of the exercise is how to find a supple way to present this and have theater companies and audiences be able to afford it."[1] The jury remains out on the downsizing of *Show Boat*. Among regional musical theater producers, the Goodspeed Opera House in Connecticut offered yet another new version in summer 2011, adjusting the scale of the show to match a modest nineteenth-century theater and employing the latest in stage technology to try, yet again, to solve the problem of act 2. And in summer 2010, the Municipal Theatre Association of St. Louis, know locally as the Muny, staged *Show Boat* on its massive 12,000-seat outdoor stage in Forest Park for the fifteenth time since 1930, hiring Broadway professionals to re-create Prince's version and Stroman's choreography. Michel Bell first sang Joe at the Muny in 1992, and with return engagements in 2003, 2008 (to sing "Ol' Man River" for the Muny's ninetieth anniversary revue), and 2010, Bell is practically an honorary citizen of St. Louis, welcomed with standing ovations in the middle of the show, part of *Show Boat*'s place in the historical memory and contemporary life of a river city that loves musicals and treasures this show with particular passion.

All these twenty-first-century productions, with the exception of Signature's reduced-scale experiment, built on trends begun earlier in *Show Boat*'s long history. The health of *Show Boat*'s ongoing life on American stages suggests a secure future for the show away from Broadway. As one critic noted in 2009, "Despite all its faults, however, *Show Boat* is about as difficult to resist as a slice of mile-high pie. . . . The fact that *Show Boat* can still move and entertain despite decades of cutting, rearranging and 'improvements' is a testament to its grandeur."[2] In short—to give in to the temptation to use a boat metaphor for the first time in *this* book—Cap'n Andy's *Cotton Blossom* isn't headed for permanent dry dock any time soon.

After the 1994 *Show Boat* closed its historically successful run, three new musicals with mixed-race casts added new dimension to the interracial stage pictures, musical encounters, and popular music plots first seen in *Show Boat*, taking their place in the small canon of shows initiated by Kern and Hammerstein's long-lived musical. These radical remakings—Ferber's plot and characters are set aside, but Hammerstein and Kern's juxtaposition of black and white characters and music remains—suggest an ongoing resonance for *Show Boat*, even as the new shows took their audiences to places *Show Boat*, no matter how it's remade, could never go.

Ragtime, a grandly imagined 1998 musical with music by Stephen Flaherty and lyrics by Lynn Ahrens, produced by Garth Drabinsky in 1998 and revived in 2009, dramatized the moment when whites first heard a syncopated vernacular music understood to be the sound of blackness. Standing in the parlor of their "house on the hill in New Rochelle," members of the show's white family respond to the genteel sound of the black pianist Coalhouse Walker Jr.'s "New Music," their strain ending with the question, "And I ask myself, why can't I sing it, too?" (During the course of the show, none of them do.) But Coalhouse is hardly singing to the whites; he's really reaching out to his estranged wife, Sarah, listening from upstairs. His strategy works. She descends to him, his musical entreaty breaking down long resistance. Sarah sings the words "Play that melody" to a tune laden with blue notes and syncopated rhythms. There was no need for the original Sarah and Coalhouse (Audra McDonald and Brian Stokes Mitchell) to sing black: the music and words made the point in this sung reconciliation. In *Ragtime*, a musical idiom that the show calls "ragtime" works at this moment on several levels, initiating varied reactions in the hearts of whites who take the time to listen across the color line and bringing together two black characters central to the story being told. One critique of *Show Boat* in 1993—"The real problem is that the show follows the wrong story. It assumes that black people are inherently less interesting than whites"—cannot be leveled against *Ragtime*.[3]

Indeed, beyond the composition of the cast, which increased the casting complexities with the addition of a third group: Jewish immigrants from Eastern Europe, *Ragtime* bears little resemblance to *Show Boat* in its use of musical style. Each racially sorted group includes dramatic principals who sing in the same idiom, a cross between Stephen Sondheim's multiple-perspective songs and Andrew Lloyd Webber's pop arias. (Klezmer inflections color the orchestrations for the Jewish characters in a long tradition of "oriental" touches.[4]) In the context of *Show Boat* history, though, one featured performer who emerges from *Ragtime*'s black cast stands out. At the close of act 1, Sarah is beaten to death by white policemen. The company responds with "Till We Reach That Day," introduced by a singer simply named "Sarah's Friend." Like Jim's "Free at Last" from *Big River*, "Till We Reach That Day" puts civil rights language and gospel singing style into the mouths of characters living decades before such words were said or such music sung. Initially only the black chorus—anachronistically called "Harlem Men and Women"—joined in on a repeat of the chorus. The original "Sarah's Friend," Vanessa Townsell-Crisp, a replacement Effie in the original *Dreamgirls*, improvised a gospel peroration above them. (On the cast album Townsell-Crisp does not sing the notes as printed in the vocal score.) After an interlude where black and white characters comment on Sarah's death, the anthem-like tune begins again, this time with two female voices rising above the voices of everyone on the stage—blacks, immigrant Jews, even the whites (with the exception of Father and Grandfather, the vocal score notes). The finale climaxes on a long held note, the two women "wailing" above it. The curtain to *Ragtime*'s first act (a funeral procession) recalls the *Porgy* saucer burial and "Mis'ry's Comin' Aroun'." Only in *Ragtime*, the injustice of the Jim Crow past is explicitly indicted in the lyrics, with powerful musical expression grounded in popular music history on its side, bringing all but the most recalcitrant white males on the stage into its irresistible orbit.

Crafted in the 1990s and like all musicals an expression of a particular moment in time, *Ragtime* wears its allegiances on its sleeve. *Show Boat* will never be this kind of unproblematic vessel of progressive sentiment, a reality that works against *Show Boat*'s relevance for African American audiences in the post–civil rights era. As Lonette McKee noted in defense of the Prince production, "It's showing how sick it is and how wrong it is and how sad it is that we had to go through this. I think maybe some young black kids might take issue with this production and not want to see themselves portrayed in certain ways—but by the same token, I think it's important that they remember where we came from, what we went through and what we're still going through on many levels."[5] This therapeutic view of *Show Boat* as medicine suggests the long arguments for the show as a valuable opportunity for black performers have finally ended. *Ragtime*'s "Till We Reach That Day" is powerful, in part, because it builds from a solemn to a defiant cry. Both "Ol' Man River" and "Mis'ry's Comin' Aroun'" begin with solemn tones but neither is open to the defiant and transcendent gospel impulse. Neither can easily invoke the passionate gospel Broadway prayer, which turned up everywhere in the 2000s, from the black-cast *The Color Purple* (2005) to the white-cast *Urinetown* (2001) to the mixed-cast *Sister Act* (2011). So while the roots of a moment like "Till We Reach That Day" may be found in *Show Boat*, Hammerstein and Kern's score can never cross over into the gospel promised land.

If *Ragtime* owes relatively little to *Show Boat, Hairspray* owes a lot.[6] This musicalized version of John Waters's 1988 film tells the story of plucky Tracy Turnblad's attempts to help integrate a teenage television dance show in Baltimore circa 1962. Reading *Hairspray* through *Show Boat*, traces of Hammerstein's popular music plot grafted onto a different era are everywhere evident. Tracy, like Magnolia, loves black culture. She gets it not by way of a black cook in her home but through radio and television. The desire to be a star animates Tracy—as it did Magnolia and Kim—and she makes connections with black people in her quest to acquire black style. "I believe in integration. It's the new frontier," Tracy cheerfully admits, and *Hairspray* believes in integration as well. Tracy's love interest is white—the difference they overcome is the revolutionary notion that a chubby girl can attract a teenage heartthrob—but the secondary couple Seaweed and Penny enact the scenario raised by generations of white opponents to racial equality: a black man claiming a white woman's love. Seaweed is Penny's "black white knight," she declares in song. Steve and Julie's love, lived in a different place and time, provides a shadowy precursor, sung by Julie in code—"He's just my Bill"—but no less resonant of the truth that love has often called individuals across the color line.

Approving and disapproving parents play a major role in *Hairspray*, as they do in *Show Boat*. Tracy's parents echo and amplify with committed action Andy's proud claim "I think the show boat has made a damn fine girl out of my daughter" when they join her in a protest march. And like Parthy, only earlier in the show and with much greater enthusiasm, Tracy's mother Edna puts away her repressed 1950s wardrobe to garb herself in flamboyant 1960s fashions. *Hairspray* climaxes with a guerrilla effort on the part of the forces for integration to crash the Miss Hairspray competition. They succeed, of course, and the winner of the contest turns out to be Little Inez, Seaweed's sister. The invisible audience in television land chooses her as the best dancer on the show, in effect choosing black music and dance performed by blacks as the model for the moment. Black style, *Hairspray* declares, is now American style. The Robeson recital, "It's Getting Hotter in the North," and Kim's version of "Gallivantin' Aroun'" would have made the same claim, had any of these made it to stage or screen. Stroman's "Montage II" and "Kim's Charleston" took the notion as far as it could go without crossing over into an overly sanguine view of American racial history. What *Hairspray* can celebrate outright—and *Show Boat* can only point to—is the idea that blacks and whites can, should, have, and must dance and sing together. Crossing the color line is an essential act in the making of America on the musical stage. This happens, at least for Magnolia, in the original kitchen pantry scene, where the young white girl shows her skill at dancing black. Tracy cements her friendship with Seaweed by way of a similar display of black dancing. In this respect, the seeds of *Hairspray*'s concluding celebration "You Can't Stop the Beat" lay in *Show Boat*'s "Can't Help Lovin' Dat Man."[7]

Memphis took the Broadway musical into unusual territory: the segregated South in the 1950s. With music by David Bryan (of Bon Jovi) and book and lyrics by Joe DePietro, *Memphis* tells the story of Huey Calhoun, a white disc jockey with absolutely no impulse control who loves black music and finds a way to play it for white kids in Memphis over the radio and on television. Huey's constant breaching of the color line—his effective refusal to recognize that it applies to him at all—drives the show to both exhilarating moments of racial reconciliation and dangerous confrontations with racism in action. In his first solo, Huey fearlessly declares to a group of blacks in a Beale Street club that their music is, for him, "The Music of My Soul." This proud embrace of black music and Huey's success at getting black music out to the white audience earns him the respect of the black characters. Huey also wins the love of Felicia, a black singer who pays for Huey's impulsiveness: he kisses Felicia on the street before it's too dark for anyone to see, and she is beaten up by racists who haunt the show. Like *Ragtime*, act 1 of *Memphis* closes with an ecstatic gospel prayer using 1960s civil rights language sung over the body of a black woman (except in Memphis circa 1954 the words and the music make historical sense). Huey repeats the interracial kiss with Felicia on television in act 2, ending the couple's forbidden (and, should they have married, illegal) relationship. Felicia goes to New York for a national career. Huey, who was supposed to go as well, remains in Memphis, unable to restrain himself enough to put on the business suit required by national television. (Dick Clark gets the job, instead.) Like James "Thunder" Early in *Dreamgirls*, who, like Huey, strips off his clothes to declare his true musical identity, or Lonette McKee as Julie, who played the "passing" role without trying to "pass," Huey refuses to change his style to fit into the way segregated America works.

Memphis pulls no punches in its depiction of the prejudice, violence, and fear necessary to maintain racial segregation. A white father abruptly ends the jubilant dance number "Scratch that Itch," where white kids move to black music for the first time, by slapping his joyously dancing daughter full across the face. Another white character's dismissive description of rock and roll as "nigger music" early in act 1 elicited a few gasps from a St. Louis audience during the *Memphis* tour. The n-word on the musical stage still has the capacity to shock. More fundamentally, *Memphis* celebrates rock and roll and gospel-inspired singing in a familiar Broadway idiom that leaps off the stage with energy and enthusiasm. Much like *Dreamgirls*, the score keeps the sounds of white music to a minimum—Perry Como and Patti Page sound-a-likes are briefly heard in the show (but left off the cast album). Even Huey's mother, Gladys, a working class Parthy, learns to sing black, leading "Change Don't Come Easy" with three black male characters singing backup behind her, simulating as best she can the gospel sounds she heard when she dared to visit a black church. The potential of the interracial Broadway musical to take basic popular music forms—the Motownesque vocal group—and embed them in stories of American life by casting an old southern white lady as the lead singer and three black men as her amused backups shines forth in this musically, dramatically, and historically satisfying number. Parthy could never make such a change. Gladys—a descendant of Parthy—can.

Show Boat, Hairspray, and *Memphis* all tell stories of race and popular music history. Among these three, *Show Boat* stands out as the boldest. The ultimate triumph of black music and dance in *Hairspray* and *Memphis* is a matter of history: rock and roll conquered popular culture and, in the age of amplified sound, much of Broadway as well. Both shows reenact a still remembered hinge in American social and cultural history, a period when white young people insisted on dancing black, and black young people insisted on being treated as citizens. This celebrated historical epoch provides both the frame and the music and dance content for compelling stories that affirm Broadway's progressive political culture at the start of the twenty-first century. The respective location of each show—Baltimore and Memphis—inflects the period differently. In *Hairspray*, the triumph is giddy, led by a chubby white girl whose silly best friend wins the love of a brilliant black dancer. Youth saves the day, and the adults join in the fun. In *Memphis*, all the main characters are adults and success exacts a higher price. Felicia becomes a star, but Huey and Memphis are left behind. The interracial romance at the heart of the show fails, mainly because it cannot see the light of day. Felicia and Huey are much like Julie and Steve, historical characters caught in a time when miscegenation was a punishable offense in the South. By the time *Hairspray* and *Memphis* came to Broadway—some fifty years after the era they re-create—the history lessons they told were old hat. It was obvious who the villains were and equally obvious who would emerge at the close to celebrate in song. Still, both *Hairspray* and *Memphis* have the capacity to move contemporary audiences, re-enacting relatively recent episodes in America's racial history that continue to ignite deep emotions and that resonate with twenty-first century concerns and challenges. Beyond the general reminder that work remains to be done in the realm of racial reconciliation, Huey and Felicia's conversations about their desire to marry despite anti-miscegenation laws can be mapped directly onto current debates about the legalization of same-sex marriage.

If *Hairspray* had been made in 1962 or *Memphis* in the mid-1950s, they would have been very different shows. Indeed, the stories they tell would have been impossible to tell before the final triumph of the music they celebrate had been won. *Show Boat*, which quite self-consciously ended in the present, attempted to tell a tale of race and popular music while profound transitions in both were still going on. Little wonder it proved so difficult to stage Hammerstein's popular music plot—however tame it might look from the perspective of the early twenty-first century. In 1927, the mere fact of putting black and white into the same show was adventurous, and black and white performers alike resisted the story Hammerstein originally wanted to tell. *Memphis*'s closing number advises the audience "Don't let anyone steal your rock and roll." Robeson refused to let his black music be blithely inserted into *Show Boat*, a choice that surely impacted the longevity of the show in positive terms, lodging Robeson's spiritual-singing persona in abstract rather than literal terms. For different reasons, Terris rejected "It's Getting Hotter in the North," Hammerstein's argument for how the races were coming together in popular music and dance. Terris's imitations—unrepeatable by later Kims—opened up a space for later productions to remake the number, to suggest other narratives whether it be the utopian mixing of black and white in the Paper Mill production or the complex expression of how white took from black in Stroman's dream ballet.

In the end, the bold choice to put black and white music, dance, characters, and themes into the same show—a show about popular music and entertainment—helped *Show Boat* endure, made it a show with the potential to address history as it passed by, made it the first in a line of shows to use music and dance to explore what it has meant to be black *and* white in the United States. This long-lived resonance makes *Show Boat* the most important musical ever made and also necessitated its remaking again and again.

This book has endeavored to show how questions of race at the heart of the American experience have played out in the story of that rare flower—a Broadway musical with blacks and whites in the cast. This has not been a theme in most writing on *Show Boat* or on the musical. And yet, as Richard Rodgers advised readers of the black newspaper the *New York Amsterdam News* in 1966, it has been a persistent theme in Broadway history. "The paradox here is inescapable. We all agree that our musicals can be just about the lightest, gayest form of theatre. Nevertheless, within its recognizable framework, it has frequently spoken out on many serious themes. And surely the theme of racial equality is one that has long been important in the development of what once was thought of as merely escapist entertainment."[8] After rehearsing the progeny of *Show Boat* (among the shows listed were his own

South Pacific and *No Strings*), Rodgers speculated that the American musical may be heading "toward a day when it is completely color blind." *Dreamgirls, Big River, Ragtime, Hairspray, Memphis,* and their collective great-grandmother *Show Boat* suggest that keeping the color line in place, depicting its operation in history, and showing how it has been crossed—most often to the sound of black music—has been fruitful artistically and commercially. These musicals form a canon of integrated shows that deny the convenient fictions of black-cast and white-cast musicals, and that cut to the heart of the American experience by telling stories where popular music and dance drives cultural change. Hammerstein and Kern's *Show Boat* initiated this tradition, and many of *Show Boat*'s remakers nurtured its survival until social and political transformations made possible more radical versions of the story of the white girl with a black voice.

APPENDIX 1 CAST OF CHARACTERS

PRINCIPAL CHARACTERS (IN ORDER OF APPEARANCE IN ACT 1, SCENE 1)

Queenie	cook on the *Cotton Blossom*
Parthy Ann Hawks	wife to Andy
Cap'n Andy	owner of the *Cotton Blossom*, husband to Parthy
Ellie	actress on the *Cotton Blossom*, Frank's partner, spelled Elly in the novel
Frank	actor on the *Cotton Blossom*, Ellie's partner
Julie	leading lady on the *Cotton Blossom*, wife to Steve
Gaylord Ravenal	gambler, leading man and later husband to Magnolia
Magnolia	daughter of Andy and Parthy, leading lady and later wife to Ravenal
Joe	stevedore on the *Cotton Blossom*, spelled Jo in the novel

SUPPORTING CHARACTERS (DISCUSSED IN THIS BOOK)

Windy	pilot of the *Cotton Blossom*
Steven Baker	leading man on the *Cotton Blossom*, husband to Julie
Pete	engineer on the *Cotton Blossom*, reveals Julie's mixed racial identity to Vallon
Vallon	sheriff, confronts Julie and Steve after learning their marriage is a case of miscegenation
Backwoodsman and Jeb	comic pair created by Hammerstein, attend a show on the *Cotton Blossom* and mistake the play for real life
La Belle Fatima	cooch dancer at Chicago World's Fair
Kim (as a child)	daughter of Magnolia and Ravenal, shares a reprise of "Make Believe" with her father just before he abandons the family

At the Trocadero

Jim	manager
Jake	piano player, accompanies Julie's singing of "Bill," assists Frank in updating Magnolia's musical style
Charlie	doorman, brings word that Julie has gone "off on a tear," opening the way for Magnolia to take her place. In the 1936 film, Hammerstein added a dialogue scene between Julie and Charlie.
Lottie and Dolly	Andy's "tarts" who accompany him to the Trocadero on New Year's Eve

| Kim (as a young woman) | a musical comedy star on Broadway, in some productions played by the actress who plays Magnolia |
| Old Lady (on Levee) | elderly woman who reminds Ravenal and Magnolia of their wedding day in the final moments of the show |

Featured Black Dance Roles Added by Hammerstein to 1946 Broadway Revival

Sam and Sal	perform the "No Shoes" dance added to "Queenie's Ballyhoo"
Dahomey Queen	lead dancer for "In Dahomey," changed to Dahomey King when LaVerne French took over the role for the national tour
Ata, Mala, Bora	supporting dancers for "In Dahomey"

APPENDIX 2 ARCHIVAL SOURCES FOR THE 1927 BROADWAY PRODUCTION

Four complete drafts of Hammerstein's libretto survive. Each provides a unique glimpse of the 1927 *Show Boat* as a work in progress. For ease of reading and to communicate a consistent sense of chronology, in the text I refer to these draft librettos by the month in 1927 during which (or by which) they were typed. The libretto for the Broadway production, which was never published, survives in several identical typescripts and is referred to in the text as the Broadway version.

JANUARY

New York Public Library for the Performing Arts, Billy Rose Theatre Collection, Flo Zieg-feld-Billie Burke Papers 5/6.

Scott McMillin was the first to detail the contents of this source in his article "Paul Robeson, Will Vodery's 'Jubilee Singers,' and the Earliest Script of the Kern-Hammerstein *Show Boat*" in *Theatre Survey* 41, no. 2 (November 2000): 51–70. McMillin refers to the item by its former shelflist RM#7430. The cast list has Paul Robeson and Elizabeth Hines penciled in as Joe and Magnolia. Contracts with both were announced in *Variety* in December 1926. On January 26, 1927, Robeson's participation was put in doubt by the *New York Times* and on February 7, the same paper announced that Ziegfeld was post-poning *Show Boat* until the fall. Hines was never mentioned again as a possible Magnolia. January seems the likely completion date for this source, which is referred to as type-script B in Katherine Axtell, "Maiden Voyage: The Genesis and Reception of Show Boat, 1926–1932" (PhD diss., University of Rochester, 2009).

AUGUST

Library of Congress, Music Division, ML 50.K43 S3 1927.

Stamped with the date August 3, 1927. Axtell, "Maiden Voyage" refers to this source as typescript C.

OCTOBER

Wisconsin Historical Society, Edna Ferber Papers 20/7.

This carbon typescript contains pen and pencil notations by Hammerstein, Kern, Fer-ber, and possibly others. I first described its contents in my 2007 University of Michigan PhD dissertation. "Black/White Encounters on the American Musical Stage and Screen

(1924–2005)." The second page of the source is a cast list that reflects final casting decisions. Almost all the principals had been cast by the time this page was typed. Only the role of Joe remained open. Progress casting *Show Boat* was consistently reported in the press during fall 1927. Three different sources—the *New York Times*, *Variety*, and the *New York Age* (a black newspaper)—all announced the start of rehearsals for the week of October 17. The *Times* announcement on October 15 ("Theatrical Jottings") also summed up casting so far. The list in the *Times* matches that found in the October typescript with the omission of Charles Winninger as Cap'n Andy. The next day, Sunday, October 16, the *Times* announced Winninger's casting ("Rialto Gossip"). Jules Bledsoe was not announced for the part of Joe until October 30. Thus the October draft can be dated to mid October 1927, around the time rehearsals began, but before Bledsoe had been cast as Joe. Axtell, "Maiden Voyage" refers to this source as typescript D.

NOVEMBER

New York Public Library for the Performing Arts, Billy Rose Theatre Collection, NCOF+ (Kern, *Show Boat*).

This carbon typescript is a copy of the October version that has been marked up in pencil with cuts and stage business, and supplemented with lyric sheets and at least one completely retyped and revised scene (the last scene in act 2). The sole surviving copies of lyrics for several rejected numbers ("Cheer Up" and "Yes Ma'am"), an early try at "Life on the Wicked Stage," and a unique version of "Mis'ry's Comin' Aroun'" are included, suggesting this draft was used both during rehearsals and in the early weeks of tryouts. The last new song to be added to *Show Boat* was "Hey, Feller!," the lyrics for which are in this draft but not the dialogue for Queenie and Joe that sets up the song. "Hey, Feller!" first appears in the Philadelphia tryout programs, suggesting it was added during the previous week in Cleveland—the last week in November 1927 (hence the short title assigned this draft). Axtell, "Maiden Voyage" refers to this source as typescript E and provides a table comparing the contents of the October and November drafts on a song-by-song basis.

By the time *Show Boat* reached Philadelphia on December 5 for a three-week stand, the show was basically frozen. No major numbers were added or cut beyond this point. In the early weeks of December, the *Show Boat* libretto was retyped, incorporating all the new numbers and revised dialogue, going from draft libretto to blueprint for performance.

THE BROADWAY VERSION

At least three identical copies are extant: two in the New York Public Library, Billy Rose Theatre Collection—RM #7787 and Flo Ziegfeld–Billie Burke Collection 5/5—and a third, with notes in Hammerstein's hand, among papers belonging to the Hammerstein family. (My thanks to Ted Chapin and Bruce Pomahac for granting access to the third copy.) The Oscar Hammerstein Collection at the Library of Congress contains a fourth typescript of the Broadway version, bound in red leather for presentation by Hammerstein to his wife,

Dorothy (his customary practice). The text differs from the above three only in small details (such as stage directions entered in pencil by Hammerstein in the leather-bound copy, which are incorporated into the typed text of the above three). A fifth typescript, identical in its contents to the first three but retyped by a London service, was placed on deposit with the Lord Chamberlain's Office anticipating the May 1928 London opening of *Show Boat* (British Library, Manuscripts Department, LCP 1928/33). This last source was likely produced by retyping a copy of the Broadway version according to British practices.

APPENDIX 3 SELECT STAGE AND SCREEN VERSIONS (1928–1998)

Remakings of *Show Boat* are listed below in chronological order. Individuals whose names appear in the text only are given. Production personnel are listed first, followed by cast members in alphabetical order.

1928 (COMMERCIAL STAGE)

London/Drury Lane (followed by UK tour)/350 performances

Sir Alfred Butt (producer), Marie Burke (Julie), Edith Day (Magnolia), Cedric Hardwicke (Andy), Alberta Hunter (Queenie), Paul Robeson (Joe), Howett Worster (Ravenal)

1929 (FILM)

Hollywood/Universal Pictures

Carl Laemmle (producer), Harry Pollard (director), Charles Kenyon (writer), Jules Bledsoe (Joe in musical prologue), Aunt Jemima [Tess Gardella] (Queenie in musical prologue), Laura LaPlante (Magnolia), Helen Morgan (Julie in musical prologue)

1932 (COMMERCIAL STAGE)

Broadway/Casino Theatre (followed by U.S. tour)/180 performances

Florenz Ziegfeld (producer), Jules Bledsoe (tour Joe), Tess Gardella (Queenie), Dennis King (Ravenal), Angelica Lawson (replacement Queenie), Helen Morgan (Julie), Eva Puck (Ellie), Robert Raines (replacement Joe), Paul Robeson (Joe), Norma Terris (Magnolia), Sammy White (Frank), Charles Winninger (Andy)

1936 (FILM)

Hollywood/Universal Pictures

Carl Laemmle Jr. (producer), James Whale (director), Oscar Hammerstein II (writer), Leighton Brill (technical director), Irene Dunne (Magnolia), Allan Jones (Ravenal), Hattie McDaniel (Queenie), Helen Morgan (Julie), Paul Robeson (Joe), Helen Westley (Parthy), Sammy White (Frank), Charles Winninger (Andy)

1940 (LIGHT OPERA STAGE)

Los Angeles/Philharmonic Auditorium/Los Angeles Civic Light Opera
Zeke Colvan (director), John Boles (Ravenal), Helen Morgan (Julie), Paul Robeson (Joe), Norma Terris (Magnolia), Sammy White (Frank)

1943 (COMMERCIAL STAGE)

London/Stoll Theatre/264 performances
Prince Littler (producer), Lucille Benstead (Queenie), Mr. Jetsam [Malcolm McEachern] (Joe)

1944 (LIGHT OPERA STAGE)

Los Angeles/Philharmonic Auditorium/Los Angeles Civic Light Opera
Todd Duncan (Joe)

1946 (COMMERCIAL STAGE)

Broadway/Ziegfeld Theatre (followed by U.S. tour and return Broadway engagement in 1948)/initial run: 418 performances
Rodgers and Hammerstein (producers), Howard Bay (set design), Helen Tamiris (choreography), Carol Bruce (Julie), Jan Clayton (Magnolia), Helen Dowdy (Queenie), Charles Fredericks (Ravenal), LaVerne French (dancer), Pearl Primus (dancer), William C. Smith (Joe), Kenneth Spencer (Joe)

1946 (ABBREVIATED VERSION IN THE FILM *TILL THE CLOUDS ROLL BY*)

Hollywood/Metro-Goldwyn-Mayer
Arthur Freed (producer), Roger Edens (music arranger), Kathryn Grayson (Magnolia), Lena Horne (Julie), Tony Martin (Ravenal), Virginia O'Brien (Ellie), Caleb Peterson (Joe)

1951 (FILM)

Hollywood/Metro-Goldwyn-Mayer
Arthur Freed (producer), George Sidney (director), John Lee Mahin (writer), Roger Edens (music director), Ava Gardner (Julie), Kathryn Grayson (Magnolia), Howard Keel (Ravenal), William Warfield (Joe)

1954, SPRING AND FALL (OPERA STAGE)

New York City/City Center/New York City Opera
    Julius Rudel (conductor), Helena Bliss (Julie), Laurel Hurley (Magnolia), Robert Rounesville (Ravenal), William C. Smith (Joe)

1954, SUMMER (LIGHT OPERA STAGE)

New York City/City Center/New York City Light Opera Company
    William Hammerstein (producer), Julius Rudel (conductor), Helena Bliss (Julie), Laurel Hurley (Magnolia), Burl Ives (Andy), Robert Rounesville (Ravenal), Lawrence Winters (Joe)

1956 AND 1957 (OUTDOOR STAGE)

New York City/Jones Beach State Park
    Guy Lombardo (producer and conductor), Andy Devine (Andy), Albert Popwell, Geoffrey Holder and Alvin Ailey (dancers)

1960 (LIGHT OPERA STAGE)

Los Angeles/Dorothy Chandler Pavilion/Los Angeles Civic Light Opera
    Carlton Johnson (featured dancer)

1961 (LIGHT OPERA STAGE)

New York City/City Center/New York City Light Opera Company
    Anita Darian (Julie)

1966 (LIGHT OPERA STAGE)

New York City/New York State Theater, Lincoln Center/Music Theater of Lincoln Center
    Richard Rodgers (producer), Barbara Cook (Magnolia), Rosetta Le Noire (Queenie), Constance Towers (Julie)

1967 (LIGHT OPERA STAGE)

Los Angeles/Dorothy Chandler Pavilion/Los Angeles Civic Light Opera
    Eddie Foy Jr. (Frank), Carlton Johnson (featured dancer)

1971 (COMMERCIAL STAGE)

London/Adelphi Theatre/910 performances
   Harold Fielding (producer), Cleo Laine (Julie), Miguel Godreau (principal dancer)

1982 (OPERA STAGE)

Houston/Jones Hall (followed by U.S. tour)/Houston Grand Opera
   David Gockley (artistic director), John DeMain, conductor

1983 (COMMERCIAL STAGE)

Broadway/Uris [currently Gershwin] Theatre/Houston Grand Opera production/73 performances
   Karla Burns (Queenie), Bruce Hubbard (Joe), Lonette McKee (Julie), Donald O'Connor (Andy)

1989 (OPERA STAGE)

Houston/Wortham Theater Center (followed by a U.S. tour and short run at Cairo Opera House, Egypt)/Houston Grand Opera
   David Gockley (artistic director), John DeMain (conductor), Michel Bell (Joe), Eddie Bracken (Andy), Karla Burns (Queenie)

1989–90 (OPERA/THEATRICAL STAGE)

Leeds, Stratford-upon-Avon, London and UK tour/Opera North and Royal Shakespeare Company
   Ian Judge (director), Karla Burns (Queenie)

1989 (SUBSIDIZED STAGE)

New Jersey/Paper Mill Playhouse (broadcast nationally on PBS Great Performances)/ Paper Mill Playhouse

Robert Johanson (director), Jim Coleman (music director), Rebecca Baxter (Magnolia/Kim), Eddie Bracken (Andy), P. L. Brown (Joe), Ellia English (Queenie)

1993 (LIMITED PRE-BROADWAY RUN)

Toronto/North York Performing Arts Centre/Livent Inc.
Garth Drabinsky (producer), Harold Prince (director), Susan Stroman (choreographer), Eugene Lee (set design), Michel Bell (Joe), Gretha Boston (Queenie), Rebecca Luker (Magnolia), Lonette McKee (Julie), Elaine Stritch (Parthy)

1994 (COMMERCIAL STAGE)

Broadway/Gershwin Theatre/Livent Inc./947 performances
Production staff same as above, Michel Bell (Joe), Gretha Boston (Queenie), Rebecca Luker (Magnolia), Marilyn McCoo (replacement Julie), Lonette McKee (Julie), Elaine Stritch (Parthy)

1998 (COMMERCIAL STAGE)

London/Prince Edward Theatre/Livent Inc./approx. 168 performances
Producti staff same as above, Michel Bell (Joe)

NOTES

INTRODUCTION

1. Camille F. Forbes, *Introducing Bert Williams: Burnt Cork, Broadway, and the Story of America's First Black Star* (New York: Basic Books, 2008).

2. Edna Ferber, *Show Boat* (New York: Doubleday, Page and Co., 1926), 291–92.

3. Ibid., 124. In the novel, the character's name is spelled without a final *e*.

4. Todd Decker, "'Do you want to hear a Mammy song?': A Historiography of *Show Boat*," *Contemporary Theatre Review* 19, no. 1 (February 2009): 8–21.

5. Commercially unsuccessful shows with interracial casts include *Great Day* (1929), *Kwamina* (1961), *1600 Pennsylvania Avenue* (1976), *Grind* (1985), *Marie Christine* (1999), *Caroline, or Change* (2004) and *The Scottsboro Boys* (2010).

6. Susan Manning, *Modern Dance, Negro Dance: Race in Motion* (Minneapolis: University of Minnesota Press, 2004), xi.

7. Langston Hughes and Milton Meltzer, *Black Magic: A Pictorial History of the African American in the Performing Arts* (New York: Prentice-Hall, 1967); David Krasner, *A Beautiful Pageant: African American Theater, Drama, and Performance in the Harlem Renaissance, 1910–1927* (New York: Palgrave Macmillan, 2002); and Allen L. Woll, *Black Musical Theatre: From Coontown to Dreamgirls* (Baton Rouge: Louisiana State University Press, 1989). These books make no or only passing mention of *Show Boat*. John Graziano's "Images of African Americans: African-American Musical Theatre, *Show Boat* and *Porgy and Bess*" in *The Cambridge Companion to the Musical*, ed. William A. Everett and Paul R. Laird (New York: Cambridge University Press, 2008) proves a noteworthy exception.

8. See Stephen Banfield, *Jerome Kern* (New Haven, CT: Yale University Press, 2006); Gerald Bordman, *American Operetta: From H.M.S. Pinafore to Sweeney Todd* (New York: Oxford University Press, 1981); Larry Stempel, *Showtime: A History of the Broadway Musical Theater* (New York: W. W. Norton, 2010); and Richard Traubner, *Operetta: A Theatrical History* (New York: Routledge, 2003). Decker, "'Do You Want to Hear a Mammy Song?'," 13–14, summarizes David Ewen's influential views on *Show Boat*.

9. Ethan Mordden described *Show Boat* as "a musical comedy with epic dimensions" in *Make Believe: The Broadway Musical in the 1920s* (New York: Oxford University Press, 1997), 216. Geoffrey Block characterized *Show Boat* as "a musical that successfully balances musical comedy and operetta" in "The Melody (and the Words) Linger On: American Musical Comedies of the 1920s and 1930s" in Everett and Laird, *Cambridge Companion to the Musical*, 110.

10. Neil Foley, *The White Scourge: Mexicans, Blacks, and Poor Whites in Texas Cotton Culture* (Berkeley: University of California Press, 1997), 11.

11. Raymond Knapp, *The American Musical and the Formation of National Identity* (Princeton, NJ: Princeton University Press, 2005); Andrea Most, *Making Americans: Jews and the Broadway Musical* (Cambridge, MA: Harvard University Press, 2004).

12. Bruce Kirle, *Unfinished Show Business: Broadway Musicals as Works-in-Process* (Carbondale: Southern Illinois University Press, 2005) speaks to the importance of performers and the theatrical event.

13. Raymond Knapp, "Performance, Authenticity, and the Reflexive Idealism of the American Musical," in *The Oxford Handbook of the American Musical*, ed. Raymond Knapp, Mitchell Morris, and Stacy Wolf (New York: Oxford University Press, 2011).

14. Lecture at the opening of the Opera Carolina production of *Margaret Garner*, Charlotte, NC, April 19, 2006.

15. Albert Murray, *Stomping the Blues* (New York: McGraw-Hill, 1976), 90.

16. Jayna Brown, *Babylon Girls: Black Women Performers, and the Shaping of the Modern* (Durham, NC: Duke University Press, 2008), 283.

17. Banfield, *Jerome Kern*, 125.

18. See Robin Breon, "*Show Boat*: The Revival, The Racism," *Drama Review* 39, no. 2 (Summer 1995); M. Nourbese Philip, *Showing Grit: Showboating North of the 44th Parallel* (Toronto: Poui Publications, 1993); Linda Williams, *Playing the Race Card: Melodramas of Black and White from Uncle Tom to O.J. Simpson* (Princeton, NJ: Princeton University Press, 2001); Knapp, *American Musical and the Formation of National Identity*; Miles Kreuger, *Show Boat: The Story of a Classic American Musical* (New York: Oxford University Press, 1977); and *Show Boat*, EMI-Angel Records CDS 7 49108 2, conducted by John McGlinn.

19. Scott McMillin, "Paul Robeson, Will Vodery's 'Jubilee Singers,' and the Earliest Script of the Kern-Hammerstein *Show Boat*," *Theatre Survey* 41, no. 2 (November 2000): 51–70.

20. I first discussed the script in Todd Decker, "Black/White Encounters on the American Musical Stage and Screen (1924–2005)" (PhD diss., University of Michigan, 2007). Frank W. D. Ries, "Sammy Lee: The Broadway Career," *Dance Chronicle* 9, no. 1 (1986) first described the conductor's score, which was in a private collection. I located a copy in the St. Louis Public Library.

CHAPTER 1

1. Edna Ferber, *A Peculiar Treasure* (New York: Doubleday, 1939), 288–89.

2. Letter, W. H. Tippitt to EF, February 14, 1925, Ferber 4/10.

3. Ferber, *Peculiar Treasure*, 297.

4. Ibid., 298–99.

5. Letter, Charles Hunter to EF, October 20, 1925, Ferber 4/10. Hunter's letter is discussed in J. E. Smyth, *Edna Ferber's Hollywood: American Fictions of Gender, Race, and History* (Austin: University of Texas Press, 2010), 75–76.

6. Edna Ferber, *Show Boat* (New York: Doubleday, Page and Co., 1926), 147.

7. Ibid., 149.

8. "Flag-Waving, Now and Then, is Reasonable," *Boston Transcript*, May 21, 1929.

9. Ferber, *Show Boat*, 70.

10. Ibid., 63.

11. Ibid., 371.

12. Christopher P. Wilson, *White Collar Fictions: Class and Social Representation in American Literature, 1885–1925* (Athens: University of Georgia Press, 1992).

13. Rogers Dickinson, *Edna Ferber: A Biographical Sketch with a Bibliography* (Garden City, NY: Doubleday, Doran and Co., 1925), 12.

14. Ferber, *Show Boat*, 121–22.

15. Ibid., 361–62.

16. Ibid., 320.

17. Donald Davidson, *The Spyglass: Views and Reviews, 1924–1930* (Nashville, TN: Vanderbilt University Press, 1963), 73.

18. MacKinley Helm, *Angel Mo' and her Son, Roland Hayes* (Boston: Little, Brown and Company, 1942).

19. Martin Bauml Duberman, *Paul Robeson* (New York: Alfred A. Knopf, 1988), 79–80.

20 *Opportunity* (November 1925), 330.

21. Duberman, *Paul Robeson*, 81.

22. Clippings, January 6, 1926, Brown.

23. "Social Progress," *Opportunity* (January 1925), 29.

24. Carl Van Vechten, "Folksongs of the American Negro," *Vanity Fair*, July 1925, 52.

25. Van Vechten, "Folksongs," 92.

26. Curtis Burlin's career is treated in detail in Michelle Wick Patterson, *Natalie Curtis Burlin: A Life in Native and African American Music* (Lincoln: University of Nebraska Press, 2010).

27. Natalie Curtis Burlin, "Negro Music at Birth," *Musical Quarterly* 5, no. 1 (January 1919): 87.

28. Ferber, *Show Boat*, 120, 291.

29. Ibid., 155.

30. Curtis Burlin, "Negro Music," 89.

31. Ibid., 87; Ferber, *Show Boat*, 121.

32. Curtis Burlin, "Negro Music," 89.

33. Ferber, *Show Boat*, 121.

34. Curtis Burlin, "Negro Music," 89.

35. Ibid., 87.

36. Ferber, *Show Boat*, 94.

37. Curtis Burlin, "Negro Music," 88.

38. Ibid., 123.

39. Ferber, *Show Boat*, 387–88.

40. Ibid., 105–6.

41. See Ferber's stories "The Leading Lady" (1912), "Cheerful, By Request" (1918), "That's Marriage" (1918), "You've Got to Be Selfish" (1920), and "Not A Day Over Twenty-One" (1922).

42. Armond Fields, *Women Vaudeville Stars: Eighty Biographical Profiles* (Jefferson, NC: McFarland and Company, 2006), 18; Trav S.D., *No Applause—Just Throw Money: The Book that Made Vaudeville Famous* (New York: Faber and Faber, 2005), 70.

43. Ferber, *Show Boat*, 362.

44. Fields, *Women Vaudeville Stars*, 154.

45. Ferber, *Show Boat*, 368.

46. Ibid., 387.

47. Campbell Playhouse, March 31, 1939.

48. Robert Van Gelder, *Writers and Writing* (New York: C. Scribner's Sons, 1946), 363.

49. Ferber, "A Few Things Altered or Abolished," *Nation*, May 30, 1928, 609–10. Ferber's 1952 novel *Giant* dealt with racism between whites and Hispanics in Texas.

CHAPTER 2

1. Flyer, Brown 5/2.

2. Walter White, "The Paradox of Color," in *The New Negro: An Interpretation*, ed. Alain Locke (New York Albert and Charles Boni, 1925), 361.

3. Ibid., 362.

4. Eslanda Robeson expressed contempt for black dramatic efforts. Diary entry, May 17, 1926, Eslanda 16.

5. Sheila Tully Boyle and Andrew Bunie, *Paul Robeson: The Years of Promise and Achievement* (Amherst: University of Massachusetts Press, 2001), 103.

6. AW to PR, n.d., Robeson 5.

7. Boyle and Bunie, *Paul Robeson*, 116.

8. April 18, 1925, Brown 5/1.

9. A. S., *NYW*, April 20, 1925.

10. Richard S. Davis, *Milwaukee Journal*, February 13, 1926; Burt McMurtrie, *Pittsburgh Press*, January 28, 1926.

11. *Evening News* (London), September 15, 1925.

12. C. S. S., *Evening Transcript* (Boston), November 3, 1926; *NYHT*, January 6, 1926.

13. O. T., *MA*, January 23, 1926.

14. *Pittsburgh Sun*, January 28, 1926.

15. R. de A.J., *Providence News*, March 1, 1926.

16. Herman Devries, *Evening American* (Chicago), February 11, 1926.

17. *Pittsburgh Sun*, January 6, 1926.

18. B. L. D., *MA*, January 16, 1926.

19. *Philadelphia Inquirer*, January 23, 1926; *Pittsburgh Chronicle-Telegraph*, January 28, 1926.

20. Glenn Dillard Gunn, *Chicago Herald Examiner*, February 11, 1926.

21. Oxted and Limpsfield Federation of Music Clubs, February 4, 1925, Brown 5/1.

22. Flyer, Robeson 1.

23. The story first appeared in the October 8, 1927, *NY*. See Dorothy Parker, *Complete Stories* (New York: Penguin Books, 1995), 77–80.

24. Elizabeth Shepley Sergeant and E. O. Hoppé, *Fire Under the Andes: A Group of North American Portraits* (New York: Alfred A. Knopf, 1927), 194–95.

25. Ibid., 197.

26. Ibid., 203, 208.

27. Ibid., 208.

28. "*Black Boy* Has Opening," *BAA*, October 9, 1926.

29. "Robeson is Praised by New York Critics at the Opening of New Play," *PC*, October 16, 1926.

30. Sergeant and Hoppé, *Fire Under the Andes*, 193–94.

31. JK to Vaughn DeLeath, May 3, 1938, Gershwin Fund Collection-Correspondence, Library of Congress, Music Division.

32. "Hopkins to Stage a Jazz Opera Here," *NYT*, January 19, 1926; *BAA*, October 16, 1926.

33. "Lady Astor in Society Vanguard at *Deep River*," New York *Morning Telegraph*, October 5, 1926.

34. Burns Mantle, *NYDN*, October 5, 1926.

35. "*Deep River* Stars Bledsoe," *BAA*, October 2, 1926.

36. Hollister Noble, "Native American Opera Proves Elusive," *NYT*, November 21, 1926.

37. J. Brooks Atkinson, "Native Opera in the South," *NYT*, October 5, 1926.

38. Miles Kreuger, *Show Boat: The Story of a Classic American Musical* (New York: Oxford University Press, 1977), 18; Ethan Mordden, *Make Believe: The Broadway Musical in the 1920s* (New York: Oxford University Press, 1997), 207.

39. *NYT*, December 5, 1926.

40. Countee Cullen, "The Dark Tower," *Opportunity*, December 1926.

41. Kreuger, *Show Boat*, 19–20.

42. Rumors persist that Ziegfeld or perhaps the costume designer John Harkrider had the idea to turn Ferber's novel into a musical. The evidence of Kern and Hammerstein's work and Ferber's own testimony argue against these stories. See Richard Ziegfeld and Paulette Ziegfeld, *The Ziegfeld Touch: The Life and Times of Florenz Ziegfeld, Jr.* (New York: H. N. Abrams, 1993), 139.

43. Kreuger, *Show Boat*, 25–26.

44. "Robeson for *Show Boat*," *Variety*, December 15, 1926.

45. Programs, Brown 5/1.

46. Boyle and Bunie, *Paul Robeson*, 179–80.

47. *New York Herald*, November 15, 1926, Brown clippings.

48. Kern 59/7.

49. Kern 59/12 contains a typescript of act 1 scene 1 that is substantially like the Broadway version. Although the lyrics for "Ol' Man River" are lacking and Joe's song is simply referred to as "SONG," the spoken song cue—"Better ask Ol' Man River what he thinks."—suggests that work on the number was well underway if not complete.

50. Review of 1929 Chicago tour, Ferber 20/8.

51. Robeson famously changed the lyrics when he sang "Ol' Man River" in concert settings and on recordings after World War II. In a subsequent study of the performance history of "Ol' Man River," I will describe in detail how Robeson used this song in his concertizing and activism after his final appearance in *Show Boat* in 1940.

52. NYPL/TC.

53. "In the Provinces," *NYT*, September 26, 1926. "Ashes and Fire" is listed as the opening number in the draft libretto.

54. AW to EF, February 23, 1933, Ferber 1/2.

55. See Joseph P. Swain, *The Broadway Musical: A Critical and Musical Survey* (New York: Oxford University Press, 1990), 43–47, for a discussion of Kern's tune.

56. Katherine Axtell, "Maiden Voyage: The Genesis and Reception of Show Boat, 1926–1932" (PhD diss., University of Rochester, 2009), notes the influence of revue on *Show Boat* but does not point out the Robeson recital.

57. The earliest surviving program to include "Ol' Man River" as part of the announced program is a March 22, 1931, concert at Carnegie Hall (programs, Brown 5/1). A July 3, 1928, concert given during the run of *Show Boat* in London has "Ol' Man River" inked in as a concluding encore (V&A Drury Lane 1928).

58. "Rialto Gossip," *NYT*, October 16, 1927. Winninger's name is missing from the typed cast list in the October draft.

59. Robeson and Brown's concert of "Musique Nègre" on October 29 was so successful that Varney organized a second Paris concert in November. Brown 5/1.

60. "Big Ziegfeld Show Here on Tuesday," *WP*, November 13, 1927.

61. Scott McMillin, "Paul Robeson, Will Vodery's 'Jubilee Singers,' and the Earliest Script of the Kern-Hammerstein *Show Boat*." *Theatre Survey* 41, no. 2 (November 2000): 51.

62. "A Footnote to *Show Boat*," *PC*, April 21, 1928.

63. "*Show Boat* Postponed," *NYT*, February 7, 1927.

64. Gwendolyn Brooks, "The Ebony Flute," *Opportunity*, March 1927.

65. Boyle and Bunie, *Paul Robeson*, 184.

66. Martin Bauml Duberman, *Paul Robeson* (New York: Alfred A. Knopf, 1988), 106.

67. Duberman quotes Eslanda that Robeson "received the news with mixed feelings." Ibid., 106.

68. Eslanda Goode Robeson, *Paul Robeson, Negro* (New York: Harper and Brothers, 1930), 99.

69. Duberman, *Paul Robeson*, 111.

70. Ibid., 58–59.

71. Diary entry, May 18, 1926, Eslanda 16.

72. Robeson, *Paul Robeson*, 111.

CHAPTER 3

1. "Theatrical Notes," *NYT*, May 2, 1927.

2. "Pop Musical Market Tied Up for Performing Talent," *Variety*, May 25, 1927.

3. *Variety*, September 7, 1927.

4. Katherine Axtell, "Maiden Voyage: The Genesis and Reception of Show Boat, 1926–1932" (PhD diss., University of Rochester, 2009), 226–27.

5. *WSJ*, June 24, 1925.

6. *WSJ*, July 28, 1926

7. Morgan's role in *Americana* reconstructed from programs in NYPL/TC.

8. Gerald Bordman, *Jerome Kern: His Life and Music* (New York: Oxford University Press, 1980), 276.

9. Oscar Hammerstein II, "Memories of First *Show Boat* Launching,' *NYT*, June 23, 1957.

10. *NYT*, January 10, 1927.

11. *NYT*, January 23, 1927.

12. *NYT*, January 25, 1927.

13. *CT*, March 13, 1927.

14. Irving Hoffman, "Helen Morgan the Magnificent," *Life*, February 1932.

15. Zeke Colvan, *Face the Footlights!: A New and Practical Approach to Acting* (New York: McGraw-Hill, 1940), 82–83.

16. NYPL/TC, NCOF+ (Bolton, *Oh, Lady! Lady!!*).

17. *WSJ*, September 5, 1929.

18. Burns Mantle, *CT*, September 15, 1929.

19. *CT*, October 20, 1930.

20. *CT*, April 16, 1929.

21. TV: *Playhouse 90*, "Helen Morgan" starring Polly Bergen and Hoagy Carmichael; film: *The Helen Morgan Story* (Warner Bros.), starring Ann Blyth and Paul Newman, both 1957.

22. Columbia 4917.

23. My thanks to Scott Paulin for raising the question of Hammerstein's stage directions.

24. Walter Winchell, "Opening Nights," *NY Graphic*, December 28, 1927.

25. *CT*, April 20, 1929.

26. *NYT*, December 31, 1927. For the larger context for Morgan's story, see Michael A. Lerner, *Dry Manhattan: Prohibition in New York City* (Cambridge, MA: Harvard University Press, 2007); and Burton W. Peretti, *Nightclub City: Politics and Amusement in Manhattan* (Philadelphia: University of Pennsylvania Press, 2007).

27. *NYT*, February 16, 1928.

28. *NYT*, May 6, 1928.

29. *NYT*, June 29, 1928.

30. *NYT*, June 30, 1928.

31. *NYT*, August 7, 1928.

32. *Life*, September 6, 1928.

33. *NYT*, August 2, 1928.

34. *NYT*, August 6, 1928.

35. *NYT*, December 3, 1928.

36. *Life*, February 8, 1929.

37. *NYT*, April 19, 1929.

38. *NYT*, September 12, 1929.

CHAPTER 4

1. *NYT*, December 12, 1927. The ad is reproduced in Miles Kreuger, *Show Boat: The Story of a Classic American Musical* (New York: Oxford University Press, 1977), 68.

2. "Brooklyn Briefs," *BAA*, December 24, 1927.

3. *NYT*, December 25, 1927.

4. "Aboard the *Show Boat*," *NYW*, June 22, 1932.

5. Edna Ferber, *Show Boat* (New York: Doubleday, Page and Co., 1926), 149.

6. Jim Lovensheimer, *South Pacific: Paradise Rewritten* (New York: Oxford University Press, 2010).

7. Review, *NYT*, March 18, 1926.

8. *Variety*, November 23, 1927.

9. Clipping, NYPL MWEZ +9993.

10. "Flag-Waving, Now and Then, is Reasonable," *Boston Transcript*, May 21, 1929.

11. The final pages of the October script are missing so it's not clear exactly when this scene was revised.

12. Kern 58/11.

13. The long white chorus number "I Would Like to Play the Lover's Part" that originally opened the scene was cut in Washington. The briefly tried "Be Happy, Too" began as "Cheer Up" in the World's Fair scene, both part of the ultimately futile effort to create a trio for Magnolia, Parthy, and Andy.

14. Ferber, *Show Boat*, 80.

15. Anthony Harkins, *Hillbilly: A Cultural History of an American Icon* (New York: Oxford University Press, 2004), chapter 4.

16. *NYT*, March 21, 1926.

17. James Randall, "Becoming Jerome Kern: The Early Songs and Shows, 1903–1915" (PhD diss., University of Illinois, Urbana-Champaign, 2004), 223.

18. "Rialto Gossip," *NYT*, November 7, 1926.

19. *Telegram*, November 28, 1926; *NYT*, December 5, 1926.

20. "Actress' Suit Up in Court," *NYT*, June 17, 1927.

21. "*Show Boat* Postponed," *NYT*, February 7, 1927.

22. *NYT*, June 27, 1927.

23. "Want *Follies* in London," *NYT*, August 21, 1927.

24. *Sunday News*, July 4, 1976, NYPL/TC clippings.

25. Ziegfeld sent Fender a telegram and the tenor's name was associated with *Show Boat* in the *NYT*, December 5, 1926.

26. Holographs in NYPL/TC show Fender's role made tenor-range requirements.

27. "Ziegfeld Engages Dennis King," *NYT*, June 18, 1927.

28. "Random Gossip of the Street Called Broadway," *NYT*, August 28, 1927.

29. My thanks to William Everett for providing copies of Schober's songs and insights on the music for Marsh.

30. William A. Everett, *Sigmund Romberg* (New Haven: Yale University Press, 2007), 54.

31. Geoffrey Block, *Enchanted Evenings: The Broadway Musical from Show Boat to Sondheim*, 2nd ed. (New York: Oxford University Press, 2009), 33–38, analyzes the musical content of Ravenal and Magnolia's meeting. Katherine Axtell, "Maiden Voyage: The Genesis and Reception of Show Boat, 1926–1932" (PhD diss., University of Rochester, 2009), 198–208, offers a novel reading of the sources through the lens of Kern's supposed devotion to Richard Wagner.

32. Kern 58/16, an underscoring worksheet, refers to the tune as being in D-flat. Kern 58/15 lays out a substantial section of the duet with C-sharp major as the notated key signature. Kern notes that the copyist should change the notation to the enharmonically equivalent—and easier to read—D-flat.

33. Kern 59/9. The flats in the first chorus's original key signature were picked out and inked over as sharps, and all accidentals were similarly changed. For as long as the duet stayed on the flat side, this method worked to transpose the music up a half step. When the original employed a sharp-side key signature—the shift to F-sharp minor for Magnolia's "Tho' the cold and brutal fact is"—the entire musical text had to be recopied.

34. Bennett's full score (Kern 57/1) directs the copyist to transpose the music "1 tone higher (E-flat)" at the start of Ravenal's solo chorus and "D'ici dans le ton originale" at the end of the vocal. The first indication was not correct—judging from the parts that go into D at this point—so the surviving sources do not tell the whole story. Perhaps Marsh requested the music start even higher.

35. Kern 58/20.

36. Kern 59/3.

37. *NYW*, December 28, 1927.

38. *Sunday News*, July 4, 1976, NYPL/TC clippings.

39. Frank W. D. Ries, "Sammy Lee: The Broadway Career." *Dance Chronicle* 9, no. 1 (1986): 73–74.

40. Block, *Enchanted Evenings*, details these links.

41. Gerald Bordman, *Jerome Kern: His Life and Music* (New York: Oxford University Press, 1980), 249–50.

42. Todd Decker, *Music Makes Me: Fred Astaire and Jazz* (Berkeley: University of California Press, 2011), 197–98.

43. Combined author credits go to Louis A. Hirsch, Gene Buck. and Dave Stamper.

44. A few years later, Dorothy Fields would write a signature lyric for Bill "Bojangles" Robinson titled "Doin' the New Low-down."

45. Kern 56/7.

46. Richard and Paulette Ziegfeld, *The Ziegfeld Touch: The Life and Times of Florenz Ziegfeld, Jr.* (New York: H. N. Abrams, 1993), 145.

47. Kern 59/7.

48. As evident on the videotape of the 1994 Broadway revival (NYPL/TOFT) and at the St. Louis Muny production in summer 2010.

49. *Sunday News*, July 4, 1976, NYPL/TC clippings.

50. *NY World Telegram*, n.d., NYPL MWEZ +9993.

51. Ries, "Sammy Lee," 76.

CHAPTER 5

1. Oscar Hammerstein II, *Lyrics (1949)* (New York: Hal Leonard Books, 1985), 39.

2. "Uncle Dud Broadcasts," *PC*, December 10, 1927.

3. Floyd Snelson, "Broadway Bound," *PC*, August 6, 1932.

4. Chappy Gardner, "Along the Rialto," *PC*, February 4, 1928.

5. Chappy Gardner, "Along the Rialto," *PC*, January 14, 1927.

6. Salem Tutt Whitney, "Timely Topics," *CD*, April 7, 1928.

7. "Dixie Jubilee Singers in *Uncle Tom's Cabin*," *NYA*, November 25, 1927.

8. Alice Dunbar Nelson, "*Show Boat* Will Go Big on Broadway," *PT*, January 5, 1928.

9. Review, *Variety*, January 4, 1928.

10. Frank W. D. Ries, "Sammy Lee: The Broadway Career." *Dance Chronicle* 9, no. 1 (1986): 68.

11. "'Hi Yaller' Girls No Longer Wanted," *Variety*, January 19, 1927.

12. Eva Jessye, conductor of her own Jubilee Singers (a group hired by Gershwin as the chorus for *Porgy and Bess*) reported the names and show business credentials for all twelve in her column. "Down Theatrical Lane," *BAA*, November 5, 1927.

13. Eddie Cantor, *Ziegfeld: The Great Glorifier* (New York: A. H. King, 1934), 144.

14. Bob Slater, "Theatrical Jottings," *NYA*, September 17, 1927.

15. Details on Rogers's and Roberts's careers taken from Bernard L. Peterson, *A Century of Musicals in Black and White: An Encyclopedia of Musical Stage Works By, About, or Involving African Americans* (Westport, CT: Greenwood Press, 1993); and Bernard L. Peterson, *Profiles of African American Stage Performers and Theatre People, 1816–1960* (Westport, CT: Greenwood Press, 2001).

16. Eva Jessye, "Music Mirror," *BAA*, September 3 and 17, 1927.

17. *Variety*, October 5, 1927, 44.

18. Vodery's association with Rogers went back to the 1910s. See Mark Tucker, "In Search of Will Vodery," *Black Music Research Journal* 16, no. 1 (Spring 1996): 134.

19. Richard and Paulette Ziegfeld, *The Ziegfeld Touch: The Life and Times of Florenz Ziegfeld, Jr.* (New York: H. N. Abrams, 1993), 146.

20. The alternate spelling "Hey, Fellah!" appears in some sources.

21. Countee Cullen, "The Dark Tower," *Opportunity*, April 1927.

22. *NYW*, October 11, 1927.

23. *NYT*, October 11, 1927.

24. Frank Vreeland, *NY Telegram*, n.d.

25. Continuity draft, Kern 58/6; full score, Kern 55/9.

26. Chappy Gardner, "Along the Rialto," *PC*, February 25, 1928.

27. Part of the *Show Boat* album—a set of four 78s—produced by Jack Kapp for Brunswick and also featuring Robeson.

28. Karen L. Cox, *Dreaming of Dixie: How the South was Created in American Popular Culture* (Chapel Hill: University of North Carolina Press, 2011), 39–42.

29. "Actress Wins $115,000," *NYT*, May 8, 1936; "'Aunt Jemima' Plea Won," *NYT*, May 11, 1937.

30. "Gossip of Vaudeville," *NYT*, September 7, 1924.

31. "News of Vaudeville," *NYT*, August 31, 1924.

32. *Variety*, January 4, 1928.

33. Nelson, "*Show Boat* Will Go Big on Broadway."

34. *NYT* obituary, January 4, 1950.

35. Columbia 4917 (recorded February 14, 1928).

36. "Frank Fay Chats and Sings at Palace," *NYT*, September 1, 1930.

37. Ries, "Sammy Lee," 71.

38. Edna Ferber, *Show Boat* (New York: Doubleday, Page and Co., 1926), 94.

39. Camille F. Forbes, *Introducing Bert Williams: Burnt Cork, Broadway, and the Story of America's First Black Star*, (New York: Basic Books, 2008), 30.

40. Ries, "Sammy Lee," 74.

41. Bob Slater, "Theatrical Jottings," *NYA*, December 3, 1927.

42. Production Statements, Florenz Ziegfeld and A. L. Erlanger, season 1925/26/27, Ziegfeld 13/36. Gates and Lee are listed in successive entries among other creative production staff.

43. This ad appears in the April 13, 20, and 27, 1927, issues of *NYAN*.

44. *NYAN*, October 26 and November 2, 1927.

45. Bradley worked out of black impresario Billy Pierce's Forty-sixth Street studio. Perhaps Gates conceived of his Harlem school as a similar institution for black performers uptown. For more on Bradley and Pierce, see Marshall and Jean Stearns, *Jazz Dance: The Story of American Vernacular Dance* (New York: Macmillan, 1968), 162–67.

46. "M. Ravel Honored at Large Reception," *NYT*, January 16, 1928.

47. "Chorus of *Show Boat* in Benefit," *NYAN*, December 28, 1927.

48. William F. McDermott of the Cleveland *Plain Dealer* quoted in "Speakin' O' Performers," *NYAN*, December 14, 1927.

49. Ashton Stevens, torn clipping from Chicago paper, Ferber 20/9.

CHAPTER 6

1. "Charm of *The Show Boat* [sic]," *Evening Standard*, May 4, 1928.

2. Libretto, LCP 1928/43.

3. Libretto, LCP 1928/38.

4. "Drury Lane's New Play," *DT*, May 4, 1928.

5. Stamper's well-marked scores for all four of Hammerstein's Drury Lane operettas, together with an explanatory letter from his granddaughter Linda McGhee, can be found in V&A.

6. "London Fashions," *LT*, May 16, 1928.

7. Columbia 9427.

8 *Sunday Express*, May 6, 1928, clipping in Robeson 28.

9. "London Show Boat, Robeson Triumph," *BAA*, May 16, 1928.

10. *Sunday Express*, May 6, 1928, clipping in Robeson 28.

11. "Fashion Changes," *NYDN*, April 26, 1928.

12. Cedric Hardwicke, *Let's Pretend: Recollections and Reflections of a Lucky Actor* (London: Grayson and Grayson, 1932), 180.

13. Ibid., 178–79.

14. Jingle, "*Show Boat*," *Bystander*, May 30, 1928.

15. Floyd Calvin, "Alberta Hunter was Sensation with Ziegfeld," *PC*, June 20, 1931.

16. "Popular Member of American Colony," *NYAN*, January 2, 1929.

17. Alberta Hunter, "Our Quarterly Letter from Alberta," *NYAN*, April 25, 1928.

18. Hunter 1/4.

19. Calvin, "Alberta Hunter was Sensation with Ziegfeld."

20. J.A. Rogers, "Rogers' Gives New View," *PC*, October 6, 1928.

21. "The Theatre," *Opportunity*, October 1928, 313.

22. "Coloured Singer's Contract," *DT*, October 4, 1928

23. "Robeson Turns Down *Show Boat* for *Porgy* Role," *BAA*, March 10, 1928; ER to LB, March 20, 1928, Brown 3/8.

24. Congratulatory telegrams, Robeson 6.

25. ER to LB, March 20, 1928, Brown 3/8.

26. PR to LB, April 19, 1928, Robeson 2 and Brown 3/8.

27. ER to LB, February 15, 1929, Brown 3/8.

28. PR to LB, April 19, 1928, Brown 3/8.

29. Eslanda Goode Robeson, *Paul Robeson, Negro* (New York: Harper and Brothers, 1930), 139.

30. Oscar Hammerstein II, *Lyrics* (New York: Simon and Schuster, 1949), 165. A subsequent edition of *Lyrics* (Hal Leonard, 1985), edited by William Hammerstein and including post-1949 lyrics, removed "Me An' My Boss." The lyric can be found in *The Complete Lyrics of Oscar Hammerstein II* (New York: Alfred A. Knopf, 2008), 119.

31. Horace Shipp, "The Wood and the Trees," *Sackbut* (June 1928); "*Show Boat* at Drury Lane," *Referee*, May 6, 1928.

32. James Agate, *Sunday Times* (London), May 6, 1928.

33. V&A Drury Lane 1928.

34. The first on July 3, 1928, subsequent concerts on September 4 and 25.

35. James Douglas, *Daily Express* (London), July 5, 1928.

36. FZ to OH, February 13, 1931, Hammerstein 19.

37. OH to FZ, February 16, 1931, Hammerstein 19.

38. FZ to OH, February 18, 1931, Hammerstein 19.

39 *BAA*, July 5, 1930.

40. The following summary of Robeson's concerts in 1931–32 taken from programs in Brown 5/2.

41. Robeson included a set of European art song and opera arias in a handful of concerts, only to drop the practice soon after.

42. "Capacity Audience Acclaims Robeson," unattributed clipping, March 25, 1931, Brown 5/1.

43. Marie Hicks Davidson, *San Francisco Call Bulletin*, 1931, Brown 5/1.

44. Edna Ferber, *A Peculiar Treasure* (New York: Doubleday, 1939), 306.

45. Review, *Variety*, May 24, 1932.

46. "Robeson Sings at Stadium," *NYT*, August 1, 1932.

47. "The Microphone Will Present," *NYT*, May 1, 1932; "Robeson Is Heard Over Radio Twice," *CD*, May 14, 1932.

48. Stirling Bowen, "A Welcome Revival," *WSJ*, May 21, 1932.

49. Burns Mantle, "Theatre Business Offers Quite a Problem," *CT*, May 29, 1932.

50. Katherine Axtell, "Maiden Voyage: The Genesis and Reception of Show Boat, 1926–1932" (PhD diss., University of Rochester, 2009), 317.

51. Gilbert Maxwell, *Helen Morgan: Her Life and Legend* (New York: Hawthorn Books, 1974), 126.

52. "Paul Robeson sails for Europe; Purpose Vague," *PC*, September 10, 1932.

53. Miles Kreuger, *Show Boat: The Story of a Classic American Musical* (New York: Oxford University Press, 1977), 102.

54. "*Show Boat* to be Heard on Air Thursday," *BAA*, October 8, 1932.

55. "Jules Bledsoe No Longer on the Air," *CD*, January 14, 1933. For more on the *Maxwell House Show Boat* radio program, see Karen L. Cox, *Dreaming of Dixie: How*

the South was Created in American Popular Culture (Chapel Hill: University of North Carolina Press, 2011), 49–50.

56. Tour information taken from Kreuger, *Show Boat*, 104–10 and Axtell, "Maiden Voyage," 324–30.

57. "Jules Bledsoe's *Show Boat* Successor was once a Dentist," *BAA*, December 17, 1932.

58. *CD*, January 14, 1933.

59. Maxwell, *Helen Morgan*, 146.

60. Ibid., 149.

61. Rob Roy, "*Show Boat* has New Find in Robert Raines," *CD*, January 21, 1933.

62. Aired May 16, 1957. Leonard Spiegelgass and Paul Monash were credited with the adaptation.

63. Mordaunt Hall, *NYT* review, April 18, 1929.

64. Kreuger, *Show Boat*, 84, describes the considerable difficulties of the premiere.

65. James Curtis, *James Whale: A New World of Gods and Monsters* (Boston: Faber and Faber, 1998), 263–64, describes the contents of the Akins version, which is in the Huntington Library (San Marino, California).

66. LBr to OH, December 2, 1935. This and all letters quoted in this section in Hammerstein 19 unless noted otherwise.

67. CL to OH, November 6, 1935.

68. Curtis, *James Whale*, 266.

69. LBr to OH, December 2, 1935.

70. OH to JW, November 18, 1935.

71. "Robeson Will Play Lead in *Show Boat*," *CD*, September 28, 1935.

72. CL to OH, October 15, 1935.

73. OH to CL, October 24, 1935.

74. Pay from Universal Pictures budget files at USC.

75. LBr to OH, December 2, 1935.

76. JW to OH, October 28, 1935.

77. JW to OH, October 14, 1935.

78. CL to OH, November 1, 1935; OH to CL, n.d.

79. LBr to OH, December 3, 1935.

80. The January draft includes mention of a duet where Ravenal would thrill Magnolia with stories of Paris.

81. LBr to OH, December 3, 1935.

82. JB to HZ, October 17, 1935, AMPAS/PCA.

83. Two copies of Hammerstein's draft script survive, both dated November 1935. One in NYPL/TC MFLM + 76–1834; the second, a retyped copy from 1950 made by MGM as part of script resources assembled for their 1951 *Show Boat*, in AMPAS/Turner 2876.f-1064.

84. JB to HZ, November 15, 1935, AMPAS/PCA.

85. HZ to JB, December 14, 1935, AMPAS/PCA. JB agreed in a letter two days later.

86. Recorded November 12, 1930 in England with Ray Noble and his Orchestra. Available on *Paul Robeson: the Complete EMI Sessions (1928–1939)*, EMI Classics 50999 2 15586 2 7.

87. JW to PR, April 28, 1936, Robeson, 6.

88. A copy of Hammerstein's script survives in Robeson 36.

89. OH to JW, November 18, 1935, Hammerstein 19.

90. Curtis, *James Whale*, 1998; Mark Gatiss, *James Whale: A Biography or The Would-Be Gentleman* (New York: Cassell, 1995).

91. Script, "adaptation and continuity" by Charles Kenyon, bearing two stamped dates (April 5 and 19, 1928), AMPAS/Turner 2876.f-1063.

92. *Universal Weekly*, April 6, 1929.

93. Kreuger, *Show Boat*, 81.

94. Robeson 35.

95. Hammerstein 19.

96. OH to JW, November 18, 1935, Hammerstein 19.

97. *Complete Lyrics of Oscar Hammerstein II*, 114.

98. *The Secret of Madame Blanche* and *Ann Vickers* (both 1933).

99. NYPL/TC MFLM + (Show Boat) 76–1834; AMPAS/Turner 2876.f-1064.

100. VHS and laserdisc versions were released in the early 1990s.

101. Many are reprinted in Kreuger, *Show Boat*, 148–50.

102. Harrison Carroll, "*Show Boat* Best Mounted Since Original Production," *LA Evening Herald*, May 14, 1940.

103. Christy Fox, "Gay Parties Mark Opening of City's Annual Musical Fete," *LAT*, May 14, 1940.

104. Clarence Muse, "What's Going On in Hollywood," *CD*, May 4, 1940.

105. Clarence Muse, "John Boles Means Zero to Paul Robeson," *CD*, May 25, 1940.

106. Sammy White would play Frank one last time in the 1946 Broadway revival.

CHAPTER 7

1. "Revival of *Show Boat*," *LT*, April 19, 1943.

2. Horace Horsnell, "The Theatre," *Tatler and Bystander*, June 2, 1943.

3. "*Show Boat* Sails Again," unattributed clipping, V&A Stoll 1943.

4. Oscar Andrew Hammerstein, *The Hammersteins: A Musical Theatre Family* (New York: Black Dog and Leventhal Publishers, 2010), 79.

5. Horsnell, "The Theatre."

6. "New *Show Boat* Arriving Tonight," *NYT*, January 5, 1946.

7. Cook on Columbia Broadway Masterworks 1962 studio cast (CD version: SK 61877) and cast album of 1966 Lincoln Center production (CD: RCA Victor 09026-61182-2). Luker on the "world premiere cast recording" of the 1994 production released by Livent (CD: Quality Music RSPD 257).

8. Snow sings his top note on the word "more" in the recitative-like passage before "When the Children Are Asleep," as he imagines the growth of his fishing business.

9. JK to OH, June 30, 1942. Thanks to Bruce Pomahac for providing access to this letter.

10. Richard Watts Jr., "*Show Boat* Sails Again," *Saturday Review*, January 26, 1946.

11. "Specter of Helen Morgan Haunts Carol Bruce in *Show Boat* Role," *NYHT*, January 20, 1946.

12. "Can't Help Lovin' Dat Man," from E-flat to A-flat; "Bill," from B-flat to E-flat. The 1946 vocal score retained Morgan's higher keys, but surely Bruce sang onstage in a lower register than Morgan had.

13. Lewis Nichols, "The Tinsel which Now Decorates the Broadway Tree," *NYT*, December 22, 1940.

14. *Life*, September 8, 1940.

15. Helen Tamiris, "Tamiris in Her Own Voice: Draft of an Autobiography (transcribed, edited, and annotated by Daniel Nagrin)" *Studies in Dance History* 1, no. 1 (fall/winter 1989): 41.

16. Susan Manning, *Modern Dance, Negro Dance: Race in Motion* (Minneapolis: University of Minnesota Press, 2004), 101–13.

17. Lynne Fauley Emery, *Black Dance: From 1619 to Today*, 2nd rev. ed. (Princeton, NJ: Princeton Book Company, 1988), 260–66; and John O. Perpener III, *African-American Concert Dance: The Harlem Renaissance and Beyond* (Urbana: University of Illinois Press, 2001), chap. 7, summarize Primus's career.

18. Julia L. Foulkes, *Modern Bodies: Dance and American Modernism from Martha Graham to Alvin Ailey* (Chapel Hill: University of North Carolina Press, 2002), 71.

19. Foulkes, *Modern Bodies*, 73–74.

20. Sam Zolotow, "News of the Stage," *NYT*, December 3, 1945.

21. Joseph H. Mazo, *Prime Movers: The Makers of Modern Dance in America, Second Edition* (Princeton, NJ: Princeton Book Company, 2000), 134.

22. Peggy and Murray Schwartz, *The Dance Claimed Me: A Biography of Pearl Primus* (New Haven, CT: Yale University Press, 2011), 29.

23. "*Show Boat*," *Life*, January 28, 1946.

24. Walter Terry, "Dances on Broadway," *NYHT*, January 20, 1946.

25. Samuel Sillen, *DW*, January 10, 1946.

26. NYPL/TC, Richard Rodgers Scrapbooks 17.

27 *Hartford Daily Courant*, October 21, 1947.

28. Tracy Silvester, *Daily Oklahoman*, January 25, 1948.

29. Paul Jones, *Atlanta Constitution*, March 1, 1949; George L. David, *RDC*, December 20, 1947; Elinor Hughes, *Boston Herald*, October 28, 1947; Mary Nash, *Buffalo Evening News*, December 26, 1947; *Baltimore News Post*, March 15, 1949; Arthur Speth, *Cleveland News*, April 19, 1949.

30. George L. David, *RDC*, December 20, 1947; Betty French, *Akron Beacon Journal*, October 19, 1948; Bruce Bohle, *St. Louis Star Times*, February 8, 1949; Gilbert Kanour, *Baltimore Evening Sun*, March 15, 1949.

31. Allen Young, *Denver Post*, January 20, 1949.

32. A recreation of "Mourner's Bench" and Primus's "Strange Fruit" can be seen on *Dance in America: Dancing in the Light*, an episode of *Great Performances* aired on June 20, 2007 and available on DVD (Kultur D4251).

33. Thomas F. DeFrantz, *Dancing Revelations: Alvin Ailey's Embodiment of African American Culture* (New York: Oxford University Press, 2004), 3–18.

34. Contract between Loews, Inc. and EF, OH, JK, et al., April 29, 1938, MGM PR-1A. Wells's script in AMPAS/Turner 2877-f.1066–68.

35. Karen L. Cox, *Dreaming of Dixie: How the South was Created in American Popular Culture* (Chapel Hill: University of North Carolina Press, 2011).

36. Contract between Loew's Inc. and OH/JK partnership, September 28, 1945, MGM PR-1A.

37. Al Block to L.B. Mayer, January 9, 1946, AMPAS/PCA.

38. Lennie Hayton made an arrangement of "Bill" in April 1946, when work on the film was still ongoing. Edens.

39. The *Show Boat* opening first appears in a script dated January 10, 1946, which begins with the blunt sentence "The picture opens with a presentation of the top scenes and numbers from SHOW BOAT" (AMPAS/Turner 3374.f-1529; Freed). Arranger's scores are dated between January 14 and 28, 1946 (Edens). Shooting took just over a week, concluding on February 7, 1946 (Freed AD reports).

40. The earliest trace of the film—a list of Kern songs—dates to April 1940. Intense work on the script began in 1943 and proceeded through October 1945, with five writers producing three substantially different scripts. Shooting of the various specialty numbers featuring MGM stars began in October 1945 but work on the framing story continued for months. Freed, production file and scripts; AMPAS/Turner, 3371.f-1504-32.

41. Wells, "THE SILVER LINING Notes," January 7, 1944, AMPAS/Turner 3372.f-1511.

42. Bolton script drafts in AMPAS/Turner, 3371.f-1504-08.

43. V-disc recorded April 4, 1945; Hollywood Bowl concert on August 4, 1945.

44. Script, dated October 4, 1945, AMPAS/MGM 3373.f-1524.

45. *Motion Picture Herald*, June 9, 1951.

46. "Cinema: The Winners," *Time*, January 7, 1952.

47. Box office report, July 19, 1951, Freed.

48. John Kobal, *People Will Talk* (New York: Alfred A. Knopf, 1985), 652. On several occasions, Sidney publicly denied the story that Horne had ever been considered for the role although Gardner did audition for Julie by mouthing to Horne's version of "Can't Help Lovin' Dat Man" from *Till the Clouds Roll By* and worked with Horne's vocal coach Phil Moore early on when having Gardner do her own singing was being considered. (George Sidney, letter to the editor, *LAT*, December 19, 1982; "Phil Moore Coaches Ava Gardner," *Los Angeles Sentinel*, November 23, 1950)

49. *Boxoffice*, June 9, 1951.

50. OH to AF, May 23, 1951, Freed.

51. Jennifer Frost, *Hedda Hopper's Hollywood: Celebrity Gossip and American Conservatism* (New York: New York University Press, 2011), 179.

52. "The Farmer's Daughter," *Time*, September 8, 1951.

53. Scripts consulted include drafts in AMPAS/Turner 2877.f-1069, 1072–77, 1079, as well as the final shooting script (AMPAS/Turner 2877.f-1069; Moorehead 26/3). A memo announcing Garland was again available is preserved in the *Show Boat* production file (September 13, 1949, Freed).

54. "Ava Gardner gets Role in *Show Boat*," *NYT*, September 22, 1950; "Garland is Freed from Metro Pact," *NYT*, September 30, 1950.

55. John Lee Mahin to legal department, October 27, 1949, Freed; reader's report by Arthur Fitz-Richard, January 5, 1951, AMPAS/Turner 2879.f-1081.

56. *Variety*, June 5, 1951; *Library Journal*, June 15, 1951.

57. "Old Perdurable," *NY*, July 28, 1951. The critic gets the song title wrong, perhaps intentionally.

58. Edens directed because Sidney was ill. Miles Kreuger, *Show Boat: The Story of a Classic American Musical* (New York: Oxford University Press, 1977), 188; Hugh Fordin, *M-G-M's Greatest Musicals: The Arthur Freed Unit* (New York: Da Capo Press, 1996), 342.

59. As a result, AMPAS/Turner—repository of the MGM writing department—contains the richest and most varied one-stop archive of *Show Boat* script materials.

60. AMPAS/Turner 2877.f-1070.

61. AMPAS/Turner 2877.f-1069, September 8, 1949.

62. Howard Keel with Joyce Spizer, *Only Make Believe: My Life in Show Business* (Fort Lee, NJ: Barricade Books, 2005), 131.

63. *Saturday Review of Literature*, June 9, 1951.

64. Keel, *Only Make Believe*, 136.

65. Otis L. Guernsey Jr., *NYHT*, July 20, 1951.

66. Neal Gabler, *Walt Disney: The Triumph of the American Imagination* (New York: Alfred A. Knopf, 2006), 497.

67. J. P. Telotte, *The Mouse Machine: Disney and Technology* (Urbana: University of Illinois Press, 2008), chap. 6.

CHAPTER 8

1. Martin Sokol, *The New York City Opera: An American Adventure* (New York: Macmillan, 1981).

2. NYCLOC subscription flyer, Ives 20/39.

3. Paul V. Beckley, "City Opera's *Show Boat* to Follow Original Score," *NYHT*, March 7, 1954.

4. EF to OH, March 26, 1954, Hammerstein uncatalogued boxes.

5. OH to EF, April 1, 1954, Hammerstein uncatalogued boxes.

6. Jo Sullivan played Magnolia in at least one performance.

7. Obituary, *NYT*, August 12, 2005.

8. William Fowlkes, "Star Smith in *Show Boat*," *Atlanta Daily World*, March 5, 1949.

9. Valena Minor Williams, "'Joe' Is a Guy Named Bill," *PC*, October 2, 1954.

10. Phyl Garland, "William Smith, Helen Dowdy Brilliant in *Show Boat*," *PC*, July 16, 1960.

11. Miles Kastendieck, "Verdi and Kern in City Center Repertoire," *Christian Science Monitor*, April 24, 1954.

12. "City Opera Troupes Offers Show Boat in New Production of Classic Musical," *NYT*, April 18, 1954.

13. Robert Coleman, "*Show Boat* at City Center on Par with Original," unattributed clipping, Ives 20/39.

14. Walter Kerr, "*Show Boat,*" *NYHT*, May 6, 1954.

15. John Chapman, "Helena Bliss, Burl Ives Stand Out in *Show Boat* at the City Center," *NYDN*, May 6, 1954.

16. "13,500 at Stadium Event," *NYT*, July 12, 1954. Hammerstein's script can be found in Hammerstein 19.

17. Robert I. Giesberg, Carl Cunningham, and Alan Rich, *Houston Grand Opera at Fifty* (Houston, TX: Herring Press, 2005), 100.

18. Sherwin N. Goldman was the force behind this operatic *Porgy and Bess*, but Gockley and the HGO were the only American opera company willing to take it on. Goldman said, "Without Houston's name on it we couldn't have done it at all. On the other hand, it was a good arrangement for them. They got a free show." Hollis Alpert, *The Life and Times of Porgy and Bess* (New York: Alfred A. Knopf, 1990), 298.

19. "HGO's *Show Boat* a very hot ticket in Cairo," *Houston Post*, February 28, 1989.

20. "HGO's *Show Boat* a hot ticket in Cairo," *Houston Chronicle*, February 28, 1989.

21. Deena Rosenberg, "*Show Boat*, an American Classic, Sails Into the Present," *NYT*, April 24, 1983.

22. Carol Lawson, "Broadway," *NYT*, May 6, 1983.

23. Michael Billington, "Roll On, *Show Boat,*" *Guardian*, August 2, 1990.

24. Clive Barnes, "*Show Boat,*" *NY Post*, April 25, 1983.

25. "Can't Help Loving that ol' *Show Boat,*" *NYDN*, April 25, 1983.

26. Review, *Variety*, April 27, 1983.

27. Brendan Gill, "The Theatre," *NY*, May 9, 1983, 109.

28. "*Show Boat*: John McGlinn Talks to Edward Seckerson," *Gramophone*, November 1988.

29. Ibid.

30. After *Show Boat*, McGlinn recorded *Kiss Me, Kate, Brigadoon, Anything Goes* (again with von Stade), *Annie Get Your Gun*, and Kern's *Sitting Pretty* with EMI before his contract went unrenewed in 1992.

31. *Gramophone*, November 1988.

32. Stephen Holden, "*Show Boat* Makes New Waves," *NYT*, September 25, 1988.

33. Michael Ratcliffe, "The Old Tub Revamped," *Observer*, October 16, 1988.

34. Massenet's *Werther* (1887) is one exception.

35. Darian on Columbia Broadway Masterworks 1962 studio cast (CD version: SK 61877); Towers on cast album of 1966 Lincoln Center production (CD: RCA Victor 09026-61182-2). Franz Allers conducted both recordings.

36. "Show Boat: John McGlinn Talks to Edward Seckerson," *Gramophone*, November 1988.

37. Edward Greenfield, "All Aboard the *Show Boat,*" *Guardian*, August 18, 1989.

38. Katrine Ames, "A Classic Reconstruction," *Newsweek*, November 7, 1988.

39. John Fraser, "Producer's Note," EMI press pack.

40. London Records OSA 13116, conducted by Loren Maazel.

41. Jay Records 1394, conducted by John Owen Edwards.

42. Holden, "*Show Boat* Makes New Waves."

43. Raoul Abdul, "Angel Records Restores 'Niggers' to *Show Boat,*" *NYAN*, October 29, 1988.

44. "Bruce Hubbard talks about *Show Boat* and 'Ol' Man River,'" EMI press pack.

45. Miles Kreuger, "Some Words about *Show Boat*," Liner note for *Show Boat*, CD: EMI-Angel 7 49108 1/2/4, 1988.

CHAPTER 9

1. "Rodgers, Hammerstein Reply to Lee Newton on *Show Boat*," *Daily Worker*, October 25, 1948. Newton's letter first appeared in the 16 September edition.

2. Jeremy Gerard, "*Show Boat* docks with $75 top," *Variety*, January 3, 1994.

3. Carol Ilson, *Harold Prince: A Director's Journey* (New York: Limelight Editions, 2000), 398.

4. Geoffrey Block, *Enchanted Evenings: The Broadway Musical from Show Boat to Sondheim*, 2nd ed. (New York: Oxford University Press, 2009), 27.

5. John Barber, "*Show Boat* a Vivid and Talented Revival," *DT*, July 20, 1971.

6. John Higgins, "*Show Boat*," *LT*, July 30, 1971.

7. *Guardian*, July 30, 1971.

8. Blurbs on the back of press photos used the term "principal dancer" to describe Godreau's role in the production. V&A Adelphi 1971.

9. The ON/RSC production premiered in Leeds in December 1989, gave twenty-five performances in Stratford between February 13 and March 3, 1990, then played London and toured the UK in August and September.

10. Foster Hirsch, *Harold Prince and the American Musical Theatre*, rev. ed. (New York: Applause Books, 2005), 199.

11. *Harper's Queen* (August 1990).

12. Rupert Tyler, "Happy Marriage . . .," *Gay Times* (October 1990).

13. Rupert Christiansen, "Can't Help Lovin' Dat Opera Singer," *Observer*, July 29, 1990.

14. Robert Gore-Langton, "All Aboard! It's Showtime," *Sunday Correspondent*, August 5, 1990.

15. Charles Osborne, "Can't Help Lovin' Dem *Show Boat* Melodies," *DT*, August 3, 1990.

16. Richard Morrison, "Show of Southern Spirit," *LT*, August 3, 1990.

17. M. Nourbese Philip, *Showing Grit: Showboating North of the 44th Parallel* (Toronto: Poui Publications, 1993), 56.

18. Garth Drabinsky with Marq de Villiers, *Closer to the Sun: An Autobiography* (Toronto: McClelland and Stewart, 1995), 479.

19. Glenn Collins, "Battle of the Big-Time Musicals," *NYT*, April 12, 1994.

20. The Paper Mill telecast, aired on October 27, 1989, can be viewed at the Paley Center or the Library of Congress. Clips can sometimes be found on YouTube. A video of the Prince version with its original cast is in NYPL/TOFT.

21. RCA Victor 09026-61182-2. The revised verse lyric was also used in London in 1971. The complete new verse lyric is reprinted in Miles Kreuger, *Show Boat: The Story of a Classic American Musical* (New York: Oxford University Press, 1977).

22. Sarah Gristwood, "A Rounded Performance," *Guardian*, July 27, 1990.

23. Valerie Grove, "A Childhood: Karla Burns," *Times Saturday Review*, April 13, 1991.

24. Gristwood, "A Rounded Performance."

25. Linda Armstrong, "Stars answer questions about *Show Boat* musical," *NYAN*, July 8, 1995, 28.

26. Linda Armstrong, "Drama Desk members discuss *Show Boat*," *NYAN*, November 18, 1994, 51.

27. Kreuger, *Show Boat*, 199.

28. Videotape, NYPL/TOFT.

29. Cleo Laine, *Cleo* (New York: Simon and Schuster, 1994), 223.

30. *Guardian*, July 30, 1071.

31. Sheridan Morley, "Cleo Laine's Conquest of America," *LT*, November 24, 1973.

32. Michael Billington, "Cleo Laine," clipping, ca. 1971, V&A Cleo Laine.

33. "Ethnically Correct," *Evening Standard*, July 26, 1971.

34. Laine, *Cleo*, 223.

35. Michael Billington, "Cleo Laine."

36. *NYHT*, May 6, 1954.

37. Nan Robertson, "Voyage to Broadway by Show Boat Singer," *NYT*, May 21, 1983.

38. Ibid.

39. *Jungle Fever* (1991), *Malcolm X* (1992), *He Got Game* (1998).

40. John Lahr, "Mississippi Mud," *NY*, October 25, 1993.

41. John Istel, "Lonette McKee: Why the Caged Bird Sings," *American Theatre* 12, no. 2 (February 1995).

42. *NY Post*, October 20, 1995.

43. Hirsch, *Harold Prince*, 203.

44. Edna Ferber, *Show Boat* (New York: Doubleday, Page and Co., 1926), 398.

45. The boogie-woogie reference appears in materials prepared by McGlinn for his recording held by the Rodgers and Hammerstein Organization.

46. Jones Beach script in NYPL/TC RM 4315.

47. My thanks to Bruce Pomahac at the Rodgers and Hammerstein Organization for access to Stroman's choreography guide and to Stroman herself for permitting me to quote from her unpublished text here.

48. Videotape in NYPL/TOFT.

49. Sarah Kaufman, "A Leg Up on Social Change," *WP*, June 5, 1998.

EPILOGUE

1. David Belcher, "The *Cotton Blossom* is Dry-docked, but Ol' Man River Keeps Rollin' Along," *NYT*, December 9, 2009.

2. Jayne Blanchard, "*Show Boat* Sails to Lush Grandeur," *Washington Times*, November 20, 2009.

3. William A. Henry III, "Rough Sailing for a New *Show Boat*," *Time*, November 1, 1993.

4. Todd Decker, "Race, Ethnicity, Performance" in *The Oxford Handbook of the American Musical*, ed. Raymond Knapp, Mitchell Morris, and Stacy Wolf (New York: Oxford University Press, 2011), 198.

5. John Istel, "Lonette McKee: Why the Caged Bird Sings," *American Theatre* 12, no. 2 (February 1995).

6. Thanks to Rosalind Early who pointed me toward the connections between *Show Boat* and *Hairspray*.

7. For a different reading of *Hairspray*, see Matthew Tinkcom, "'Dozing Off During History': *Hairspray*'s Iterations and the Gift of Black Music" in *The Sound of Musicals* ed. Steven Cohan (NewYork: Palgrave Macmillan, 2010). Tinkcom faults *Hairspray* for employing "essentialist notion[s] of black identity" (208). As noted throughout this book, racial stereotypes—essentialist notions that are themselves in constant transformation—are the engines that drive the depiction of racial identity and the American racial scene on the Broadway musical stage.

8. Richard Rodgers, "Negro Theme Lined Many a Top Musical," *NYAN*, July 9, 1966.

REFERENCES

ABBREVIATIONS

ARCHIVAL COLLECTIONS (REFERENCED IN ENDNOTES BY SHORT TITLE AND BOX OR BOX/FOLDER, I.E., HAMMERSTEIN 19, BROWN 3/8, ETC.).

AMPAS/PCA	Production Code Administration files, Margaret Herrick Library, Academy of Motion Picture Arts and Sciences, Beverly Hills, California
AMPAS/Turner	Turner/MGM Script Collection, Margaret Herrick Library, Academy of Motion Picture Arts and Sciences, Beverly Hills, California
Bledsoe	Jules Bledsoe Papers, Schomburg Center for Research in Black Culture, New York Public Library, New York
Brown	Lawrence Brown Collection, Schomburg Center for Research in Black Culture, New York Public Library, New York
Edens	Roger Edens Collections, Cinematic Arts Library, University of Southern California, Los Angeles
Eslanda	Eslanda Robeson Papers, Moorland-Spingarn Research Center, Howard University, Washington, D.C.
Ferber	Edna Ferber Papers, Wisconsin Historical Society, Madison
Freed	Arthur Freed Collection, Cinematic Arts Library, University of Southern California, Los Angeles
Goodland	Recordings, Writings, and Ephemera Relating to the Life and Works of Paul Robeson, 1935–1985 (collected by Ken Goodland), LMA/4231, London Metropolitan Archives, London
Hammerstein	Oscar Hammerstein Collection, Library of Congress, Music Division
Hunter	Alberta Hunter Papers, Schomburg Center for Research in Black Culture, New York Public Library, New York
Ives	Burl Ives Collection, Billy Rose Theatre Collection, New York Public Library for the Performing Arts, Lincoln Center, New York City
Kern	Jerome Kern Collection, Library of Congress, Music Division
LCP	Lord Chamberlain's Plays, Manuscripts Reading Room, British Library, London
Moorehead	Agnes Moorehead Papers, Wisconsin Historical Society, Madison
NYPL/DC	Dance Collection, New York Public Library for the Performing Arts, Lincoln Center, New York City
NYPL/TC	Billy Rose Theatre Collection, New York Public Library for the Performing Arts, Lincoln Center, New York City
NYPL/TOFT	Theatre on Film and Television, New York Public Library for the Performing Arts, Lincoln Center, New York City

Robeson	Paul Robeson Papers, Moorland-Spingarn Research Center, Howard University, Washington, D.C.
MGM	MGM Music Department Collection, University of Southern California, Cinematic Arts Library, Los Angeles
V&A	Theatre And Performance Collection, Victoria and Albert Museum, Blythe House, London
Ziegfeld	Flo Ziegfeld /Billie Burke Collection, New York Public Library for the Performing Arts, Lincoln Center, New York City

NAMES

AW	Alexander Woollcott
CL	Carl Laemmle Jr.
EF	Edna Ferber
ER	Eslanda Robeson
FZ	Florenz Ziegfeld
HZ	Harry Zehner (Universal Pictures)
JB	Joseph Breen
JK	Jerome Kern
JW	James Whale
LB	Lawrence Brown
LBr	Leighton Brill
OH	Oscar Hammerstein II
PR	Paul Robeson

NEWSPAPERS AND MAGAZINES

BAA	*Baltimore Afro-American*
CT	*Chicago Tribune*
DT	*Daily Telegraph (London)*
DW	*Daily Worker*
LAT	*Los Angeles Times*
LT	*London Times*
MA	*Musical America*
NY	*The New Yorker*
NYA	*New York Age*
NYAN	*New York Amsterdam News*
NYDN	*New York Daily News*
NYHT	*New York Herald Tribune*
NYT	*New York Times*
NYW	*New York World*
PC	*Pittsburgh Courier*
PT	*Philadelphia Tribune*
RDC	*Rochester Democrat and Chronicle*

WP   *Washington Post*
WSJ   *Wall Street Journal*

BIBLIOGRAPHY

(Newspaper and magazine articles referenced in notes only.)

Alpert, Hollis. *The Life and Times of Porgy and Bess*. New York: Alfred A. Knopf, 1990.

Axtell, Katherine. "Maiden Voyage: The Genesis and Reception of Show Boat, 1926–1932." PhD diss., University of Rochester, 2009.

Banfield, Stephen. *Jerome Kern*. New Haven, CT: Yale University Press, 2006.

Block, Geoffrey. "The Melody (and the Words) Linger On: American Musical Comedies of the 1920s and 1930s." In *The Cambridge Companion to the Musical*, 2nd ed. Edited by William A. Everett and Paul R. Laird. New York: Cambridge University Press, 2008.

Block, Geoffrey. *Enchanted Evenings: The Broadway Musical from Show Boat to Sondheim*. 2nd ed. New York: Oxford University Press, 2009.

Bordman, Gerald. *Jerome Kern: His Life and Music*. New York: Oxford University Press, 1980.

Bordman, Gerald. *American Operetta: From H.M.S. Pinafore to Sweeney Todd*. New York: Oxford University Press, 1981.

Boyle, Sheila Tully, and Andrew Bunie. *Paul Robeson: The Years of Promise and Achievement*. Amherst: University of Massachusetts Press, 2001.

Breon, Robin. "Show Boat: The Revival, The Racism." *Drama Review* 39 (Summer 1995): 86–105.

Brown, Jayna. *Babylon Girls: Black Women Performers and the Shaping of the Modern*. Durham, NC: Duke University Press, 2008.

Cantor, Eddie. *Ziegfeld: The Great Glorifier*. New York: A. H. King, 1934.

Colvan, Zeke. *Face the Footlights!: A New and Practical Approach to Acting*. New York: McGraw-Hill, 1940.

Cox, Karen L. *Dreaming of Dixie: How the South Was Created in American Popular Culture*. Chapel Hill: University of North Carolina Press, 2011.

Curtis Burlin, Natalie. "Negro Music at Birth." *Musical Quarterly* 5, no. 1 (January 1919): 86–89.

Curtis, James. *James Whale: A New World of Gods and Monsters*. Boston: Faber and Faber, 1998.

Davidson, Donald. *The Spyglass: Views and Reviews, 1924–1930*. Nashville, TN: Vanderbilt University Press, 1963.

Decker, Todd. "Black/White Encounters on the American Musical Stage and Screen (1924–2005)." PhD diss., University of Michigan, 2007.

Decker, Todd. "'Do you want to hear a Mammy song?': A Historiography of *Show Boat*." *Contemporary Theatre Review* 19, no. 1 (February 2009): 8–21.

Decker, Todd. *Music Makes Me: Fred Astaire and Jazz*. Berkeley: University of California Press, 2011.

Decker, Todd. "Race, Ethnicity, Performance." In *The Oxford Handbook of the American Musical*. Edited by Raymond Knapp, Mitchell Morris, and Stacy Wolf. New York: Oxford University Press, 2011.

DeFrantz, Thomas F. *Dancing Revelations: Alvin Ailey's Embodiment of African American Culture*. New York: Oxford University Press, 2004.

Dickinson, Rogers. *Edna Ferber: A Biographical Sketch with a Bibliography*. Garden City, NY: Doubleday, Doran and Co., 1925.

Drabinsky, Garth, with Marq de Villiers. *Closer to the Sun: An Autobiography*. Toronto: McClelland and Stewart, 1995.

Duberman, Martin Bauml. *Paul Robeson*. New York: Alfred A. Knopf, 1988.

Emery, Lynne Fauley. *Black Dance: From 1619 to Today*. 2nd rev. ed. Princeton, NJ: Princeton Book Company, 1988.

Everett, William A. *Sigmund Romberg*. New Haven, CT: Yale University Press, 2007.

Ferber, Edna. *Show Boat*. New York: Doubleday, Page and Co., 1926.

Ferber, Edna. *A Peculiar Treasure*. New York: Doubleday, 1939.

Fields, Armond. *Women Vaudeville Stars: Eighty Biographical Profiles*. Jefferson, NC: McFarland and Company, 2006.

Foley, Neil. *The White Scourge: Mexicans, Blacks, and Poor Whites in Texas Cotton Culture*. Berkeley: University of California Press, 1997.

Forbes, Camille F. *Introducing Bert Williams: Burnt Cork, Broadway, and the Story of America's First Black Star*. New York: Basic Books, 2008.

Fordin, Hugh. *M-G-M's Greatest Musicals: The Arthur Freed Unit*. New York: Da Capo Press, 1996.

Foulkes, Julia L. *Modern Bodies: Dance and American Modernism from Martha Graham to Alvin Ailey*. Chapel Hill: University of North Carolina Press, 2002.

Frost, Jennifer. *Hedda Hopper's Hollywood: Celebrity Gossip and American Conservatism*. New York: New York University Press, 2011.

Gabler, Neal. *Walt Disney: The Triumph of the American Imagination*. New York: Alfred A. Knopf, 2006.

Gatiss, Mark. *James Whale: A Biography or The Would-Be Gentleman*. New York: Cassell, 1995.

Giesberg, Robert I., Carl Cunningham, and Alan Rich. *Houston Grand Opera at Fifty*. Houston, TX: Herring Press, 2005.

Graziano, John. "Images of African Americans: African-American Musical Theatre, *Show Boat* and *Porgy and Bess*." In *The Cambridge Companion to the Musical*. Edited by William A. Everett and Paul R. Laird. New York: Cambridge University Press, 2008.

Hammerstein, Oscar Andrew. *The Hammersteins: A Musical Theatre Family*. New York: Black Dog and Leventhal Publishers, 2010.

Hammerstein, Oscar II. *Lyrics*. New York: Simon and Schuster, 1949.

Hammerstein, Oscar II. *Lyrics (1949)*. Edited by William Hammerstein. New York: Hal Leonard Books, 1985.

Hammerstein, Oscar II. *The Complete Lyrics of Oscar Hammerstein II*. Edited by Amy Asch. New York: Alfred A. Knopf, 2008.

Hardwicke, Cedric. *Let's Pretend: Recollections and Reflections of a Lucky Actor*. London: Grayson and Grayson, 1932.

Harkins, Anthony. *Hillbilly: A Cultural History of an American Icon*. New York: Oxford University Press, 2004.

Helm, MacKinley. *Angel Mo' and her Son, Roland Hayes*. Boston: Little, Brown and Company, 1942.

Hirsch, Foster. *Harold Prince and the American Musical Theatre*. 2nd ed. New York: Applause Books, 2005.

Hughes, Langston, and Milton Meltzer. *Black Magic: A Pictorial History of the African-American in the Performing Arts*. New York: Prentice-Hall, 1967.

Ilson, Carol. *Harold Prince: A Director's Journey*. New York: Limelight Editions, 2000.

Keel, Howard, with Joyce Spizer. *Only Make Believe: My Life in Show Business*. Fort Lee, NJ: Barricade Books, 2005.

Kirle, Bruce. *Unfinished Show Business: Broadway Musicals as Works-in-Process*. Carbondale: Southern Illinois University Press, 2005.

Knapp, Raymond. *The American Musical and the Formation of National Identity*. Princeton, NJ: Princeton University Press, 2005.

Knapp, Raymond. "Performance, Authenticity, and the Reflexive Idealism of the American Musical." In *The Oxford Handbook of the American Musical*. Edited by Raymond Knapp, Mitchell Morris, and Stacy Wolf. New York: Oxford University Press, 2011.

Kobal, John. *People Will Talk*. New York: Alfred A. Knopf, 1985.

Krasner, David. *A Beautiful Pageant: African American Theatre, Drama, and Performance in the Harlem Renaissance, 1910–1927*. New York: Palgrave Macmillan, 2002.

Kreuger, Miles. *Show Boat: The Story of a Classic American Musical*. New York: Oxford University Press, 1977.

Kreuger, Miles. "Some Words about *Show Boat*." Liner note for *Show Boat*, conducted by John McGlinn. EMI-Angel, 1988.

Laine, Cleo. *Cleo*. New York: Simon and Schuster, 1994.

Lerner, Michael A. *Dry Manhattan: Prohibition in New York City*. Cambridge, MA: Harvard University Press, 2007.

Lovensheimer, Jim. *South Pacific: Paradise Rewritten*. New York: Oxford University Press, 2010.

Manning, Susan. *Modern Dance, Negro Dance: Race in Motion*. Minneapolis: University of Minnesota Press, 2004.

Maxwell, Gilbert. *Helen Morgan: Her Life and Legend*. New York: Hawthorn Books, 1974.

Mazo, Joseph H. *Prime Movers: The Makers of Modern Dance in America*. 2nd ed. Princeton, NJ: Princeton Book Company, 2000.

McMillin, Scott. "Paul Robeson, Will Vodery's 'Jubilee Singers,' and the Earliest Script of the Kern-Hammerstein Show Boat." *Theatre Survey* 41, no. 2 (November 2000): 51–70.

Mordden, Ethan. *Make Believe: The Broadway Musical in the 1920s*. New York: Oxford University Press, 1997.

Most, Andrea. *Making Americans: Jews and the Broadway Musical*. Cambridge, MA: Harvard University Press, 2004.

Murray, Albert. *Stomping the Blues*. New York: McGraw-Hill, 1976.

Parker, Dorothy. *Complete Stories*. New York: Penguin Books, 1995.

Patterson, Michelle Wick. *Natalie Curtis Burlin: A Life in Native and African American Music*. Lincoln: University of Nebraska Press, 2010.

Peretti, Burton W. *Nightclub City: Politics and Amusement in Manhattan*.
    Philadelphia: University of Pennsylvania Press, 2007.
Perpener, John O. III. *African-American Concert Dance: The Harlem Renaissance and
    Beyond*. Urbana: University of Illinois Press, 2001.
Peterson, Bernard L. *A Century of Musicals in Black and White: An Encyclopedia of
    Musical Stage Works By, About, or Involving African Americans*. Westport, CT:
    Greenwood Press, 1993.
Peterson, Bernard L. *Profiles of African American Stage Performers and Theatre People,
    1816–1960*. Westport, CT: Greenwood Press, 2001.
Philip, M. Nourbese. *Showing Grit: Showboating North of the 44th Parallel*. Toronto:
    Poui Publications, 1993.
Randall, James. "Becoming Jerome Kern: The Early Songs and Shows, 1903–1915."
    PhD diss., University of Illinois, Urbana-Champaign, 2004.
Ries, Frank W. D. "Sammy Lee: The Broadway Career." *Dance Chronicle* 9, no. 1
    (1986): 1–95.
Robeson, Eslanda Goode. *Paul Robeson, Negro*. New York: Harper and Brothers,
    1930.
S. D., Trav. *No Applause—Just Throw Money: The Book that Made Vaudeville Famous*.
    New York: Faber and Faber, 2005.
Schwartz, Peggy, and Murray Schwartz. *The Dance Claimed Me: A Biography of Pearl
    Primus*. New Haven, CT: Yale University Press, 2011.
Sergeant, Elizabeth Shepley, and E. O. Hoppé. *Fire under the Andes: A Group of North
    American Portraits*. New York: Alfred A. Knopf, 1927.
Smyth, J. E. *Edna Ferber's Hollywood: American Fictions of Gender, Race, and History*.
    Austin: University of Texas Press, 2010.
Sokol, Martin. *The New York City Opera: An American Adventure*. New York:
    Macmillan, 1981.
Stearns, Marshall, and Jean Stearns. *Jazz Dance: The Story of American Vernacular
    Dance*. New York: Macmillan, 1968.
Stempel, Larry. *Showtime: A History of the Broadway Musical Theater*. New York:
    W. W. Norton, 2010.
Swain, Joseph P. *The Broadway Musical: A Critical and Musical Survey*. New York:
    Oxford University Press, 1990.
Tamiris, Helen. "Tamiris in Her Own Voice: Draft of an Autobiography (transcribed,
    edited, and annotated by Daniel Nagrin)." *Studies in Dance History* 1, no. 1 (Fall/
    Winter 1989): 1–64.
Telotte, J. P. *The Mouse Machine: Disney and Technology*. Urbana: University of
    Illinois Press, 2008.
Tinkcom, Matthew. "'Dozing Off During History': *Hairspray*'s Iterations and the
    Gift of Black Music." In *The Sound of Musicals*. Edited by Steven Cohan. NewYork:
    Palgrave Macmillan, 2010.
Traubner, Richard. *Operetta: A Theatrical History*. New York: Routledge, 2003.
Tucker, Mark. "In Search of Will Vodery." *Black Music Research Journal* 16, no. 1
    (Spring 1996): 123–82.
Van Gelder, Robert. *Writers and Writing*. New York: C. Scribner's Sons, 1946.

White, Walter. "The Paradox of Color." In *The New Negro: An Interpretation*. Edited by Alain Locke. New York: Albert and Charles Boni, 1925.

Williams, Linda. *Playing the Race Card: Melodramas of Black and White from Uncle Tom to O. J. Simpson*. Princeton, NJ: Princeton University Press, 2001.

Wilson, Christopher P. *White Collar Fictions: Class and Social Representation in American Literature, 1885–1925*. Athens: University of Georgia Press, 1992.

Woll, Allen L. *Black Musical Theatre: From Coontown to Dreamgirls*. Baton Rouge: Louisiana State University Press, 1989.

Ziegfeld, Richard, and Paulette Ziegfeld. *The Ziegfeld Touch: The Life and Times of Florenz Ziegfeld, Jr*. New York: H. N. Abrams, 1993.

INDEX

Page numbers in **bold** indicate illustrations.

Abdul, Raoul, 210
Abyssinia, 107
The Adventures of Huckleberry Finn,
    229
"African Ceremonial," 173
The African Queen, 195
"After the Ball"
    in 1927 production, 91, 99–100, 109
    in later versions, 126, 157, 161,
        193, 221
Agate, James, 135
The Age of Innocence, 149
Ager, Milton, 120
"Ah Still Suits Me"
    in 1936 film, 147, 150
    in stage revivals, 164, 215–16,
        219, 221
Ahrens, Lynn, 244
Aida, 179, 242–43
Ailey, Alvin, 178–79, 215
"Ain't Misbehavin'," 96
Ain't Misbehavin', 221
Akins, Zoe, 146
Albert, Donnie Ray, 204
"All God's Chillun Got Wings" (song), 2,
    18–22, 49, 97, 155
All God's Chillun Got Wings (play), 21, 31,
    34–35, 49, 55
Ambrosian Chorus, 209–10
American Grand Guignol, 61
An American in Paris, 183
Americana, 59–60
Ames, Winthrop, 13
Cap'n Andy (character)
    in films, 149, 159–63, 179–80
    in novel, 16
    in stage musical, 48, 73–75, 90–93,
        117, 198

Ann Vickers, 149
Annie Get Your Gun, 172, 187
Armstrong, Louis, 96, 115, 143
"Arrangement in Black and White," 38
"Ashes and Fire," 44–45
Astaire, Adele, 76, 79
Astaire, Fred, 59, 79, 94
"At a Georgia Camp Meeting," 238
Atkinson, Brooks, 40, 109
Aunt Jemima, 114, 195
    See also Gardella, Tess
Axtell, Katherine, 57–58, 140

backwoodsman, 78, **79**
Baker, Josephine, 96
Balanchine, George, 197
Un Ballo in maschera, 198
Banfield, Stephen, 6
The Barefoot Contessa, 187
Barney Google, 78
Baxter, Rebecca, 237
Bay, Howard, 226
Beatty, Talley, 174–76, 178
Beggar's Holiday, 178
Bell, Michel, 165, 183, 204, 243
La Belle Fatima (character), 117, 173
Benchley, Robert, 68
Bennett, Robert Russell, 95–96, 107,
    112–14, 117
Benstead, Lucille, 143
Bergen, Polly, 145
Bergman Ingrid, 185
Berkeley, Busby, 93, 238
Berlin, Irving, 34
Bernie, Ben, 171
Bernstein, Leonard, 198, 204, 206
Big Boy, 106
Big River, 5, 228–29, 245, 250

"Bill"
  in films, 146, 147, 152, 181, 189
  in 1927 production, 30, 57–58, 62–64,
    70, 107
  in 1988 recording, 208
  in stage revivals, 165, 171, 201, 231, 234
  in television biography of Morgan, 145
Billington, Michael, 231
The Birth of a Nation, 20
Black Boy, 31, 39–42, 139, 218
black-cast Broadway shows, 4–6, 33, 49,
    54, 84, 107, 120, 122, 139, 179,
    201–2, 221, 227, 245
blackface, 1, 76, 98, 114–15, 126, 157–62
Blake, Eubie, 49, 96
Bledsoe, Jules
  concert career, 20, 38
  dramatic career, 21, 104
  in *Deep River*, 40, 44–45
  in *Show Boat*, 8, 53–54, 71–73, **74**, 103,
    121, 133, 142–43
Bliss, Helena, 198–99, 201, 208
Block, Geoffrey, 215
Blossom Time, 83, 87, 168
The Blue Paradise, 51
Blumenthal, A. C., 142
Boles, John, 165
Bolton, Guy, 182–83
Boone, Pat, 228
Boston, Gretha, 223–25, **235**
Bottomland, 120
Bowen, Stirling, 140
Bracken, Eddie, 198
Breen, Joseph, 149, 152
Breon, Robin, 7
Brice, Fanny, 62
The Bribe, 188
Bride of the Lamb, 56
Brill, Leighton, 143, 146–47, 148
Brohn, William David, 238
Brooks, Gwendolyn, 53–54
"Brotherhood of Man," 230
Broun, Heywood, 35, 38
Brown, Anne, 7
Brown, Ashley, 242

Brown, P. L., 220–22
Brown, Jayna, 6–7
Brown, Lawrence
  background, 37
  partnership with John C. Payne, 34, 37
  partnership with Paul Robeson, 31,
    35–38, 42, 48, 132–33, 135, 139–40
Bruce, Carol, 170–71, 208, 227, 234
Bryan, David, 247
Bubblin' Brown Sugar, 221
"The Bully Song," 99–100
Burke, Marie, 127
Burleigh, Harry T., 38, 135
Burlin, Natalie Curtis, 22–24
Burns, Karla, 222, **223**, 237
Butt, Sir Alfred, 34, 56, 126–27, 130, 132–34
Butterbeans and Suzie, 150

"Cadillac Car," 228
Cage, John, 173
Calamity Jane, 195
Call Me Mister, 199
Cambridge, Alyson, 242
Campbell, Maurice, 68
Candide, 198
"Can't Help Lovin' Dat Man"
  and stereotypes of black couples, 150
  as evidence and/or celebration of black
    identity, 65–66, 89, 95, 100, 112,
    150, 190, 246–47
  changes to lyrics, 220
  in 1927 production
    composition of, 42, 57, 111
    in act 2, 62, 91, 93, 98–100
  in films, **66**, 146, **148**, 150, 157, 180, 182,
    185, 189–90, 192
    kitchen pantry scene, 65, 155
  in stage revivals, 129, 134, 165, 201, 215,
    220–22, 231–36
    use in wedding scene, 89–91
  performers' approaches to, 58, 65–66,
    127, 171, 189–90
  recordings of, 65–66, 114–15, 127, 171
  shuffle dance to, 66, 148, 155, 160,
    231–34, **235**, 240, 246

Cantor, Eddie, 69, 78, 105–6
Carerras, José, 206
Carmen, 197–98, 203
Carousel, 169–71, 197–98, 201
Castle, Irene, 81
Chaliapin, Fyodor, 121
Chapman, John, 201
"Change Don't Come Easy," 248
Charleston (1920s social dance), 76, 78,
    126, 237–38, 240
"Cheer Up," 75, 270n13
Cherry Blossoms, 52, 83, 87–89
Cherniavsky, Joseph, 145, 155
Chicago, 67–68, 215
Chicago Lyric Opera, 242
Christiansen, Rupert, 216
Cimarron, 149
The Circus Princess, 82
The Clansman, 20
Clayton, Jan, 169–70, 237
Coalition to Stop Show Boat, 217
Coates, Albert, 140
Cohan, George M., 80
Coleman, Jim, 261
Coleman, Robert, 201
Coleridge-Taylor, Samuel, 135
The Color Purple, 245
Colvan, Zeke, 62
"Come, Boys," 87
Como, Perry, 248
Compton, Betty, 59
Connie's Hot Chocolates, 60
Cook, Barbara, 169
Cook, Donald, 152
Cooke, Sam, 228
Coolidge, Calvin, 69
coon songs and singers, 18–19, 26–27, 59,
    99, 156–57, 159
Coppola, Francis Ford, 233
The Cotton Club, 233
Cowling, Bruce, 180
Cox, Karen, 180
Crawford, Joan, 194
Crazy for You, 238–39
"Crazy Words, Crazy Tune," 120

"Creole Love Song," 87, 98, 146, 207
Criss Cross, 41
Crosby, Bing, 115
Cullen, Countee, 109
Cunard, Nancy, 142

Daffy Dill, 82
Dale, Alan, 39
Dalrymple, Jean, 197
"Dance Away the Night," 237
"Dancing in the '20s," 237
Dankworth, John, 231
Danse Negre, 135
Darian, Anita, 208
David and Bathsheba, 183
Davidson, Donald, 19
Day, Edith, 126–28, 237
Dazey, Frank Mitchell, 39
"De Old Clay Road," 44–47
"Deep River," 19–20, 155
Deep River, 40–41, 44–47, 87, 105
DeLavallade, Carmen, 179
DeMain, John, 203
DePietro, Joe, 247
The Desert Song, 83, 126, 168
Deutsche Grammophon, 206
Devine, Andy, 198
"Didn't I Tell You (That You'd Come Back),"
    115
Dietz, Howard, 60
Dixie Jubilee Singers, 104
Disney, Walt, 195
Disneyland, 195
Dixon, Thomas, 20
Domingo, Plácido, 203
Don Giovanni, 197–98
Douglas, James, 137–38
Dowdy, Helen, 171, 199, 213
Drabinsky, Garth, 214–15, 217–18, 236, 244
Dreamgirls, 5, 228–29, 245, 247, 250
DuBois, W.E.B., 36
Dudley, Caroline, 54, 130
Dudley, S. H., 120
Duncan Sisters, 126
Duncan, Todd, 7, 165

Dunham, Katherine, 172, 175
Dunne, Irene, 147–49, 159–61, 163–64, 195
Durbin, Deanna, 231
Dvořák, Antonín, 45, 135

The Earl and the Girl, 99
Earth, 109
East Side, West Side, 188
Eddy, Nelson, 149
Edens, Roger, 181
Edwards, Cliff "Ukelele Ike," 49
Edwards, John Owen, 210
Elkins, William C., 106–7
Ellie/Elly (character)
    in films, 180–81, 193
    in novel, 15–16, 77
    in 1927 production, 15, 71–73, 76–81, 86,
        92, 96–97, 98–100, 109, 116
    in stage revivals, 99, 175, 202, 237–38
Ellington, Duke, 107, 164, 173
EMI-Angel, 204–11
The Emperor Jones, 21, 31–32, 34–35, 55,
    104, 133
English, Ellia, 220–22, 225, 227, 237, 242
Etting, Ruth, 62
Eubie, 221
Everett, William, 84
Excuse My Dust, 194
Eyen, Tom, 229

Falstaff, 197
Fanny Herself, 25
"Fascinatin' Rhythm," 49
Fender, Harry, 82
Ferber, Edna
    literary circle, 34
    reaction to idea of musical, 41
    reaction to musical, 138–40, 198
    stereotypical depiction of black
        characters, 2, 14
    typical plot, 15–16, 25–27, 229, 244
    See also Show Boat (novel)
Fielding, Harold, 215
The 5th Dimension, 236
Finck, Hermann, 135

Finian's Rainbow, 178
The First, 233
Flaherty, Stephen, 244
Die Fledermaus, 197, 201
Floradora, 82
Mr. Flotsam. *See* Bentley Collingwood
        Hilliam
Forata, Asadata, 173
Ford, John, 152
42nd Street, 238
Foulkes, Julia, 173
Foy, Eddie Jr., 237
Frank/Schultzy (character)
    in films, 155–56, 158–59, 193
    in novel, 15
    in 1927 production, 71–73, 76–79, 86, 92,
        94, 96–100, 109, 116
    in stage revivals, **79**, 99, 175, 202, 237–39
Franklin, Aretha, 228
Fraser, John, 209
Fredericks, Charles, 170
"Free at Last," 229, 245
Freed, Arthur, 184–85
Freed Unit (at MGM), 180, 183
French, LaVerne, 174, 176, **177**, 178, 215
Friml, Rudolf, 82
From Dixie to Dover, 105
Funny Face, 79

Gable, Clark, 188
"Gallivantin' Aroun'," 160–63, 207, 246
Gardella, Tess [Aunt Jemima]
    in 1927 production, 9, **74**, 111, 115–17,
        122
    in 1929 film, 120, 146
    in 1932 stage revival, 142–44
    in 1936 film, 149–50
    vocal style, 65–66, 115–16, 127, 129, 167
    show business career, 98, 114–15,
Gardner, Ava, 168, 184–92, **193**, 232,
        278n48
Gardner, Chappy, 102–3, 106, 113
Garland, Judy, 162, 182, 186–88, 192, 231
Gates, Aaron, 108, 119–20
Gates, Henry Louis Jr., 217

Gaylord Ravenal (character). *See* Ravenal (character)

Gentlemen Prefer Blondes, 80

George White's Scandals, 58, 115

Gershwin, George and Ira, 7, 49–51, 59, 75, 81, 96, 106, 165

Gilbert, Julie, 243

Gilpin, Charles, 34, 133

Gilson, Lottie, 26

Girl Crazy, 96

The Girl Friend, 76, 78

Glyndebourne, 204, 210

Gockley, David, 202–3

Godreau, Miguel, 215, **216**

Go-Go, 107

"Goin' Home," 45, 135

The Gold Diggers, 80

Golden Boy, 5

Golden Dawn, 106

Gone with the Wind, 150

"Goodbye, My Lady Love," 77, 100, 109

Goodspeed Opera House, 243

Gordon, Dexter, 233

gospel music and singing style, 227–28

"Got My Eye on You," 151, 158–59

Grayson, Kathryn, 180, 189, **193**, 194

The Great Caruso, 183

Great Performances (PBS), 218

The Great Sinner, 188

The Great White Hope, 218

The Green Pastures, 107

Grey, Mark, 242

Gubbay, Raymond, 242

Guinan, Texas, 60, 67–69

Gunn, Nathan, 242

Guys and Dolls, 218

Hadley, Jerry, 88, 207–8

Hairspray, 5, 228, 230, 246–50

Hall, Adelaide, 107

Hall Johnson Singers, 104, 107, 109, 121, 142, 159, 164

"Hallelujah" (song), 98

Hallelujah (film), 144

Hammerstein, Arthur, 106

Hammerstein, Oscar I, 75, 167–68

Hammerstein, Oscar II

  1927 production, 3–4, 7–8, 23, 27–28, 39, 41–44, 57, 72–73, 76, 80–82, 86–87, 89–93, 98–99, 100, 115, 122, 219, 228–29, 236–37

    black chorus in, 105, 108, 111, 113, 116–18, 121, 222

    Helen Morgan as Julie in, 30, 58–59, 62–66, 235

    Paul Robeson as Joe in, 29, 33, 35, 42–43, 45, 48–50, 53–54, 134–35

  1928 London production, 126, 128–29

  added song for Paul Robeson, 134

  1929 film, 145

  1932 revival, 140, 143–44

  1936 film, 8, 125, 146–55, 157, 159–64, 180, 219

  1946 revival, 168–74, 197, 237

  1954 revival, 198

  1951 film, 179, 185, 191

  1954 revival, 198

  1920s vogue for Negro spirituals, 20, 25, 29, 31, 42, 113

  and *Deep River*, 40–41, 44–45, 87

  and Ferber's novel,

    attraction to, 25

    revisions to, 14–16, 49, 52, 73–75, 77–78, 93, 97–98, 213

  as director of *Show Boat*, 65, 108, 213

  other musical shows of, 41, 63, 82–83, 106, 126, 169–70, 198

  plan for *Show Boat* sequel, 138

  post-1960 revisions to "Can't Help Lovin' Dat Man," 220–21

  show business biography inserted into *Show Boat*, 75

  use of black dialect, 65, 95, 134, 225

  use of the word *nigger*, 101, 112, 152, 209–11

  view of *Show Boat* and race, 213, 225–27, 235

  See also popular music plot, in Hammerstein's hands to 1946

Hammerstein, William, 196–201, 206

Handel, Georg Frederic, 20, 45
Hansel and Gretel, 203
"Happy, the Day," 89–90
Hardwicke, Cedric, 128
Harlem Renaissance, 2, 29, 55, 227
Harling, Frank, 40, 45, 87
Hart, Lorenz, 76
Hayes, Roland, 20–21, 35, 37, 55
Hayworth, Rita, 185
"Heav'n, Heav'n." *See* "All God's Chillun
        Got Wings" (song)
"Helen Morgan," 145
Hello, Dolly! 202
"Hello, Ma Baby," 100
"Hey, Feller!"
    in 1927 production, 108, 115, 119–20, 254
    in 1929 film, 146
    in revivals, 129, 203–4, 215, 237, 243
Heyward, DuBose and Dorothy, 109
Hilliam, Bentley Collingwood
        [Mr. Flotsam], 166
Hines, Elizabeth, 80–81
Hines, Gregory, 233
Hirschfeld, Al, 178
Hit the Deck, 98
Holder, Geoffrey, 178–79
Holiday, Billie, 173, 231, 233–34
Holliday, Jennifer, 229
Holman, Libby, 60
Hopkins, Arthur, 40
Hopper, Hedda, 185
Horne, Lena, 168, 180–82, 189–90, 233,
        278n48
Houston Grand Opera, 202–5, 210, 215,
        242
House of Flowers, 179
"How Blest We Are," 229
How Long Brethren? 172, 179
*How to Succeed in Business Without Really
        Trying*, 230
"How'd You Like to Spoon with Me?" 99
Hubbard, Bruce, 165, 204, 209–11, 216
The Hucksters, 188
Huey, R. J., 121
Hughes, Langston, 173

Hunter, Alberta, 125, 129
Hunter, Charles, 13–14
Hurley, Laurel, 198–99

"I Am Changing," 228
"I Can't Be Bothered Now," 238
"I Got Rhythm," 238
"I Got Shoes." *See* "All God's Chillun Got
        Wings" (song)
"I Have the Room Above Her," 149, 219
"I Might Fall Back on You"
    in 1927 production, 77–78, 91–92, 109,
        116
    in stage revivals, 197, 201
"I Want to Be Happy," 73
"I Would Like to Play the Lover's Part,"
        109, 270n13
Illusions, 233
"I'm Just Wild About Harry," 96, 105
"In Dahomey"
    in 1927 production, 108, 117–19
    in stage revivals, 172, 174, **175**, 176, **177**,
        178–79, 201, 215, 241
In Dahomey, 106–7
In Old Kentucky, 104
"In the Good Old Summertime," 99
In the Good Old Summertime, 194
Inside U.S.A., 175
interracial musical, 4–5
Irwin, May, 99–100
"It's Getting Dark on Old Broadway,"
        95–96
"It's Getting Hotter in the North"
    in 1927 production, 94–97, 105, 120, 249
    in relation to later 1920s numbers, 163,
        237, 246
    on 1988 recording, 207
"(I've Got the) You Don't Know the Half
        of It, Dearie, Blues," 59
Ives, Burl, 198

Jackson, Mahalia, 227
The Jazz Singer, 145
The Jamie Foxx Show, 220
The Jeffersons, 220

Jessye, Eva, 199, 272n12
Jesus Christ Superstar, 202
Mr. Jetsam. *See* McEachern, Malcolm.
Joe/Jo (character)
    and the performance of blackness, 8, 25, 33, 65, 139, 165, 209–10, 216, 220–22
    in 1927 production, 8–9, 29, 41, 43–45, 48–49, 51–54, 71–72, **74**, 84, 89, 97, 109, 111, 118, 253–54
    in films, 66, 147, 150, 153, 155–57, 189–92
    in novel, 2–3, 18–19, 22–25, 28, 97
    in *Show Boat* sequel, 138
    in stage revivals before 1941 (with Robeson), 32, 34, 56, 125, **131**, 134–35, 138, **141**, 142–44, 165
    in stage revivals post 1941, 165–67, 199, **200**, 204, 208–11, 216, 219–22, 224, 226, 231, 234, **235**, 237, 240, 242–43
    origin in Ferber's research, 14
    size and importance of role, 132–33, 200, 202
    sung in blackface, 166–67
Johanson, Robert, 218–22, 225–27
John Henry, 139
Johnson, Carlton, 179
Johnson, James P., 107
Johnson, Van, 198
Jolson, Al, 106
Jones, Allan, 147, 149, 163–64
Jones, James Earl, 218
Judge, Ian, 215
Julie (character)
    and the performance of race, 7–8, 60, 65–66, 111–13, 145, 150, 154, 182, 186, 219, 232–36
    Hammerstein's revision of novel, 73–75, 213
    in films, **67**, 144, 146–47, **148**, 150, 154, 156, 180–82, 184–92, **193**
    in novel, 14–17, 28, 64, 73–74
    in 1927 production, 30, 43, 57–61, 62, 64–67, 69–71, 76, 80, 84, 86, 98, 108, 111–14

    in stage revivals before 1941 (most with Helen Morgan), 125, 127, **136**, 140, 144, 165
    in stage revivals post 1940, 170–71, 198–99, 202, 208, 213, 215, 219, 220, 222, 225, 227, 230–34, **235**, 236, 242, 247
    parallels with twenty-first-century Broadway characters, 246–48
    relation to her mixed-race identity, 186, 213, 234, 247
    vocal style, 65–66, 127, 208, 171, 208, 232, 242
June Days, 81
"Just Like a Butterfly (That's Caught in the Rain)," 61

Kahn, Aly, 185
Kahn, Michael, 203
Kalman, Emmerich, 82
Kander and Ebb, 67
Kasha, Lawrence, 226
Kaufman, George S., 13, 24
Keel, Howard, 192, **193**, 194
Kentucky Singers, 107
Kenyon, Charles, 154–57, 159
Kern, Eva, 183
Kern, Jerome, 29, 40, 164
    1927 production, 3–4, 7–8, 23, 27, 41–43, 53, 57, 65, 72, 80, 84, 94, 109, 122, 236
        black chorus in, 111–13, 117–18, 121
        Parthy underscoring in, 75
        interpolated music in, 49–51
    1929 film, 145, 155, 157
    1936 film, 125, 145, 147, 149–50, 157, 160
    1951 film, 193
    and black music in *Show Boat*, 7, 20, 29, 65, 98, 105–6, 108, 135, 159, 229
    and *Deep River*, 40, 45–47
    and Helen Morgan, 30–31, 58–60, 63, 145
    and Howard Marsh, 83, 85–88
    and jazz/dance music, 94
    and Norma Terris, 90–92, 97, 100

Kern, Jerome (*continued*)
  and 1920s operettas, 51, 83, 85–88
  and Negro spirituals, 31, 49–50
  and Paul Robeson, 29, 33, 35, 39–43,
    53–54, 133, 182
  and Puck and White, 75, 77, 80
  and Tess Gardella, 115–16
  and *Till the Clouds Roll By*, 168, 180–83
  and stage revivals to 1946, 7, 134, 140,
    164, 170, 231, 237
  attraction to novel, 25, 41
  death, 169, 18
  on Ravenal's vocal identity, 170
  other Broadway shows of, 41, 49, 58, 63,
    80, 99, 187, 205
  plan for *Show Boat* sequel, 138
  post-1980 stage revivals and Kern's
    musical structures in act 1 scene 1,
    224–27
  post–World War II reputation, 201–3,
    205–6, 210–11, 214, 216, 218, 244,
    250
Kerr, Deborah, 188
Kerr, Walter, 201
The Killers, 188
Kim Ravenal (character)
  in 1927 production, 25, 29, 50–53, 75, 91,
    93–97
  in films, 146, 150, 157, 159–60, 162–63,
    180, 184, 193, 246
  in novel, 2, 17, 23–26
  in planned *Show Boat* sequel, 138
  in stage revivals, 201, 204, 218–19, 224,
    231, 236–41, 246, 249
"Kim's Charleston," 238–41, 246
King, Dennis, 82, 140, **141**, 142
Kiss of the Spider Woman, 218
Knapp, Raymond, 5–7
Kreiger, Henry, 229
Kreuger, Miles, 7
Kykunkor, 174

Lady, Be Good, 49
Lady Day at Emerson's Bar and Grill, 233
Laemmle, Carl, 145

Laemmle, Carl Jr., 146–47
Lafayette Players, 33
LaGuardia, Fiorello, 196
Lahr, John, 234
Laine, Cleo, 215, 219, 227, 230–34, 236
Lancaster, Burt, 188
"Land Where the Good Songs Go," 183
LaPlante, Laura, 157
The Last Waltz, 82
Lawrence, Gertrude, 76, 81
Lawson, Angelica, 143
Le Noire, Rosetta, 220–21
Lee, Doris, 8–9
Lee, Eugene, 226
"The Lee Family," 107
Lee, Sammy, 95, 119
Lee, Spike, 234
"Let Me Awake," 87
Let's Pretend, 128
Lewis, Aylene, 195
Lewis, Theophilus, 105
"Life Upon the Wicked Stage," 78, 80, 86,
  109, 180–81, 201
Light, James, 34–35
Lil' Abner, 78
The Lion King, 215
The Little Colonel, 151
Little Nelly Kelly, 80
The Little Show, 60
Littler, Prince, 168
The Littlest Rebel, 151
Live at Carnegie Hall, 231
Livent Inc., 214
Lloyd Webber, Andrew, 216, 244
Locke, Alain, 32
Loftus, Cissie, 26
Lombardo, Guy
London Sinfonietta, 209
"The Lord Done Fixed Up My Soul," 171
Los Angeles Civic Light Opera, 164–65, 179
Lost in the Stars, 5
Louie the 14th, 82
Louisiana Purchase, 171
Lovelace, Henrietta, 113
Lucky, 49

Luker, Rebecca, 169, **235**
Lulu Belle, 59
Lyrics, 134

Maazel, Loren, 210
MacDonald, Jeanette, 149
The Magic Flute, 197, 242
The Magic Melody, 51
Magnificent Obsession, 159
Magnolia Hawks Ravenal (character)
    and the performance of blackness, 1–3,
        14–15, 17–19, 27, 65, 94, 98–100,
        154–62, 232–34, **235**
    and the performance of whiteness, 7–8,
        100
    casting and vocal style of, 7, 80–82,
        88–92, 169, 198, 207–8, 242, 253
    in 1927 production, 3, 8–9, 29, 43, 48–52,
        57, 62, 65–66, 71–74, 76, 79–82,
        84–85, 87–95, 97–100, 109, 111, 117,
        253
    in films, 145, 147–48, 151, 154–63, 165,
        179–80, 184, 189, 191–92, **193**,
        194–95
    in novel, 2–3, 14–19, 22–28, 57, 236
    in stage revivals, 125–27, **136**, **141**,
        169–70, 202, 218–19, 221–22,
        224, 230, 232–33, 237, 239–40,
        246
    parallels with twenty-first-century
        Broadway characters, 246
Mahew, Stella, 98
Mahin, John Lee, 186–87
"Make Believe," 8, 43
    adjustments to key, 84–87, 127, 170,
        270–71nn32–34
    in films, 146, 149, 180, 184
Manhattan Mary, 80
Manning, Susan, 5
Mantle, Burns, 40, 63, 139–40
Marjorie, 80
March, Frederic, 149
Marchant, Claude, 174, 176
The Marriage of Figaro, 199, 203
Marsh, Howard, 8, 71–73, **74**

and subsequent Ravenals, 127, 170, 198,
    207, 242
    casting as Ravenal, 82–83
    Ravenal as written for, 84–92, 122, 201,
        209
Martin, Tony, 180
Mary Poppins, 242
Mason, James, 189
Maxwell House Show Boat, 142
Maytime, 51
McAnuff, Des, 230
McClendon, Rose, 40
McCoo, Marilyn, 236
McDaniel, Hattie, 125, 150, **151**, 223
McDonald, Audra, 244
McEachern, Malcolm [Mr. Jetsam],
    166–67
McGlinn, John, 7, 88, 113, 203–11, 213, 215
McKee, Lonette
    as Julie, 171, 186, 219, 227, 230, 233–34,
        235, 236, 247
    background and career, 233–34
    defense of 1994 production, 245,
McMillin, Scott, 7
"Me an' My Boss," 134–35
Memphis, 5, 230, 247–50
Metro-Goldwyn-Mayer (MGM), 144,
    179–88, 226
Midnight Frolic, 69
The Mikado, 223
Miller, Marilyn, 81–82, 182
Miller, Roger, 229
Mills, Florence, 96, 105
Minick, 13–14
"Mis'ry's Comin' Aroun'"
    in 1927 production, 15, 108–9, 111–16,
        254
    in stage revivals, 203, 215, 223
    relation to black-themed concert music,
        135
    relation to twenty-first-century
        Broadway shows, 245
    use of themes from, 145, 190
Miss Saigon, 226
Mitchell, Abby, 121

Mitchell, Brian Stokes, 244
"Moanin' Low," 60
Mogambo, 188
"Montages I and II," 239–41, 246
Morgan, Helen
  and Prohibition, 30, 64, 67–70, 145, 186
  and subsequent Julies, 127, 170–71, 186,
    189, 208, 231, 234
  in 1927 production, 29–31, 62–72, **74**, 84,
    122
  in 1929 film, **67**, 146
  in 1932 revival, 139–40, **141**, 142–44
  in 1936 film, 146–47, **151**, 152
  in 1940 revival, 164–65
  in historical memory, 144–45, 170–71,
    188, 201
  Julie as written for, 57–58, 62–63, 125,
    127, 165, 209, 235
  nightclub career and persona, 30–31, 58,
    60–64
  stage career excluding *Show Boat*,
    58–61, 187
  vocal approach to the role of Julie,
    65–66, 114, 129, 227, 234
Morrison, Toni, 6
Moses, Ethel, 142
Most, Andrea, 5
The Mountain Boys, 78
"Mourner's Bench," 178
"Muddy Water," 229
Muny (Municipal Theatre Association of
  St. Louis), 243
Murray, Albert, 6–7
Muse, Clarence, 164–65
"The Music of My Soul," 247
Music Theatre of Lincoln Center, 197, 220
"My Coal Black Lady," 99–100
My Magnolia, 107

"The Negro Speaks of Rivers," 173
Negro spirituals
  as sung by Paul Robeson, 31, 34–38, 48,
    55, 132–33, 135, 137–39 , 147, 165
  in musical *Show Boat*, 33, 44, 48–49, 51,
    134, 138, 147, 164–65, 249

  in 1929 film *Show Boat*, 155
  in novel *Show Boat*, 2, 18–20, 22–25, 27
  mid-20s vogue for, 2, 14, 20–22, 37–38,
    40, 42, 45, 55, 60, 104, 107, 109–10,
    121, 126, 172, 227–28
  dances set to, 172–73, 179
Nelson, Alice Dunbar, 104, 115
New Dance Group, 174
The New Moon, 83, 126
"New Music," 244
The New Negro, 32
New World Symphony, 45, 135
New York City Ballet, 197, 215
New York City Light Opera Company
  (NYCLOC), 197, 200
New York City Opera (NYCO), 197–99, 201
Newton, Lee, 212
nigger
  word as used in *Show Boat*, 101–3,
    111–12, 129, 152, 209–11, 223
  word as used in *Memphis*, 247
"Niggers all work on de Mississippi"
  (opening chorus of "Ol' Man
  River"), 43, 101, 191
A Night in Paris, 81–82
A Night in Spain, 81–82
No, No, Nanette, 73
"No Shoes," 174, 176, 239
No Strings, 249
"Nobody Else But Me," 187, 231, 237
"Nobody Wants Me," 59–60

O'Brien, Virginia, 180–81
O'Brien, Pat, 198
The O'Brien Girl, 80
"The Oceana Roll," 194
O'Connor, Donald, 198
Oh, Boy, 80
Oh, Kay! 59, 81
Oh Lady! Lady!! 58, 63
Oklahoma! 75, 169, 171–72
"Ol' Man River," 236, 245
  and 1920s vogue for spirituals, 111, 113
  and *Deep River*'s "De Old Clay Road,"
    44–47

and Ferber's novel, 28
audience impact of, 39, 121, 164–65, 167, 210–11, 216, 242
as expression of protest, 204, 210, 217, 267n51
Hammerstein's view of, 213
in 1928 London production, 134–35, 167
in 1929 film, 145–46, 155–57
in 1936 film, 125, 148, 150, 152–54
in 1951 film, 168, 190–91
in *Till the Clouds Roll By*, 180–83
Robeson as inspiration for, 39–41, 53, 182
Robeson's initial reaction to, 55
musical numbers in other shows modeled upon, 229, 245
lyrics, 44, 134
musical analysis, 44–45
orchestration of, 206
use by Robeson in concert career, 50, 136, 139–40
use in *Show Boat* advertisements, 71–73, 140
use in stage musical, 5, 8, 29, 43–44, 49, 57, 109, 125, 132–34, 218, 226, 240, 243, 267n49
Old Lady on the Levee (character), 236
"Old Man Minick," 13–14
Oliver, Edna Mae, 9, 71–73, **74**, 75–76, 93, 143, 149
Oliver Blackwell's Jazz Orchestra, 120
Olivotti, Eva, 157
O'Neill, Eugene, 21, 31–32, 34–35, 38, 49
"Only a Few of Us Left," 166
Only Make Believe, 192
Opera North, 204, 214–16
operetta
and whiteness, 7, 84, 122
in the 1920s, 40, 51, 82–83, 126, 168, 195
Magnolia and Ravenal as unlikely operetta lovers, 52, 81–82, 84, 93, 163–64, 170, 198, 207, 218, 236
Show Boat as, 5, 43, 86–89, 91, 109, 126–27, 163, 197, 202, 205, 211

Otello, 203
Othello, 139

Pete (character), 14–15, 76, 86, 225, 227
Page, Patti, 248
Paper Mill Playhouse, 198, 218–22, 225–27, 236–37, 242, 249
"The Paradox of Color," 32–33
Parker, Dorothy, 38
Parthy Ann Hawks (character)
in 1927 production, 9, 15, 43, 48, 71–75, 80, 87, 90–93, 116–18
in films, 149, 150, 154–55, 159–60, 162–63, 189
in novel, 16–17, 23, 27, 236
in stage revivals, 149, 224, 237–38
parallels with twenty-first-century Broadway characters, 246, 248
Passing Show, 76
Paul Robeson, Negro, 54–56, 133
Payne, John C., 34, 37, 127
Peck, Gregory, 188
A Peculiar Treasure, 13
performers, importance of, in history of *Show Boat*, 6, 33, 58, 72–73, 84, 90–91, 121, 213
"People Will Say We're in Love," 169
Pete (character), 14–15, 76, 86, 225, 227
Peterson, Caleb, 180, 183
The Phantom of the Opera, 226
Philip, M. Nourbese, 7, 217
Phillips, Helen, 199
Pidgeon, Walter, 149
Playhouse 90, 145
"Po' Lil' Black Chile," 44
Pollard, Harry
"Polonaise in the Mall," 166
popular music plot
in Hammerstein's hands to 1946, 3, 29–30, 50–52, 84, 91, 93–95, 97, 100, 125, 138, 162–64
in the hands of others after 1946, 185, 214, 220, 239–41, 246, 249–50
Porgy, 109–13, 121, 131, 181, 245

Porgy and Bess
    and the performance of blackness, 7
    reference to in Stroman's 1994
        choreography for *Show Boat*, 239
    revival in opera house and on records in
        1970s and '80s, 202–4, 206, 210–11,
        214, 280n18
    role in careers of black singers, 165, 178,
        199–200, 204, 223
Popwell, Albert, 178–79
Powell, Joan, 194
Powell, Michael, 198
Pressberger, Emeric, 198
Price, Leontyne, 224
Primus, Pearl, 172–74, **175**, 176, 178–79, 239
Prince, Harold, 149, 205, 214–20, 223–26,
    229–30, 234, 238–41, 243
Production Code Authority (PCA), 149–50,
    152, 154
Prohibition, 30–31, 50, 58, 64
Provincetown Players, 34, 55
Puck, Eva, 71–73, 76–80, 92, 142, 181
Purlie, 228

Queen O' Hearts, 82
Queenie (character), 7, 15
    as blackface role, 72, 74, 98, 114–17,
        143–44, 149–50, 167
    as played by black performers, 125, 129,
        143–44, 199, 213
    in 1927 production, 8, 49, 52, 55, 65–66,
        71, 89, 108, 111, 114–19, 197, 199,
        254
    in films, 147, **148**, 149–50, 154–57, 182,
        189
    in novel, 2, 18, 22–24, 28
    in stage revivals, 125, 127, 129, 134, 143,
        150, 171, 174, 199, 203–4, 213, 216,
        219–22, **223**, 224–27, 231, 232–34,
        235, 237, 241–43
"Queenie's Ballyhoo"
    in 1927 production, 108, 115–18
    in 1951 film, 187
    in stage revivals, 129, 172, 174, 178, 197,
        201, 215, 222

race
    as performed in American musical
        theater, 5–9, 72, 195, 212–13, 228
    as performed in Hollywood musical
        film, 160, 194–95
    performing blackness, 18–19, 27, 30–31,
        38, 49, 84, 115–16, 134–35, 144, 167,
        196, 210, 221–22
    performing mixed-race identities (i.e.,
        Julie), 65–66, 227, 230, 232–36, 186
    performing whiteness, 8, 30–31, 65,
        78–80, 84, 128, 227–28
    See also blackface; Negro spirituals;
        torch song and singing
Ragtime, 5, 228–29, 244–47, 250
Raines, Robert, 142–43
Rainger, Ralph, 60
Raisin, 228
The Rake's Progress, 198
"The Rap," 228
Rattle, Simon, 204, 206
Ravel, Maurice, 121
Ravenal (character)
    and the performance of whiteness, 8,
        84, 161, 179–80, 224
    casting of, 82–83, 147–49, 207, 242
    in 1927 production, 8–9, 29, 43, 48, 53,
        71–73, 76, 79, 84–91, 93–94, 98,
        109, 116
    in films, 147, 151, 155, 157, 159–61, 163,
        179–80, 184, 186, 191–92, **193**, 194
    in novel, 3, 16–17, 48
    in stage revivals, 125, 127, **136**, 140, **141**,
        165, 198, 201, 202, 218–19, 221, 224,
        239
    on 1988 recording, 207, 209
    rehabilitation at end of story, 42, 48, 52,
        97, 159–60, 163, 191, 218–19, 236
    silence in wedding scene, 89–90
    vocal range and style, 7, 82–90, 169–70,
        192, 198, 201, 207, 209, 242
Raymond, Lizzie C., 99
Razaf, Andy, 60
Reagan, Ronald, 195, 210–11
"Red Ball Express," 199

Revelations, 179
revisals, 169
Rhapsody in Blue, 50–51, 96
Rich, Frank, 205
Richardson, Ron, 229
Ride, Vaquero! 194
The Rider of Dreams, 107
Ries, Frank W .D., 92, 105, 116
Ring cycle, 206
Ring, Blanche, 99
"River in the Rain," 229
Roberta, 149
Roberts, C. Luckyeth, 106–8
Robertson, Guy, 82
Robertson, Lanie, 233
Robeson, Eslanda, 32, 35, 53–56, 131–34,
    142, 147
Robeson, Paul
  activism, 173, 267n51
  and 1927 production, 38–39, 72, 84, 122
    as inspiration for "Ol' Man River,"
      39–40, 44
    casting as covered in press, 41, 52–54,
      253
    efforts to feature in, 29, 33, 43, 48–49,
      111, 246
    resistance to, 29, 53–56, 249
  and Greenwich Village, 34–35, 55
  and London, 34, 135–38
  and New Negro ideology of the
    Talented Tenth, 30, 36, 55
  as object of sexual desire by whites, 38,
    152–54
  childhood and education, 31, 37
  concert career, 2, 20–22, 31–32, 42, 107,
    172, 209, 227
    critics reaction to concert
      appearances, 35–37, 137–38
    efforts to feature as concert singer in
      Show Boat, 42–43, 48–50, 135, 147
    incorporation of "Ol' Man River" into
      recital repertory, 50
    use of *Show Boat* for concert career,
      132–33, 138–40, 176
  dramatic career, 21, 31–35, 39, 107, 139

  in 1928 London production, 8, 125,
    128–30, **131**, 134–35, **136**,
  in 1932 revival, 125, 138–40, **141**, 142
  in 1936 film, 125, 146–47, **148**, 150, 215,
    221, 226
    "Ol' Man River" in, 152–54, 163
  in 1940 Los Angeles production, 125,
    164–65, 215
  in historical memory, 167, 170, 204, 210,
    217–18, 226
  in *Till the Clouds Roll By*, 182–83
  plan for *Show Boat* sequel, 138
Robeson, Paul Jr., 54
Robinson, Bill "Bojangles," 150–52, 159
Robinson, Jackie, 233
Robinson, Morris, 242
Rodgers, Richard, 76, 176, 197
  view of *Show Boat* and race, 213, 249–50
Rogers, Alex C., 106–8
Rogers, J. A., 129
Romberg, Sigmund, 51–52, 83, 85, 87
Romeo and Juliet, 149
Rooney, Mickey, 162
Rosalie, 81
Roseanne, 33
Rose-Marie, 82, 126, 168
Rossellini, Roberto, 185
'Round Midnight, 233
Rounesville, Robert, 198–99
The Royal Family, 24
Royal Shakespeare Company, 204,
  214–16
Royce, Ruth, 99
Ruby, Harry, 40
Rudel, Julius, 197, 206
Runnin' Wild, 105

Salemme, Antonio, 35, 152, 154
Salome, 197
San Francisco Opera, 242
Sanders of the River, 154
Saunders, Gertrude, 120
Schuller, Gunter, 202
Seeley, Blossom, 99
"Serenade," 83, 85

"Serenade Creole (When Your Eyes Looked Into Mine)," 87
Sergeant, Elizabeth Shepley, 38–39
Sharlee, 107
Shore, Dinah, 184
SHOW BOAT
Novel (1926)
  Ferber's thematic use of black music, 17–19
  Ferber's use of Natalie Curtis Burlin on black singing, 22–24
  "passing" plot, 14–15
  relation to Ferber's earlier work, 15–16, 25–27
  writing of, 13–14
New York commercial productions
  1927, 8–9, 29–122, 219, 229, 237
    "A Paul Robeson Recital," 45, 48–50, 52–53, 151, 246
    black dancing chorus (Jubilee Dancers), 96, 105, 116–17
    casting of, 52–53, 57–59, 73, 75–76, 80–82
    contracts for, 41–42
    chorus, 104–5, 108–9, 117–18
    extant draft librettos, 42, 254–55
    large-scale form, 110, 116, 118–19
    references to Ferber's novel, 50, 116
  1932, 125, 138–40, **141**, 142–45, 237
  1946, **79**, 168–74, **175**, 176, **177**, 178, 180, 197, 212, 231, 237, 239
  1956/57, **xviii**, 168, 178–79, 198–99, 237
  1983, 198, 204–5, 210
  1994, 214, 217–20, 223–26, 230, 234, **235**, 236, 238–41, 243
London productions
  1928, 125–30, **131**, 132–35, **136**, 237
  1943, 166–68
  1971, 215, **216**, 226, 230–33, 237
  1989–90, 204, 214–16, **223**, 281n9
  1998, 215
Hollywood film versions
  1929, **67**, 70, 120, 125, 145–46, 154–57

  1936, 65–66, 125, 146–47, **148**, 149–50, **151**, 152–54, 157–64, 215, 219, 226, 236, 240
  1951, 160, 168, 183–92, **193**, 194, 237
Light opera and opera productions
  1940 (LA), 125, 164–65, 215
  1944 (LA), 165
  1954 (NY), 196–202, 206, 208–9
  1960 (LA), 179
  1961 (NY), 197, 208
  1966 (NY), 197, 208, 220, 226
  1967 (LA), 179, 237
  1982 (Houston), 198, 203, 237
  1989 (Houston / Cairo), 198, 203, 223, 237
  2012 (Chicago), 242–43
Televised productions
  1989 (Paper Mill Playhouse), 198, 218–22, 225–27, 236–37, 249
Recordings
  McGlinn (1988), 88, 205–7, **208**, 209–11, 213, 215, 222
  Showing Grit: Showboating Above the 44th Parallel, 217
Shuffle Along, 49, 96
Sidell Sisters, 109
Sidney, George, 184, 190
Signature Theatre, 243
Sillen, Samuel, 176
Simon the Cyrenian, 107
Simpson, Angele Renée, 242
Sinatra, Frank, 168, 183, 185, 189, 191, 194
Sissle, Nobel, 49, 96
Sister Act, 245
Sitting Pretty, 94
1600 Pennsylvania Avenue, 204
"Slap that Bass," 238
Slater, Bob, 106, 119
Smith, William C., 165, 199, **200**
Smith, Oliver, 226
Snelson, Floyd, 102
So Big, 25
Sobel, Bernard, 70
Solti, Georg, 206
Solomon-Glover, André, **235**

"Some Day," 88–89
Sondheim, Stephen, 216, 244
Song of the Flame, 82
Sophisticated Ladies, 221
soubrette, 26
South Pacific, 218, 223, 250
Southern Landscape, 175, 178
Souvaine, Henry, 60
Sparkle, 233
Spencer, Kenneth, 165, 199
Spialek, Hans, 107
Stagecoach, 152
Stallings, Laurence, 40, 87
Stamper, Frank, 127, 134
Stanwyck, Barbara, 188–89
Steve (character), 248
  in films, 152, 154, 180, 185–87, 189–90,
    192
  in novel, 14–15
  in stage versions, 64, 76, 114, 225, 236
  parallels with twenty-first-century
    Broadway characters, 246, 248
"Stiff Upper Lip," 238
Still, William Grant, 199
"Strange Fruit," 173
Stratas, Teresa, **208**, 227
Stravinsky, Igor, 198
Strike Up the Band, 75
Stritch, Elaine, 149, 224
Stroman, Susan, 171, 214–15, 218, 238–41,
    243, 246, 249
The Student Prince, 83, 85–87, 90, 168, 198
Sunset Boulevard, 219
Sutton, Alma, 174, 176
Sweet Adeline, 63, 187

Taboo, 33, 107
Take Me Out to the Ball Game, 194
Talbert, Florence Cole, 121
Tales of Hoffmann, 198
Tamiris, Helen, 172–75, 179, 239
Tavernier, Bertrand, 233
Taylor, Robert, 149
Te Kanawa, Kiri, 206
"Tell Me, Cigarette," 87

Telotte, J. P., 195
Temple, Shirley, 151
Terris, Norma
  and subsequent Magnolias, 157, 242
  casting as Magnolia, 81–82
  in 1927 production, 8, 51, 71–73, **74**
  in stage revivals, 140, **141**, 142, 164–65
  Magnolia as written for, 27, 84, 89–94,
    97, 99–100, 122, 127, 207, 209, 237,
    249
  stage career outside *Show Boat*, 81–84,
    115
Terry, Walter, 176
theaters, cinemas, concert venues,
    nightclubs (New York City unless
    otherwise noted)
  48th Street, 35
  Adelphi (London), 215
  Aeolian Hall, 20
  Albert Hall (London), 147, 242
  Auditorium (Chicago), 143
  Belmont, 59–60
  Café Society Downtown, 173
  Cairo Opera House, 203
  Capitol, 104, 143
  Carnegie Hall, 31, 139, 173, 205, 242
  Casino, 139, 143
  City Center, 196–97, 199, 212
  Club Alabam, 3, 105
  Connie's Inn (Harlem), 105
  The Cotton Club (Harlem), 118
  Drury Lane (London), 56, 126–28, 130,
    135, 167
  Gershwin, 203–5, 214
  Greenwich Village, 21, 35
  Hammerstein's Victoria, 75
  Henry Miller, 56
  Hippodrome, 115
  Hollywood Bowl, 183
  Kennedy Center (Washington, D.C.), 242
  Lewisohn Stadium, 140, 202
  Mounds Club (Cleveland), 143
  New Amsterdam Roof Garden, 69–70
  New York State Theatre, Lincoln Center,
    197

theaters, cinemas (*continued*)
   North York Performing Arts Centre
      (Toronto), 217
   The Palace, 60, 115
   Philharmonic Auditorium (LA),
      164
   Plantation Club, 105
   Prince Edward (London)
   Princess, 120
   Radio City Music Hall, 203–4
   Roxy, 104
   Stoll (London), 167
   Town Hall, 20, 139, 199
   Uris. *See* Gershwin
   Ziegfeld, 62–63, 68–70, 105, 130, 145,
      148, 175
The Three Musketeers, 82
"'Til Good Luck Comes My Way," 86–88,
   109, 169
Till the Clouds Roll By, 168, 180–83, 189,
   278nn39–40
"Till We Reach That Day," 245
Topsy and Eva, 126
torch singing and singers, 30–31, 62, 66,
   234
Tosca, 197
Towers, Constance, 208
Townsell-Crisp, Vanessa, 245
Toye, Wendy, 215
La Traviata, 197
Treemonisha, 202–4
Tropic Death, 175
Troubled Island, 199
Tucker, Sophie, 98
Tully, Jim, 39
Twain, Mark, 229
Two Weeks with Love, 194

Ulric, Lenore, 59
Uncle Tom's Cabin (film), 104
Uncle Tom's Cabin (novel), 20, 154
Universal Pictures, 145–46
Up in Central Park, 172
Urban, Joseph, 106, 170
Urinetown, 245

The Vagabond King, 82, 168
Vallon (sheriff character), 86, 226–27
Van Vechten, Carl, 21–22, 38
Varney, Walter K., 54, 132
vaudeville, 26–27
Verdi, Giuseppe, 197, 209
Vidor, King, 144
Virginia, 126
Vodery, Will, 107–8
"Vo-do-do-de-o Blues," 120
"Volga Boat Song," 121
von Stade, Fredericka, 88, 207, **208**
Voodoo, 34
Vreeland, Frank, 110–11

Wagner, Richard, 206
Waldorf, Willela, 100
Walker, George, 106, 118
Waller, Thomas "Fats," 60
Warfield, William, 165, 190
Warren, Annette, 189
Washington National Opera, 242
Waters, John, 246
Watkins, Maurine, 67
Watts, Richard, 170
Wayne, John, 152
Weissmuller, Johnny, 153
The Well of Romance, 83
Welles, Orson, 27
Wells, George, 179, 182
West, Mae, 222
Westley, Helen, 149, 160
Whale, James, 146–48, 150, 152–54, 157,
   226
"(What Did I Do to Be So) Black and Blue,"
   60
"Where's the Mate for Me," 84, 86, 94, 180
White Cargo, 144
White, Lillias, 230
White, Sammy, 71, 73, **74**, 76–78, **79**, 80,
   92, 98, 142, 159–60
White, Walter, 32
White, Willard, 165, 210
white-cast musical, 5
Whiteman, Paul, 49, 69

Whitney, Salem Tutt, 103–4, 113
"Why Do I Love You?"
   in 1927 production, 75, 91–93, 96, 109, 114,
   in stage revivals and films, 149, 201, 237–38
"Why D'ya Roll Those Eyes?" 59
"Why Was I Born?" 187–88
The Widow Jones, 99
Wildflower, 82
Will Vodery's Jubilee Singers, **67**, 71–72, 104, 120–21
Willebrandt, Mabel Walker, 68, 70
Williams, Burt, 1, 106, 118
Williams, Linda, 7
Wilson, Edith, 120
Winchell, Walter, 69
Windy (character), 14, 75
Winninger, Charles, 53, 71–73, **74**, 75, 93, 96, 142, 149, 161, 254
Winters, Lawrence, 199
The Wiz, 228
Wodehouse, P. G., 63
Woollcott, Alexander, 34, 39, 45, 53, 109
"Worlds Apart," 229
Worster, Howett, 127
Wycherly, Margaret, 33

Yellen, Jack, 120
"Yes, Ma'am," 86

"You Are Love"
   in 1927 production, 53, 88–89, 92, 98, 155
   in films, 146, 148–49, 163–64, 236
   in stage revivals, 127, 170, 218, 230, 236
   on 1988 recording, 208
"You Can't Stop the Beat," 246

Zambello, Francesca, 242–43
Ziegfeld, Florenz
   1927 production, 7–8, **74**, 267n42
      and casting of Magnolia and Ravenal, 80–82
      contracts for, 41–42, 80, 84, 119, 253
   1929 film, 70, 145–46, 155
   1932 revival, 140–42
   advertisements for *Show Boat*, 71–72, 140
   and blacks, 31, 102–3, 105–8, 121–22, 129
   and Helen Morgan, 30, 58–60, 62, 68–70
   and Paul Robeson, 35, 53–55, 125, 130–33, 135, 140
   and subsequent *Show Boat* producers, 126–27, 142, 214, 215
   in *Till the Clouds Roll By*, 182–83
   plan for *Show Boat* sequel, 138
   revue and musical comedy aesthetics in *Show Boat*, 43, 49, 76, 80, 90–93, 105–6, 119–22, 243
   show business biography inserted into *Show Boat*, 18, 75, 117–18
Ziegfeld Follies, 1, 95, 107